Twigs *of* a Tree
A Family Tale

Twigs *of* a Tree

A Family Tale

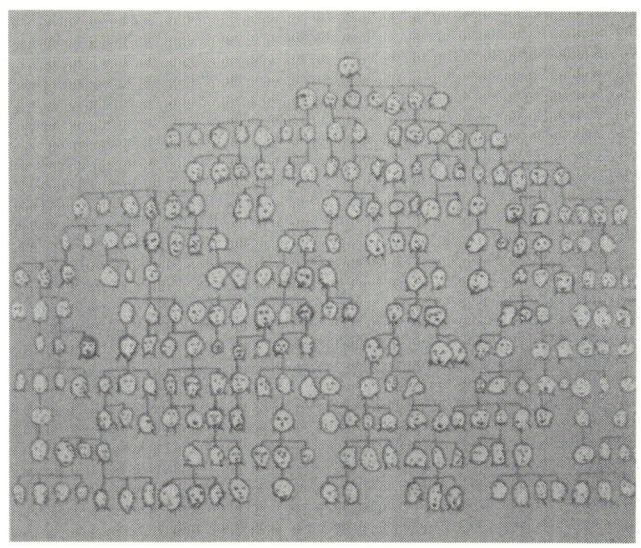

From a priest defrocked by the French revolution to English pioneering on the Pampas: connecting Walkers, Cattys, Goodbodys, Dysons, Adams, Eggars, Bradys and many more.

Lin Widmann

AuthorHouse™
1663 Liberty Drive
Bloomington, IN 47403
www.authorhouse.com
Phone: 1-800-839-8640

© 2012 by Lin Widmann. All rights reserved.

No part of this book may be reproduced, stored in a retrieval system, or transmitted by any means without the written permission of the author.

Published by AuthorHouse   03/23/2012

ISBN: 978-1-4670-0719-1 (sc)
ISBN: 978-1-4670-0720-7 (hc)
ISBN: 978-1-4670-0721-4 (e)

Any people depicted in stock imagery provided by Thinkstock are models, and such images are being used for illustrative purposes only.
Certain stock imagery © Thinkstock.

Because of the dynamic nature of the Internet, any web addresses or links contained in this book may have changed since publication and may no longer be valid. The views expressed in this work are solely those of the author and do not necessarily reflect the views of the publisher, and the publisher hereby disclaims any responsibility for them.

DEDICATION

Fertility among the British tribes ain't what it used be. Nevertheless, there are impressive numbers of descendants hailing from great-grandparents, John and Alice Walker: some sixty young people in the two latest generations alone. Of these, a mere five come from my own family: three great-great grandchildren—Christie, John and Sebastian—and two great-great-great grandchildren: Sebastian Oliver and Julian Linley. It is to them, and to all of JG and Alice Walker's youngest descendants—twigs and sprouts of many different names and several nationalities—that this chronicle is especially dedicated. If not now, perhaps somewhere down the line one or the other may want to know something about their adventurous ancestors and the family's long connection to South America. This tale is also in memory of my mother Noreen Adams and her sister Molly Dyson, whose Estancia La Susana gave me a small child's insight into the delights—if not the difficulties—of that Pampas life first opened to the family by John George Walker and his wife Alice Catty.

ACKNOWLEDGMENTS

There are many to thank for enabling me to put together this sprawling chronicle—most of all *John Briton Walker,* from whom all the present Walkers descend. Over the course of his long life Briton did much to record his own and his parents' youth on the Pampas. He also left accounts of his adventures in the Brazilian Mato Grosso and in South Africa during the Boer War.

Thanks to her research into the Catty family, *Meryl Catty* has unearthed precious information on Alice Catty Walker's distinguished father, Frederick Adam Catty, and on the fascinating 'French Connection' in our ancestry. *Claire Dulanty*—with her site on Ancestry—has provided me with an instant means of checking many dates and relationships.

Patrick Brady has tracked down, looked up, double-checked and sent on to me countless details: dates, maps, photographs from libraries and archives in London and even a leafy grove of family trees. *Diana (Eggar) McClure* has passed me many papers including a vivid account of her parents' Pampas life. *Brian Dyson* has made notes on *estancia* life in the 1930's and his daughter, *Susie Cogan,* has kindly sent me photographs. She and her sister, *Tania Dyson,* also had the good sense to interview their grandmother Molly (Goodbody) Dyson on videotape. *Angela and Matt Huber* made a great discovery in the memoirs of film-director David Lean. *Gillian Finlay* unearthed a number of documents on JG Walker's schooling and rowing. My brother *Jim Adams* contributed the painting for the cover.

Michael Goodbody's work on the Irish and Quaker background of the widespread Goodbody clan has been very valuable indeed. *Jorge Luis Rojas Lagarde,* an avid admirer of JG, talked to me at length over drinks in Buenos Aires. Though not the first to do so, he has inserted 'Facón Chico' into Argentine history. *Andrew Graham-Yooll*, former editor of the Buenos Aires Herald and author of *The Forgotten Colony*, has very kindly passed on to me copies of letters from JG and his friends to Edmund Goodhall, one of the original colonists and later British Consul in Bahia Blanca.

Mariano Correa sent me a great find: historical photographs of his estancia *La Mancha*, where JG and Alice passed their final years in Argentina before returning to England.

As the only surviving member of Molly's generation, *Barbara (Walker) Brady* has patiently answered countless questions. Enormous thanks must also go to *Ruth (Brady) Coxon*, Barbara's daughter, who had the generous idea of bringing together JG and Alice's many descendants for a Hampshire *asado*—particularly important since many of the young people did not know one another and met at her house for the first time in July 2010. Last but not least, affectionate thanks to my long-suffering husband, Carlos. He has long weathered, with grace and humour, more family and Pampas lore than most, even an *Argentino*, should have to endure.

CONTENTS

INTRODUCTION xi

CHAPTER I	BEGINNINGS AND A FIRST LONG JOURNEY 1
CHAPTER II	ROWING—AND SAILING AWAY 27
CHAPTER III	THE FRENCH CONNECTION 37
CHAPTER IV	THE ADVENTURES OF A SURGEON 56
CHAPTER V	GO SOUTH, YOUNG MAN! 73
CHAPTER VI	ON THE INDIAN FRONTIER 83
CHAPTER VII	LIFE AND DEATH BY THE WILLOWS 97
CHAPTER VIII	ALICE IN MACHOLAND 117
CHAPTER IX	UNCIVILIZED CLASHES 135
CHAPTER X	BABIES, BULLETS AND BOLEADORAS 145
CHAPTER XI	REALITY AND LITERARY LICENCE 166
CHAPTER XII	BETWEEN BOOM AND BUST 172
CHAPTER XIII	OLD ENGLAND, NEW ARGENTINA 180
CHAPTER XIV	CHILDREN'S PARADISE 190
CHAPTER XV	BRITON, BOERS AND BULLETS 208
CHAPTER XVI	THE ENGLISH TOWER 226
CHAPTER XVII	DEATH IN THE TRENCHES 238
CHAPTER XVIII	YOUTH BETWEEN THE WARS 272

SOURCES & BIBLIOGRAPHY 318

INTRODUCTION

I began to think of writing up one branch of our family's history only a few years ago, when by chance I came across some papers by John Briton Walker, John George Walker's eldest son. These papers, that I had copied out in the seventies and then forgotten in the bustle and hustle of daily life, dealt mainly with Briton's youth on the Argentine Pampas. Looking through them I was suddenly hit by the fleeting nature of existence, by the speed with which the hands of the human clock spin from youth into age, by human presence being suddenly replaced by final absence. My mother's mind had already receded into dementia, and then, all too suddenly, people I loved and esteemed—parents, relations, friends, and colleagues—began to disappear into the hereafter. With them went mysteries about their identities, personalities, and many details of their lives and times that will now remain forever unknown.[1]

The original idea was simple: to answer a question that might occur to a very young or, even, still unborn member of the family. I pictured someone several decades on, perhaps in England, the Netherlands, Germany, Italy, Poland, the United States, or Australia—but, strangely enough, probably not in Latin America, neither in Brazil nor Argentina. I imagined him or her wondering about the family's once close South American connection. How and where did it begin; how did it develop and unfold; how and why did it—almost—come to an end?

I hope I shall be forgiven for sometimes launching into the subjective, even autobiographical, manner of the first person singular. My insistence on supplying a historical context—familiar enough to many old-timers—is

---

[1] The latest addition to my little gallery of loss, is a young cousin, Geoffrey Burns, killed at 19 in a car crash a few weeks after we met him at an Adams get-together in Portland, Oregon in August, 2011.

Twigs of a Tree

intended for the newer generations. I hope that allusions to those other wanderers in my ancestry, the Adams tribe, may also be forgiven.

For my immediate family and myself, the link to South America was sundered at about one o'clock on July 30, 2009. It was then, on that winter afternoon in Argentina, that the long life of Kathleen Mary Dyson, known to us all as Molly, came to an end. Her brother, Patrick Goodbody, had died in 1975 and left no children. Molly's sister Noreen, my mother, had died four years earlier, on July 15, 2005, at the age of 93 in São Paolo, Brazil, and there are no members of the family left there. For me, Molly's death represented the end of a long connection with—and sentimental attachment to—Argentina, my birthplace and the scene of my earliest memories and childhood experiences. This is not so for my Argentine-born husband, Carlos, who still has nieces and nephews and close friends in Buenos Aires, or for Molly's sons, Derek and Brian Dyson, who—although they, their children and grandchildren all live in the United States—still have a strong and active connection to the Pampas through the estancia *La Susana*. My brother David has a new connection to Brazil in his wife, Maria Lucia Ferreiro.

On the day of her death, Molly Dyson—who, like my mother, was born in Uruguay—was approaching her 103rd birthday. But her link to South America had begun almost a century and a half earlier, in 1868. It was then that her grandfather, John George Walker, had for the first time boarded a boat—then still a means of locomotion subject to tilting masts, flapping sails and the vagaries of the winds—to carry him from London to Buenos Aires.

My own fondness for Argentina has much to do with my grandmother Melrose Goodbody, and with her brother, my great-uncle Briton, surrogate grandfather to me. My own maternal grandfather William Robinson (known as 'Patrick') Goodbody had died in 1928. My other, Australian, grandfather, Oliver Linley Adams, an engineer/surveyor, spent some ten years in Argentina. I never knew him, but two of his sons, including my own father, Oliver Huxley, joined him there from Tasmania in the nineteen-thirties. Oliver Linley himself and his son, Noel Darwin, eventually returned to Australia. My father stayed on in Argentina after having met and married my mother in 1939.

My own affection for the countryside after so many years of city life—Buenos Aires, São Paulo, London, Rio de Janeiro, New Delhi, Rome, Washington and Paris—finally brought my husband and me permanently

Introduction

to Italy, a happy compromise between Latin America and Northern Europe. There we found the exquisite hills, vineyards and medieval villages of Umbria. This rural affection originated, to some extent, in that Pampas world of Molly and Charles Dyson's, represented by the *Susana*. It was a world that—although undoubtedly replete with problems and difficulties for the adults—seemed, through the eyes of a child, nothing less than Arcadian, even magical.

However, the nostalgia for the country of my birth may well have been tinged by the very tenuousness and infrequency of my later connections to it. True, I was born in Buenos Aires, but even that is not quite official. So that my parents could christen me with a paternal family name that circumvented the Argentine law that all children born there be given names with a Spanish equivalent (Charles became Carlos; Mary, Maria; William, Guillermo), they registered me as born, not in Buenos Aires, but in Rosario. Rural officialdom was seemingly less rigid in the matter of monikers. Who knows, Rosario bureaucrats might even have bent the rules so that a homesick Welshman from Chubut could name his new-born Argie daughter Argylwyddes (meaning Lady) or Blodeuwedd (meaning Flowerlike). I became a more modest and pronounceable 'Linley'.

Those were the days when, in spite of an Empire already in an advanced stage of dissolution, not to be quite British was still something of a regrettable lapse of propriety. So I was given not only the gift of life but also that of Englishness: I became a true (if not blue) Brit thanks to a second registration with the British Consulate in Rosario.

Although living with my parents in Rosario and therefore growing up as a city kid, I somehow, in my very early youth—mostly through visits to the *Susana* and later to the estancia in Tandil run by Martin Eggar—soon learned something about the country and the countryside of my birth: of the Pampas with their vast flatness and immeasurable skies; of the beauty and mystery of great gardens and ancient trees; of gauchos and *boleadoras*, of horses—catching, saddling, riding and falling from them; of chickens and *caranchos*; of *tero-teros* and oven birds, of locusts and lagoons; of fields merrily waving with wheat, corn and alfalfa, and of storms—those mighty *pamperos*, both the wet and, even worse—much worse—the dry.

My early Argentine experience was short, for in 1946, when I was not yet seven, my father was transferred to Brazil by *Swift's*, the company for whom he worked. (All the family men seem to have been involved, in one way or another, either in the farming, cattle, meat-packing or railway business.) We, my parents and my brother David, made a strange and silent journey in a shrouded ship of war to the country up the coast. My vagrant gypsy life had begun.

Childish Spanish, turned into housemaid's Portuguese, afterwards occasionally sliding back into Spanish vernacular on a few journeys back to the Buenos Aires of Briton and my grandmother, Melrose; to the estancia of the Dysons. In those days of the late forties and early fifties, the plane from Sao Paulo to B.A. was a wheezing propellered machine that took, not today's two hours, but—with a short stop in Curitiba, Florianópolis or Porto Alegre—almost a full day. Passengers lunged about in the vibrations of the cabin, gagging into brown paper-bags inscribed 'Cruzeiro do Sul'.

At the age of twelve or so, in 1953, travel was by ship, this time to England. Once on board, I had never heard so much and such varieties of English. During the two-week journey a friendly ship's hand prepared me for arrival. Alan Pottle, while he washed glasses in the pantry or spliced ropes on the deck, did his best to teach me what he considered 'proper' English. His tutoring in Cockney jargon readied me for 'home', the country I had never seen but of which, I had been assured, I was a citizen. Although my grandparents were born in Australia, Argentina and Ireland, my mother in Uruguay and my father in Tasmania, I had a passport to prove it.

"Naiow Linlay", instructed Alan, "*not* How aaaaahhhh you, but Ow aarhhh yiewe!" I would show off my new skills at dinner (on the ship I had, for the first time, to 'dress for dinner', wear my smart red frock for the evening meal)—but my mother, amused and tolerant as always, did not appear to appreciate my progress in the dropping of aitches.

Then the meeting with my long-suffering English kinsmen, who had kindly agreed to have me—and later various other 'South Americans'—during the long holidays from boarding school. In my case it was Joan and Norman Walker with their children, Angela and her brother—another John Briton—who so generously housed me. School was Berkhamsted, where my mother had been a pupil one generation before, in the days when Graham Greene's father was the headmaster of the far more venerable boy's section of the school. When I arrived, my teacher of geography was Miss Danby. To me she seemed as ancient as those Himalayas she waveringly pointed out on the world map. Miss Danby was then in her last term of teaching at Berkhamsted before retirement, but

Introduction

she still remembered the tall and slender Noreen Goodbody and as a result smiled on me with especial kindness.

When John George Walker's son, young Briton, travelled from Buenos Aires to England in 1880 with his mother, Alice, the little boys in Melrose Road teased him as a 'foreigner', a condition even worse than being a 'colonial'. When I, in the 1950's, approached my fellow students in my new green uniform—an inelegant garment known as a 'vile bile'—I was not merely a foreigner but surely, although Alan Pottle's Cockney lessons were now faded, a savage. My schoolmates would make me laugh by banging their chests, like wild men of the woods, or they would whoop, like Indians—the wrong Indians, those of the American Wild West. I was sometimes asked, with genuine—even concerned—interest, whether, coming from Brazil, I lived in a tree. But of course, I said, walloping my own chest obligingly, and lunging as if swinging from a branch.

As a result of choices made for, by and in spite of me my vagrant existence continued: a couple of years in London, learning that staple of female employment, typing and shorthand, a couple of jobs, then back to Brazil, followed by marriage, seven years in the Netherlands and, then, divorce and re-marriage. In my early thirties it was briefly Brazil again, followed by six years of India, seven of Italy, then the United States (my longest place of abode to date—eleven years), then France and again Italy. As a result, I am now the rootless and somewhat astonished owner of no less than five driving licenses from five different countries (the latest, the Italian, acquired only in the spring of 2010). I can also stumble, rather than glide, through some half a dozen languages.

Through all of this there were only a few occasional trips back to Argentina, twice with our son, Sebastian, once as a baby and again when he was in his late teens. Meetings with Carlos's old friends and family in Buenos Aires enriched the trips as did long bus rides to the town of Venado Tuerto to see my grandmother, Melrose, and Molly and Charles Dyson at the *Susana*.

The last visit to Venado was relatively recent: in February 2007. Carlos and I travelled, as did Angela and Matt Huber, to Argentina for the celebration of Molly's 100th birthday. An elderly local told me that the passenger trains that used to link Venado Tuerto to Buenos Aires had not run for almost thirty-five years, an inconvenience that has also rendered obsolete the acronym, homage to the 'Liberator', that was part of Molly's

Twigs of a Tree

old address—La Susana, San Eduardo, F.C.N.G.S.M.[2] In times past, all addresses in Argentina proudly carried the initials of the nearest railway line. The whole system had been built by British companies—with one or two family members involved—and was as widespread as the railway network of British India. The decay began after World War II, when the Perón government started the nationalization of the lines. There are now many parts of Argentina that can no longer be reached by train. The tracks lie dead, buried deep in Pampas vegetation.

To get to Molly's estancia, Angela, Matt, Carlos and I were driven the six or seven hours from B.A. to Venado Tuerto by Brian Dyson's charming Brazilian friend Ricardo Carvalho. He too had come from the United States for the birthday celebrations.

*La Susana and the giant magnolia,
photo Susie Cogan*

The afternoon we arrived we drove out to *La Susana* to see Molly for tea, before the full excitement of the celebrations of the following two days. The roads are still, as they were once described in the 19th century, 'unacquainted with Macadam'. That afternoon a *tormenta*—a storm—had

---

[2] Ferrocarril Central Nacional General San Martín—San Martin's Central Nacional Railway.

xvi

transformed the dirt and dust into rivers of sludge. We pitched and heaved our way through the mire that flew past the windows and coated the windshield; so thickly that the wipers almost gave up in despair. We did get there, but only because Ricardo's car had a four-wheel drive. Later on, in the evening, when Brian and his wife, Penny, tried to join us for dinner in Venado Tuerto, the winds and rain were too much for their vehicle; they had to turn back. Two days later, another 'torment' sent Johnny Foster, one of the birthday guests, off the road into a deep ditch, a dangerous plunge that he and his wife miraculously survived, unhurt.

When we arrived at the *Susana*, Molly, though born in Uruguay of a mother born in Argentina, was still clearly, even officially, a true Brit. She sat at the dining-room table, drinking tea and contemplating a birthday card that had arrived on the Pampas from Buckingham Palace.

I am so pleased to know that you are celebrating your one-hundredth birthday on 5th February, 2007. I send my congratulations and best wishes to you on such a special occasion. signed Elizabeth R.

Molly reaped much delight from these words sent by Her Majesty. Having just seen the film *The Queen*, with Helen Mirren playing Elizabeth, I remarked teasingly: 'You know, Molly, you have something in common with Elizabeth II.' 'What's that?' she inquired. 'It's that you share a turn of phrase'.

I went on to describe a scene in the film. While tooling about on the moor around Balmoral Castle, Elizabeth's Range Rover gets stuck in the mud. Climbing out of the vehicle, she then inspects, chin in hand, the damage. For a moment she is silent and then, 'Oh bugger!', exclaims the Queen of England. 'Just like you, Molly, when you are particularly vexed.' Molly waved the Royal card triumphantly and then, with a giggle, reached for her tea.

The *casco* or main building of the estancia was overflowing joyously with Molly's immediate family, including her delightful grandchildren, offspring of her sons Derek and Brian. There was Tania, who has the look of her pretty great-grandmother Melrose in an early portrait, and her sister Susie; Kathleen, Derek's daughter, and his son Patrick were also there. Patrick looking much as the young Derek did when he was, so many years ago, at Cambridge.

*Tania Dyson, Susie Dyson Cogan,
Patrick Dyson, Kathleen Dyson Davis, photo ELW*

Other birthday guests, like ourselves, were housed in style at the *El Molino* country hotel in Venado Tuerto. The owner, now old and frail, still reigned from the lobby. Faded posters and pictures attested to his glory days on the racing circuit.

The estancia looked wonderful, although—in this age of almost industrial soja production—it no longer has the horses, milk cows, chicken-runs and the large staff that gave it so much life when I was a child. The tennis court has long been invaded by the woods surrounding it, and the once smooth outside walls of the old box-like pool are now exuberant with ivy. But the tall windmill is still pumping water, even if the round 'Australian' tank is no longer replete with gold-, pink-flashing fish.

Introduction

La Susana Windmill, photo Susie Cogan

I introduced myself to Johnny Forster, an old hand of the area and family friend. He studied me in silent disbelief—after some sixty years—and launched into a torrent of finger-wagging rebuke. It seems that I was still notorious in those parts for having one day climbed almost to the top of the *Susana* windmill. 'The other thing you did was to swing on the end of a horse's tail. You were a very naughty little girl and had to be spanked regularly.' I, a dowager of almost three score years and ten, remembered nothing of this reckless behaviour and could only accept the news of my disrepute in silent remorse, alleviated by a gulp of *vino tinto*.

There is now a new pool, built especially for Molly, who delighted in swimming into her very old age. The circular flowerbed she lovingly tended for over seven decades, still dances with blooms and butterflies, and the magnolia tree facing the veranda is now, in its more than mature magnificence, almost as high as a three-floor house. The skirts of the ancient conifers trail on the emerald lawns of the vast park and beautiful garden. The house glows in new paint to the accompaniment of the double bass refrain of the frogs and toads that still lurk in the nether regions of the veranda. Brian describes Molly and Charles' 'happy legacy',

Twigs of a Tree

> *Look for it in the clean sweep of parkland and elegant mix of old trees that surround the house; or in an avenue of eucalyptus, clean-limbed and graceful, that cuts through the evergreens and opens up a view of the fields and sky beyond. Now venture out to the neat and efficient layout of fields and enclosures that taper down to the south, where a brave knot of trees still stand on a windy knoll that overlooks the saltwater lake and the boundary fences.[3]*

If there is anything that can perhaps alleviate the pains and difficulties—and add a touch of enrichment and joy—to the ambivalent triumph of reaching one's hundredth year, this was a celebration to do it. The dinner at *El Molino* the following evening was a lively event for some hundred-and-sixty people sitting at tables gaily decked in yellow. The guests came from the *Susana* itself, from the nearby village of San Eduardo, from neighbouring estancias, from Venado Tuerto and Buenos Aires; but also from the furthest reaches of the world; the United States, Europe and New Zealand among them. Molly, an elegant pink blouse setting off her white hair, a broad smile on her face, was obviously revelling in the stylish and delicious dinner, the speeches, the merriment and attention.

Molly with her granddaughters Tania Dyson and Susie Cogan, February 2007

---

[3]   Brian Dyson, *Estancia La Susana in the 1930's*

Introduction

Molly's grandparents, John George Walker and his wife Alice, would have enjoyed all this—the highly civilized estancia, the elegant dinner, the croquet games and, on the following day, the *asado*, the outdoor barbecue, ably conducted by Jorge Simonovich. This youthful and amiable man, the present manager or *mayordomo* of the *Susana*, had inherited the job from his father, who in turn was the son of, no longer British or Basque, but Croatian immigrants.

But what Alice and JG might have enjoyed most, apart from the 21st century comforts of the place, was the Englishness of the affair, emphasized by the acknowledgement from Queen Elizabeth herself. Although, as early pioneers, they might have smiled, rather than laughed, at the sardonic humour of Barney Miller's 'Anglo-Argentine National Anthem'. It describes—even celebrates—the many years, the generations, that the British take to shed their Britishness, to speak correct Spanish, to become Argentine. Argentine enough goes the song, to finally acknowledge the hero of the Republic's independence, General San Martín. An entirely self-congratulatory ditty about the British and their reluctant assimilation, it is sung in turn by representatives of four different generations and begins with the oldest:

Some talk of Alexander and some of Hercules
Of Hector and Lysander, and such great names as these
But of all outstanding figures there's none compares to date
With the British pioneers who came to live by the River Plate[4]

One of those early pioneers, John George Walker, was born in the City of London in 1841, some 167 years before his granddaughter's Argentine centenary birthday party. As mentioned, he is the triple-great grandfather, not only of my grandchildren Julian Linley and Sebastian Oliver Van Witsen but also of a great number of other young people. Numbers and names increase almost exponentially both back into the past and forward into the future. JG and Alice had, from their two surviving children, Briton and Melrose, six grandchildren (Molly, Pat and Noreen Goodbody and Betty, Norman and Barbara Walker) and fourteen great grandchildren (my generation). Next come some twenty-eight great-great grandchildren (my children's generation) who are then followed by some thirty-seven great-great-great grandchildren (Julian and Sebastian's generation). In this

---

[4] Written by Harry Duggan in the 1960's and kindly sent to me by Barney Miller

Twigs of a Tree

last large group of twigs there are no Adamses, but there are—among many other names—Blakemores, Bradys, Coxons, Cogans, Davises, De Veulles, Dysons, Eggars, McArees, McClures, Offords, Olivers, Postlethwaites, Tealls, Van Witsens and Walkers. JG and Alice's 'great' grandchildren to the power of—not three, but four—will soon be on the horizon.

Looking backwards, any one of these many young people have, like Julian and Sebastian, not one, but sixteen great-great-great-grandfathers. Numbers backwards double with each generation: from two parents to four grandparents to eight great-grandparents to sixteen great-great grandparents, thirty-two great-great-great grandparents and so on . . .

With families extending (both backwards and forwards) across generations, the dizzying multiplication of chessboard and rice comes to mind. Put a grain of rice in the first square, then double up each time: two grains into the second square, four in the third, eight in the fourth and keep on going. By the eighth square you will have 128. By the time you have filled the 64 squares of the entire board you will have (the Internet tells me) no less than 18,446,744,073,799,551,615 grains of rice, a number even a mathematician might have no language to express, but large enough to fill (the Internet again) a 'container of some 37 cubic kilometres'. It is enough to make anyone believe that the entire globe was indeed, as Genesis insists, populated solely by the reproductive energies of Adam and Eve and their immediate descendants.

Moreover, like all of JG's young descendants, the grand-fathers, too, all had different names (not to mention the grand-mothers): among them Walker, Catty, Christie, Mignolet, Trouvé, Edgecumbe, Adams, Axford, Goodbody, Edwards, Chamberlen, Bovill, Battanta—to mention only a few on only one of the many branches of the family.

One startling (and sobering) curiosity for the many descendants of John George Walker and his wife Alice Catty, is that none of us would be walking the surface of the globe if not for the fate of one of Alice's two grandfathers. This man who was also one of sixteen triple-great grandfathers to me and many cousins, was a priest ordained into the Catholic Church. He had to endure a rude and sudden divestment of his orders by the anti-clerical French Revolutionaries. Marriage became his consolation.

Even if you, my three children and two grandchildren, had miraculously been living at the same time as all these people, you couldn't possibly have known them all. Your own thirty-two triple-great grandparents were scattered all over the world: in Austria, in France, in the Netherlands, in Germany, in England, in Ireland, in Australia, possibly in Wales and even in Italy. Nor would you have been able to speak to them all. You would have had to know at least French, German, Dutch, English, Italian, probably Polish and even some Yiddish. Yet strangely enough: in spite of our long South American connection, there are no ancestors who spoke Spanish or Portuguese as their mother-tongue. Each of the thirty-two triple-great grandparents—here represented by JG and Alice Walker—also symbolize a genealogical path. Most of these thirty-two paths, with their own innumerable offshoots like the hundreds of branches and twigs on a large tree, cannot be followed or traced. The personalities each represents are entirely lost in the dense thickets of the past.

Of many of our distant ancestors we know nothing, or almost nothing; at best their dates of birth and death. Like most of us, they have disappeared into the impenetrable anonymity of the hereafter, leaving no mark. In the vast universe of the dead most stars have no identity. All but a very few—like some of the Huguenot Chamberlens[5] and the Edgecumbes of Devonshire, of my father's family—probably came not only from rural, but even illiterate peasant backgrounds. Some were merchants or landowning farmers, there was a knight or two, one who distinguished himself in the battle of Bosworth. More recently, on the side-lines, there is a famous actor, a priest, even a nun. Most, however, were probably modest country people or, who knows, miners, ironmongers, founders, candlestick-makers, builders, blacksmiths, joiners, cart—or wheelwrights, or, most certainly, soldiers; more recently, there were a couple of diamond cutters. One Peter Chamberlen (1560-1651), a physician, son of William, is credited with having invented the forceps that revolutionized midwifery and saved the lives of countless mothers and new-borns. But the family rather meanly kept this invention secret, even blindfolding the women whose babies they were delivering, so as to retain their exclusive rights (and the profits).

---

[5] George Sherwood's 'Pedigree Register' of June 1915 tells us that the Chamberlens of London were 'A Norman family of 22 sons and 1 daughter, whose father was the Comte de Tankerville, became known in England through the escape thither from St. Bartholome's massacre of William Chamberlaine, a younger son, one of a race of captains and great commanders'. The refugee's wife was Jeneveva Vignon of France.' Sherwood has William settled in Southampton in 1569. There are some inconsistencies here: the St. Bartholomew's massacre occurred in 1572.

In the 19th century, there were some solicitors, a dentist, doctor and surgeon—Alice's father, Frederick Adam Catty; there were lawyers, professors, mathematicians and, in William Mahoney Christie, an Astronomer Royal. JG Walker's own father ran a modest livery stable in London's Coleman Street.

The Goodbodys have brought a touch of non-conformism into the family. The Society of Friends, or Quakers—an initially pejorative term for quaking or 'trembling before God'—were long barred from law and politics. Although they had fiercely opposed the slave trade, eventually banned, after some thirty years of effort in 1807, they remained shut out, until 1870, from advanced education in the universities. Blocked from the professions, and, as pacifists, from the army, they necessarily went into business. Quakers like the Cadburys and Rowntrees 'conquered the sweet shops' and made fortunes in chocolate. The Goodbodys became merchants of, among other things, flour, tea, coffee, jute, tobacco, drapery.

Not many of our forebears have left a trace, written or otherwise, of their passage through life. And when it comes to character and personality, there is almost nothing to tell us what sort of men and women even some of our closest ancestors were. As far as records are concerned, chance can play unkind tricks.

Alice's mother, Ann Edwards (1812-1896) was the daughter of a Cambridge professor. But although her life spanned 86 years, including a couple of decades knocking about Europe, she has gone down in family history as no more than a 'pious woman with a sharp tongue'. Ann's sister-in-law, Sophia Stacey (1791-1874), married to Frederick Adam's brother, James Patrick Catty (1794-1839), was more fortunate. Her beauty has been immortalized in an ode composed by none other than the poet Percy Bysshe Shelley.

But for the most part, our ancestors' likes and dislikes, their tastes, their joys, sorrows and reactions to the world in which they lived, the people they knew, have all been irretrievably torn from us by the oblivion of death. In one or the other case, the best one can offer is an educated guess.

However, one or two wrote books—others, at least for a while, kept diaries that survived. There is a journal by Robert Goodbody (1781-1860), a merchant of County Clara, Ireland, written in 1851. JG Walker wrote a log of his journey to New Zealand—but this was the adventure of a very young man. In Argentina, where JG helped to fight off the Indians and became the legendary 'Facón Chico', he was probably struggling too hard for life and limb to have the leisure for literary pursuits. After New Zealand, there are no logs or diaries from him. All he left in writing from his eventful Argentine period are a few official letters.

Later, the sorrows of World War I and the bitterness of much family loss might have stymied any thought of recording the details of his adventurous life. But JG's son, John Briton, did what he could to record his memories of his parents' pioneering and has left accounts of his own exploits. Of the women, we know almost nothing.

JG's wife, Alice, must have written scores of letters to her family from Argentina—nothing was more important to the settlers than the *galera*, or post chaise, that carried news from home and back again—but those letters are gone, lost by the recipients through moves, change of house, death and war. Or, perhaps, because they would have described mainly domestic matters, letters from women were not considered worth keeping. Appreciated at the time, they were possibly not treasured enough to preserve for the future. Today, those details of daily life in a world so different from our own would be of the greatest interest and fascination.

In Puglia, where we once spent a few weeks enjoying the Italian south, we stayed on a farm that belonged to a once grand Neapolitan family that had been somewhat genealogically obsessed for centuries. One of the walls of the stately house was painted with a vast family tree set against the symbolic background of the bay of Naples. The dynasty sprouted from the earth, set low near the floor, in the form of a thick tree-trunk marked with the year 1205 and one called simply 'Giovanni'. From Giovanni's loins down by the skirting board the tree (to mix metaphors) climbed up and across the huge wall, its countless branches stretching high and far to ceiling and distant corners. Instead of apples or cherries, the tree carried names, hundreds of them. Most were just first names; representing the ordinary, everyday apples that most of us are. But there were also a few Cardinals and Condottieri,—their worldly importance, if not their virtue, indicated by richly curlicued capitals—there were princes, counts, and priests, there was even a branch that ended with the very large apple of a Pope. No doubt, as on every tree, there were some bad apples, too, since the branching was endless.

But there was something odd: every name was male. 'Where are the women?' I asked. 'How did these men reproduce over the past 800 years?' 'Oh,' said the Contessa Lancelotti, who was running the farm, 'the women don't count, they are not part of the tree that endures: the wood, the branches. If you look very closely, you can see a few women's names, very pale, on the leaves. The leaves, of course, like the women themselves, fall away.' The Contessa reminded me of Molly—no shrinking violet she—and how she once made me laugh with a remark about the women in our family. 'Lin, what you must realise is that we all come from a long line of doormats.'

JG Walker, the Cattys, Goodbodys and Adams were all wanderers, people who set forth, mostly in the nineteenth century, to set up lives in what were then some of the furthest reaches of the globe. We do not have to be told that if they had not eventually had young women, wives who shared their often difficult and even dangerous lives, none of us would be here today. It is also their wanderings that have left several of us, including myself and my two brothers, even now, rootless, vaguely vagrant.

If some young men, like the writer Cunninghame Graham, or JG on his trip to New Zealand, set off through a sense of adventure, most emigrants travelled to escape the considerable difficulties and miseries of life in the Old World. It was a world where—in spite of industrialization and a developing middle class—even the most ordinary comforts were still very much in the hands of the very few. The young Charles Dickens with his ten-hour days in the blacking factory, already as a child, had had a taste of the harshness of much of English life. In 1844 the situation in Manchester was to shock twenty-four year old Friedrich Engels into publishing his *Conditions of the Working Class in England,* the work that inspired his friend Karl Marx's theories of communism.

Not many emigrants of the period made the fortunes they may have hoped for when they set sail, and many came to grief, particularly if they were poor and uneducated. JG and his cousin, Harry Edwards, had very little capital, but at least some education, and managed to attain, after much time and labour, not riches but a reasonable standard of living in the very difficult circumstances of early camp life.

After giving up on the pioneering 'frontier' adventure of the Sauce Grande colony, JG for a time used his experience managing the huge properties of wealthy entrepreneurs like Ernesto Tornquist. Eventually, in the 1880's, he seems to have bought an estancia of his own. We know nothing of this property except that it was called *La Mancha* but we now have a photograph of it. JG, after having sailed to England around 1906, seems to have returned briefly to Argentina around 1910, probably in

Introduction

order to sell it. If he did not become rich he was eventually able to retire to his own house on the Thames.

When John George Walker was born, John Adams and his supposedly aristocratic wife, Susana Edgecumbe, had already left Cornwall and sailed for Australia.[6] Another branch of that same Adams family had settled long ago in Braintree in the United States, where a couple of them—extremely distant kinsmen—had already left their mark in the history books.

Frederick Adam Catty—whose own father had abandoned France for England as a result of the Revolution—was working as a doctor at the spa town of Bad Ems in Germany, where his daughter Alice—JG's future wife—was born in 1848. Alice would follow JG to the Argentine, and so eventually would her brother George. Another brother, Arthur Bovill Catty, would set up, in the 1880's, a school in Heidelberg, then under Prussian control; yet others would join the army and go to India, or South Africa. About many of these we know almost nothing, but, thanks to a lifetime of research by Meryl Catty, we do know something about Alice Catty's family, especially her father. Alice's mother, Ann Edwards, remains an enigma.

After his many years in Europe, Alice's father, Frederick Adam Catty, would move back to London and provide a home for his grandchildren—JG and Alice's offspring—when they were sent to school in England from Argentina. When JG Walker was born, Robert Goodbody—whose great grandson William Robinson Goodbody would later marry JG's daughter Melrose Walker in Buenos Aires—was in Ireland running his many businesses in Clara, a town made prosperous by the commercial activity of the Quakers.

We have been for generations a peripatetic family and much has gone. I never knew either of my grandfathers—one from Ireland, the other from Tasmania, both by all accounts rather bookish men—and I only knew one of my grandmothers. Melrose was to me—her only granddaughter—a close friend. She taught me to read, to sew and to laugh at the ridiculous, though we saw little of each other after my parents moved to Brazil from Argentina shortly after the end of the Second World War. But I visited her a couple of times in Argentina before I went to England in 1953, she once or twice came to stay with me when I was living in the Netherlands. We corresponded intermittently until her very old age.

---

[6] She is said to have been the 13th child of the Earl of Edgecumbe but I have found no evidence to prove this.

Twigs of a Tree

The last time I saw Melrose was in 1974, when Sebastian was a year-old baby and Carlos and I went on a visit to Argentina. JG's daughter was by then ninety years old and living at the *Susana*—or rather next door at the *Magnolias*. I begged her to write down details of her life that had begun on the Pampas. She had a rather stoical attitude to her by no means easy existence but she promised to do so.

If she ever wrote anything it is lost. Although many years later I searched for it, I could not find the notebook she is said to have had with her when she died in a nursing home in Buenos Aires in 1977. At her death we were still living far away in India. In 2006 I found her grave in the Chacarita cemetery of Buenos Aires, together with that of her, husband Patrick, and her brother, John Briton Walker.

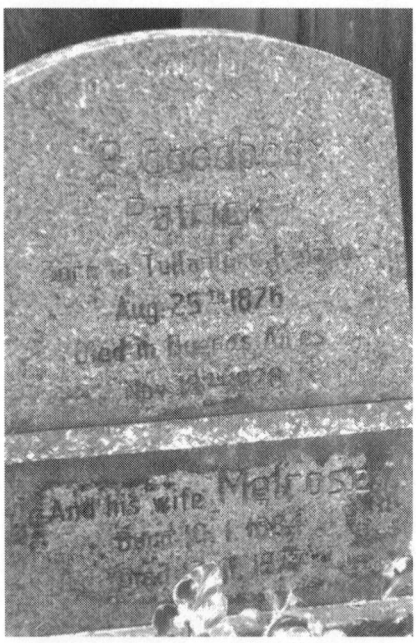

Melrose and Patrick Goodbody's,
grave in the Chacarita Cemetery, Buenos Aires

This, then, is mostly the story of Melrose and Briton's father, John George Walker, who, with his wife Alice Catty, added the South American dimension to the family saga. As said, much of what we know comes

Introduction

from Briton, who was himself fascinated by his father's early pioneering in Argentina and throughout his own life did what he could to reconstruct it.

I can still see Briton, some sixty years ago, typing away on a battered machine almost lost in the paper-strewn mess of a great roll-top desk. His study in the Patricios house in Hurlingham, also functioned as a workshop for the carpentry that was his hobby. The little farm houses that I, Diana and Christie Eggar played with as children were the result of this pastime of his.

Angela (Walker) Huber at the Chacarita grave of her grandfather John Briton Walker—2007

I have set this story out in vaguely chronological order with a few leaps both backwards and forwards, beginning with JG, his youth and his voyage to New Zealand and ending with Alice's death in 1939. I have attempted to tell the story of JG's life in the context of the times through which he lived. There are a few interludes—one is for the younger ones: a short account of the South American Indians and the catastrophe of their confrontation with the Europeans after the accidental arrival of Christopher Columbus in the West Indies in 1492.

Sometimes, without enough material about John George and Alice's daily lives, I have had to use the writings of others, or even a bit of imagination. Jorge Luis Rojas Lagarde, writer and former lawyer and rancher, has, in books on the Indian attacks of 1870 and 1875, done much research into the newspapers and records of the time. His account of the attack of 1870—*El Malón de 1870 a Bahía Blanca y la colonia de Sauce Grande*—tells us much about JG's early life in Argentina and lays out Rojas Lagarde's own admiration for both JG and his cousin Henry Edwards.

Unfortunately there are gaps, many things we will never know. But we do know something about JG Walker—and about the French connection that came through his wife, Alice Catty.

CHAPTER I

BEGINNINGS AND A FIRST LONG JOURNEY

John George Walker was born in North London, on April 5, 1841. His father William (1789-1850), possibly from Nottingham, ran a livery stable in Blue Anchor Yard, Coleman Street, near Moorgate.[1] He grew up in the district around the inn of *The Swan and Hoop* (now renamed *The John Keats*), where some sixty years before the poet's father had worked, in just such a stable, as an ostler. Like the poet, JG grew up surrounded by the horses and carriages his father let out for hire.

This part of North London, sometimes called Moorgate or Lothbury, is now part of the city's financial district. In JG's time it was a neighbourhood of modest craftsmen: upholsterers, weavers, cabinet-makers, braziers.[2] Coleman Street is not far from the church of St Margaret Lothbury and

---

[1] livery stable— A stable where one could hire or board carriage or riding horses. In the 19th century a livery stable posted along a busy stagecoach route might have had as many as a thousand horses.

[2] The Bethlam hospital was also nearby. Formerly a priory, it was acquired by the City Corporation in 1547 and re-established as a lunatic asylum. It became a popular tourist attraction with people flocking to see the patients chained in their cells. However, in 1770 it was decided that 'the tranquillity of the patients' was being disturbed, so admission was restricted to ticket holders only'. In the lower walks of Moorfields in the mid-16th century inhabitants stretched cloth and dried linen. By the early 17th century the area had been established as 'a garden of this City and a pleasurable place of sweet ayres for Citizens to walk in'. The elegant houses of the early 19th century gave way to the offices of modern times, but 'Finsbury Circus Gardens remain and provide an enjoyable space for city workers'.

the Guildhall where Frederick Adam Catty, JG's father-in-law, held a prominent position for some twenty years.

In the summer of 2005 while I was pottering about the area looking for the Guildhall, I blundered through an imposing entrance into the uniformed arms of a young doorman. 'Is this the Guildhall?' I innocently asked. Drawing himself to his full height, he looked down on me with the mute pity accorded to imbeciles. Then he relented and affectionately replied: 'No, love. This is the Bank of England.' After a little more searching I found the Guildhall. Built in the 15th century to assert the power of London's merchants, it is still an imposing piece of architecture although the buildings that flanked it in Frederick Adam's time are gone.

The Guildhall photo ELW

Coleman Street was once graced with the ill-starred church of St. Stephen. First destroyed in the London fire of 1666, the church was afterwards rebuilt by the great architect of St. Paul's Cathedral, Christopher Wren. JG must have known it well. Later, bombed flat during the Second World War, St. Stephen's was never reconstructed. However, the Armourers'

Hall of the 'Worshipful Company of Armourers and Braziers', founded in 1346, is still to be seen at 81 Coleman Street.[3]

John George Walker had a sister, Marianne (1836-1928), who never married, and two brothers: William (1838-1906) and Alfred (1844-1880). When William Walker *père*, the stable keeper, died in 1850, his wife Ann Thorrowgood was—as noted by JG's son, Briton—left to bring up on her own a fifteen-year old daughter and three sons, aged between six and twelve.[4] About Ann Thorrowgood (1806-1870) we know almost nothing, although she seems to have inspired JG with great affection, judging from the tone of his letters from New Zealand.

William Walker, JG's father, was a Freeman of the City of London, that is, he enjoyed the full citizenship that membership in one of London's guilds or trade associations conferred.[5] Until the early 19th century, only such membership accorded the privilege of earning a living in London. Frederick Adam Catty was also to become a Freeman.[6] As such both

---

[3] According to John Stow's 1603 *Survey of London*, at the end of Queen Elizabeth's reign Lothbury was "possessed for the most part by Founders, that cast Candlesticks, Chafingdishes, Spice mortars and such like Copper or Laton workes, and do afterwards turne them with the foot and not the wheele, to make them smooth and bright . . . making a loathsome noice to the by-passers, that have not been used to the like and therefore by them disdainedly called Lothberie." Ben Johnson refers to the street as a source of copper and candlesticks. In 1678 the street still had founders, two pewterers and a tin smith. Stow tells us that Coleman Street was "a faire and large street, on both sides builded with diverse faire houses."

[4] Her brother Sam Thorrowgood, who never married and lived in Petersham, assisted her in this task. William Walker's family appear in Coleman Street in the 1841 census but not in that of 1851, which may mean that the stables were sold or handed to another keeper after William's death. The death certificate, found by Patrick Brady, reads: *8 April 1850. Sarah Giles, nee Thorrowgood*—his sister-in-law—*present at the death*. In the 1851 census we find a 7 year old Alfred Walker—nephew—at 52 King's Rd. Brighton with, a Henry Edwards, solicitor, his daughter Ellen and his wife Susette, sister of Ann Thorrowgood Walker.

[5] The trade association, guild, or livery system is once again flourishing and the 108 livery companies of London include the 'Worshipful Companies' of Barbers, Surgeons and Dentists; of Fishmongers; of Loriners (harness makers); of Paviors (road pavers). They have now been joined by, among others, the more up to date Worshipful Companies of Air pilots and Navigators, of Security Professionals, and the undoubtedly most useful 'Worshipful Company of Tax Advisors'.

[6] Tradesmen usually bought their Freedom status in the city of London but there is also a Freedom of the City status conferred as an honour.

men enjoyed the rare and useful right to drive a flock of sheep across London Bridge. Moreover, if the law caught up with them for any serious misdemeanour, they could look forward to the honour of being hanged, not with any old hangman's rope, but with one of silk.

When JG's father, William Walker, died on April 8, 1850, a few days after JG's 9th birthday, he left a will with precise instructions for his wife and the Big Brothers, the trustees, who were to control her and his business:

> *My wife Ann Walker may in the discretion of my said trustees carry on my business of Livery Stable Keeper and Job Master during so long of her widowhood as my said trustees shall think fit, and for that purpose shall have the use and occupancy of such parts of my estate, including my house hold furniture, as may be employed therein at my bequest.*[7]

It was because of his status as a Freeman that, after William's death, his orphaned sons were given sponsored and reasonably good educations. JG's older brother, also William, seems to have been sent to a mission school in Germany run by the protestant Moravian sect. This choice may have reflected not only necessity, but also a degree of religiosity in his mother. He might, possibly, have attended the Moravian charity school in Neuwied, near Koblenz.[8] William eventually went into the stock market. JG's other brother, Alfred, became a doctor, practising, possibly, at Guy's. He recorded a trip to Africa.[9]

JG, on the other hand, was sent to Christ's Hospital—not a hospital, in spite of its name, but a school, popularly known as the Blue Coat School. Founded in 1552 as a charity school for the poor by Edward VI in 1552,

---

[7] The complete will, not easy to read, is in my possession.
[8] Like the writer George Meredith. Set up in 1756 as a charity school it became very popular during the 19th century with the British and the Scots. In his log describing his arrival in New Zealand in 1860, William refers to the New Zealand port of Lyttleton as similar to 'a German village'.
[9] I have not discovered where he trained.

Beginnings And A First Long Journey

Charles II added, in 1673, its Royal Mathematical School.[10] By the 19th century some distinguished pupils had passed through its halls.[11] JG, still in his ninth year, was admitted on September 3, 1850. Gillian Finlay has unearthed a copy of the 'humble petition' that Ann Walker, JG's mother, presented to the school on August 23, 1850 on behalf of her ten-year old son. It tells us that Ann, just after the death of her husband, carried on the stable business from which she derived an income of 120 pounds sterling a year. Ann virtually falls to her knees as she

> *Humbly beseeches your Worships in your usual Charity to Widows, Orphans and Families, who stand in need of Relief, to grant admission to . . . John George Walker . . . to be educated and maintained among other poor Children; and instructed in the Christian Religion.*

JG was to attend the school until just before his 15th birthday. He was discharged 'for ever' in March 1856, his mother Ann agreeing to provide him with a 'master', presumably for an apprenticeship of some kind.

The school, first in London and after 1902 in Sussex, was at that time housed in a grand building not far from where the family lived. To be admitted was to be 'clothed' and clothed JG certainly was. Pressed into the uniform designed for the impecunious in the days of the Tudors, three hundred years before, he wore an ankle-length blue coat held together with silver buttons embossed with the head of the boy king, Edward VI. Knee britches, bright yellow stockings and a white bib-like neckpiece completed the outfit. These remain, even today, part of the school uniform.

---

[10] "The three classes of poor" are described somewhat quaintly in the sixteenth century school annals as "the poor by impotency, by casualty, and the thriftless poor. For the innocent and fatherless was provided *Christ's Hospital* . . . in London; for the wounded and diseased, the hospitals of St. Thomas and St. Bartholomew; and for the idle and vagabond, Bridewell where they might he chastised and compelled to labour. Decayed householders, and the poor, afflicted with incurable diseases, were to be relieved at their own homes".

[11] Samuel Taylor Coleridge, Warren Hastings, Charles Lamb and Leigh Hunt. More recently it schooled Colin Davis and Bernard Levin.

Twigs of a Tree

Christ's Hospital School in the 1770's

Edward VI buttons of the Blue Coat Uniform

Leaving school just short of his fifteenth birthday, JG did not have the opportunity to become a 'Grecian'—one of the sixth-form high achievers who were then sent on to university. But he left with a love of books that endured into his old age.

To whom he was apprenticed is not clear. Unlike Alfred, the young doctor, neither JG nor his brother, William, seem to have had a real profession, although William eventually became a stockbroker. We do not know how he was earning his living during the six years between leaving the Blue Coat School and setting off for New Zealand in 1862 at the age of twenty-one.

Rats, Lice and Fish that Fly

Although JG was eventually to add the South American component to the family history, in 1862 the River Plate was the last thing on his mind. America was lost, but the British Empire, already encompassing the vast and still almost empty spaces of Australia, New Zealand and Canada, was approaching its heyday. It offered novelty, adventure, the possibility of farming and the—generally false—lure of easy wealth in strange and wonderful lands. Even for young men with some education, interesting and remunerative employment in nineteenth-century London was not easy to find. At this point JG, who did not have the connections nor indeed the schooling to go into diplomatic or colonial service, may well have worked, as did so many young men, as a commercial clerk in one of London's many businesses.

His brother William, soon tiring of office work, had sailed for New Zealand two years before, in 1860, on the *Gananoque*. Two years later JG, eager for excitement and novelty, decided to join him.[12] He was ready to leave London, at least for an adventure, if not for good. He may even have had the glint of gold in his mind's eye, hoping not only for excitement but also for a quick fortune.

Those were the days of the great gold rushes—mainly in California, but also in Australia and New Zealand. JG might well have heard the tales, most of them fables, of the vast quantities of gold that could be dredged from the rivers, dug from the mountains of the New World. William, JG's brother, after having tried his luck at sheep farming, had indeed begun searching for gold in New Zealand.

Whatever the reason, John George Walker bid his family goodbye and on July 3, 1862 climbed aboard a triple-mast ship in Gravesend, London. The wood vessel, royally named *Queen of the Mersey*, partly 'fastened with iron bolts', was only two years old. There is a presumed sketch of the ship—chartered for two journeys to New Zealand—by one of the many emigrants stowed away in its hold. The sketch does not show that it had been 'sheathed in yellow metal' a year before.[13]

American built, the ship weighed 1227 tons. Its commander was a Captain Aitken, a man described by JG as something of a grouch, who was to have his own serious setbacks during the voyage. Apart from

---

[12] See Gillian Finlay's transcriptions of William and JG's letters home.
[13] Contributed by Glenn Newton and drawn by his grandfather William Charles Brown

Twigs of a Tree

the cabin passengers, the ship carried 349 emigrants. It would be 108 days—well over three months—before the *Queen of the Mersey* sailed into New Zealand's Lyttleton harbour on October 19th. It was to be an adventurous trip.

Presumed sketch of the Queen of the Mersey

JG seems to have anticipated a difficult and even dangerous life in New Zealand. He carried in his luggage not only a compass borrowed from his brother, some nuts and—like William before him—a small stock of his mother's delicious plum puddings, but also two revolvers—one his own and 'a small one' of Alfred's. They were to come in handy for bringing down birds for food. JG's stay was to be a relatively brief couple of years. Still very attached to his family, he seems, at least at the beginning, to have had no intention of leaving England for good.

The ship's bowels were crammed tight with entire families who had pulled up stakes to brave the long and difficult voyage in search of new and better lives: work, livelihood, and perhaps free land. Many clearly had no plans—or even the possibility—of ever returning to their native land.

HERE AND THERE;
OR, EMIGRATION A REMEDY.

The illustration entitled *Emigration a Remedy* shows the Dickensian miseries the emigrants were abandoning and the modest abundance and conviviality of the lives they were being promised.

The passengers in the hold of JG's ship were among almost 50 million men, women and children who left Europe between 1820 and 1930. With barely more than the clothes on their backs not only individuals, but whole families set forth from the Old World to the dangers and uncertainties of a new life across the seas.

Life in England for much of the population, both in town and country, was harsh. People were streaming off the land into the cities—London, Manchester, Liverpool—where, in spite of the new factories, there was little hope of work. Some nine million left from Liverpool alone, part of the huge exodus from the great, industrialized cities of England that could no longer accommodate or provide work for the vast numbers of rural poor that had flocked into them during the previous two generations. In Ireland, the terrible potato famine of the 1840s had put hundreds of thousands to flight, first to England and then to far-off destinations across the seas.

Twigs of a Tree

The emigrants would have had to save long and hard for their passages to a new life. In those days a London artisan earned about 36 shillings for a ten-hour day and six-day week. Sailors earned about 15 shillings a week. Senior clerks, or employees in a firm, probably the kind of work that JG may have started in, earned about 150 pounds a year.[14] A professional man—doctor or lawyer—made about 700 pounds. The 'Constables' who kept order on the immigrant ships worked for their passages and received, for work well done, no more than a small gratuity at the end of the voyage. JG seems to have been well off enough to carry a saloon class ticket, worth about 30 guineas, the equivalent of what one of the *Mersey's* sailors earned in a year.

The colonies, eager for labourers and skilled artisans, often lured emigrants onto the ships with the promise of work and often-mendacious tales of the rosy nature of life across the seas. So eager were they that they sometimes offered free passages. These frequently failed to materialize.

The conditions on the steam-ships that began crossing the seas around 1860 were more comfortable than the sailing ships they eventually replaced. The older ships, designed mainly for cargo rather than passengers, had scarce amenities or comforts. A few provisions would be brought on board. A temporary deck was then laid over the cargo and on this narrow and flimsy berths were constructed. Like the deck itself, these could be dismantled after the voyage. Passengers on sailing vessels, regardless of the class in which they travelled, had to endure not only seasickness but also overcrowding, disorder, foul air, and poor, even scarce, food.

> 1 Adam street, Adelphi,
> 14th August, 1839.
>
> FREE PASSAGE.
>
> EMIGRATION to NEW ZEALAND.
> The Directors of the New Zealand Land Company hereby give notice that they are ready to receive applications for a Free Passage to their FIRST and PRINCIPAL SETTLEMENT, from Mechanics, Gardeners, and Agricultural Labourers, being married, and not exceeding 30 years of age. Strict inquiry will be made as to qualifications and character. The Company's Emigrant Ships will sail from England early in September next.
> Further particulars and printed forms of application may be obtained at the Company's Offices.
> By order of the Directors,
> JOHN WARD, Secretary.
> No. 1 Adam street, Adelphi,
> June 15, 1839.

---

[14] For those unfamiliar with old British money: 12 pennies (or pence) equalled 1 shilling; 20 shillings equalled 1 pound; and 21 shillings equalled one guinea.

Beginnings And A First Long Journey

The men in the steerage class of JG's ship were mostly country people: farmers, labourers, ploughmen, blacksmiths, gardeners, shepherds, cart-wrights, and bricklayers.[15] The single women on board were listed mostly as 'domestic servants', dairymaids, a few cooks, laundresses, one or two nurses or nursemaids.

The steerage passengers were harshly crammed into a few square feet of space. Each had a bed, but so restrictive that the occupant could barely turn over. Since there were generally no toilet facilities and no windows, sanitation and ventilation were serious problems. The luggage of the steerage passengers was stored below and it was only at long intervals and with special permission that they could open their boxes for something to relieve their discomfort. Orders were that:

Luggage will be put in the Hold. Emigrants will have access to their boxes once in every three or four weeks, as the Captain may direct.

Moderately more comfortable in the 'cabin' class, JG nevertheless notes in his log that he had to stretch a 'network' across his entire cabin, with the help of nails and screws, to store his things.[16] He even had to construct shelves for his books. He preferred to make his own bed (just before turning in) rather than have the steward enter his cabin. He sometimes cleaned out the cabin himself 'with a hard brush' to get at the filth that the 'dirty old man' missed.

The ship's public spaces were little better. JG writes that during a period of 'stiffish weather', when the cabin-class passengers congregated in the saloon to escape the rain and wind, it was 'so close and smells so nasty that I keep out of it as much as possible'.

On board the sailing vessels of the sixties it was frequently dark. The electric lighting we take so much for granted only began to be commercially viable with Thomas Edison's bulb, invented in the 1880s. Before that light came from wax or tallow candles or, presumably, oil or kerosene lamps. Some towns in England were still—as in Argentina—lit with lamps fuelled with mare's fat. The *Queen of the Mersey* ran short of lights. JG and his fellow passengers tried to improvise with a dangerous and ultimately

---

[15] The New Zealand *Lyttleton Times* passenger list for the voyage is clearly not complete. Neither JG nor any of the other saloon passengers are mentioned.

[16] JG. Walker, *Journey to New Zealand* All quotations about the journey come from this log.

fruitless concoction of brown paper, gunpowder and water. 'The solution was not strong enough, so we shall have to try again,' comments JG.

Fires, set off by candles and open cooking fires, were common on board ship. JG describes a small one in the steward's room that consumed 'two or three of the steward's coats'. But generally they were far more hazardous. Fire, in addition to shipwreck and disease, was one of the great perils of voyage by sea. In 1874, the ship *Cospatrick* caught fire on its way to New Zealand; with scarce and inadequate lifeboats, only three of the 477 people on board survived.

To escape the conditions in the cabins, particularly in times of intense and suffocating heat, JG and his friends, although privileged saloon passengers, often camped out on deck. However, this was not free of discomfort. 'The worst of it is that they bundle us up at about 5 o'clock to wash the decks,' writes JG. Mrs Frankish, one of JG's fellow saloon passengers, was so sea-sick she was unable to stay in her cabin at all and spent most of her time 'in all weathers' on the decks outside.

If sanitation and ventilation were difficult, food was basic and often scarce. The provisions were generally flour, potatoes, oatmeal, tea, salted fish. JG describes boxes of rice, sago, raisins and preserved meat during a storm: they fly 'all over the outer saloon, (turning) the passage between our cabins into a kind of skittle alley'. Refrigeration not yet invented, meat was on the hoof. Pens and coops held live sheep, pigs and poultry for the table. Sometimes even the saloon passengers' rations were cut and one can imagine that the steerage passengers actually went hungry. ' . . . They positively cut us off in porridge and sugar and such little things as that,' JG writes.

John George Walker suspected that his 'brute of a steward' received a 'commission on surplus stores'. On the other hand, he and his fellow passengers were able to fish from the ship. One day, 'unfortunate in (their) fishing', they lose most of their large catch, including a dolphin and a bonito, but nevertheless manage to reel in a small king fish that they had 'curried for dinner'. JG glances longingly at the plum puddings he had brought with him, but resists temptation, wanting to keep them, perhaps for Christmas, 'although the wretches keep us short of pastry'. Aunt Giles' jam is 'very respectable', but he is eager to have some 'directions for making plain things in the cookery department'. Water was often stored in rancid casks used previously for oil or worse. The water, as a result, is frequently fetid and foul. JG is grateful for the filtering device he had brought along. 'My filter is invaluable. The water is filthy.'

The ship was also alive with vermin; rats in such numbers that the men 'came to a general agreement not to go onto the main deck'. On September 7th, two months into the journey, the quantities of lice found in the beds of some of the single women in the steerage class were such that the Captain ordered both beds and bedding thrown overboard. 'The women', says JG, 'came to him in great tribulation to know where they were to sleep.' The captain did not mince words; he ordered the women to 'sleep on the boards'.

The ship moved excruciatingly slowly, at a rate of about 8 knots or 14 kilometres an hour.[17] Even a trip to America from Europe could take anywhere from five weeks to two months; a few recorded trips, like JG's to New Zealand, took 100 days or more. A bad wind could push the boat wildly off course. On the other hand, when the wind dropped, the vessel simply bobbed about on the sea surface, hardly moving. 'We have only made 20 miles of our proper course in 24 hours,' he observes on one windless day.

The vessel was the plaything of the winds. A storm, with the boat pitching, decks awash, hatches battened down, people retching everywhere, was a miserable experience; a calm brought the ship to a standstill. 'You can hardly imagine,' JG writes,

the depression of spirits there is on board when we have either a foul wind and have to turn our backs to the shore, or a calm. And then you should see the difference when a fair wind comes up. The fellows started capering about all over the poop today when the wind came.

Slow and uncomfortable certainly, but in those days travel by sea was also, apart from fires, dangerous in other ways, especially for children. Epidemics were common and frequently fatal. Outbreaks of measles, typhoid or 'ship fever'—spread by lice—killed by the thousand. In 1847, the worst year of the Irish famine, some 7000 emigrants died of typhus at sea and 10.000 more expired after arrival in Quebec. Another scourge was Asiatic cholera, caused by an intestinal microbe spread by contaminated water. The worst attacks were in 1853, when ten to fifteen percent of the

---

[17] (Knot = 1.15 statute mile. 1 kilometre = 0.621 miles).

passengers on some ships succumbed to the disease. The dead were simply thrown overboard.

JG's trip, ten years later, was marked by relatively few deaths; nevertheless, he several times records the loss of children. On his trip they died mostly of whooping cough or measles; they were unceremoniously dispatched. 'The captain', JG writes, 'gabbles them overboard while we are at dinner.' Once he watches, from the top of a mast, the disposal of one of these children. From his high perch, he sees the 'buried' child end in the jaws of a shark. Mrs Frankish, who was always out on deck because of the foul air inside, came down with dysentery. Her little girl, Nellie, whom JG had earlier described as the 'most noisy, senseless child on board', first caught the measles but this, he records, also turned to dysentery. 'She is not expected to live. There are all sorts of smells coming from their cabin.' JG's own severe bouts of seasickness soon abated.

The doctor on board could clearly do little for his patients. After having conscientiously noted the outbreak of the measles in his letters home to his 'darling mother', JG describes a visit, in the company of the doctor, to the steerage class and the ship's 'hospital'.

The stench and dirt, were something awful . . . The hospital . . . is about 6ft by 6ft with two bunks for adults and two for children, an immense medicine chest takes up one side and the doctor uses one of the children's bunks to mix his medicine on . . . with the smell of chloride of lime, medicine, bad ventilation and the natural smell of a sick room, it is certainly not a place calculated to improve the health of the patient.

Little Nellie Frankish did indeed die—at 3am on Sunday, September 28th: one of ten children who succumbed to the conditions of the journey and had to be thrown, by way of burial, into the sea.

Nevertheless young JG and his friends found much to amuse themselves on board. He was healthy, energetic and interested in his surroundings. Perched on a crossbar on one of the ship's tall masts, he surveyed the ocean, the fish, the birds, the stars, the skies, once 'a magnificent sunset, the first really good one we have had'. In the kind of competition that young men take on with their friends, JG came first in crowning the highest mast with his cap. He helped with the sails, took the wheel, fished from the bowsprit, and tried to outdo his friend, Kitson, in gymnastics on a horizontal rope stretched by the captain.

There were plenty of books passed about between the cabin passengers, among them a supply of novels. They could not have included translations of the 1862 publications of Dostoevsky's *House of the Dead,* Turgenev's *Fathers and Sons* or Victor Hugo's *Les Miserables,* but JG was delighted to get his hands on a *History of Greece.* They captured birds and made bait for the line he shared with 'Mr Faraday' weighted with 'sardine boxes cut to look like a fish and tied over with lead to make it sink'. His friends drew, etched or did watercolours. He enjoyed the birds and marvelled at their markings.

The albatross is a beautiful bird with a white head and body, wings white underneath, tipped with black and dark brown, with a white spot near the body . . . The cape hens are dark speckled birds with a clear white ring around the head and eyes, and the flying fish look like silver in the sun.

He also caught birds, killing them by 'holding them over the side of the ship and pressing their breasts' and then, in the way of 19th century naturalists, tried to turn them into 'specimens'. The skull and feet of a Cape pigeon, the skin of which he had accidentally 'ruined', were preserved to be sent home to his brother Alfred, the future doctor, who clearly had a scientific turn of mind. The great naturalist Darwin had published his *The Origin of Species* three years before. It had become a bestseller and might have provided JG with inspiration for his specimen collecting.

There was none of the ubiquitous sound paraphernalia that today makes silence so rare a luxury. There was, however, a band; not much of one—a fiddle, two concertinas and a triangle—just enough to encourage the passengers to spend their evenings singing. The Frankish daughters, including poor little Nellie, according to JG, 'persist in singing dreadfully high and so awfully out of tune on the Poop all evening . . . that it is impossible to sit in the saloon.' He describes how he and a group of 'ungallant' friends retaliated with an 'opposition song, a tremendous chorus which very soon shut them up'. JG was to enjoy singing sea shanties for the rest of his life. He liked practical jokes and highly appreciated the antics of a Mrs Thornton, 'a very nice party', who evoked much merriment by pouring a teaspoon of brandy over her husband's hair when he fell asleep, head on the dining table.

Communication with families left behind was difficult and expensive. The recipient paid postage in those days and the normal post was avoided whenever possible, presumably because of cost. I remember that my grandmother, JG's daughter Alice Melrose, many years later still had the habit of sometimes writing in both directions across her flimsy writing paper. After covering the paper in the ordinary way she would turn it and write, at a right angle, across the previous script. Thus the weight of only one rather than two sheets of paper would be charged. Whether anyone could easily read such letters I don't know. Postage became more efficient and reliable with steam-ships and eventually planes. The 1946 complaints by Lucas Bridges, the author of *The Uttermost Part of the Earth*, about his publishing house in London 'firing many hundreds of questions' at him 'by air-mail' makes even us old-timers of the email-generation smile.

JG had to content himself with much less. Whenever a ship was sighted, there was a rush for writing materials, so that letters could be handed over to the homebound vessel. The captains would sometimes agree to carry the post, but often they did not. On September 1st they captured a pigeon on the deck of the *Queen of the Mersey;* its leg tagged 'Resolute'. The captain was delighted. The bird indicated that a ship commanded by an acquaintance was nearby. JG wrote to his family in London that the *Resolute*

. . . started 6 days before us for Melbourne and is a very fast ship. We expect to catch her tomorrow when I hope we shall be able to send letters by her through Melbourne, which would save a post, and you would get a letter before Christmas.

This, written in September, demonstrates the excruciating slowness of 19th century communication—one that widened the distances between travellers and emigrants and those left behind so greatly that they frequently lost touch with their friends and families altogether.

When the *Queen of the Mersey* passed Tasmania in late September, the captain nearly stopped at Hobart, the island's capital. JG liked the idea because he was curious about the town, and 'it would save a mail and you would get letters before Christmas.' In the end they went straight on to Lyttleton in New Zealand.

By the time JG Walker was sailing past Tasmania, John Adams from Devon had been settled there on his farm—with his wife Susanna

Edgecumbe—for almost thirty years.[18] Their great grandson Oliver Huxley Adams would one day cross to the other side of the world and marry JG's granddaughter, Noreen Goodbody, in Argentina.

Mutiny on the Mersey

Strict rules controlled the behaviour of the young men and women in the steerage class and put them to 'useful work'. Married men were rotated on three night watches; young boys over fourteen were required, in turn, to assist the cook. The married and unmarried, both male and female, were kept strictly segregated, with plenty of finger-wagging regulations.

Single women are to be on the poop, and upon no pretext whatever will they be permitted to go to any other part of the Ship.

So go the rules for emigrants to New Zealand drawn up in 1868.

The matron is instructed to permit no communication with the Single Women on the part of the Ship's Company or the other passengers. It is hoped that a sense of propriety on their part will prevent any attempt to infringe this rule.

Nevertheless, when the vessel reached the Equator, the authorities relaxed for the celebration and ceremony of the crossing. There was a 'grand bachelors' ball' and JG and his friends were permitted to invite some young women up from the steerage for the afternoon. By present-day standards, it was a somewhat staid affair.

There was dancing from 4.30 till about 7pm when the girls went down into the fore part of the saloon for refreshments, which consisted of preserved salmon, ham and sherry and soda water. Then dancing again till 8.30 when the girls had to go below.

---

[18] John Adams (1794-1859) had arrived in Perth on September 9, 1830, with 'plants, animals and indentured servants'. Finding conditions too difficult, he abandoned the 850 acres he had been granted and in January 1831 moved on to Tasmania with his wife, several children and his brother, Oliver. He acquired several properties including a farm, called Mount Edgecumbe after the English home of his wife's family. He also opened an Inn. He seems to have done well. After his death in 1859 his daughter Elizabeth Edgecumbe Adams writes to her relations in Werrington, Cornwall: 'You ask how my father left us? John, Charley and Edward have a farm each and my sister and I have about 100 pounds a year.' 'Charley' was to have thirteen children. One of these was my grandfather, Oliver Linley Adams (1870-1949), who would himself eventually spend about ten years in Argentina.

Twigs of a Tree

JG adds that, 'Single women are generally locked up at 8 but they were allowed half an hour last night.' After that there was supper, 'a glorious turnout, eating and drinking and songs till about midnight'. Clearly such evenings could turn rowdy; JG records that Captain Aitken was extremely gratified that this particular crossing of the line had been so 'peaceful'.

Captain Aitken himself was neither easy nor likeable. 'The skipper gets more and more grumpy every day, I never speak to him and he very seldom troubles me or anyone else,' writes JG. Aitken also had serious difficulties controlling his crew. Replacement of meagre meals with bread and water was the usual punishment for defiance and insubordination, but on one occasion a drunken member of the crew abused the Captain so fiercely that he was put in irons.

On October 6th there was an actual mutiny. A number of sailors, again befuddled with grog, jumped the Captain, knocked him soundly on the head, pushed him over and trussed him up. This little rebellion provided JG and his friends with considerable excitement.

Four of us went forward (into the forecastle) *and found the steerage passengers all around the door. But the sailors had posted a sentry at the door, one of us engaged him in conversation and the rest pushed by . . . . The men were nearly naked and all drunk. There is hardly room to move in there* (in the forecastle), *it is almost dark and a precious nasty place for a row. They had kicked* (the captain) *in the groin, and just as we got in one them had hit him two hard blows on the head with a pair of handcuffs . . . I wish we had had a revolver. We had to beat a retreat, because none of the steerage fellows followed us, but we got the captain out with us.*

A little later, while at lunch, the Captain discovered that the ship was 'going all sorts of ways'. He found the steersman dead-drunk and tried to take the wheel. The drunken man resisted. The Captain had him clapped in irons, putting the man into such a rage that he ran at the carpenter, splitting open his head with a blow of the handcuffs. JG took charge of the drunkard and 'popped him in the lock-up' although he considered him 'one of the best men on the ship when sober'. After the mutiny JG and his friends stood watch. At one time they feared that the single men travelling steerage were in league with the sailors, 'If that is the case it will be war to the knife.'

Beginnings And A First Long Journey

JG, critical of the Captain, felt that he only 'took half measures' and that it had been a serious mistake to throw the first mate into irons. He and his friends finally persuaded Aitken to release him. JG admired the effectiveness of the mate's discipline: 'He is the proper man for sailors, so long as they do their duty well and good, but if they are cheeky he knocks them down.' The Captain gave in reluctantly and JG reports that, immediately after the mate was released, 'there was a change in the ship'. Nevertheless, the passengers, including JG, continued to carry loaded weapons.

JG was also at war on another front. He had a running quarrel with the little Frankish girls that turned into a real 'fight'. Amie Frankish, driven to distraction, gave him a devastating blow 'in the eye with a thimble'.

At the end of their journey they spent a tantalizing day becalmed just outside the port in New Zealand, until the right breeze carried them into Lyttleton harbour. Police came on board with guns and marched off the mutineers, rooting one out of a hiding place. Two days later the arrival made headlines.

<u>ARRIVAL OF THE QUEEN OF THE MERSEY</u>
Lyttelton Times, October 22 1862

The Queen of the Mersey, 1226 tons, Captain Aitken with immigrants, arrived off the heads on Friday morning, but was unable to enter the harbour till night. She brings a large number of passengers who have arrived in good health. The deaths of ten infants have occurred on the voyage, measles having at one time being prevalent among the children. The Queen of the Mersey sailed from Gravesend on July 3rd, passed the Lizard on the 12th, sighted Madeira on the 24th, but did not pass the line till August 16. Since then she has experienced more favourable winds, having passed the Cape on September 12, and sighted the Snares on the 14th inst.

A serious mutiny took place amongst a portion of the crew during the voyage. The cause of the offence was the old story "grog" some of the crew having contrived to broach cargo and get at the spirits. After the men were in irons we hear that the Captain was violently assaulted and struck by one of the sailors with the handcuffs, by which he was seriously hurt. The men, five in number, were handed over to the police as soon as the vessel anchored.[19]

Lytleton Harbour

Arriving in Lyttleton Harbour on Saturday, October 19, 1862, after a journey of over three months, JG was probably disappointed not to find his brother William waiting for him. Undeterred, he immediately set off for Christchurch in the region of Canterbury with a group of friends. His friend Kitson had got hold of a horse. JG, eager to have a mount of his own, took a turn on it, but then, for lack of cash, set off on foot. However, after a short while a dogcart, driven by a 'Chinese coolie' who understood no English, appeared. It had been sent for another friend, Wilson, and they were able to ride into town. Horses were expensive. William writes in his New Zealand log that a horse worth 15 to 20 pounds in England cost 40 or 50 in New Zealand. As a result, most of JG's travelling in New Zealand and Australia was done on foot.

Eager for news from home, their first visit was to the Post Office in search of letters. Then they called on a few people to whom they had introductions of some kind. The wife of a Mr J. Hall claimed to be JG's cousin. What they wanted of this gentleman or what they received from him is not clear. In Christchurch they attended an agricultural show and a ball with about three hundred people. The women seem to have been scarce and grandly out of JG's range,

> *I believe it is very difficult to get partners. All the women I have seen are great swells. Nothing less than a silk dress will do for them out of doors, and all together they dress very expensively. Men dress all anyhow, and are very civil to 'new chums'.*

By November 10th, three weeks later, JG had met up and was travelling with his brother, William. Two years before, William had already thought about sheep farming. The idea had been to lease some 10.000 acres of land, getting someone to stock it with sheep, and—in return for the shepherding—repay the investment with 35% of the increase in the flock. But it seems not to have worked out, since JG does not mention the matter again.

As they journeyed together the brothers often had nothing better than floorboards to sleep on, but once they found decent lodgings for 35

---

[19] Found on the net. The entry also gives the steerage class passenger list, but not that of the cabin class.

shillings a week. They soon moved on, however. They cut each other's hair, scrabbled for food, found a few books to read and searched for something remunerative to do. Soon they were shearing sheep with a 'clergyman's son' who had been reduced to shepherding real rather than human sheep. The shearing was an experience that did not last long, but that perhaps proved useful many years later, in Argentina.

Then there was the constant moving about, the endless trudging through rough country, the sore feet. They foot-slogged, their only means of locomotion, for hundreds of miles. It was rough going, whether in summer or in winter, but they kept their sense of humour.

Cold and raining, fearful walking . . . roads covered with deep greasy mud and full of holes . . . Heavy fall of snow in the night, making the walking bad, made half way house to breakfast, about five miles.

Or again:
Walking on the plain is nasty work . . . The dust is fearful, I had to put my handkerchief over my face, which by the way I have lost—the handkerchief not the face—and it was the best of those two jolly silk ones . . .

They spent the night in tents, the only 'hotels' en route. Once they applied for accommodation, only to be told that 'We could sleep in the tent but they could not supply us with blankets and the next tent was 15 miles on.' On that particular night they managed to borrow a couple of blankets, so were spared the 15-mile walk in the dark. One tent was not only shared but was also overrun with rats: 'We saw a fine fellow running over the two men who were in the opposite corner to us.' They walked burdened by their heavy 50-pound 'swags'. JG's mother, Ann Thorrowgood, worrying perhaps that her sons were becoming a little rough, objected to JG's use of the word 'swag'; she preferred the more refined 'luggage'. JG explained to her that

For such things as a blanket, pick shovel, pot for boiling, frying pan etc. swag is a more appropriate word'. He added obligingly: *'Nevertheless, as you do not like it, I will not use it to you.*

If JG was not thinking of gold when he left England, it soon enough entered his mind after his arrival. Small quantities had been discovered in New Zealand over the past ten years, but in May 1861 Gabriel Read, an

Australian prospector who had travelled as far as California in his search for the precious metal, suddenly made a find in the bed of a creek in the Otago area. For Read it was no less than poetry:

> *At a place where a kind of road crossed on a shallow bar I shovelled away about two and a half feet of gravel, arrived at a beautiful soft slate and saw the gold shining like the stars in Orion on a dark frosty night.*

Gillian Finlay, who has arranged JG's correspondence over the two years he spent in New Zealand and Australia, has also found permits showing that William, having tried his hand at sheep farming, was looking for gold in Otago by September 10, 1861, about a year before JG's arrival. William's attempt at prospecting was part of the furious gold rush that began with Read's discovery. By the time it was over, in 1864, some 18.000 hopefuls had flocked to the Tuapeka area near Dunedin. This settlement (founded only in 1848) turned almost overnight into New Zealand's largest town.[20] The University of Otago, New Zealand's first university, was founded in 1869 with wealth from the goldfields.

A little over a month after JG's arrival, on December 8, 1862, William Walker applied for a second permit to search for gold in Dunstan in the south of New Zealand's South Island. By Christmas Day 1862, the two brothers were at the Dunstan Diggings. As a Christmas treat they finally opened the carefully preserved plum pudding that had been travelling with JG since the previous July. It was a disappointment; the 'gentleman' had turned into a 'mass of corruption'. Smuggled out under a coat it was 'dropped down a bank'. Their prospecting was to be no more successful than the peripatetic pudding.

Either JG or his brother might have heard about, if not read, John Sherer's *The Goldfinder of Australia*. In 1853, this book had laid out the exaggerations and distortions of the gold frenzy that caused, within the seven years from 1851, an eightfold explosion in Melbourne's population of 80.000. Sherer describes the rumours that sent men of all classes to the other side of the world.

> *Everyone was bustling about, getting his things together to be off to the 'Diggings', lest all the gold be gathered before his arrival. I, among the rest, was not idle, for there were news arriving every hour*

---

[20] An unsigned article on the web tells me that 'Many of the city's stately buildings date from this period of prosperity... The rapid decline in gold production from the mid 1860s led to a sharp drop in the province's population.'

of the immense findings, which some unfortunate fellows were happy enough to light upon without much trouble. We heard little of the failures of any; consequently success was in some measure, assured in one's own mind before he had even applied himself with his pick to dig the ground.

It was a frenzy that caught the imagination of men of all classes, and many thought nothing of crossing the globe in the hope of finding gold.[21] Polish miner Seweryn Korzelinski, born 1804, found the mining experience in Australia the ultimate leveller in terms of class, race and multiculturalism:

This very large society comprises men from all parts of the world, all countries and religions, varying dispositions and education, all types of artisans, artists, literary men, priests, pastors and soldiers, sailors, wild tribesmen with tattoos markings and those deported for crimes—all mixed into one society, all dressed similarly, all forced to forget their previous habits, learnings, customs, manners and occupations.[22]

Korzelinski is a keen, though racially and socially conscious, observer: *As they dig shafts next to each other . . . a colonel pulls up the earth for a sailor, a lawyer wields not a pen but a spade; a priest lends a match to a Negro's pipe; a doctor rests on the same heap of earth with a Chinaman; a man of letters carries a bag of earth; many a baron or count has a drink with a Hindu, and all of them hirsute, dusty and muddy, so that their own mothers would not be able to recognise them. Many a one would not, a short while before, bother to look at a fellow with whom he now works. Here we are all joined by a common designation: digger. Only various shades of skin colour and speech denote nationality and origin, but it is impossible to guess their previous station in life or background.*

JG records news of some of the ship's passengers. Frankish, 'who has plenty of money', is looking for land. Thompson and Mac have joined a surveyor: 'I can hardly imagine poor Thompson, a Cambridge man,

---

[21] Charles Adams, one of John and Susana Buse Adams' children, prospected for gold in Tasmania with some success.
[22] Korzelinski, Seweryn: *Memoirs of Golddigging in Australia*, Stanley Robe (ed. and trans.), University of Queensland Press, St Lucia, 1979.

trudging through a swamp with a chain, measuring.' The Faradays have been disappointed in their expectations: 'He is thinking of commencing practice as a lawyer in town.' JG wishes that his cousin, Henry Edwards—who much later was to go out to Argentina—were with him, but begs his mother not to tell him, as he is certain that Edwards would drop everything and race out to join him.

Prospecting is not easy, and the roads to the diggings are littered with animal carcasses. Walking on the rough ground is not made easier by the burdens tied to their backs. At times the rain is so heavy that they have to spend whole days crouched in their tents; they amuse themselves reading 'Fred's *Punches* and Aunt's *Illustrateds*'.[23] At other times they camp but are unable to find drinking water. Some days they trudge through knee-deep snow with nothing to keep them warm but heated stones. For beds they are often obliged to collect grass. They tramp on. Once they lose their bearings and are unable to find their campsite, but the compass borrowed from brother Alfred helps them find their way in this place for which there are no maps. Life is hard and expensive and they are always in danger of running out of food.

However, the brothers seem to be enjoying themselves. They write that they are in 'capital health, good spirits' that they have 'enough money to last them a couple of months'. Once they hit 'colour'—but it is not gold.

Most prospectors like William and JG find either nothing, or veins that they cannot, for lack of capital, exploit. JG describes the huge numbers of men sitting on river banks for months waiting for the waters to subside so they can pan for gold. 'If the river should not go down or the ground not turn out well (ie. yield no gold), there will be terrible poverty,' he remarks. Elsewhere he writes: 'Some of these fellows have but one meal a day, and that very often nothing but flour.' Much later, when they arrive in Australia, they hear that an avalanche at the New Zealand diggings had killed forty men.

Finally the brothers find the prospecting in New Zealand so hopeless that they decide to begin a store, bringing in provisions to sell to the diggers. It was not a bad idea. Better money was often made in the business of supplying goods and services to the captive market of thousands of prospectors than panning the rivers. In California, Levi Strauss had made his fortune selling miners those tough and now ubiquitous denim jeans

---

[23] *The Illustrated London News*, perhaps?

that still bear his name. The intrepid Ellen Clacy travelled in the early 1850s from England to Australia with her brother and had even panned for gold herself. In her description of this experience she remarks:

Carters, carpenters, store men, wheelwrights, butchers, shoemakers etc usually in the long run make a fortune quicker than the diggers themselves, and certainly with less hard work or risk of life.[24]

Many men were simply not suited to the hard life on the diggings, she writes. She knew of one man

More fitted for a gay life in London, who found the diggings too dirty and uncivilised and so turned to his childhood hobby of woodwork and earned a massive £400 a year from his work as a carpenter...

She quotes British miner Henry Brown who, while visiting the diggings, remarked:

Often have I heard men, who have carried off honours at their colleges say, Oh! If my father had but brought me up to anything useful, either baker, butcher or stonemason, what a fortune I would make.

JG clearly considered himself a 'gentleman' but thought nothing of 'being a labourer', proud of his ability for physical work. He remarks that he and William had 'a name for working': 'Only people do not like to take gentlemen to work because most of them will not work and so spoil it for others.'

Eventually they give up prospecting and buy themselves a black bull called Johnny, a porter to carry their gear and the stores—bags of flour and sugar—they plan to sell across the mountains. JG doesn't seem to mind being a bullock driver. In about two months they make enough to pay the £50 price of the bull and rake in £46 more. But they don't expect

---

[24] Mrs Charles Clacy, Thompson, Patricia (ed): *A Lady's Visit to the Gold diggings in 1852-1853*, Lansdowne Press Pty Ltd, 1963. She begins her 1853 bestseller almost falling over with apologies: "It may be deemed presumptuous that one of my age and sex should venture to give to the public an account of personal adventures in a land which has so often been descanted upon by other and abler pens; but when I reflect on the many mothers, wives and sisters in England, whose hearts are ever longing for information respecting the dangers and privations to which their relatives at the antipodes are exposed, I cannot but hope that the presumption of my undertaking may be pardoned . . ."

Twigs of a Tree

such good fortune to last. They are thinking of home. If they could make a thousand pounds each, JG writes, they would return to England.

Months pass without letters or news from London, but in January 1863 the brothers receive some more copies of *Punch*. They are delighted, because otherwise, they say, most of their reading matter is 'trash'. JG writes home sitting on the floor of the tent. A tin dish for ink on his knees, he holds down the canvas with his other hand so that it doesn't blow about. He is so entranced with some of the wild flowers he sees about him that he sends seeds back to his family. At one point the brothers build a store and a dwelling that sounds like one in a Rio *favela*, but to JG 'It is a jolly comfortable little place with sod walls and calico roof, a fireplace and 2 bunks composed of a wooden framework with sacks nailed across and a sack stuffed with brushwood as a mattress.' But 'business is bad', they are losing money and finally make their way back to Dunedin.

Finding nothing there by way of employment, their clothes stolen, including JG's 'gold pin', their hopes of making a living are decidedly dented. They pack up what they have left, sell Johnny the bull, and decide to try their luck in Australia. Before leaving they go to church and take part in the celebrations—triumphal arches, bullocks roasted in the streets, a fishmongers' procession—for a royal marriage. The following day, July 1, 1863, they board the *Omeo* for the seven-day journey to Melbourne. They have funds to keep them going for a couple of months and admit that there is plenty of amusement in the city, 'if we could only afford it'. They watch a river race but are unimpressed with the standard of the rowing.

After several months more of hard labour as bullock drivers, sheep shearers and panners of gold, the young men eventually make their way back to England. The story goes that JG was interested in staying in Australia. William, however, is in love. Afraid of losing the object of his passion, William sails back to England, and his brother goes with him. JG is no longer in cabin class, teasing little girls armed with deadly thimbles. They now travel 'before the mast'—JG as a ship-hand and William as cook. JG gets his hand 'busted up' under a falling anchor. William's precipitous return home makes no impression—he loses his young woman to 'another chap'.

CHAPTER II

ROWING—AND SAILING AWAY

By 1868, John George Walker had been back from Australia for about four years. He was now twenty-seven and had been working, at least for some of the time, at an office job in London for the wine merchant Lightly & Simon.

Rowing clubs had been springing up all over the country, and the British were introducing sports—rowing, polo, soccer, tennis, and rugby—into the furthest reaches of Empire and beyond. For enterprising young men, clubs in England had become important venues both for sport and social contact. In his free time, JG developed a passion for both serious rowing and pottering about in boats. This passion was to endure into his extreme old age and it possibly contributed to his final return to England around 1906. After almost four decades in the far away Pampas, he was eventually to die in his house in Teddington, by the River Thames. Competitive rowing was a taste and talent that would be passed on to several of his descendants.

JG had soon become a member of the London Rowing Club—LRC—that is today one of the oldest boat clubs on the Thames. Founded in 1856, it declared its aim to be 'the encouragement of rowing on the River Thames, and the bringing together of gentlemen interested in that Sport'.[1] It was based—until the permanent clubhouse was built in 1871—at *The Star and Garter* pub in Putney, not far from where Frederick

---

[1] All my rowing information comes from another boatman, my cousin Patrick Brady, who here cites Christopher Dodd's history of the London club, *Water Boiling Aft*.

Twigs of a Tree

Adam Catty lived with his large family. Through this club JG was to meet many young men—and some women—from the extended family into which he would eventually marry: Cattys, Shearmans and Christies.

John George Walker as a young man c. 1865

Some of these had long been rowing enthusiasts. Patrick Brady tells us that the mathematician Samuel Hunter Christie (1784-1865)—maternal uncle of JG's future bride, Alice Catty—when at Trinity, Cambridge, was one of the first to organize a racing boat crew in the early years of the 19th century. Montague Shearman (1815-1865), married to Alice Catty's older sister, Mary Beardmore Catty (1837-1929), was a founding member of the London Rowing Club. His son Jack (1855-1940) as a small boy coxed the Thames Rowing Club crew in 1870 at Henley. JG's cousin Henry Edwards joined the club in 1866 and from 1870 became a 'member abroad'.

We learn from the notes of JG's eldest son, John Briton Walker, that in about 1860 Frederick Adam Catty—Alice's father, now working in the Guildhall—moved with his family from Peckham to Essex House.[2] Alice was then about twelve. This house, in spite of its history soon to be destroyed, stood not far from the Thames in what is now Putney's High Street.

Essex House

James Edwards Catty (1844-1923) and Frederick Henry Bovill Catty (1835-1903), Alice's brothers, were also rowing men, and it was undoubtedly through them that JG was first introduced to Essex House. George Ernest Christie Catty (1850-1935), another brother, would go pioneering with JG in Argentina. Years later Briton Walker remarked that Essex House developed into a 'resort for many young rowing men: George and William Cross, William Dobson, JG Walker and Tom Radmall among them'. Several of these young men were to marry into Frederick Adam Catty's family.

The Regatta for amateur oarsmen at Henley, later the Royal Regatta, was first held on June 14, 1839 and—excepting the intervals of the two

---

[2] British History Online tells us "Essex House is generally believed to have been built and occupied by Queen Elizabeth's ill-starred favourite, Robert Devereux, Earl of Essex, about the end of the sixteenth century. The royal arms, with the initials E. R., appear in the ornamentation of the drawing-room, and also in one of the bedrooms. The wainscoting of the various rooms is stated to be of wood which formed a portion of one of the ships of the Spanish Armada'. The house was sold and demolished with several others in the 1870's, during the building of the bridge at Putney

world wars—has continued ever since, expanding from a one- to a five-day event, very high on the calendar of English amateur sports. In 1858 Frederick Henry Bovill Catty, Alice's oldest brother, had been part of a crew rowing in the Henley Regatta. But as a clerk in the Bank of England, his employers seem to have had scant sympathy with his achievements on the water. 22-year old Fred did a no-show at Henley, failing to turn up for the coveted Grand Challenge Cup, the Regatta's main event. He caused a commotion; the London Rowing Club had to reshuffle its crew on the morning of the race because the number three

> ... *did not show up. There was a fearful argument about Catty's absence, some accusing London of orchestrating a last-minute substitution of a better oarsman ... The argument was fuzzy, and rumbled on despite Catty's explanation of his action ...* "Because the governor of the Bank of England, in which I am a clerk, seeing by the newspapers that I was about to row, expressly forbade me from leaving the bank and if I had disobeyed this injunction I should have been dismissed from my appointment ... I sent a telegraphic message to Henley on the day of the race and my brother-in-law Mr Shearman who was at Henley the same day explained to the crew the reason of my absence ... I have no desire to incur the censure of the club in addition to the mortification I have already suffered."[3]

JG was more fortunate than poor Frederick, his future brother-in-law. In 1868, just before leaving England, he was in the London Rowing Club crew that won Henley's Grand Challenge Cup in the final race against Eton. In that year many rowing clubs were so recent that there were still no rules regulating the size and weight of the coxswains, the boys who steered and set the pace and rhythm for the oarsmen. Both teams were angling for the same boy, a lightweight of under five stone. After much argument they agreed on two others for the helms of the competing boats, much heavier, but of identical weights.

Argentina Beckons

In spite of his triumph at Henley, however, and either bored with his office-job, doubtful of its prospects, or aware that other employment in

---

[3] Patrick Brady quoting Dodd's *Water Boiling Aft*. Fred's career in the Bank of England carried him into retirement, but at 22 he was probably not especially well paid, and he was put on the 'black list' for failing to pay his dues to the London Club.

London was notoriously difficult to find, JG began once more looking overseas. He was now about twenty-eight and already engaged to be married to Frederick Adam's musical daughter, Alice Catty.

George and Fred's indomitable sister was then barely twenty years old. But even Alice may already have known something about Argentina. Her mother, Ann Edwards, was a cousin of the prolific novelist and journalist George Alfred Henty. His first children's book, curiously enough, dealt with emigration to Argentina and pioneering in the Pampas.

Henty's *Out in the Pampas, or The Young Settlers*, set in the 1850's and written in 1868, before his arrival in Argentina, cannot have owed anything to letters home from JG. But since Henty, although widely travelled, never seems to have gone to Argentina himself, he must have based the book on reports and stories currently circulating in England about the dangers and delights, the opportunities and obstacles of life in those faraway parts of the earth. JG had, no doubt, also heard tempting stories from his cousin, Henry Edwards, who had left England two years before.

Edwards, with a little money in his purse, had left England on the *Halley* two years earlier.[4] He had, according to his daughter, taken a job on an estancia to learn the farming business and was now writing to say that the Argentine government was making offers of land on attractive terms. Apart from what he had heard from Edwards and despite the disappointments he had experienced and witnessed in New Zealand and Australia, JG seems to have been tempted, as were dozens of young men, by the glowingly presented prospects of cheap land and of a living—even of getting rich—in sheep farming.

---

[4] In the 1851 census a Henry Edwards, solicitor, and his wife Susette are recorded as living at 52 King's Road in Brighton, with their son, daughter Ellen, and a seven-year old nephew, Alfred Walker. William Walker, JG's father had died by this time. In 1861, Susette (51) is registered in Islington at 10 Willow Terrace, in a household with her daughter Ellen (20), Louisa (15), and Henry J. (18). Her solicitor husband is not mentioned. Susette herself is registered as having died in 1868 at the age of 58. Patrick Brady has found Henry Edwards in 1871 as a widower, with his children Ellen, Louisa and Frederick (Ancestry.com) at 46, Canonbury Park South. In 1881 he is still with Ellen and Louisa as a 'retired gentleman'. This seems to contradict the information from Briton that the solicitor's son, Henry, went to Argentina in the eighteen-sixties with money he had inherited from his deceased father. Perhaps it was money he had inherited from his mother.

Henty shows, too, how difficult things could be in England even for men with some education. The father in his *Out on the Pampas* is no labourer, but an architect. Concerned for the future of his two sons, aged fourteen and fifteen, he lays out for his wife the meagreness of their prospects at home:

There seems to be no opening here in England for young fellows. The professions are crowded, even if they were not altogether beyond our means; and as to a clerkship, they had better have a trade, and stick to it: they would be far happier, and nearly as well paid . . . I think the best thing for ourselves, would be to emigrate . . . You see, my dear, I am just, and only just, earning enough for us to live upon. Nor is there any strong probability of an increase of business. The boys, as you say, are growing up, and I see no prospect of giving them a fair start in life. Abroad it is altogether different: we can buy land and stock it for next to nothing. We should live roughly, certainly; but at least there is no fear for the future, and we should start our boys in life with a fair certainty of success.[5]

The concept of the 'gentleman farmer', of farming as a profession, was still a powerful one, whether one tilled the soil in England or in the farthest corners of the earth. This persisted in spite of the enormous exodus from the English countryside by the impoverished peasantry, largely pushed from their land by the aristocracy and great landowners in the new craze for sheep farming.[6] For most, such dreams of a life as prosperous farmers

---

[5] *Out on the Pampas*, p.2

[6] Robert Heilbronner in *The Worldly Philosophers* tells us that the process of enclosure, whereby landowners turned arable commons land into pastureland for sheep and cattle-rearing had been going on for centuries. It destroyed the medieval peasantry, and in the 19th century the process, by then almost complete, deprived thousands of landless labourers, farmers and peasants of their means of a livelihood. Without his land, the peasant could no longer maintain himself as a 'farmer'. Factories were not ubiquitous and even if they had been a peasant could not easily metamorphose into a factory worker overnight. Instead he became 'that most miserable of social classes, an agricultural proletarian', and where 'agricultural work was lacking, a beggar, sometimes a robber, usually a pauper'. Heilbronner relates that 'In 1820, the Duchess of Sutherland dispossessed 15.000 tenants from 794.000 acres of land, replaced them with 131.000 sheep and by way of compensation rented her evicted families an average of two acres of submarginal land each.'

did not materialize, and many returned defeated, disillusioned and with empty pockets.

One such young man was George Reid (1842-89). Almost the same age as JG, he was lured to the shores of Argentina's Rio de la Plata by dreams of 'sheeping on the River'. Reid had sailed to Buenos Aires in 1867, only a few months before JG's departure from England, and left a series of letters covering the three years he remained in Argentina. They provide a valuable insight into how JG's own camp experiences must have unfurled. Also eager for adventure, Reid wrote of himself as one of many young Englishmen who, not finding employment in his own country, was impelled by a vague and, as it turned out, highly romanticized notion of the Pampas. It was a place from which other men

> *had returned rich and sunburnt after a few years of galloping over boundless prairies after countless flocks and herds, and (with) a strong expectation that they might succeed in doing the same.*[7]

For JG, too, the opportunity and adventure of rural life in the new world beckoned yet again, so insistently that he set off once more, this time to join 27-year old Henry Edwards in Argentina. Young Alice would not see her future husband for five years.

Unfortunately, unlike the Australia trip, no letters home from JG—neither to Alice, his fiancée, nor to his family—appear to have survived. And, apart from a few official letters, some transcriptions of JG's *Yarns from the Camp* and the *On the Frontier* recollections written many years later by his oldest son, Briton, we have no account of his South American experiences. But George Reid's letters to his parents, who were in the textile business in Portugal, give us a good idea of the journey, of Argentina at the time of JG's arrival, of the difficulties and the pleasures that he and other young Englishmen encountered in their own attempts to farm.

Those who could afford it often returned to their homeland. Another young Englishman, Richard A. Seymour, had sailed to Argentina in January 1865, and returned to England in 1868. He had some capital and on reaching home still had high hopes for the land he had bought

---

[7] *A South American Adventure, Letters from George Reid 1867-1870*, collected and edited by his granddaughter, Valerie Boyle, London 1999.

Twigs of a Tree

in Argentina, in spite of the dangers from the Indians. He published an account of his experiences in 1869.[8]

As with the colonies of the Far East, the need for capital and manpower of all kinds was so great in Argentina that its post-Rosas government[9] and its agents in Europe were exerting themselves mightily, and not always honestly, to attract investment and immigrants, particularly labourers—shepherds, smiths, carpenters, farmhands—into the country's vast unpopulated spaces.[10] Like George Reid, JG had probably read the dispatches of M.G. Mulhall, founder and editor of *The Standard*, the Buenos Aires English language paper.[11] Mulhall's *Handbook of the River Plate* became something of a bible for prospective settlers. But even this was suspected of exaggeration, if not deception, in its presentation of bucolic life on the great plains of the Pampas as a sure road to riches and Arcadian content. From Reid, in his account of his three-year sheeping adventure, we learn that Mulhall, who called Argentina 'the poor man's Eldorado', was rumoured to be 'paid for cracking up the place'. Even the very poor were fair game for this kind of bait. Mulhall enticed the penniless with inducements like these:

The class of immigrants by far the most numerous and most successful consists of those who land on our shores without a shilling. They begin as peons or servants, living with some estanciero at £30 a year to mind a flock of sheep . . . It often happens that when a man has proved himself steady and sober, the estanciero gives him a flock of

---

[8] Seymour Richard A., *Pioneering in the Pampas, or the First Four Years of a Settler's Experience in the La Plata Camps*.

[9] Juan Manuel de Rosas, dictator from 1832 to 1852, had earlier vigorously, even murderously opposed immigration into Argentina.

[10] Graham-Yooll tells us that Britons arriving in Argentina between 1857 and 1915 to make a new life amounted to only one per cent of the approximately six million immigrants of that period. The 1869 census showed that there were 10.637 Britons resident in Argentina, while by the 1895 census the figure had risen to 21.788. There were 29.772 in 1910 and 27.692 in the 1914 census. In the latter year the total population stood at close to eight million, and three-quarters of the adult male population in Buenos Aires was foreign-born.

[11] The first edition of M.G. Mulhall's *Handbook of the River Plate*, came out in 1863

sheep on thirds, that is the peon gets one third of the increase of the flock and the same proportion of the net proceeds of the wool.[12]

Mulhall goes on to describe the joys of rural life for better-educated men like JG and George Reid:
Life in the camp has a peculiar charm for young men emancipated from the office desk. The complete liberty of thought and action induces a buoyancy of feeling that compensates for all the hardships undergone. Fortunes have been made in the camp, and are still being made, minding sheep . . .

After his initial enthusiasm, George Reid would eventually paint a very different picture of what he came to call 'this infernal country', full of roaming young Englishmen, many of them lonely, bewildered, broke, drunken and desperate, unable to return to the shores they had left with such high hopes. But in 1868, when JG set off for Argentina, his cousin Henry Edwards was already participating in a farming venture, in an agricultural colony not far from the outpost harbour of Bahía Blanca in Buenos Aires province. At first it was so successful that the venture attracted the attention of Mulhall himself, who dedicated a chapter of his book to the colony on the River Sauce Grande or Large Willow.

Edwards' initial adventures in Argentina were to become something of a family enterprise. Not only Henry Edwards and JG, but also Alice's brother, George Ernest Christie Catty, and Samuel Giles, a maternal cousin of JG's, joined the group of families near Bahía Blanca.[13] The story told by JG's son, Briton, was that in 1870—after Edwards' six-month trip to England to buy agricultural machinery—Alice's brother, George

---

[12] By 1911 *Whitaker's Almanac*—discovered by Matt Huber—had a different opinion: "The immigration of the British working-man (is) not being attended with success."

[13] George Ernest Christie Catty, born 1850. He returned to England in 1882 and married Mary Barbara Wilson (née Cross), widow of Captain James Wilson. Their two children were born in Argentina, and JG's oldest son, Briton, would marry George's daughter (and his own first cousin) Annie Alice (Elsie), mother of Barbara Walker Brady, Betty Walker Eggar, and Norman Walker.

Twigs of a Tree

Catty, travelled back with him and enlisted in the colony.[14] In fact, Alice's brother George seems to have been in Argentina from the beginning. A map of the colony shows George Catty already registered in the Sauce Grande area in 1868. But before moving to the Pampas, let us first cross the channel to France and the French Connection.

---

[14] If JG ever wrote an account of his voyage and arrival in Argentina, it is lost. What we do have are some letters preserved by a granddaughter of one of the settlers, Henrietta Brackenbury, to their agent and consul Goodhall in Buenos Aires and an account of his youth by JG's son, Briton. There are also a few letters from Edwards to his sister Louise in London. Both JG and Edwards appear, with thinly disguised names, as characters in some of the stories of rural Argentina by Cunninghame Graham. *Yerba Vieja* (1936) by Henry Hogg, written with the co-operation of Briton Walker, also provides some details of their life around Bahia Blanca. Rojas Lagarde recently very kindly (2007) gave me copies of an account of her childhood on the Sauce Grande by Elinor Barber, the daughter of one of the other settlers. George Catty's children were her playmates. Edwards' visit to England seems to have been in 1872.

CHAPTER III

THE FRENCH CONNECTION

According to romantic family legend, Louis François Catty (1759-1824) fled the French Revolution from Paris reaching the safety of England 'with the help of the Scarlet Pimpernel'. Catty Jr., as I shall call him, was the grandfather of Alice, JG's future wife, but—although it is true that he left France in the heyday of Robespierre and Saint-Just—the Scarlet Pimpernel had no hand in the matter. This royalist nobleman, engaged in saving French aristocrats from the guillotine during the Reign of Terror, was not a contemporary counter-revolutionary but a fictional Superman, invented at the beginning of the 20th century by the novelist, Baroness Orczy. That aside, this tale, with its implications of patrician flight from the murderous sans-culottes, requires considerable revision.

The young Frenchman Louis François Catty Jr was indeed in London by 1791. But, in all probability, he had by then a long-standing, though often disrupted, connection with the British Isles both through his uncle, Michel Talma, and perhaps even through his own father. The father, also Louis François Catty (1736-1814), had set up various business partnerships in England as early as the 1770's.

Catty Sr. was no aristocrat, but rather a merchant, a wholesaler, who specialized in 'the fashions and articles of Paris'. This unhappy man, however, eventually went bankrupt and never recovered. At the end of his life he lived, according to Madeleine Ambrière, biographer of his famous nephew, 'in the most modest circumstances'. Catty Sr. was to die in Paris in 1814 leaving nothing but a sad little entry in the Paris Archives:

Twigs of a Tree

> Catty Louis-François, 78 years old.
> Deceased 24th January 1814.
> No assets. No testament.[1]

His bankruptcy was largely the result of the political upheavals of his time—much of it unrest that originated across the Atlantic, in part through the activity of an extremely remote connection of the Australian Adams tribe.

In 1773, Samuel Adams and his radical mates, 'dressed unconvincingly' as Mohawk Indians, hurled, with much whooping and yelling, several valuable cargoes of British tea into Boston harbour. The colonial protest of this particular Tea Party eventually, in 1776, escalated into the American War of Independence. French support for the Americans led to almost forty years of hostilities and intermittent warfare with Britain. This, and the Revolution that followed, seriously disrupted commerce between the two countries until the end of the Napoleonic Wars in 1815. Peace treaties of brief duration—such as those of Versailles in 1783 and of Amiens in 1802—provided only short-lived respite from the antagonisms that played havoc with cross-channel trade and Catty Sr.'s business.

A Brush with *Gloire*

If Catty Sr. died a ruined man, he did at least have a small link with celebrity, even with *gloire*: he was the uncle of the famous French tragedian, François-Joseph Talma (1763-1826). Known simply as Talma, this man, friend of Danton's, became the most eminent actor of his day, the 'Garrick of France', pal and favourite player of Napoleon.

Talma

---

[1] Found and kindly sent by Ambrière

The *gloire* of the stage was not then universally endorsed. The Catholic Church in France, particularly in Paris, bracketed the immorality of actors with that of harlots and hangmen. Denying them all sacraments, actors were even refused burial in consecrated ground. Talma, declining to abjure his profession, was—in 1790—refused the right to marry in the church of Saint Sulpice.

Talma as Racine's Cinna in the classical dress he introduced to the French stage.

Catty Sr. and Talma's father, Michel Talma, were married to two sisters, Anne and Marguerite Mignolet. These daughters of Pierre Mignolet and Marguerite Trouvé of Verdun had in the late 1740's moved to Paris. There they lived with their uncle, Joseph Mignolet, who owned a fashionable clock and jewellery shop at the Palais Royal.

On February 2, 1758, Marguerite married Louis François Catty Sr., 'a man from the north', a merchant who travelled frequently to London. Two years afterwards, in April 1760, Marguerite's sister, Anne, married Michel Talma (1733-1806) in the Parisian church of Saint Nicolas des Champs, a few blocks from where Carlos and I now live, in the Marais.

Twigs of a Tree

Michel Talma was in 1760, at age 27, a *valet de chambre*, still not launched into his future career as a dentist. Before the Revolution, Ambrière explains, the nobility with its enormous households was able to offer men of some education a considerable range of employment: artists, musicians, composers, doctors, even priests could all make a living on the estates of a rich nobleman. Those with intellectual leanings often worked as secretaries, teachers or librarians. Even the *valet de chambre*, Jeeves to an important nobleman, was often not a mere servant but rather manager of the household:

> *a privileged man, keeper of the secrets of his master, and if he did not yet have the insolence of Beaumarchais' Figaro, he enjoyed a certain liberty of speech and an enviable position. He was the 'homme de confiance', often charged with delicate missions for his master. The master, in return, became both the generous benefactor, protector and patron of his man.*[2]

Michel Talma was employed, however, not by a French but an English nobleman.[3] Sir Oliver Clinton would remain his protector in France and later in England.[4]

Obviously, the higher placed the employer, the better the position as his *homme de confiance*. Catty Sr.'s occupation at his death was still described as an *homme de confiance*, but, since he died so poor, possibly the household in which he worked after his bankruptcy was itself, in the wake of Revolution and war, also much reduced.

Michel Talma, by contrast, initially engaged in the same business, did rather better than his brother-in-law: he soon turned what may, at first, have been a strange hobby, into a highly lucrative profession. He became a dentist, opening a practice in Paris at his home in the Rue Mauconseil. His son tells us in his *Mémoires* that Michel Talma had

> *a large family: three daughters and two sons, and the goodness of his heart had augmented his charges, because he had also adopted a nephew. Competition was great: the vanity of us Parisians, the especial care they have for their teeth, had multiplied at this time the numbers*

---

[2] Ambrière, 29, *Talma ou l'Histoire du Téâtre*.
[3] *Mémoires de J.F. Talma, 1850,* ed. by Alexander Dumas, p.15
[4] Hicks, Peter, *Napoleon and the Théâtre*

of dental surgeons. My father was dreaming of a new establishment when chance heeded his call.[5]

Apart from adopting his nephew, Louis François Catty Jr., Michel Talma was also a generous man who early in his career did all he could to salvage Catty Sr.'s increasingly precarious financial position. A document cited by Ambrière testifies that on April 27, 1771 Michel Talma lent his brother-in-law the not inconsiderable sum of 2.360 *livres*, to be invested, with a partner, in a tile works. A few days after this transaction Michel gathered up his entire family and crossed the channel to London where he set up a dental practice in an elegant part of the city at 13, Old Cavendish Street.

According to Ambrière, his wife Anne, to whom he was unhappily married, persuaded him that he would be able to augment his income by serving as an intermediary for his brother-in-law's businesses. Michel Talma, on the other hand, hoped that Catty Sr.'s familiarity with London would lead clients to his new dental enterprise.[6] Michel Talma was indeed to do very well as a dentist in fashionable London, with the future King of England among his patients.

In his *Mémoires,* Michel's son, the tragedian, relates how his father, who clearly already had influential friends in Paris, came to leave his home town for London:

Lord Harcourt arrived at my father's house to have one of his teeth pulled. He was so satisfied with the way the operation was carried out that he persuaded (my father) to leave Paris, to place his establishment in the hands of one of his students and move to London. My father, seduced by the promises of Lord Harcourt, followed his advice, and went to live on Cavendish Square. Lord Harcourt had not fooled my father: his recommendations brought him riches and numerous friends, among them the Prince of Wales, who later became George IV. It was not only a great favour but a hugely lucrative one to be the dentist of the future sovereign of England.[7]

Although he had left France, Michel Talma maintained his Parisian dental practice in the Rue Mauconseil. His brother-in-law, Catty Sr., remained in

---

[5] *Mémoires*, p. 15 (my translation)
[6] Ambrière, p.39
[7] Talma, *Mémoires*, p.15

Paris with his wife and his two children, Louis François and a daughter, Anne Sophie (1760-1835). But Catty Sr.'s business enterprises—ranging from tiles to French scent—became increasingly unstable as commerce between France and Britain deteriorated with the outbreak of war in 1778. In 1779, like many other merchants who could not collect their debts, Catty Sr. found himself in grave financial difficulties.

A document dated January 4, 1779, published by Ambrière, shows the bankruptcy of one Jean Honoré Fargeon, *'Parfumeur de la Reine et de la Cour*, supplier of scent to the Queen and the Court. Catty Sr., listed among Fargeon's creditors, was owed the vast sum of 20.839 livres. Ambrière relates how some well-placed businessmen—like Fargeon himself—managed to get through the crisis. Catty Sr. however—who, according to Ambrière, possibly 'did not have the connections of the others'—lost whatever still remained to him in the general bankruptcy of 1781. That year Catty Sr.'s own creditors were made public. Among them was his brother-in-law; Michel Talma was listed as owed 2.100 livres.[8]

This came as a shock to Michel, still across the channel, in London. Five years before, his wife Anne had told him that Catty had repaid the money lent him in 1771. Believing his wife, Michel Talma had even gone to a London notary and on March 7, 1776 he had had a receipt—an official acknowledgment of repayment—drawn up. Michel Talma now realised that Anne, in an effort to help or shield her sister, to whom 'she was very close', had lied.

Michel Talma's not very edifying opinion of his in-laws, to whom he believed he had been sacrificed by his estranged wife, are recorded in an angry letter written to Anne in 1785, almost ten years later, and four years after Catty's bankruptcy in 1781.[9] In the letter he refers to the debt and to his nephew Louis François Jr., who by then had entered the priesthood. He also mentions Catty Jr.'s sister, Sophie, who eventually fled from her problematic household into a nunnery. Of Sophie, the nun, he writes:

> *The daughter of this man, your niece—did I not arrange for her to come to England, did I not pay for her trip, did I not find a place for her here, and afterwards did I not receive her in my home, did I not see that at different times she had all that she needed, did I not lend her about 40 louis that she still owes me?*

---

[8] Ambrière, p.48

[9] The complete text of this letter was kindly sent to me by Madeleine Ambrière in the summer of 2009 and translated by me from the French.

Then he goes on with a series of angry questions:
One summer, while we were both in Paris, did she (Sophie) *not treat you badly . . . steal the best of your things? For fear of upsetting you did I not let all that pass in silence? The mother, your own sister, has she ever tried to soften the faults of her daughter? Was it not so that her only concern was to blacken me in your eyes . . .*

Michel Talma, who according to his son was an admirer of Rousseau and Voltaire and a professed atheist, is unimpressed with his niece's religiosity:
This daughter returned to Paris and, well settled, stole from the house where she was, escaped, and not knowing where to turn became a nun, good riddance.

Michel then turns his anger and wounded pride on his nephew, Louis François Jr., the neophyte priest:
The abbé Catty, your nephew, whom I have long loved and whom I thought had a sense of what his parents owed me—I said nothing to him about the matter because I do not wish to imitate you in lightly passing judgement without proof on a man about whom I have only suspicions, founded solely on the silence that he has maintained with me after these last discussions. He is a minister of religion, and his role should be that of a peacemaker. He has kept quiet however, and this is enough to make him appear a hypocrite. Without reproaching him for the moment directly, he will never have from me either love or trust. One must be, dear Madame, the master of one's sentiments.

Catty Sr., his brother-in-law, comes next:
The father who has robbed me at your request; this daughter who did the same and who is now a nun, the most hypocritical of all; that mother who has never deigned to acknowledge by a single word that which she owes me, on the contrary who has always tried to get between us. Monsieur the abbé who (after the friendship that he wished to show me (crossed out) *keeps his silence over a matter as important as this one; look, Madam, I say, look at those to whom you have sacrificed your husband, these your oracles, your source of guidance (you know I have reproached you for them and this is not the first time). To follow your own advice, I look into myself and I*

Twigs of a Tree

find there a recognition of what I owe you, and the obligations that I owe them.

Michel Talma follows with a general, less than flattering sketch of his in-laws, the entire Catty family:
All these people are however very religious, they confess every 8 days, go to mass, always have the word virtue, the name of God on their lips. You have often joked that I am wicked. I take pride in being and thinking differently from them. The only true religion that I know and practice is to do good to others and no harm, to love my fellows. I disdain those who engage in flattery, in futile ceremonies and who, behind the mask of pity, speak of peace, of virtue, without practising it.[10]

The deception by his wife rather than the loss of the money was a severe blow that festered. Talma's marriage had always been, 'unlike the Catty's', a stormy and unhappy one. Nevertheless, there was much coming and going by the family and their children between England and France. In 1775 the young Talma, now age twelve, had been sent back to Paris for schooling at an institute run by a Monsieur Verdier.[11] Catty Sr. sheltered his nephew in his own home and introduced him, young as he was, to the French theatre.

The boy was already, under the influence of his father, an admirer of Voltaire. Three years on he attended the famous performance of Voltaire's last play, *Irène*, when the writer's bust was carried to the stage and crowned 'by all of France'. When Voltaire was afterwards carried in triumph to his carriage, young Talma, now fifteen, assisted with the horses. Two months later, on May 30, 1778, Voltaire died; the Catholic hierarchy in Paris, knowing that he had professed that the Church was an 'infamous thing' that should be 'crushed', refused the great man burial.

Monsieur Verdier had in the meantime engaged a priest to prepare the children for communion. Young Talma, deeply affected by the insult to Voltaire, repudiated the priest's opinions with a highly dramatic exposition

---

[10] All from the letter sent from London by Michel Talma to his wife Anne Mignolet Talma in Paris in 1785.

[11] Talma, in his *Memoires*, says he was nine, but since he was born on January 15, 1763, he must have been in, or nearing his twelfth year. One of his biographers mentions that he sometimes concealed his true age, perhaps for reasons of vanity.

The French Connection

of his own unfashionably liberal views. Verdier, outraged, expelled him from the school.

Talma was not surprised at the scolding he received when he was deposited at his uncle's house, for Catty Sr's 'philosophical views were less advanced' than his own. Young Talma then re-joined his father in England.

On returning to England, Talma alternated a dental training from his father with enthusiastic explorations of English literature. In the company of other young Frenchmen and under the aegis of his father's protector, Sir Oliver Clinton, he also became familiar with English theatre.[12] The young men, too, had their 'protectors'. Talma writes:

Almost all of us had powerful patrons in London; almost all of us had people in whose eyes we wished to shine.[13]

Anne visited her husband, Michel, three years later, in 1781. There was a row over her lying, but Anne, by this time, had discovered that Michel was embroiled in a deception of his own. He had an English mistress, Charlotte Sterne, by whom he had two children. The upshot was that Anne returned to Paris, taking her son with her. Talma tells us that the journey from London to Paris took three days 'In one of those carriages with six horses that ply the road from London to Dover in so rapid and agreeable a way.'

That even Michel's affair with Charlotte Sterne was marked by his deep unhappiness with his wife Anne can be seen in the wording directed to his mistress in his will. When he died in 1806 Michel Talma left nothing to Charlotte, the mother of his two illegitimate children, declaring:

It will no doubt be considered surprising that I do not leave to Charlotte a specific legacy, but my Heart revolts at all the good I should wish to have done her. I trust that this will amend her for the rest of her days. My two Natural children have a disposition to learn everything, but the mother who pretends to know better than anybody is not capable of governing them. I entreat my Executors earnestly to watch her and give her advice therefore as I have given to my Children a share of my Heart.

---

[12] Hicks, He also joined a group, trying to introduce French theatre to the English and tells us that his father's principal protector was Lord Harcourt.

[13] Talma, *Memoires*

Twigs of a Tree

Nevertheless, he had clearly overcome his anger at the 'hypocrisy' of his nephew. Louis François Catty Jr. (his name now anglicised to Lewis Francis) was one of the executors of Michel's will and inherited a 'portrait of my son and of his wife'.

In spite of the perpetual quarrelling between his parents, Talma had a careful and extensive French and English education, spoke both languages fluently and developed a passion for Shakespeare that he later exploited on the French stage.[14] Talma's sister, on the other hand, who had lived mostly with her mother, seems to have had barely any schooling at all. Father Talma at one point accuses his wife of having neglected the child's education to the point that at the age of nine she was still unable to read or write.

After returning to Paris with his mother in 1781, young Talma threw himself into his dental studies. The somewhat disreputable profession of dentistry had been accorded in the 18th century the lustre of entry into the Royal College of Surgeons. Even so, dentistry—like surgery—was not then what it is today. There were no drills, no anaesthetics, and teeth for the living were wrenched from the mouths of the dead.

One of Talma's sisters, Anne Gertrude, known as Manette, wrote to her brother from the London she hated in her capacity as assistant to her father. She asked him to please visit the Paris morgues, the *salles des morts*, for a supply of fresh teeth. Manette especially sought canines and molars that were still 'white and beautiful'. [15]

Already agonizing over his desire to go into the theatre, he was nonetheless tempted to accept a position as a dentist in the household of the Duc de Chartres. Talma's remarks on his decision throw a light on the changing social realities of the dying days of the Ancien Regime. After consulting his father he tells us that, on learning that

I would have to leave both the Rue Mauconseil and my home at the Palais Royal, my father, who no longer loved either princes or priests, insisted that I not place myself in the pay of a grand nobleman.

---

[14] For Talma Shakespeare was 'le Dieu de ma jeunesse, mon maître, mon guide dans l'étude des passions humaines'. 'The God of my youth, my master, my guide in the study of human passions'.

[15] Ambrière, p.49

Eventually young Talma—who had been engaged in other studies, including rhetoric and philosophy at the celebrated Collège Mazarin—followed his inclinations and abandoned dentistry for the stage.

From Paris to Woolwich

What Talma's cousin Louis François Catty Jr. was doing, where he lived, or what kind of education he obtained after his father went bankrupt when he was around 21 years of age, we do not exactly know. But he, too, seems to have acquired a sound education. Perhaps the generous Michel Talma financed his studies. Or possibly, by joining the priesthood, Catty Jr. had his tertiary schooling underwritten by the Church.

It was at the Collège Mazarin that Talma met, among other distinguished men of the future, Nicolas-Francois Bellart (1761-1826), who would become one of France's famous Crown attorneys. Since Bellart, the future lawyer, turned into a close friend and 'brother' to Louis François Catty, it is possible that Catty Jr., also studied at the Collège Mazarin with his cousin. He also developed the literary abilities to later produce a number of books.[16]

Talma, at least at first, had a 'good revolution'. The theatre as popular, rather than as aristocratic, entertainment took off. He became a personal friend of a young military firebrand then roaming Paris, Napoleon Bonaparte.

Talma's cousin Louis Francois Catty, the priest, had a more difficult time. Immediately after the Revolution the Church, the biggest landowner in France, was stripped of its possessions; monasteries and nunneries were closed down. In July 1790, a year after the fall of the Bastille, the clergy lost its special rights; nuns and priests were required to swear an oath of loyalty to the Civil Constitution of the Clergy, i.e. acknowledge not the Pope but the French State as head of the Church. The nobility occupied most of the upper echelons of the Catholic Church. As a result the Church, the First Estate, was seen as intimately linked to the hated Second Estate, the aristocracy.

Catty Jr. was forced to become an *assermenté*, to take the oath. He was also de-frocked and forced to hand over his letters of ordination. Not long afterwards, the revolutionaries began a massacre of the clergy, both male

---

[16] He wrote *Elements of French Grammar*, 1803; *Exercises on French Grammar*, 1810, for his students at Woolwich, and a revision of Voltaire's *Histoire de Charles XII, Roi de Suede'*. All can be found in the British Library.

Twigs of a Tree

and female.[17] Catty Jr., not surprisingly, seems to have found the situation so intolerable that, like some 30.000 others, he left France. His friend Bellart rose to eminence in 1792 as 'counsel for individuals brought by revolutionary passions before the sanguinary tribunals of that unhappy time'. It is possible that Bellart attempted to defend Catty Jr. when he was forced into the oath that stripped him of his vocation.

Meryl Catty believes that Louis François Catty Jr. remained a royalist sympathiser and that he may have escaped from France and obtained his job in England with the help of the Duke of Richmond. The Duke had been Ambassador in France, but by the time young Catty arrived in England he had become Governor of the Royal Military Academy of Woolwich and Captain of the Company of Gentleman Cadets. Apart from the Duke, the connections and 'protectors' of his uncle Michel Talma Sr. might also have been of help to the young priest.

By November 1791—now in his very early thirties—Louis François was registered as Master of French at the *Academy for Gentleman Cadets* at Woolwich with a starting salary of £100 per year. Light and warmth were provided for with '4 chaldrons of coal and 6 dozen lbs of candles'.[18] To augment his salary, the young Frenchman soon set up, with a partner, a short-lived private Academy at Prospect Place, Walworth Common.[19] This Academy, possibly partly financed by his uncle, Michel, offered cadets private tuition outside the Woolwich Academy hours.[20]

It was about then that Louis François anglicised his name to Lewis Francis. Not long afterwards, on January 25th, 1794, the former priest accepted the hand of Mary Ann Christie at the Anglican Church of Saint Anne Soho in Westminster. Mary Ann was an older sister of Samuel Hunter Christie, one of Woolwich's future and most distinguished professors of

---

[17] A favourite form of massacre became 'marriage' between the clergy: a priest and a nun were tied together and thrown into a river to drown.

[18] He replaced a Mr. Felix Hugonin as French Master on November 1st 1791.

[19] In 1809 Talma, in a letter to a nephew, refers to his cousin Catty, whom he had asked for a loan; he tells us that Louis François (Lewis Francis) Catty Jr. lived at Prospect Place, Walworth Common, Kent, in 1809.

[20] The partnership was dissolved on January 25, 1794, and the Academy closed down. See Meryl Catty's *Descendants of Pierre Mignolet*, p. 5

mathematics.[21] Michel Talma, his anger at the family clearly over, was witnesses to the marriage. Relations between the Talmas and Cattys across the channel were maintained.[22] Mary Ann and Lewis Francis were to name their second son, Robert Bellart Catty (1796-1826) after Crown Attorney Nicolas Francois Bellart (1761-1826).

In 1802 the treaty of Amiens established a brief peace between the French and the English. Meryl Catty tells us that Sir George Smart, in Paris in July 1802, remembered 'the great French actor, the Garrick of the place', whom he met in the city's National Library. Smart also records meeting 'a Mr. Catty' who introduced him to Mr. Bellart, 'the first counsel at the bar'. Smart goes on to say that Catty had with him 'a son who, though but ten years old, speaks English, French and Latin well'.[23]

Lewis Francis Catty Jr., now back in Paris with his wife and three small children, had serious business to attend to in his hometown. In 1801 the French State had decided to make peace with the Church and the Papacy. A Cardinal Caprara was sent to Paris to settle the complications of the Concordat with the Vatican. On January 25, 1802, his eighth wedding anniversary, Lewis Francis added his own petition to some 5.000 others submitted to Caprara. It reads:

Louis François Catty, priest of Paris, aged forty-three and a half years, took the oath of the Constitution of the Clergy, (but) carried out no functions afterwards and was married before the (sic) protestant minister in London to Marie Anne Christie of the Anglican religion on the 25th of January, 1794 and has three children.
He asks his Eminence to reconcile him to the Church, to absolve him from censure, to lift any irregularities and to give him permission to

---

[21] Samuel Hunter Christie's (1784-1865) younger son, William Henry Mahoney Christie, became England's Astronomer Royal for the years of 1881-1910. See Meryl Catty's Notes on the History of the Catty Family and the Astronomer Royal's recently discovered obituary.

[22] In 1806 Michel Talma died, leaving a portrait of his famous son to Lewis. In 1810 the bankrupted Catty Sr. and Talma were both witnesses at the marriage—in the church of St. Germain de Pres—of the actor's youngest sister, Euphrosine (Ambrière 469, 127).

[23] This information comes from Meryl Catty; she thinks that the son mentioned must be James Patrick Catty, but the dates do not match. James Patrick, Lewis oldest son, could not have been 10 years old in 1802, since his parents had married in 1794. His birth elsewhere is given as 1795. He might of course have been a very precocious seven.

marry, according to the rites of the Catholic Church, (Catholiquement) Maria Anne Christie, in spite of the fact that she is not yet inclined to abandon the Anglican religion.
He has never wished to agree to the Test Act, in spite of it having been proposed to him as a condition for obtaining employment.
He has been in Paris for three weeks and he must return in the first days of August.
In the hope of a favourable reply he has signed,
L.F. Catty[24]

Six months later, on August 3, 1802, Lewis and Mary Anne Christie were married once again. This second marriage took place in the heart of Paris in the Church of St. Sulpice, the same church that had turned away Lewis' cousin, the actor Talma, some ten years before. Now that the Revolution had, for a time, converted it into a 'Temple of Reason', St. Sulpice seemed not to mind bestowing the sacraments on an unfrocked priest with an uneasy conscience and a Protestant wife.[25] The groom's father, Catty Sr., was one of the witnesses.

Unlike his uncle Michel Talma's 'infernal union', this twice-celebrated marriage between Catholic priest and staunch Anglican seems to have been an unusually happy one. In his will Lewis Francis was to declare:
I give and bequeath to my dear and beloved wife Mary Ann all my goods and chattels and personal property of every description. At the same time, I take this opportunity to declare my most grateful acknowledgement for the happiness I have enjoyed with her, and that I have always had reason to bless the day we have been united

---

[24] The petition to Caprara is in the National Archives in Paris. The Test Act was a 17th century penal law that required all holders of public office to swear their allegiance to the official Church of England. No 'popish' recusants or non-conformists like Quakers were allowed.

[25] St. Sulpice has no record of the marriage. I was told that probably, since Mary Ann was and remained staunchly Anglican, the church probably gave the couple a blessing rather than an actual marriage. A 'blessing' would not have entered the records.

together. If ever I have given her any moment of pain, I hope she will forgive me in favour of the tender love I bore her.[26]

In 1808 Lewis, now known as the 'Premier maître de la langue Française a l'académie Royale et Militaire de Woolwich' edited a new 'stereotyped' edition of Voltaire's Charles XII, King of Sweden. Any difficulties Lewis might have suffered in France because of his marriage or his father's bankruptcy seem to have been nullified by the early success of his own career and by his own circle of influential friends, many of whom, like Bellart, he could have met at the Collège Mazarin. Ambrière writes that the younger Catty came to be considered 'trés honorable'. When he and his wife travelled to France in July of 1819, a minister of the central government went to the trouble of ordering the authorities at the port of Dieppe to extend especial care to the visitors with 'all the attentions due to foreigners who arrive in France'.

Lewis died at Woolwich in 1824 and was buried in the Churchyard of St. Mary Magdalene, Woolwich. His tombstone was later moved and placed against the walls of the church. It reads:

'Sacred to the Memory of Lewis Francis Catty, Esq., of the Royal Military Academy Woolwich, who departed this life February 1st 1824 in the 64th year of his age'.

Lewis Francis' wife, Mary Ann Christie, was to die over fifteen years later, not in England but in Germany. His famous cousin, François-Joseph Talma, would pass into the hereafter on October 19, 1826.

---

[26] Meryl Catty, from an article in the *Guardian* on Last Wills and Testaments, April 14, 2007. I now have a copy of the will in my possession. Bellart is to be 'the distributor of my tender sentiments to my dear adopted family, and to assure them that in spite of all the events which have prevented us from enjoying one another's Society, my heart has always been with them. Their love has been a source of happiness, and the idea of being loved by them has made me bear quietly the injustice of some people . . .' The family he refers to may be the illegitimate English family of Michel Talma and Charlotte Sterne.

Twigs of a Tree

Talma's tomb in the Père Lachaise cemetery ELW

The actor lies in the Père Lachaise Cemetery in Paris; companion to Oscar Wilde, Colette, Chopin, Gertrude Stein, and, before their remains were moved to Italy, to Cherubini and Rossini. The tragedian's tomb has no dates, no details of his life or death. It reads simply: TALMA.

A Brush with Eng. Lit.

Lewis Francis Catty and Mary Anne Christie had four sons. Their oldest, James Patrick (1795-1834), became an army officer. In 1823, he married an orphaned heiress, Sophia Stacey. His life was short, but he holds a small place in English literary history—thanks to the beauty of his wife. Sophia, with the 'soft clear fire' of her eyes, has been immortalized by no less a poet than Percy Bysshe Shelley in his memorable *Ode to Sophia*.

Sophia was born in Maidstone, Kent, daughter of a prosperous local businessman and sometime mayor of the city. She lost both her parents at an early age and spent three years of her youth living with a Mr and Mrs Charles Parker. Mrs Parker was Percy Shelley's aunt. An attractive and musical girl with some fortune, Sophia did not marry young. According to *Wikipedia*, all portraits of her show 'very strong eyes'.

In 1819, Sophia Stacey set out on a grand tour of the Continent with an older companion, Corbet Parry-Jones, later to be described by Mary Shelley as 'an ignorant little Welshwoman'. In November they reached

The French Connection

Florence, where the Shelleys were living. They called on the poet at his *pensione* on the Via Valfonde. After striking a rapport, the two women moved into the same digs. Mary Shelley was heavily pregnant and soon after their arrival gave birth to a son. Sophia is credited with suggesting he be named Florence, and indeed, he became Percy Florence Shelley. (The following year, an English child born in Florence was also named after the city—and so, from no other than Florence Nightingale, it was promoted into an established name for English girls.)

For two months the poet Shelley showed Sophia around the city. At the *pensione* she played the harp and sang his verses, but there is no evidence of the relationship being anything other than entirely respectable. Well, except for Shelley's beautiful lines:

Ode to Sophia

Thou art fair, and few are fairer
Of the Nymphs of earth or ocean;
They are robes that fit the wearer—
Those soft limbs of thine, whose motion
Ever falls and shifts and glances
As the life within them dances.
Thy deep eyes, a double Planet,
With soft clear fire,—the winds that fan it
Are those thoughts of tender gladness
Which, like zephyrs on the billow,
Make thy gentle soul their pillow.
If, whatever face thou paintest
In those eyes, grows pale with pleasure,
If the fainting soul is faintest
When it hears thy harp's wild measure,
Wonder not that when thou speakest
Of the weak my heart so is weakest.
As dew beneath the wind of morning,
As the sea which whirlwinds waken,
As the birds at thunder's warning,
As aught mute yet deeply shaken,
As one who feels an unseen spirit
Is my heart when thine is near it.

Twigs of a Tree

Shelley presented Sophia with his Ode around Christmas 1819. She and her companion then travelled on to Rome, where Sophia received a lengthy letter from Mary with the *Ode to a Faded Violet* by Shelley inscribed on the back. The Bodleian Library in Oxford has some letters Sophia exchanged with the poet in the months to follow. They never met again. Shelley was drowned, at the age of 29, when his boat capsized off the coast of Livorno two years later.

Sophia Stacey eventually married, in 1823, the army Captain James Patrick Catty of the Royal Engineers. Four years her junior, he was undoubtedly trained at Woolwich where his French father, Lewis Francis Catty, had been teaching for so many years.

The wedding of Sophia and James Patrick was a rather grand affair, followed by a reception given by Maria Fitzherbert, George IV's morganatic wife. Sophia and James Patrick had three children who lived to adulthood—a daughter and two sons. The daughter married a Royal Marine officer, the younger son, Corbet, spent time in the Household of the Lord Mayor of London and then retired to the family home, Hill Green House, in the village of Stockton near Maidstone. The elder son, Charles, followed his father into the army, where he participated in the Zulu wars in South Africa, rising to the rank of Major-General.

But James Patrick Catty died, aged only thirty-nine, in 1834, and Sophia—then well into her forties—married the following year a Charles Hamond, who had recently lost his own wife. Apparently Sophie continued to call herself Mrs Catty. A family note says she was always a devoted mother and her children 'adored' her. She died in London in 1874 and was taken to Stockton for burial. An obituary in the *Kentish Times* makes much of her friendship with Shelley and its importance in her life. James Patrick Catty's military coatee is in the National Army Museum in Chelsea, the collection's 'oldest piece of Engineers'' uniform.

Lewis Francis Catty's and Mary Ann Christie's second son, Robert Bellart Catty (1796-1839), was accepted in 1810, at the age of fourteen, into the 'superior class of shipwright apprentices in His Majesty's Dockyards'—together with a close friend, Charles Bonnycastle. He served, presumably in the navy, and in 1818 was, according to Meryl Catty, appointed assistant secretary to Sir Frederick Adam, later the Lord High Commissioner of the Ionian Islands, another former student at Woolwich. Robert Bellart's friend Charles Bonnycastle, on the other hand, had a distinguished career as a soldier and writer of books and mathematical

The French Connection

treatises. Robert Bellart's middle name was clearly a tribute to Talma's (and Lewis Catty's) old university friend, the notable French lawyer Nicolas Bellart.

The naming of his son after the man he referred to in his will as 'my friend, my brother Bellart', (rather than Talma) may also be an indication of royalist, or anti-revolutionary political leanings in Lewis Francis, particularly after the horrors of Robespierre's Reign of Terror.[27]

Lewis Francis Catty and Mary Anne Christie's third son, Louis Bonnycastle Catty, born in 1798, appears to have drowned very young together with his uncle, Robert Munster Christie. He may have been named after John Bonnycastle (1751-1821), also a mathematics professor at the Woolwich Academy. It is to their youngest son, Frederick Adam, that we now turn.

---

[27] Ambrière declares that the attorney Bellart's monarchist ideas (and defence of condemned victims of the Revolution) eventually distanced him from Talma, the actor, who embraced with enthusiasm both the Revolution and Napoleon.

CHAPTER IV

THE ADVENTURES OF A SURGEON
Frederick Adam Catty (1803-1891)

Frederick Adam Catty—Mary Ann and Lewis Francis' youngest son and future father of Alice Walker—was baptized in the Church of St. Mary Magdalene, Woolwich, on September 18, 1803. He was named after his godfather, his father's star pupil, Frederick Adam (1781-1853), who later became a colonial official and soldier, distinguishing himself in the Battle of Waterloo. Sir Frederick Adam later possibly became the employer of Frederick Adam Catty's elder brother, Robert Bellart.[1]

We know nothing of his youth but Frederick Adam Catty was apprenticed on April 3, 1820, aged seventeen, to an apothecary at Woolwich for five years. Seventy-one years later, his obituary in the *City Press* tells us that

> *Mr Catty, after receiving his education at a local school, studied at Guy's Hospital with the object of entering the medical profession. Subsequently he visited Paris, with a view to studying the treatment of gunshot wounds. As a boy, he was a constant visitor to Paris, staying while there as a guest of Talma, the great tragedian, and M. Bellard, the eminent advocate. On returning from France, fully qualified to enter upon the practice of his profession, Mr Catty took up his residence at Cambridge.*[2]

---

[1] See Meryl Catty's notes
[2] The obituary was discovered by Meryl Catty

By 1832 Frederick Adam was registered in Cambridge as a surgeon and in 1833 as a member of an association for the 'Advancement of Science'. The following year, on February 13, 1834, in St. Michael's Church, Cambridge, Frederick Adam married Ann Edwards (1812-1896), daughter of a Dr James E. Edwards of Downing College, Cambridge and granddaughter of Benjamin Bovill of Durnford Lodge, Wimbledon.[3] Ann Edwards, as noted, was a cousin of the journalist and novelist George Alfred Henty.

Frederick Adam Catty had many interests besides surgery. His love of music is recorded by Temple. In 1835 he was elected into the Cambridge *Garrick Club*, recently founded to 'facilitate the performance of theatrical works' and the 'diffusion of a taste for polite literature and rational amusement'. He is also listed as a member of the British Association for the Advancement of Science. By then he had been a surgeon in Cambridge for several years.

Although he seems to have lived in some style, he began planning, in his early thirties, to leave England. Meryl Catty has found an advertisement for the sale of all the possessions of 'Mr. F.A. Catty' in the *Cambridge Chronicle* of September 23, 1837. They give us an idea of the man and his rather comfortable circumstances. The contents of his drawing room are described as

fitted with well-manufactured rosewood furniture . . . 12 Trafalgar chairs, circular loo table, pair of card tables, 3 cheffioneers (sic), 2 Turkish couches, noble chimney glasses, 3 sets of amber damask curtains and gilt cornices, Brussels carpet, reclining chair . . . also a very rich toned Broadwoods horizontal piano-forte with metallic bars . . . which cost £ 120 . . . (and) is considered, by eminent judges, to be one of the finest the celebrated house of Broadwood ever made . . .

The dining room and other furniture comprises . . . a set of beautiful Spanish mahogany patent dining tables, rich carved legs, and 4 extra leaves, ditto pedestal sideboard, circular library table, 10 prime Spanish mahogany chairs, morrocco leather seats . . . several ounces of modern plate, a costly set of table and dessert cutlery with ivory carved handles, and part silver blades enclosed in handsome mahogany brass bound case, containing upwards of 100 pieces; expensive dinner, breakfast, tea and dessert services; cut and plain glass, tea urn, Books, table and bed linen . . . also a useful brown Hackney 'gig horse' quiet in harness.

---

[3]   Frederick Adam Catty—International Genealogical Index / BI
Gender: Male, Marriage: 13 Feb 1834 Saint Michael, Cambridge, England

Twigs of a Tree

Having divested himself of all these goods and chattels and paid off his creditors, the Cambridge surgeon, now 34 years old, set off with his wife and two children on a peripatetic life across the channel that would last for approximately twelve years. He was to have a number of children abroad, including his daughter Alice.

Surgeons and Barbers

It is interesting to speculate on how Frederick Adam carried out his profession, for he was practicing before the great 19th century breakthroughs that changed surgery—and indeed medicine—forever: the discovery of anaesthetics, of the connection of dirt and bacteria with disease, of antiseptics to create the essential microbe-free environment of asepsis.

Surgery, like dentistry, was originally a craft with a history that went back to the medieval barber-surgeons. As with the grocers and drapers, barbers and surgeons were grouped together in the same guilds. The red and white stripes of the traditional barber's pole were originally symbols of the blood and bandages of his work—not with razor and scissors, but with knife and bloodsucking leeches. As late as the 18th century, not only shaving and haircutting, but also tooth pulling, leeching and amputation were all part of the same trade, that of the 'snippers and shavers'.

In those far-off days, surgeons as often as not carried out their operations—removal of gall stones and amputations—in the chaos of the marketplace. A taste of this can still be found in India today, where dentists still perform in the open markets, between tottering piles of vegetable merchandise. Like the medieval barber-surgeons of Europe, they are showmen who, in attempting to relieve their patients, also perform for an audience. As one foot pumps a (painfully slow) treadle drill, the market dentist repairs or removes teeth with a theatrical flourish that brings applause from the onlookers obstructing the stalls around them. The harder the patient squirms, the louder he screams, the more entertaining the performance, the more delicious the audience's *Schadenfreude*.

The Adventures Of A Surgeon

By the early 19th century the status of the surgeon, like that of the dentist, had risen somewhat. In 1745 an official divorce had been declared from the barbers, and a New Company of Surgeons was formed. This was followed, in 1800, by a Royal College of Surgeons. But although they had gone up in the world, surgeons were still somewhat despised by physicians. These, though not licensed to prescribe drugs, were university trained. Potential surgeons, however, were instead apprenticed to apothecaries, the pharmacists of the day. Indeed, on July 23, 1836, the *London Medical Gazette or Weekly Journal of Medicine and Collateral Sciences* published a list of ten 'gentlemen' who had received a certificate from the Apothecaries' Hall on July 14, 1836; Frederick Adam Catty was among them.

But even the market dentists of today's India are aware of a number of essentials still unknown at that time even to Frederick Adam himself. The humble open-air dentist with his foot-pedal drill knows about anaesthetics, about how dirt is linked to infection. In the 19th century however, surgery—usually amputation—in the absence of anaesthetics was a brutal business that often required, besides the surgeon, several strong men to hold down the unfortunate patient. The first successful anaesthetic for surgery was applied in 1847, only four years before Frederick Adam Catty gave up his profession.

If the patient survived the shock of the operation, he often died of a subsequent infection because nothing was washed or disinfected. The connection between germs and disease had not yet been established. Surgeons usually operated with unwashed hands, wearing filthy, blood-soaked dress clothes, 'the filthier the coat proclaiming the busier their practice'. It was only in 1865 that James Lister, convinced of the necessity for cleanliness, began to use carbolic acid as an antiseptic for his operations. Surgeons themselves remained sceptical for another fifteen years. Lister's ideas were 'widely derided as finical, ladylike and affected'.[4] What Frederick Adam Catty thought about this controversy we do not know.

---

[4] See Richard Gordon, *The Alarming History of Medicine*, 1993

Robert Goodbody of Clara (1781-1860)
'Who made this town?
Mr. Goodbody made the most of it, Sir'[5]

We do, however, have a fascinating little insight into the profession from within the extended family. In 1855, the wealthy Quaker, Robert Goodbody of Clara, now 'within three months of seventy-four years old', decided to write a journal of his life.[6] He was interested in medical matters. In his world, the grim reaper is perpetually at work, striking down both old and young. The journal is, in part, a long compendium of death and disease: tumours, cholera, smallpox and the 'scarlitena' that killed his young son, Richard.

In 1800 his mother, Elizabeth, developed a lump in her breast. A surgeon in Dublin recommends rubbings of 'dandelion juice'. Ten months on, her

---

[5] Quoted by Michael Goodbody. Robert Goodbody of Clara was great, great, great grandfather (one of sixteen) to Derek and Brian Dyson and to me and my two brothers David and James Adams.

[6] Michael Goodbody tells us that Robert began a profitable jute and flour milling business in Clara in 1826. He and his family were at the time the only Quakers in Clara. Robert was the father of the 'five brothers' in the famous Goodbody portrait. The Goodbodys who went to Argentina—Edward Gaynor, Jonathan, Ebenezer and William Robinson, all descend from him.

The Adventures Of A Surgeon

case is deemed hopeless. Two surgeons, a Dr. Jacob and Dr. Bathwick, a 'rough scotch man', reject the dandelion juice and decide to operate. Elizabeth does not go to a hospital; the surgeons come to the house. Their equipment includes a couple of heavy ropes. As the surgeons sink their unwashed knives into unwashed flesh it is these that, in lieu of anaesthetics, are to keep the patient still. The stoical Elizabeth, however, waves the ropes away as an indignity. The removal of the tumour is soon over.

Several friends were in the room . . . The doctors proposed that my mother's arms should be bound as she sat on a chair, for the knife being used, but she objected. Mary Bewley stood by her all the time, and she bore it without attempting to raise her hands. It might be ten minutes before they were done. They did not take away much of the outer skin, perhaps 1 1/2 inches square, but scraped out the lump about the size of a large potato.

Ten months later, in spite of taking the waters, and 'because a gland under her arm became diseased and cancerous', Robert Goodbody tells us that his mother underwent yet another operation.

It was,

full bad as the first . . . her life being in much danger from a sudden bleeding of an artery, the part to be taken away adhering to the artery.

As well as courageous, Elizabeth Goodbody was lucky. Her son records that in the end 'She favoured to recover, as her death would have been a sure loss to her young family'. Elizabeth Goodbody, surviving all the surgeons, managed to reach the age of 81.[7] However, when next attacked, 'It did not last more than half an hour until she was gone.' The third operation took place on the 16th of 'the eleventh month' of 1834. Robert's own wife, Margaret, was less lucky. Often ill, she had died in her forties in 1824 leaving Robert with six sons. One of these, Richard, was gone a year after his octogenarian grandmother, in 1835, at the age of eighteen.

---

[7] Robert Goodbody Journal, found in the attic of his house by Tony Lynch.

Twigs of a Tree

Robert Goodbody's five surviving sons 1882
From left to right: Marcus, Lewis Frederick, Jonathan,
Thomas Pim (seated), Robert James[8]

Michael Goodbody tells us that Robert Goodbody's 'fascination with medicine' led him to help alleviate the suffering of the poor during the terrible famine years of 1846-48. The Earl of Charleville, owner of large estates around Tullamore, presented him with a silver tea service in gratitude for the work he had done, as an amateur doctor, amongst his tenants. With his flourmills, jute factory and gas works, he was able to leave Clara a Quaker Meeting House, and a burial ground for the exclusive use of his descendants. Nobody, even if a dead body, may be buried there unless he is also a Goodbody. At his death in 1860, his funeral procession was, according to Michael's sources, more than two miles long. In 1834, the year that Elizabeth, Robert Goodbody's mother, died Frederick Adam

---

[8] Thomas Pim, great great-grandfather to Derek and Brian Dyson and to myself and my two brothers David and Jim, was the father of William Robinson Goodbody Sr. whose son of the same name married Melrose Walker. Another direct descendant of Thomas Pim was Mary Ann (Buzz) Goodbody, the first woman director of the Royal Shakespeare Company. In spite of her great and early success she committed suicide at the age of 28 in 1975. A particularly horrible irony, since she was one of the few, if not the first, women in the extended family to receive a proper education. Jonathan, brother of Thomas Pim, was grandfather to the brothers Ebenezer Pike (1880-1957) and Jonathan (1883-1957) who would go out to Argentina and, for a time, run the *Susana*.

married Anne Edwards. And a few years later, between May 1837 and May 1839, according to family legend, he became medical attendant to Sarah, the Countess of Warwick, travelling with her family throughout Europe.[9]

It was still not then uncommon, even after the French Revolution, for doctors—like literary men who functioned as tutors, secretaries, or even *hommes de confiance*—to join the households of the aristocracy, accompanying them to the various spas and watering holes of Europe. Frederick Adam seems to have had the time for his practice and for literary pursuits. A publication called *Jugel's Universal Magazine*, published in Frankfurt and edited by Frederick Adam himself, in 1844 ran a number of English book reviews ranging from articles on *The Use of Elephants in War* to the dangerous enticements flaring between vice and virtue of *The Siren and the Friar*. It also carried a review of a three-volume work, entitled *The Life of a Travelling Physician, from his First Introductions to Practice; including Twenty Years' Wanderings through the greater part of Europe*. It gives us an idea of the medical career as it could be practiced at the time. In the review one reads that the young doctor

after three or four more years of hard study, anxious expectations and no fees . . . accepts a situation with Prince . . . at Paris, as family physician for five years.

The young doctor, with his master, the Prince, spends winters in Paris and summers in Dieppe, visiting various watering holes in between, in the hope of curing tuberculosis (or consumption as it was then known) with changes of air and climate. We learn that English physicians had not yet attained that

melancholy level of learning with which they now estimate the several varieties of air and temperature in the regions to which they recommend the victims of that appalling complaint.

Frederick Adam, as we have seen, carried with him his entire family. Several other children in what was to become a very large brood of four sons and five daughters were born abroad. One, Charlotte (1839-1928), was born in Dunkirk and four, including Alice were born in the Nassau district of the Rhineland.

---

[9] Meryl Catty has so far been unable to prove this piece of family legend but Temple, who knew Frederick Adam well, mentions it.

Twigs of a Tree

In 1841 Frederick Adam's widowed mother, Mary Ann Christie, visited him in Germany. Meryl Catty speculates that she may have been there for the birth of Frederick Adam's fourth child, Emily Fordbowes Catty (1841-1930) and of a possible twin brother, John, who seems to have died at birth. Mary Ann never returned home. The *Gentleman's Magazine* for January-April 1841 announces Mary Ann Christie's death in Neuwied near Bad Ems not by her name, but merely as her husband, Louis Francis Catty's, remnant or leftover, his 'relict'.[10] It was in Neuwied that Alice, the sixth of Frederick Adam's nine surviving offspring, came into the world in 1848.

Frederick Adam eventually became Bad Ems' resident English physician. He must have been enchanted with the beautiful little town on the river Lahn near Koblenz. In 1844 he published a guidebook to the spa and its surroundings.[11] The book is a rich compendium on the beauties of the countryside, the ancient towns, villages and castles. He is fascinated by the history, the botany and the geology of the area. He covers the chemical content of the waters, their effects and their superiority to the waters of Cheltenham.

> The waters of Ems pour
> *In unceasing streams from inexhaustible resources supplied by the liberal hand of a beneficent Creator ... and yet so bountiful is nature, that although all the springs issue from the rocks within a very short distance one from another the character of them is so modified in their chemical proportions, and degree of heat as to adapt them to the alleviation, if not the cure, of various classes of disease, or to enable them to be applicable to the peculiar idiosyncrasy of different constitutions.*

But Frederick Adam strongly disapproves of the 'crying evil' of the gambling tables, the 'evil passions and covetousness' of the men who run them. With its casinos and its 'Schloss Balmoral', Bad Ems was then one of the most elegant spas in Europe. Princes and intellectuals—Turgenev, Delacroix, Victor Hugo, Clara Schumann, Gogol—all passed summers in

---

[10] 'Lately, at Neuwied-on-the-Rhine, aged 73, the relict of Lewis F. Catty esq., formerly of the Royal Military Academy Woolwich'.

[11] F.A. Catty *Handbook for Ems and its Environs*, Bad Ems, 1844. The book is in the British Library and I have managed to get it copied.

Bad Ems. Frederick Adam says that no 'watering place offers such brilliant assemblages of rank and fashion as this'. These, he tells us, move about in

picturesque groups of parties on their donkeys . . . those who are fond of the proximity of the high and mighty may be delighted by meeting upon every turn . . . a queen or a princess, it may be even an empress or a king . . . or even an emperor riding on a donkey.

He writes 'of the crowds of elegantly dressed and beautiful women of all nations in full toilette'; of how the 'whole fashionable world of Ems' promenades, or listens to the 'chorals of the Bohemian musicians . . . in the required intervals between each glass of water'.

The 'familiar recollections of historical lore' inspired by the vast and exquisite extensions of 'hill wood and dale' and distant castles, are wiped out by the wonder inspired by the ancient geological upheavals represented by the stones at his feet,

If we but stoop to pick op a small portion of the rocks scattered at our feet, how must all this sink into oblivion in the thought of our own nothingness, and the power of the mighty hand which has arranged all so well and so providentially; at the same time given us at every turn the power of learning how entirely dependent we are on his all-seeing goodness; evidence which our own blindness and wilfulness prevent us from turning to our advantage, and which are often only used as the means of forming evil and unholy speculations.

In spite of these providential arrangements, 1848, the year of Alice's birth, was a time of revolutionary upheaval across most of Europe. In that year Wilhelm I of Prussia ousted all foreigners, including Alice's father, from the Rhineland.[12] After his expulsion Frederick Adam, now back in England, relinquished his medical career and in 1851 began a new life as private secretary to a series of Lord Mayors of London. In 1859, he became a Freeman of the City of London.[13] In the same year, he accepted a post as Principal Clerk in the Town's Clerk's office of the Corporation

---

[12] Temple in 1914 remarked on the coincidence of three generations of Cattys driven from the continental cities in which they lived. Louis François, from revolutionary France; Frederick Adam from Prussia, where he worked in Bad Ems and Baden Baden; and Frederick Adam's son, Arthur B. Catty, from Heidelberg in Germany, where he ran a school until his expulsion at the outbreak of the Great War in 1914.

[13] I am grateful to Meryl Catty for most of this information.

Twigs of a Tree

of London, a job he held until his retirement in 1881, when he was well into his seventies.

It was here that Frederick Adam met his much younger friend and admirer A.G. Temple,[14] who tells us that he had a 'great faculty for languages and fluently spoke several'. Frederick Adam's grandson, Briton, son of JG Walker, remarks that in his work for the various Lord Mayors his grandfather's languages were essential, especially for the reception of the many foreign dignitaries visiting London. A.G. Temple records in 1818 some of the receptions, balls and banquets that took place when Frederick Adam Catty was the Guildhall's 'chief clerk',

To this old Guildhall, hoary with age, come kings and Rulers, and those in every walk of life who have risen supreme above their fellows.

The Guildhall complex c.1805. Engraving by E. Shirt after a drawing by Prattent.

Among 'all the visiting royalty', remembers Temple in 1914 with 'indignant regret', was the 'perfidious Kaiser of Germany'. In 1867, the Sultan of Turkey arrived in London. The arrangements for this grandest of receptions cost the Guildhall no less than £21.641. The programme included a carefully planned concert to be followed by a dancing

---

[14] A.G. Temple, author of "Guildhall Memories", London, John Murray, 1918

performance. The Sultan, on his throne and in the company of Prime Minister Benjamin Disraeli and most of England's royal house, heard out the first aria of the concert. But then, Temple relates, just as Rigoletto's *Un di, se ben rammentomi* (One day if I remember well) was about to begin, there was a commotion: the Sultan leaned over; the Lord Mayor, the Prince of Wales, the conductor, all panicked and scuttled into a huddle; the concert was stopped. Not interested in music, the Sultan wanted to skip straight to the—perhaps more voluptuous—dancing. Temple found it 'heart-breaking' to scrap the music that was to be the highlight of the evening 'at the bidding of this obese Eastern potentate'. But some of the singers, all prepared for Rossini and Donizetti, began to laugh. Frederick Adam Catty, who seems to have had an independence of mind and a healthy sense of the ridiculous, might well have laughed with them.

The former surgeon was, according to Temple, greatly liked at the Corporation. He remarks that,

coming into the department somewhat late in life, he (Frederick Adam Catty) was not straitened and trammelled by stringent rules and customs, through which the trained bureaucrat becomes in time a piece of human machinery. He treated affairs that were wont to run in grooves with an originality unfamiliar to the customary practices at the Guildhall. It gave to the hard routine of things a vitalisation, which paid small regard to precedent . . .

When Frederick Adam's daughter Mary Beardmore Catty Shearman lost her husband in 1865, she and her three children moved in with her parents. Her father put up with the pranks of his two grandsons, Little John (Jack) (1855-1940) and his brother Montague (Tont) Shearman (1858-1930) with smiling equanimity.

Tont was later, after Oxford, to become a judge and to be knighted, but as children he and his brother are described by Temple as two little terrors with a fondness for practical jokes. They often visited, their grandfather, Frederick Adam, in the august precincts of the Guildhall. Their 'worst joke' was to have published in the *Times* the demise of an old black cat as 'the death of Magog Catt, of the Town Clerk's Department, Guildhall'. For days the Guildhall employees had to deal with a flood of condolences on the loss of 'good old Catty' who all the time, says Temple, 'was in his room in perfect health and busy at work'.

Twigs of a Tree

Temple later describes a speech by little Tont, by then Sir Montague Shearman, given in the Guildhall in 1912 and showing that his taste for wit had remained untarnished by the eminence he had achieved.

When asked to propose a toast to Science he said that he detested after dinner speaking, but that if he had to speak he infinitely preferred to speak upon a subject he knew nothing whatever about, and that he would therefore with pleasure propose the toast to 'Science'[15]

Frederick Adam Catty's own humour and agreeable nature somehow shine through the portrait—whether a painting or a photograph is not quite clear—that Temple includes in his book.

Frederick Adam Catty as he appears in Temple's book, Guildhall Memories

Frederick Adam and Ann Edwards had ten children: five daughters and five sons, one of whom died at birth. Two daughters, Jessey and

---

[15] Temple, p.319 goes on: 'Strange as it may seem, it was the speech of the evening for knowledge, speculation, and humour'.
Montague Shearman was not only a rowing man but fond enough of football to have written two books on the subject. *Football: its History for Five Centuries* (1885) with J.E. Vincent, and *Athletics and Football* (Badminton Library, 1887).

Emily, never married, another, young Montague Shearman's mother, was soon widowed. Their daughter Charlotte married William Dobson, one of the young oarsmen who rowed with JG Walker. Another son, James Edwards Catty (1844-1923), was to marry Sophia Radmall, sister of the redoubtable Lucy and of Tom Radmall, another oarsman at the Thames Rowing Club.

Lucy Radmall, like Sophia Stacey a connection rather than a direct relation, was hardly a girl typical of her times, and so perhaps deserves a parenthesis. Described as the 'daughter of a box-maker who worked in a warehouse', Lucy, known in the family as Poppy, became a professional dancer, then a chorus girl. At the tender age of sixteen she eloped with a married man. He, after a tumultuous affair, left her rich: with £6.000 a year for life. Poppy then passed through several marriages, including one to the 'bankrupt 9th Baron Byron of Rochdale' in 1901. Poppy was to play a small role in my mother, Noreen's, life in the 1930's.

In 1887, some time after leaving Cambridge[16], another son of Frederick Adam, Arthur Bovill Catty (1854-1920), founded an English school, Heidelberg College, in Germany. The school was a partnership with his German friend Albert Holzberg. Arthur's father, Frederick Adam, had perhaps taught him—or saw to it that he learned—the German language. Yet another son, George Ernest Christie Catty (1850-1935), was to go pioneering with JG Walker in the Argentine. But not yet: JG's younger brother Alfred was to board ship before him.

---

[16] Cambridge University Alumni, 1261-1900
Name: Arthur Bovill Catty
College: CHRIST'S
Entered: Michs. 1873
Died: 1920
More Information: Adm. pens. at CHRIST'S, Oct. 7, 1873. S. of Frederick Adam, gent. B. Dec. 4, 1854, in London. School, St Paul's. Matric. Michs. 1873; Scholar, 1874; B.A. 1877; M.A. 1889. Adm. at the Middle Temple, June 15, 1877, as s. of Frederick Adam, M.R.C.S., of Peckham Rye, Surrey. Mathematical and English Master at Oxford Military College, 1880-6. English Principal of Heidelberg College, Germany, 1888-1914. On the outbreak of the Great War interned for a short time, but released and returned to England. Assistant Master at Cheltenham College. Married and had issue. Died June 3, 1920. (Peile, II; Schoolmasters' Directory, 1919.)

A Jaunt to South Africa

On a Saturday in April 1866, Alfred Walker, aged about 22, was patrolling the wards in the hospital where he worked, when he was approached and offered a job as a ship's surgeon on a voyage to the Cape. Thinking it a good if rather sudden idea, he raced about London in a horse cab—to Canonbury, to his house at Albion Road, to Guy's, to Holloway (then a 'hospital for the insane of the middle classes')—collecting certificates, registrations, permits, his surgical outfit and even his bath tub. Before packing he just had time to dine and enjoy a drink with his brothers John George (JG) and Bill, and his cousin Harry (Edwards). By the following Monday he was on a train to Plymouth. After a transfer to another train because the luggage train ahead of them had run into a 'landslip and was smashed to pieces', he managed to board the *Briton*. Although he had his baggage with him, he objected that there were no surgical instruments on board. They were quickly fetched and by the following day young Alfred was enjoying the company of both passengers and ship's officers.

The passengers sustained the rolling seas of the Bay of Biscay without mishap but Alfred, the medical man, became sea sick. However, by Friday he is enjoying the attentions of a pretty girl called Miss Damant. He seems to have had little doctoring to do and is soon dividing his time between Scott's *Rob Roy*, the 'she-males', and smoking sessions on the deck. On Sundays he acts as Chaplain. Miss Damant seems to be 'spoony on the doctor' and later makes him a pair of slippers.

After passing the islands of St. Vincent they land on 'St. Antonio' and do a bit of sightseeing. Alfred, with some others, tries to see the British Consul but the official was busy so they only 'left our cards'. He remarks on the inhabitants of the island, 'all sorts of colours from the real nigger native to the true Portuguese, some very pretty . . .' By now he is being addressed as 'Pills' or 'Spoony', and when he returns to the ship he finds half the men dead drunk. A dance is organized and the 'little Damant girl' is dancing enthusiastically, 'much to my disgust . . .' For music the only instrument available is a comb. Eventually he falls out with little Damant and, in spite of the slippers, barely speaks to her.

He admires the seas, the night skies, the porpoises, seals, the whales including the 'fin-backs' and birds. They stop in 'beautifully luxuriant' St. Helena, but have no time for Napoleon, 'no time to see the tomb'. When they finally arrive at the Cape, Table Mountain is wrapped in fog, but the following day Alfred climbs to the top with a companion and afterwards 'liquors' with his friends. He stays a few days in the Parkes Hotel and then sails on to Port Elizabeth.

He would have liked, but has little time to explore the region and makes no comment on South Africa, its tense political situation, its appearance, its government or even its volatile mix of people; the Dutch, the English and the native Africans. Once he mentions a 'wretched Dutchman' who found himself in a boat on such rough sea that he couldn't reach the shore.

Alfred is basically a tourist. He goes sightseeing, shopping, to a museum and library, dines and 'liquors' with friends; he goes fishing, walking, hunting, finds 'the little nigger had not kept the fire going and quilted him accordingly'. He continues to conduct prayers and services and visits the 'jolly little hospital' in Port Elizabeth, the next port of call. He seems, however, to have done singularly little doctoring himself. Once, with a dose of opium and digitalis, he calms down the Captain of another ship who had been 'liquoring frightfully' for a fortnight and 'was shaking and seeing devils'.

On their return to Cape Town the drowning of Captain Ridesdale, commander of the ship *Natal,* is a nasty shock. The flags in the harbour are all flying half-mast. 'It threw a tremendous gloom over Cape Town and indeed over everybody.' As a doctor Alfred was taken to examine the body; 'a fine man, light hair and complexion, very *aneurismic*'.

As they take their last look at the beautiful sight of Table Mountain, Alfred longs to spend another month in the country. The ship is now loaded with exotic cargo: 'three lions, two tigers, and any amount of monkeys'. On the way home he delivers a premature seven-month-old baby, and pulls a tooth for the Captain. After a round trip of about three months, the *Briton* finally sails back into Plymouth on about July 15, 1866 and Alfred's journal ends.

Twigs of a Tree

Picnic about 1867 with Cattys, Shearmans and JG

A year or so after Alfred's return, the Cattys are photographed before a couple of tents at what looks like a family picnic, supposedly on Wimbledom common. Some of the sitters have been identified. Frederick Adam (the Guvnor) sits at the extreme right. The other seated man, on the left, is the writer G.A. Henty. Mumsie, Frederick Adam's god-fearing wife, Ann Edwards, is also on a chair; her children, by now all adults, are at her feet on the grass. Alice, her sisters, Charlotte and Jessey on the right, and her nephew, the mischievous prankster Jack Shearman behind her, as well as her brothers, JG's rowing colleagues, Fred and James Catty. The future pioneer, John George Walker, not yet a member of the family, sits not next to Alice, his future wife, but just in front of a top-hatted Frederick Adam.

It was not much longer after the picnic on Wimbledom common that JG threw up his job in London and set off for Argentina. He would never see his brother Alfred again; the young doctor, died in 1880, at the age of 36.

CHAPTER V

GO SOUTH, YOUNG MAN!

The journey to Argentina in 1868 was nothing like as long, arduous, or as adventurous, as the trip to New Zealand that JG had undertaken six years before. However, sailing could still be dangerous, particularly for very poor emigrants.[1] We have, unfortunately, no descriptive log of the trip from JG himself. However, his contemporary George Reid had slapped down £35 (over a whole year's worth of wages for one of Mulhall's prospective peons) for a ticket on the *SS Newton* (the initials suggest a steamship). Reid writes that he spent his time mainly lying 'reading and smoking in armchairs', playing quoits and billiards, telling stories, singing and making music. A huge table served Reid and twenty other men as a collective bed for their siestas: 'Here we sleep a good deal between lunch and dinner.'

Like the *Queen of the Mersey* that had taken JG to New Zealand a few years before, the *Newton* was swarming with rats; they made a meal of Reid's fine kid boots. Otherwise the food on board was well-cooked and clean and the drinking water came not from the usual filthy casks but was 'Condensed by the engine and is quite fresh and free from taste or smell . . . The quantity is unlimited, the condenser is always at work.'[2]

---

[1] The Buenos Aires paper, *La Nación*, on 18 January 1874 reported the severe ill-treatment and appalling accommodation of a thousand passengers who arrived in the ship *La France*; thirty of them died within twenty-four hours of disembarkation.

[2] Reid, pp.2-3

After his few years as a London clerk, we hope that JG travelled in similar comfort.

After about fourteen days of steamship sailing, JG would have arrived in São Salvador da Bahia de Todos os Santos, once Brazil's capital and its oldest town. Today, with its wealth of baroque churches, Salvador is one of Brazil's architecturally most beautiful and interesting cities. George Reid in 1867 dismissed it as a 'most filthy, muddy, ill paved, badly lit place'. Sedan chairs carried by two bearers provided the only transport, but at least the chairs were 'splendidly decorated with scarlet and gold, or blue and silver curtains'. The lush and unfamiliar vegetation of the country is still staggering to a European. Some thirty years before, Charles Darwin had been deeply moved by the beauties of the forest that bordered the shores of Salvador:

Delight itself, however, is a weak term to express the feelings of a naturalist who, for the first time, has wandered by himself in a Brazilian forest. The elegance of the grasses, the novelty of the parasitical plants, the beauty of the flowers, the glossy green of the foliage, but above all the general luxuriance of the vegetation, filled me with admiration. A most paradoxical mixture of sound and silence pervades the shady parts of the wood. The noise from the insects is so loud, that it may be heard even in a vessel anchored several hundred yards from the shore; yet within the recesses of the forest a universal silence appears to reign. To a person fond of natural history, such a day as this brings with it a deeper pleasure than he can ever hope to experience again.

The fascinations of the forest and the baroque beauties of the old churches passed young Reid by, but Brazil was still—as a shocked Darwin had already observed—a country of slaves (until 1888). Slavery had been abolished in the United States in 1865, after the bloodletting of a ferocious civil war, only three years before JG's voyage. Brazil, too, had over the centuries imported slaves from Africa, some three million, to work its plantations and mines. George Reid remarks on their numbers in the streets of Salvador da Bahia:

The proportion is about 10 black to one white man. The black women shine most brilliantly, owing to much anointing with castor oil, the smell of which in the streets is over-powering.

In Salvador the ship took on a passenger who gave Reid and his companions the bad news that, of the dozens of 'sheep-farming fellows' who go out to Argentina, nine out of ten return within three months. But Reid remained unperturbed and optimistic.

Rio de Janeiro, the next port of call, was about three days sail further south. Here the only form of transport was not sedan chairs, but *tilburies*, carriages drawn by a lone mule. Apart from the driver, they carried only a single passenger. The mule, goaded into a gallop with shrieks and stings of the whip, set the *tilburies* racing at a pace that had pedestrians jumping for their lives into the nearest shop. What JG Walker himself did when he passed through Rio the following year we do not know.

Curiously enough, however, his cousin Henry Edwards was in Rio de Janeiro at the same time as Reid, in July 1867. Edwards mentions in letters to his sister Louise the flag-draped ships in the Guanabara bay and the festivities arranged for the arrival of the Duke of Edinburgh, Prince Alfred. Reid spent a 'fortune' on gloves for a ball given by the English residents in honour of the Prince, whose ship was anchored in the beautiful harbour. In spite of the presence of the Brazilian Emperor, Dom Pedro II, and assorted princes and ministers, Reid was unimpressed:

It was just like a Factory Ball, only with finer rooms and uglier women. I never saw such a collection of ugly women in my life, not one decent-looking one or one pretty dress in the room, though the most wonderful diamonds.

Henry Edwards, staying in the bay of Botafogo on some unexplained 'sheep business', did not attend the ball, but he remarks on the beauties of the bay and the stately, soaring palms in the Botanical Gardens. He, like Reid, was astounded, appalled at the expense of the city. He eventually took a steamer back to the River Plate, stopping at Santa Caterina and Rio Grande in Southern Brazil on the way. These were both places he was curious to see, where he imagined he could sharpen his knowledge of sheep and 'sheeping'.

From Rio, Reid's ship sailed on to Montevideo and finally to Buenos Aires. In Montevideo, after attending church, Reid met one of those extraordinary adventurers of the 19th century, a Scot who had been experimenting with rural life all over the globe. Seven years of sheep farming in Queensland and New Zealand were followed by nine years in different places in the Argentine. This McLachlan was currently the owner of an estancia in the Banda Oriental—now Uruguay—along the Uruguay river. Reid, McLachlan assured him, had arrived at the perfect moment: sheep could not be cheaper, and he, McLachlan, would be happy to teach him the business first hand

You will never repent having come out... You will live the jolliest life in the world for the next 10 years and then clear out with a fortune...

The next day Reid sailed—as JG was to do a few months later—into Buenos Aires, Mulhall's 'Athens of South America'. This new-world Athens that was by the early 20th century, with the addition of some Hausmannian architecture, also to be known as the 'Paris' of South America, was a city of perfectly regular streets arranged in the grid-fashion of the ancient Romans. Along them were low, single-storied houses. Many of these Spanish-style dwellings were built around courtyards or gardens, often with flat roofs on which the inhabitants would pass the steaming summer evenings.

Many years later, when I was a child, JG's son Briton and his sister Melrose—both long widowed—lived together in such a house in the Belgrano district of Buenos Aires. Its rooms traced an L-shape around a corner of the street and faced, through a covered veranda running the whole length of the house, a gardened courtyard or *patio*. [3] My cousin, Diana (Eggar) McClure, who spent much more time there than I, has recently filled out the garden for me. There was, besides an ancient fig, a 'tall palm tree and a bougainvillea creeper (Santa Rita) which covered the boundary wall with its purple flowers'. At siesta time, while my elders slept off the rigours of the morning, I would curl with a book in the fig tree or nestle, reading behind the tall bars of a broad window-sill that looked into the street. Sometimes, as I sailed the seas to Treasure Island, the silence of the sleeping city would be shattered by the clatter of six beautifully paced horses.

Their necks aristocratically curved, they pulled, I later discovered with some dismay, the carriages of the dead on their way to Chacarita Cemetary. Nevertheless this last ride was princely and magnificent, even, it seemed to me, boisterously joyful. The carriages, columned and richly carved were

---

[3] I tried to find the Moldes house when I was in BA in 2003, but it had been replaced by a block of flats. The house next door was still in the old Spanish style, built around a courtyard. I have recently discovered from Diana (Eggar) McClure that this house belonged to George Catty and was bought by Briton and his sister Melrose after George's death in 1935.

black for adults and pure white for children, with horses to match. At about four o'clock the only slightly more cheerful Laponia ice-cream man would appear pushing his little cart before him. Awakening the grownups, as he cried out the flavours of his *helados*, I would be allowed to scamper into the street clutching a coin for an ice-cream.

When John George Walker arrived in Buenos Aires, the city was already 250 years old. In 1776 it had become the capital of the Viceroyalty of the Rio de la Plata, the last—following those of Colombia (Nueva Granada) and Peru—of Spain's three South American Viceroyalties or colonial administrations. The city's chequered history included two invasions by the British—in 1806 and 1807; attempts to pluck advantage from a Spain weakened by the Napoleonic invasions. Confidence from the ousting of the British (considered then to be the greatest fighting force in the world) by a handful of local civilian militias, and revulsion for the rule of the Bonapartes in Madrid, eventually drove Buenos Aires to depose Viceroy Sobremonte and declare its liberation from Spanish rule on May 25, 1810.

Formal independence in 1816 brought neither unity nor peace, but was followed by over half a century of dictatorships (some of them openly murderous) and civil warfare, engendered by rival *caudillos* or local leaders. The Provinces, including the Province of Buenos Aires itself and, in particular, the Northwest provinces—many still royalist and loyal to Spain, or protective of the autonomy of their own caudillos—refused to accept centralized rule (or taxation) from the city of Buenos Aires.[4]

The country was split, roughly, between the sometimes more liberal and sophisticated Unitarians, who favoured centralized rule, and the Federalists of the provinces, who clung to their local powerbase. Uruguay declared its own independence in 1828, whereas the long resistance of Paraguay to integration with the new republic of Argentina ended in war.

This war, the 'bloodiest in Latin American history', was in full swing when JG arrived in 1868. Fought from 1865 to 1870, it left the Argentine government so desperately short of soldiers that it withdrew its forces from the line of forts that protected the farmers—among them JG and

---

[4] The four Latin American viceroyalties of Spain: New Spain (Mexico), Peru, Granada (Colombia) and Rio de la Plata (Buenos Aires) eventually became no less than eighteen separate republics. The Plate Viceroyalty included what are now Bolivia, Paraguay, Uruguay and Argentina.

his pioneering friends—from the attacks of the nomadic Pampas Indians. JG was to write many letters of protest to get this military protection reinstated or reinforced.

The British had appropriated the Malvinas or Falkland Islands in 1833, during the long and bloody dictatorship (1828-1855) of the powerful cattleman Juan Manuel de Rosas. The rivalry between the Buenos Aires Unitarians or Centralists and the Federalists of the provinces continued. Many of the Federalists in the countryside, often rich and well-armed *estancieros,* the *caudillos* of their regions, were able to muster formidable private militias among the *gauchos*, the cowboys—often part Spanish, part Indian—who roamed the Pampas. The Federalists, including Rosas himself, continued to reject all authority from the city for over two decades. The city of Buenos Aires was only to become the capital of a unified Argentina in 1880.

Nevertheless, by the time JG arrived, the city already had a free public library (founded in 1810 by Mariano Moreno), hospitals, theatres, concert halls, a couple of Italian opera houses and a number of impressive churches.[5] In the central Plaza were the public offices, the Cathedral, the fortress, and the old palaces of the Viceroys. St. John's Anglican Church, where JG was eventually to be married, had been founded in 1828. There were banks, a selection of daily papers in five languages, and a few clubs—like the *Strangers' Club*—for foreigners.[6] A good deal of the town's commerce was already in the hands of the British.

Vast tracts of land had been sold or granted to the *criollos*, the Argentine-born descendants of the first Spanish settlers. When the rural economy began expanding and developing seriously in the 1860's, the fertile regions of the Pampas were divided into huge *estancias,* often covering hundreds of thousands of acres, owned, it seems, by no more than 300 families. The very rich *estancieros* were mostly of Spanish origin and often lived in Buenos Aires as absentee landlords. Their mansions, first in the style of the Spanish, were later modelled after the Haussmannian residences of Paris. Rosas had turned himself into one of the richest landowners in the country, and General Justo José de Urquiza, who overthrew him and

---

[5] The first Teatro Colón, founded in 1857, opened with Verdi's *La Traviata*, closed down in 1888, and was replaced in 1908 by the new and soon world-famous Teatro Colón.

[6] Rosas allowed the official founding of the club to take place in 1841 on the condition that Argentines be excluded. He was afraid they would plot against him.

became his successor as President, had an estate in Entre Rios 'the size of Belgium'. Urquiza was assassinated in his Pampas palace in 1870. In this sparsely populated country he put his leisure to good use. During his lifetime, he is supposed to have fathered over a hundred children.

The Buenos Aires markets were lavishly stocked through the efforts of Italian market gardeners and Basque dairy farmers. The city was, however, still a small one. In 1869, the first census of Argentina, a country only slightly smaller than today's India, registered a population of a mere 1.7 million. The city of Buenos Aires held some 180.000 citizens.[7] Of these only a minute fraction were British but their numbers, even then, were belied by their importance in trade and commerce.

The city still had no drainage or water supply. Those without private catchment cisterns for rainwater had to buy water by the bucket—murky with clay deposits—from roving watermen. Even the cistern water was dubious. The writer W.H. Hudson, an almost exact contemporary of JG and Reid's, born on the Pampas in 1842, suffered greatly, when in Buenos Aires, from a 'hateful town feeling of lassitude' and from the stench—mostly from untreated sewage—that pervaded the city. He, however, calmly swallows the cistern water with its lively population of 'wrigglers and all'. Briton tells us that almost fifteen years later, in 1881, when he and his mother returned from a trip to England with a new baby, Harold Saxon, they stayed in the Hotel Provence, 'the only one in Buenos Aires with a bathroom'.

George Reid's arrival in the port, coming from Montevideo, was 'handkerchief to nose'—scant protection against the emanations of the city's slaughter and salting plants, the *saladeros,* that exuded a ' . . . smell as of a thousand horrible butcher's shops pervading everything . . . I am nearly stifled'.

The sixteen *saladeros* of the city salted the flesh and hides of some 10.000 heads of cattle a day and boiled down sheep and mare's flesh into tallow, for lighting. On one of his visits to Buenos Aires, Reid watched fifty mares slaughtered in half an hour and noted that some were beautiful beasts that would go for '£40 in Porto'. Among the travellers who were shaken by the 'abomination' of the *saladeros* was Charles Darwin:

---

[7] The British in Argentina numbered, in 1869, 10.637. Of immigration into Argentina between 1857 and 1915 they formed a tiny 1 percent.
(Andrew Graham-Yooll, *The Forgotten Colony*, p. 169)

> When the bullock has been dragged to the spot where it is to be slaughtered, the matador with great caution cuts the hamstrings. Then it is given the death blow; the bellow a noise more expressive of fierce agony than any I know. I have often distinguished it from a long distance, and have always known that the struggle was then drawing to a close. The whole sight is horrible and revolting: the ground is almost made of bones; and the horses and riders are drenched with gore.[8]

The killing, in the days before refrigeration, was mostly for hides, but *charque*—or salted flesh—was also prepared and exported, much of it to Brazil, as nourishment for the slave population. Mare's tallow still provided fuel for lighting the city as late as the 1870's. Bones were discarded and scrounged for building or even for making furniture. Hudson has left a picture of the gruesome walls, in this 'stoneless land', that in Buenos Aires protected the market gardens and orchards near the slaughterhouses:

> These (walls) were built entirely of cows' skulls, seven, eight, or nine deep, placed evenly like stones, the horns projecting. Hundreds of thousands of skulls had been thus used, and some of the old, very long walls, crowned with green grass and with creepers and wild flowers ... had a strangely picturesque but somewhat uncanny appearance.[9]

According to Hudson, Buenos Aires in the 1870s was the 'chief pestilential city of the globe'. 'The Argentine capital,' he writes, 'was later obliged to call in engineers from England to do something to save the inhabitants from extinction.' Reid himself eventually pronounced this Athens of the good airs a 'beastly place', 'a horrid hole' and 'ruinously expensive'. The streets of the city were still mostly unpaved, and outside every shop stood horses, either hobbled or tethered to rings in the walls, as they still were in Venado Tuerto and San Eduardo in my youth. In August 1867, a month after his arrival, Reid remarks on the numbers of

> fellows going home in disgust. It is a terrible shame the way in which people are induced in all sorts of ways to come out here with the idea that they are going to make fortunes ... The editor of the Standard will get shot some day by some of the scores of men he has ruined by persuading them to come out ...'

---

[8] *Voyage of the Beagle*, Chapter 6
[9] Hudson, *Far Away and Long Ago*, p. 288

Go South, Young Man!

George A. Henty, with his popular book of pioneering adventure, was perhaps as culpable on this point as Mulhall. The Hardys, his fictional family in *Out on the Pampas,* did indeed prosper as pioneers, raising cattle and sheep. But they had no intention of remaining in Argentina.

The architect and his sons were after cash, not a new homeland. Henty's tale relates that part of the family soon returned, investing its Pampas profits in the English countryside. The two boys took turns travelling to and fro for a few years, managing both the English and the Argentine farms. Selling out their faraway *estancia* at a healthy profit, both eventually returned rich, to a life as gentlemen farmers on their newly acquired country estate in England.

Such happy endings, however, were mostly the stuff of dreams. In May 1868, just before JG's arrival, Reid returned yet again to Buenos Aires. Now the city seemed, to him, like a veritable 'hell' that sent young men like himself 'body and soul to the devil'. By this time he was ready to start a campaign: writing to the papers to prevent young fellows without money from going to Argentina at all—'for all they do,' writes Reid, 'is drink, drink, drink . . . from morning to night.'

When he arrived in Argentina, Reid had an advantage over JG: he spoke Portuguese. This made the local Spanish far more accessible. Edwards, two years before, had immediately realized the importance of being able to communicate in what had become the local language (although few Indians were able to speak it) and had taken pains to learn. Edwards grasped any opportunity, like 'attending to the stores', as a means of improving his Spanish. Cunninghame Graham, writer and aristocratic adventurer—fluent in Spanish and with some money in his pocket, actually did make a tidy fortune cattle ranching in Argentina. He compared the linguistic abilities of the two cousins in a short story written over fifty years after meeting them.[10]

According to Cunninghame Graham's unlikely tale, JG never learned Spanish but through a liaison with an Indian woman he did accomplish the feat of learning the 'Pehuelche' language. Then, perhaps abandoning literary licence, the writer describes the two cousins—with Edwards, nicknamed 'Facón Grande' (Large Knife), as getting on well with

a strange phonetic Spanish, blameless of grammar and full of local words, as easily as English. A short half league away, his cousin lived, known to the

---

[10] If, that is, the writer can be believed on this point, for in the same tale he made claims that Alice was to dismiss as nonsense.

Twigs of a Tree

> *Gauchos as Facón Chico . . . Though he had lived for twenty years in the republic, he hardly knew more than a few coherent sentences in Spanish, and those so infamously pronounced that few could understand them.*[11]

Reid soon discovered that not every region of Argentina was equally accessible. Santa Fé, where some fifteen years later the Davison family was to buy the land on which the Dyson's *Susana* now stands, was in 1868 'out of the question' because of the Indian peril. Santa Fé was still a place where, Reid says, 'you dare not ride about your camp alone'. Venado Tuerto, in Santa Fé province, today the biggest town near the *Susana*, did not yet exist. It would only be founded in 1884, after the final defeat of the Indians.

The province of Buenos Aires, its safer regions presumably those nearest the capital city, was so expensive that, according to Reid, it was 'impossible to go in and make it pay'. The Banda Oriental (Uruguay) was 'so choke-full of rich men that there is no opening left . . . '. The provinces of Entre Rios and Corrientes, east of the Paraná river, were safe from the Indians, but the price of land—recently doubled—was again prohibitive. Reid remarks on the make-up of his countrymen, who consisted of

> *only two kinds of men . . . either very big 'swells', many from the army, civil service, or else unmitigated snobs. There seems to be no middle class. I am happy to say the first mentioned kind* (says Reid snobbishly if somewhat ungrammatically) *seem to preponderate by much.*[12]

JG and his cousin fell somewhere in between. In the three years he was in Argentina, Reid tried out several places but on arrival he travelled to the area around Gualeguaychú, north-east of Buenos Aires. About a year later JG, knowing exactly where to go to meet his cousin Henry Edwards, travelled in the opposite direction—south, towards Bahia Blanca.

---

[11] Cunninghame Graham, *Mirages,* in which JG is re-named 'Hawker' pp.171-2, 1936,

[12] The word 'snob', sine nobilitatis, without nobility, was, I am told by my Random House dictionary, originally used to describe a cobbler or cobbler's apprentice. It later 'evolved' into a description of one 'who pretends to have social importance, who slavishly imitates, cultivates, or admires those with social rank, wealth, etc.'

CHAPTER VI

ON THE INDIAN FRONTIER

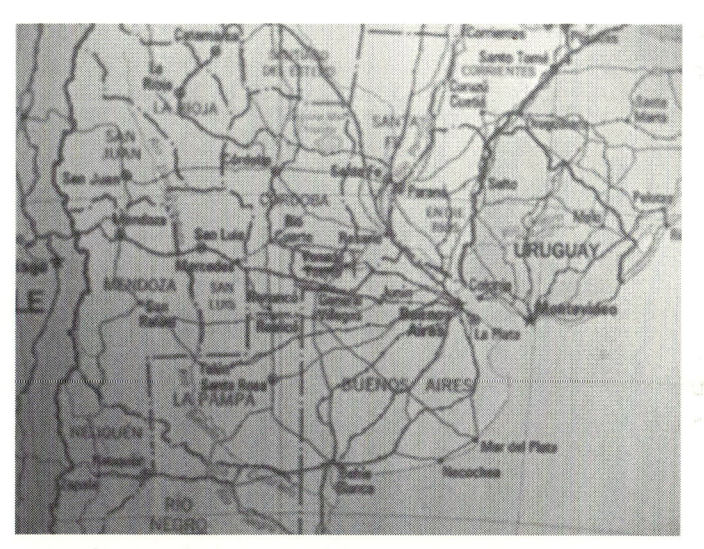

Map showing the province of Buenos Aires between the cities of Buenos Aires and Bahia Blanca

When JG arrived in the Province of Buenos Aires in 1868, it was separated and protected from Indian territory by a long line of primitive forts. The army was constantly trying to push this frontier forward into the areas still dominated by different Indian tribes. The town of Bahía Blanca, standing well to the southwest of the fortified border, was not easily reachable from Buenos Aires.

Twigs of a Tree

The 115 league (575 kilometre)[1] journey on horseback was, although only half as long as the distance by water, tedious, difficult and even dangerous. There had once been a *galera* or diligence service, but it had been suspended for years because of Indian attacks that often left passengers and drivers dead and abandoned on the road. The service was only reinstated five years later, in 1873, the year of Alice's arrival. Nevertheless, the house-high wheels of clumsily built bullock carts, roughly covered with skins, crawled periodically through the dust—or, in the wet season, knee-deep mud—of the long unmade roads. The carts travelled in convoys of ten or twelve, transporting necessities like sugar, oil, salt, flour, soap and liquor from the city of Buenos Aires to the outlying towns and forts. These were exchanged for farm produce of wool and hides for the return journey. In the 1860's, the round trip in a bullock cart from Buenos Aires to Bahía Blanca could take as long as three months.

Bullock Cart, 1854,
Principal means of transport for goods before the railways.

Inaugurated in 1828 as a fortress town for protection from the Indians, Bahía Blanca, not far from the Atlantic coast, could also be reached from

---

[1] The Argentine league is equal to about 5 kilometres or 3.1 miles. The league was originally the distance a man or horse could walk in an hour.

Buenos Aires by sea in a few days.[2] JG got a passage on a coasting steamer. After five or six days of 'avoiding the captain', who spent most of his time drinking with a 'tame' Indian *cacique* or chief, he finally arrived. Harry Edwards had come to meet him.[3] They threw JG's baggage into a cart and together drove out to the Paso Grande in the Naposta Valley, north-east of Bahia Blanca.

Just as Reid was to do, Edwards had first learned about farming in Argentina by apprenticing himself to an old hand—in his case a Mr Leighton who owned the estancia Santa Kilda, in the Banda Oriental. We have a few transcriptions of letters from Henry Edwards—now known, he tells us, as *Don Enrique*—written from St. Kilda's to his sister, Louise. 'Mrs L. is the jolliest lady I have seen since I left England, plays the guitar and sings in 7 languages', he wrote in August 1866. From Leighton, Edwards learned to run a sheep shearing: to catch and fleece the animals, to pick over the wool and press it into bales with a 'screw press'. After his stint at St. Kilda's he bought himself a couple of horses and went south, 'stopping at estancias on the way in search of work'. Eventually he took a job near Azul on a spread belonging to a Mr Keen.[4]

According to his daughter, Edwards was the sort of adventurer who actually enjoyed tracking Indians down. His wife, Hélène, indicates an eagerness for the excitement of a fight so lively that he often hoped to find himself in Indian territory: fists presumably clenched, Remington at the ready.

After a time of apprenticeship at Keen's, Edwards joined about twenty-five other Englishmen in an offer from the government of Buenos Aires province. In return for building a house, digging a well and stocking the property with sheep, the young men were promised, on easy terms, a

---

[2] Darwin in 1831 described the town's troubled and, no doubt, bloody beginnings. "Bahía Blanca scarcely deserves the name of a village. A few houses and the barracks for the troops are enclosed by a deep ditch and fortified wall. The settlement is only of recent standing (since 1828); and its growth has been one of trouble. The government of Buenos Ayres unjustly occupied it by force, instead of following the wise example of the Spanish Viceroys, who purchased the land near the older settlement of the Rio Negro, from the Indians. Hence the need of the fortifications; hence the few houses and little cultivated land without the limits of the walls; even the cattle are not safe from the attacks of the Indians."

[3] John Briton Walker, *On the Frontier*.

[4] Translated back by me from *Datos sobre la vida del Sr. Henry John Edwards . . . Facón Grande* by Hélène de Bernardy and translated into Spanish by her daughter.

suerte, or 6.700 acres, of land. This was part of a new government effort to attract Europeans to the wilder, still dangerous parts of Argentina. The dictator Rosas, overturned in 1852 and exiled in England until his death in 1877, had discouraged immigration, but the subsequent Urquiza government, in 1863, initiated a new attempt to rehabilitate the area, after years of Indian devastation, through the encouragement of newcomers.

By 1869, a year after it was inaugurated, the little colony of Sauce Grande, north of Bahía Blanca, had caught Mulhall's attention. He mentions, in that year's *Handbook of the River Plate*, the Englishmen Edwards, Goodhall, Mildred, Barber and Grieve as among the earliest of the new settlers in the Naposta Valley. Mulhall portrays the region as something of an agricultural paradise, with land that is lush, fertile, well watered and cheap. Cunninghame Graham, however, describes the same territory as wild and as dangerous as the 'Apacheria in Arizona', with

> rare estancias that were like islands in the great sea of grass that flowed around them, just as waves surround atolls in the South Seas. Most of the estancias were fortified with a deep ditch . . . and some had a small brass cannon that was chiefly used to signal to the sparse neighbours . . . .[5]

Moreover, according to Cunninghame Graham, the Indians owed 'little to the Apaches in fierceness, cruelty, skill in horsemanship and general devilry'.

Mulhall, on the contrary, and much to the eventual disgust of Reid, plays down the danger of the area. If the Indians were, indeed, the 'greatest inconvenience', this minor *contretemps* could be easily dealt with through the breeding of sheep—of no interest to the marauders—rather than cattle, for which the Natives would attack and kill. Mulhall then goes on to describe the easy terms on which land could be obtained—land for which ownership deeds would arrive after two years.

Trying his luck further north, George Reid remarks that the Indians 'get worse every day', and in September 1867 he reports that an English estancia near Rosario, where Henty had set his glowingly successful pioneering story, had been invaded. The Indians, firing the thatch of the cooking hut where the farmers had taken refuge, cut them all down as

---

[5] *Mirages*, 169

they fled the flames. In 1869, a year after JG's arrival and after a long lull, the Indians began to make themselves felt around Bahía Blanca.

John George Walker and Henry Edwards were to become legendary local figures for their courage, intrepidity and unswerving assistance and support to the local military in the long battle against the Indians. It was the Natives, impressed by the blades they carried—Gaucho fashion—under their belts, who, according to Hélène de Bernardy, Edwards' French wife, coined the cousins' gaucho-like *noms de guerre* of *Facón Chico* and *Facón Grande*—Small Knife and Big Knife. The adjectives did not refer to the identical 18-inch knives in their silver tipped sheaths, brought by Edwards from England when he went on his machine-buying expedition in 1872, but to the physical appearance of the two men. JG was the smaller man.

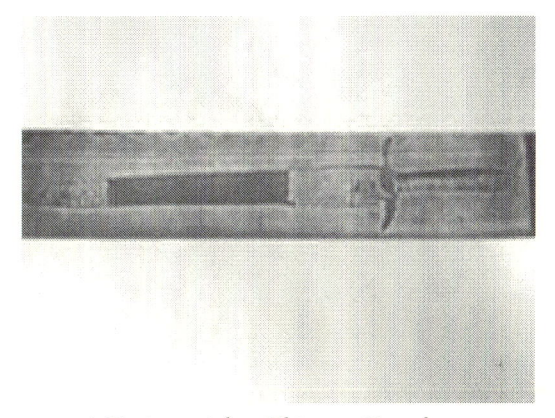

A Facón—either Chico or Grande . . .

So persistent and dauntless were the cousins in the defence of their settlements against the Indian attackers that, in his *Yerba Vieja*, the author Henry Hogg ends his essay about the two men with a glowing commendation. They deserved, writes Hogg, a 'memorial in bronze' in recognition of their 'services to civilization'. The men's courage and decency may appear unquestionable on a personal level. However, the larger picture of the 'civilizing' of the Americas in which, in its final days, they played a small part—and for which the Natives paid so dearly—was always and remains today fraught with moral ambiguity.

Twigs of a Tree

Attitudes of Empire

JG and his cousin Henry Edwards were Victorians, and, like most Europeans of that era, they were probably not only 'imperialists' but also what one might today call white supremacists. They carried unassailable certitudes and a deep belief in the superiority of their own race, ethnicity and culture; in the worth of their own civilizing mission. For all of the emphasis on *liberté, fraternité, égalité*, the Revolution did not turn all Frenchmen into democrats over-night: women, as inferior beings, were excluded from political participation, and so, as in the United States, were blacks. As Julian Barnes points out, a profoundly humanist writer like Gustave Flaubert (1821-1880) hated democracy as no more than a dream 'to raise the proletariat to the level of stupidity attained by the bourgeoisie.'[6] Darwin, for all his anthropological knowledge and curiosity, was no less certain about the current inferiority of the Indians he encountered than he was of the possible 'evolution' of their descendants in the distant future.

In popular parlance, the native peoples of the Americas, Asia, Australasia or Africa, territories more or less appropriated by the expanding empires of Europe, were 'darkies', 'browns', 'wogs', 'japs' 'goons', 'chinks', 'niggers' or simply 'savages', to be quelled by persuasion where possible, but otherwise by force. Men considered by history as highly honourable held ideas about the natives of the occupied lands that today seem shocking. As Jared Diamond points out, for George Washington the 'immediate objectives' regarding the Indians were the

> *total destruction and the devastation of their settlements. It will be essential to ruin their crops in the ground and prevent their planting more.*

Benjamin Franklin had another, simpler but more insidious idea:
If it be the Design of Providence thence to Extirpate these Savages in order to make room for Cultivators of the Earth, it seems not improbable that Rum may be the appointed means.

The third president of the USA, Thomas Jefferson, threw up his hands in despair—for him slaughter became the only option:
This unfortunate race, whom we had been taking so much pains to save and to civilize, have by their unexpected desertion and ferocious

---

[6] Julian Barnes, *Flaubert's Parrot*, p. 85

barbarities justified extermination and now await our decision on their fate.

John Quincy Adams denied the peoples who had inhabited their lands for thousands of years any concessions at all:
What is the right of the huntsman to the forest of a thousand miles over which he has accidentally ranged in quest of prey?

In the 20th century, U.S. president Theodore Roosevelt, by now influenced with ideas of 'Manifest Destiny' agreed:
The settler and pioneer have at bottom had justice on their side; this great continent could not have been kept as nothing but a game preserve for squalid savages.[7]

What ultimately made the subjection possible was the invention of faster and deadlier weapons. Primitive early muskets were followed in the 19th century by first the breech loading rifles—*Remingtons, Snider-Enfields*—of the 1870's and then the deadly machine gun—the *Maxim*—of the middle 80's. The Maxim could fire 500 rounds a minute; a distribution of death equivalent to that of one hundred men behind as many rifles. But, as Karl Meyer points out in his *Dust of Empire,* not everyone was delighted with the methods behind the growth of Empire and the incursions of the whites. As time passed, a few individuals became appalled. Hillaire Belloc (1870-1953) ended a sardonic piece about empire with 'Whatever happens, we have got/ The Maxim Gun and they have not.' Kipling's (1865-1936) famous celebration of empire, *The White Man's Burden*, originally written for Victoria's jubilee in 1899, was parodied in the same year with *The Brown Man's Burden* by an anti-imperialist British politician, writer and journalist, Henry Labouchère:

> *Pile on the brown man's burden;*
> *And, if ye rouse his hate,*
> *Meet his old-fashioned reasons*
> *With Maxims up to date.*
> *With shells and dumdum bullets*
> *A hundred times made plain*

---

[7] Collected and quoted by Jared Diamond, in *The Third Chimpanzee,*

Twigs of a Tree

> *The brown man's loss must ever*
> *Imply the white man's gain.*
> *Pile on the brown man's burden,*
> *compel him to be free;*
> *Let all your manifestoes*
> *Reek with philanthropy.*
> *And if with heathen folly*
> *He dares your will dispute,*
> *Then, in the name of freedom,*
> *Don't hesitate to shoot.*[8]

To counter the constant attacks by the Indians, the Argentine government had long begun building fortress towns like Bahía Blanca and lines of simple defences. These defences had, by 1860, evolved into a frontier line that divided the Province of Buenos Aires into two almost equal parts. The long chain of simple, indeed usually inadequate, defences—of *fuertes* and *fortines*—ran roughly along the Salado river.[9]

In 1869 a new *fortín* was built near the Sauce Grande river, where Edwards had settled, and a short time later the *Fortín Pavón* on the eastern bank of the Sauce Grande, after its destruction by fire, was reoccupied and restored. First constructed for 100 men, this fortress was rebuilt in 1873 to hold only 30. A mere 594 men, including 123 'tame Indians', manned the whole line of fortifications.[10]

Briton Walker much later described JG's land as being 12 leagues east of Bahia Blanca and five from the recently restored *Fortín Pavón*, where the local military had its headquarters. He describes the *fortín* as a 'square-built' earth tower, 12-feet high, used as a lookout over the flat

---

[8] A few verses from *The Brown Man's Burden* Henry Labouchère, Truth (London); reprinted in Literary Digest 18 (Feb. 25, 1899).
Ramon Lista in 1894 wrote a plea to save the disappearing Tehuelche race. "The poor Tehuelches! Would you not be happier again if you woke up tomorrow and somebody told you that the white men had left, never to return.'

[9] Rojas Lagarde in *El Malón de 1870 a Bahia Blanca y La Colonia de Sauce Grande*, p.14 tells us that in 1870, Buenos Aires province had five fuertes or forts, simply a collection of mud houses encircled by a moat and a parapet constructed with the earth taken from the moat. There were twenty *fortines*, generally a rectangular or circular pit with a high central lookout tower that provided shelter for no more than five to ten men. Together, these made up the line of the 'frontier.'

[10] Rojas Lagarde, *El Malón de 1870*, p. 114

Pampas. The bigger forts were stockade-like, large enough for a horse-corral and quarters for the officers.

JG Walker found himself among a group of Englishmen who had settled about fifty kilometres from the Atlantic coast in an area richly watered by four rivers. The Sauce Chico flowed into the Bahia Blanca Bay; further east were the rivers of the Naposta Grande and Chico, and finally the Sauce Grande river. The oceanic flatness of the Pampas territory was relieved on the northern horizon by the hills of the Sierra de la Ventana. To the south was the large Colorado River, boundary of an area marked, on a map dated as late as 1875, as *tierra inexplorada,* unexplored territory. To the South flowed the Rio Negro, marking the border between the unexplored territory and Patagonia.

North of the Colorado River, but to the west, were the settlements of various Indian tribes: closest were the Mapuches, then under the leadership of Calfucurá; further off were the tribes of Pinzen, the Ranqueles and Tehuelches. To the east, and north of the Colorado, the land was dry and barren, marked on the same map as *campos estériles sin agua,* sterile land without water. The area northeast of Bahía Blanca, along the Sauce Grande river, where JG and his friends had settled, appears—on the 1875 map—as slightly behind the line of fortified defences. They were not far from the Indian *tolderías,* encampments of rough, oven-shaped shelters constructed of posts and animal skins, from which the attacks took place. The map shows that the frontier had already edged forward and that the government was already planning to move it even deeper into Indian-occupied territory.

During the long dictatorship of Juan Manuel de Rosas the Indians were kept at bay through a combination of combat and cajolement, by peace treaties (sometimes respected, but often broken) and the payment of bribes or tributes. The Mapuche Cacique, Calfucurá, who had not been above throwing in his hand with Rosas against other Indian tribes, was the most formidable Native leader of the time. From Araucania in the recently established Republic of Chile, he had considerable military and diplomatic skills and, for over forty years, became the virtual lord of the Pampas, fighting both white settlers and fellow Indians. José Bengoa, historian of the Mapuches, describes how the Argentine Pampas attracted and fascinated the Indians across the Chilean border:

It was a place of easy riches, of great military adventure, where men could cover themselves in honor and glory. In the 18th and 19th centuries the *journey to the Pampas became an initiation ritual for young warriors; a period away from the family for young men who—formed, hardened and tested by war—returned transformed into adult men.*[11]

Calfucurá, like Louis XIV, invoked, for his leadership, the concept of divine right and was believed, by his people, to have magical powers. More pertinently, he had managed to negotiate deals by which the Rosas government paid him an annual tribute—several thousand horses and cattle—for keeping the area safe from attack. Mares, according to Briton 'a glut on the market', were the principal subsidy the Indians received. Mares were valued only for food; riding a female horse was entirely beneath the 'macho' dignity of any self-respecting Indian or gaucho. Dismayed at the high price of stallions, George Reid tried to overcome this prejudice against the equine female by introducing mares for the saddle. He caused a sensation, but was not imitated.

'El Señor Gobierno', Mr Government, also kept Calfucurá and his people stocked with necessities like poultry, yerba mate, sugar, tobacco, matches, gin, hair-oil and—curiously—guitars and guitar strings. For his personal use Calfucurá obtained silk handkerchiefs, knives, and heeled boots. Briton Walker was aware that the practice of giving Indians tributes was open to much corruption by middlemen. They often handed over inferior goods or simply appropriated items destined for the Indians that they sold elsewhere. JG's son grew up with a low opinion of Calfucurá and much later described his impression of this leader's not very pretty methods towards the other caciques, or chiefs, after meetings where the Chileans bartered their *vicuña* skins and *ponchos* for Argentine cattle and horses.

> *The meetings usually finished up with drunken feasts . . . But a new Chief, Caful Curá (Blue Stone) . . . while many of his braves just got drunk, kept a select body back from the bottle, and when all the Pampa chiefs were incapacitated, he and his trusty teetotallers cut the throats of the Pampas caciques and took over the command. The Pampas Indians followed the new masters without a murmur. They were not so 'vivo', although just as bloodthirsty, and probably found more opportunity for loot and slaughter than they had under their own chiefs who had been suppressed firmly by Rosas.*

---

[11] José Bengoa: *Historia del pueblo Mapuche*. LOM-Ediciones. Santiago de Chile, my translation.

More recent history tends to recognize in Calfucurá an impressive power of leadership and even sincere attempts to keep the peace. Briton was perfectly aware that there were uneasy consciences about the treatment of the Indians, but he justified the resistance to Calfucurá on the grounds that he was 'Chilean', an interloper into Argentine territory who had himself conquered and subjugated the native Pampas Indians. The Indians who had been nomadic for generations recognized no frontier between the two new Republics. The historian Dionisio Schoo Lastra tells us that, in 1870, the high number of Indians crossing the border from Chile and settling in the Province of Buenos Aires was causing considerable alarm to the authorities.[12] The official border was only to be formally established in the 1880's.

When JG arrived in Bahía Blanca in 1868, the town had a population of about 2000—a mixture of Argentines, Italians, French, Germans and a handful of about thirty-five Englishmen.[13] The town was undergoing something of a resurgence after a long series of attacks that had begun in 1852 when the overthrow of Rosas put an end to the tributes extended to the Indian chiefs. In these attacks many of the farmers around Bahía Blanca had either lost their lives or abandoned their farms—often burnt to the ground—to the ostriches, ovenbirds and *tero-teros*.

The Indian attacks on Bahía Blanca had culminated on May 19, 1859 with the sacking, torching and near destruction of the town itself by Calfucurá and a contingent of three thousand lances. It was an assault motivated by revenge rather than loot. The new garrison of Italian troops, armed with modern rifles, fought back hard. The Indians eventually fled, leaving some two hundred dead. The skies above the main square of the city were darkened for days by smoke from the Dantesque pyres into which the glut of corpses had been cast.

---

[12] Dionisio Schoo Lastra, *El Indio del Desierto 1535-1879*, Goncourt, Buenos Aires, 1928.

[13] Graham-Yooll tells us that Britons arriving in Argentina between 1857 and 1915 to make a new life amounted to only one per cent of the approximately six million immigrants of that period. The 1869 census showed that there were 10,637 Britons resident in Argentina, while the census for 1895 saw the figure rise to 21.788. There were 29.772 in 1910 and 27,692 in the 1914 census. In the latter year the country's population stood at about eight million; three-quarters of the adult male population in Buenos Aires was foreign-born.

After this, there was much confidence that the Indians could be held off with the new breech-loading *Remington* and *Snider-Enfield* rifles that made faster and more efficient shooting possible. There were already government plans for more defences and a shifting of the frontier further south and west. However, these plans were scuttled by the war with Paraguay that had broken out in 1864 and that for five years drew heavily on the country's already scarce military resources. Two thirds of the available military forces were manning the front with Paraguay, leaving the neophyte farmers on the lines of the Indian frontier vulnerable and unprotected.

Anything from a handful to a few thousand Indians—armed with lances, knives and stones—could be involved in a *malón*, a surprise attack on a town, settlement or estancia. When swung and thrown through the air, their *boleadoras* (two or three leather-covered stones attached to thongs) could, by entangling its legs, bring down a galloping horse.[14] Calfucurá had the power, when necessary, to recruit men from across the Andes, many days journey away, and the Chilean government had no objections when they returned with a good herd of stolen horses.

One of Rosas' largest estancias—as a man hugely enriched by his *saladeros* he had several—was a spread of 74 square leagues, protected from the Indians by no less than three hundred armed men.[15]

The poorer farmers, however, with no firearms, had few defences even against a small band of attackers. Their modest thatched houses were sacked and set alight, their horses and cattle easily driven off; babies' brains were dashed out, men's throats were cut. Young women and children were often kidnapped to incorporate into the Indian tribes (several of the caciques of the day were the offspring of captured Christian mothers). For Richard Seymour, who settled in Córdoba, living near the Indian encampments was like life on the 'slopes of a constantly erupting volcano'.

---

[14] Darwin notes of the Indian men: "One of their chief indoor occupations is to knock two stones together till they become round, in order to make the bolas. With this important weapon the Indian catches his game, and also his horse, which roams free over the plain. In fighting, his first attempt is to throw down the horse of his adversary with the bolas, and when entangled by the fall to kill him with the chuzo. If the balls only catch the neck or body of an animal, they are often carried away and lost. As the making of the stones round is the labour of two days, that's a considerable loss."

[15] Voyage of the Beagle, Chapter 6

While contemplating Hadrian's wall, now a symbol of another conflict between invaders and invaded, W.H. Auden was unable to make a moral choice between the invading imperialism of the Romans and the barbarity of the natives. He concluded bleakly:

That man is born a savage, there needs no other proof than the Roman Wall. It characterizes both nations as robbers and murderers.

Here, too, as all through history, the brutality was on both sides. During his visit to Bahía Blanca in 1832, in the early days of Rosas' rule, Darwin had recorded very little sympathy for the Indians.

I never saw anything like the enthusiasm for Rosas, and for the success of the "most just of all wars, because against barbarians." This expression, it must be confessed, is very natural, for till lately, neither man, woman nor horse was safe from the attacks of the Indians.[16]

The military itself was, however, made up of rough, tough men; often social outcasts, former prisoners or even 'tame' Indians. JG's son, Briton, recalled Darwin's description of his encounter with Rosas' soldiers and his remark that 'Such a villainous *banditti*-like army was never before collected together.' But Briton on the whole approved of the order Rosas, known as the Nero or Caligula of Argentina, was able to maintain.

He may have been a tyrant, but the country was much better governed ... Supplies were regular in Rosas' time, but under the new authorities there was a lot of leakage and rakeoff.

In an attack, Indians were shot on sight, like marauding animals, and rewards were paid for Indians killed, even for Indian ears collected, counted and consigned. Darwin himself learned another aspect of the story in a conversation with a veteran of the long war. He was told that after a battle, 'All the (Indian) women who seemed above twenty years old are massacred in cold blood.' When the naturalist exclaimed that this 'appeared rather inhuman', the reply was: 'Why, what can be done, they breed so!' Darwin registered his horror: 'Who would believe that in this age such atrocities could be committed in a Christian civilized country?'[17]

In short, in this particular confrontation over space and soil, over life and livelihood, between radically different peoples, civilizations and

---

[16] *Voyage of the Beagle* Chapter 6
[17] *Voyage of the Beagle* Chapter 5

Twigs of a Tree

cultures, there appears to have been no horror—on whatever side of the battlefield—that was not regarded, at least by some, as legitimate warfare. These were, very roughly, the conditions—a little over three centuries after the fall of the Incas—that JG and Henry Edwards faced when they arrived in Bahía Blanca: when they unwittingly became participants in the final stages of the resistance to the catastrophe that had been unleashed upon the native populations with the arrival of the Spaniards.

The next serious attack on Bahía Blanca, after that of 1859, would be in 1870, two years after JG's arrival—but this time under the leadership of Calfucurá's son, Namuncurá.

CHAPTER VII

LIFE AND DEATH BY THE WILLOWS

For the moment, however, JG Walker could concentrate on getting his new life organized. We have a plan from the Bahia Blanca archives published by Rojas Lagarde that shows how the land along the banks of the Sauce Grande river was divided among the Englishmen.

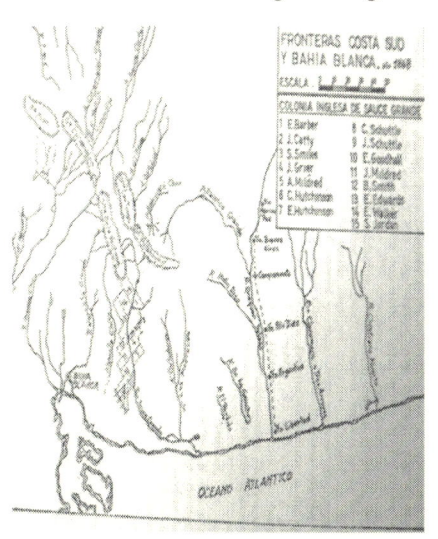

Although there are mistakes with the initials,[1] the plan shows that George Catty, Henry Edwards, 'E.' Walker as well as Barber, Mildred

---

[1] Some of the mistakes are the result of Spanish translation, as E. for Enrique or Henry and J for Jorge or George.

Twigs of a Tree

and Jordan already had allotments as early as 1868. Lots 1 and 2 are in the names of Barber and Catty. Their immediate neighbours, on lots 10, 11, 13, 14, 15, are registered as E. Goodhall and Arthur Mildred, who seem to have been the principal promoters of the colony. Edwards, Walker, and Jordan follow. From the same plan of 1868 one can see that the settlement, though east of the town of Bahía Blanca, was considerably to the west and far in advance of the line of fortifications that established the frontier—marked as dashes—between the 'civilized world' and the lands of the Indians. It was still considered highly dangerous territory and earlier attempts to develop it had been made and failed.

Mulhall in 1869 gives a list of roughly thirty Englishmen settled on the banks of the Sauce Grande River, about fifty kilometres northeast of Bahia Blanca.[2] In time, some eighty men were induced to join them, either as settlers or—with their passages underwritten—as labourers. Briton tells us that the colony stretched some 14 leagues (70 kilometres) along both banks of the Sauce Grande. The land was made doubly attractive by the fact that each property had some direct frontage onto the water.

The land did not, however, come free and different settlers, presumably for reasons of finance, formed companies among themselves. Henry Edwards and JG went into business with Alice's brother, George Catty and with Sam Giles, a maternal cousin of JG's. The land beyond the line of the frontier had been taken on terms of *emphyteusis*—a system of (no or very low) long term rental—that they hoped would eventually lead to outright ownership or to favourable buying rights in return for *poblando*, or settling, improving, stocking and developing the land.[3]

---

[2] Among them he cites Mildred, Goodhall, Sinclair, Grieve, and Barber, but not yet Walker. Mulhall *Handbook of the River Plate*, 2nd edition.

[3] In *Argentina 1516-1982* David Rock explains that the ancient Roman custom of emphyteusis was introduced by Rivadavia in 1826 to open land, taken from the Indians, to development; ownership and income remained with the State. It was a failure. There was no mechanism in place to evaluate the land or to collect the expected rental income. Land attracted speculators who obtained it on a long-term basis by paying neither purchase price nor rental. There was no limit on the land that could be claimed so some 6.5 million acres ended in the hands of some 122 persons. When Rivadavia's leases ran out in 1836, renters were given the option of purchase. The elites increased their transfer from commerce to land. Rosas himself owned 800.000 acres, the Anchorena family obtained almost two million acres. Rosas also rewarded the military with conquered land that was often passed on to the great cattle ranchers.

Mulhall gives an explanation of how the system worked. Each man could take a 'suerte', 6.700 acres of land, in *propriedad* at an initial cost of £40. In return he had to build a house or 'rancho' and place a flock of 1.000 sheep on the land.

After allotment of camp a deposit is required of $10.000 mc. or £80, to be made with the Provincial Bank, which is returned when the above conditions have been complied with, but is forfeited should the depositor fail to comply. The Provincial Bank allows six per cent per annum on this deposit. At the end of two years, when the Justice of the peace of the district has certified that all conditions have been duly carried out, the title deeds are forthcoming. It must be distinctly understood that the land must be occupied during the whole of the term of two years.[4]

When JG arrived at the Sauce Grande, Edwards and a friend, Robert Grieve, had already nearly completed the construction of the house imposed by the government, an *azotea* house of brick. This single-floor, flat- or terraced-roofed dwelling, was equipped with towers, for defence, lookouts for overseeing the animal corrals and the plains from which the Indians could appear. It had taken them a full year to build.

JG's house as published by Hogg.[5]

---

[4] Mulhall, *Handbook of the River Plate*, 1869 p. 66
[5] Lagarde, however, has doubts about whether this is the house but does not explain why.

Twigs of a Tree

Building on the Argentine Pampas, where there is neither wood nor stone, was never an easy task. The ancient Tehuelche or Patagon Indians in the Deep South had been obliged to squat for shelter in caves or even, before the animals became extinct, in the shells of giant armadillos. In the 19th century they lived in primitive huts of hides and wood generally built by the women.

The Pampas Indians still dwelled in crude oven-shaped shelters of posts and animal skins. The gauchos, who roamed the country on horseback, and many of the poorer settlers inhabited adobe mud huts thatched with thistles.

A reconstruction of a Tehueulche dwelling in El Calafate ELW, February 2007

Settlers with a little capital built better houses but had to encircle them with protective fortifications and wide ditches, six feet deep. Bricks were a luxury, so difficult to obtain and transport that they usually had to be made by hand. Elinor (sic) Barber—daughter of one of JG's fellow pioneers and a playmate in the 1880's of George Catty's children, Gordon and Elsie—reports her father's 'Lets knock off work and make bricks.'[6] First an area was cleared of all vegetation, the soil was then dug up, wetted and crushed by bullocks or, according to Elinor, by

---

[6] *La Leña*. Memoirs of her childhood by Elinor Barber, from a copy given to me by Rojas Lagarde in February 2007.

unbroken, restive horses rapidly trampling the clay earth, being driven round and round in an enclosure

The trampled mud was then shaped with wooden moulds, turned out and spread to bake, not in an oven, but in the intense heat of the summer sun. Slow, tedious, backbreaking work; but Seymour relates that it was possible to make a thousand bricks a day. Once the walls were up, there was only more mud available to plaster them. In the heat of summer the mud-plastered interior walls choked the inhabitants with clouds of fine dust.

Tiles were another unobtainable luxury. Houses with sloping roofs, like the modest adobe 'ranchos', could be thatched with thistles, but these were easily set alight. Ras tells us that, in the 1870's, the new metal roofing from England was eagerly adopted—by those who could afford it—as a powerful defence against firing by the Indians. To this day the *Susana*, built many years later and not unlike the Barber's own house in the Naposta valley, has a corrugated iron roof.

Seymour tells us that a friend of his in Argentina, desperate for a dwelling, had put down eighty pounds sterling for an absolute novelty, an 'iron house'. This uncomfortable abode, with walls that absorbed and reflected the faintest changes in temperature, was a sensation, bringing its owners much envious respect.

The banks where JG and Edwards had settled were lined with willows, hence the names of the rivers, Sauce Grande and Sauce Chico, Large and Small Willow. The willows, the only trees in the area, yielded wood—but it seems to have been suitable only for fence posts.

Once a house was built, furnishing it was no easier. Carpenters were known as 'wood butchers'. Their services and the wood itself were so costly and so difficult to find, that the skulls of dead cattle and horses often provided the only furniture for seating. For hanging clothes Reid describes walls bristling with antlers, cheaper and easier to obtain than wooden pegs. Trestle beds—*catres*—were knocked together from wood and hides.

For water, wells had to be dug by hand, but often they yielded water so salty that it could not be used. Today, flying over the Sierra de la Ventana area, one can still see lakes and waterholes in the vast flatness around the hills. Some are so thickly rimmed with salt that from the air its whiteness, even in the heat of summer, looks like snow. Far to the north the lagoon water on the edge of the Susana territory is also salt laden.

Twigs of a Tree

Labour was so difficult to obtain that most work was done by the settlers' own hands. Reid, who at one point invested in a flock of sheep, could get no peon to watch them so shepherded them himself, lying all day in the long grass 'reading Ruskin', relieving, perhaps, the monotony of the Pampas with dreams sparked into life by the *Stones of Venice*.

Mulhall in his handbook advises against native labour as 'scarce and expensive'. To save money, he says, 'Potential farmers should get English workers.' Seymour actually brings out some labourers from England—a gardener and a cook—as did several of the Sauce Grande colonists. Mulhall lays out what they should be paid (between 200 and 300 pesos or two to three pounds sterling per month) and finishes with the pious sentiment that European energy and capital will in a short time carry out the work of 'civilization'. Later, after the Indians had been defeated, it became common for bands of Italians to go out to Argentina for seasonal work that lasted a few months. They became famous for their shearing abilities.

Far away in Tasmania, into which England had emptied its prisons, John Adams describes the very different labour conditions on his farm, a few years earlier.

The price of labour is very high. To the prisoners I give from 9 pounds to 15 pounds per man per year and the greatest part of them are Irish. Their allowance per week is 11 lbs. of meat, 12 lbs of flour, 11 lbs of sugar and 3 ounces of tea. I wish the free men were treated as well. It makes my heart bleed to see those scoundrels so well served and then discontented.

John Adams' son, Charles, was to name one of his properties Idlewild, a somewhat backhanded tribute to the unfortunate convict labourers who worked it—the idle and the wild.

Drawing on infrequent articles in the Buenos Aires *Standard*, Rojas Lagarde concludes that in 1868, the year of JG's arrival in the Bahía Blanca area, things went relatively well. Mildred's later summary of the Colony's first eight years, however, tells a different story. For, although flocks and wheat and maize at first flourished, the crops, that year, were nearly all 'lost in a storm'. The work of ploughing, sowing and reaping without the agricultural machinery that had been held up in Patagones, and without the help of labourers was desperately, excruciatingly hard.

In the first year the colonists had time only to build a single house and sow a few fields with grain. Even this, with no machinery and scant labour, was extremely difficult. An Indian invasion and bad weather also took its toll.

Life And Death By The Willows

A reporter for *The Standard* in April 1869 mentions that most of the settlers' houses remained un-built because the shipping company held up the building materials for a full six months. Ordered farm machinery had also gone undelivered by the same firm. The reporter is, however, impressed by the settlers' firearms, and he doubts that the Indians would risk straying into the range of the new *Snider-Enfield* and *Spencer* breech-loading rifles.[7]

On January 20, 1869, according to Mildred, the settlers lost all their horses to the Indians. An interminable drought made the sowing of any crops impossible. But in September rain came, and the sowing went through. Not sowing their wheat crop would have been a 'stroke of very bad luck', writes Edwards in October. He adds that they have also sown potatoes, peas and pumpkins, the latter as feed for the pigs they wish to buy. But their work was for nothing. The crops of 1869, sown so late because of the dryness, were then lost almost entirely—not to renewed drought, but to continuous rain.

Nevertheless by the end of 1869 the settlers had, with their own hands, put up five brick *azotea* houses. According to Goodhall, each house had its sheds, its corrals and its fenced-off areas for animals.[8] Throughout the year new settlers, at first supported by the established colonists, were arriving in large numbers. There were about eighty of them, all English, as well as numerous labourers. Some machinery was introduced and JG finished his own house.

The following year, 1870, the wheat crop turned out well. JG and Edwards now had nine hundred sheep, not a huge flock. Continually dreaming of marriage, and having heard that 'a man should own about 20.000 sheep' before he can even think of embarking on family life, Henry Edwards nevertheless remarks that he is glad they have no more. 'They do not pay for the trouble of shepherding them.' The sheep they do have are to keep them stocked with meat, and they are happy if they can sell the wool for enough to cover the costs of the shepherding.

The colonists begin buying cattle and look forward—'as soon as we can afford it'—to fencing in at least part of their land. Fencing was costly and difficult.[9] These were the days when a man could be killed for stealing

---

[7] Rojas Lagarde, 1870, p.28
[8] In a letter to the Government of the Province of Buenos Aires, dated September 27th, 1875, quoted by Lagarde.
[9] Barbed wire or *fer de fil barbelé* had been invented by a Frenchman in 1865. Patented in 1874 in the US, it transformed Argentina's estancia economy in the late 80's and 90's.

Twigs of a Tree

a fence-post for use as firewood. For the Sauce Grande settlers it was possible to use the wood from the willows growing along the river bank. But it was only later—in the late seventies—that the recently patented barbed wire was to make possible the effective and relatively cheap fencing of huge tracts of land for the confinement of large numbers of animals.

For the time being, with no fencing, horses were *correnced*. George Reid explains how a herd of ten to twenty horses could be left to run free but be kept conveniently nearby. Correncing hinged on the unflagging affection of a troop of stallions for a single mare. The correnced mare, bell around her neck, was never without the admirers that she could lead down whatever primrose path she fancied. But this object of general desire was trained to remain near the estancia house; her followers clustered about her so closely that they were easily captured when needed. A problem arose if the bell-mare and her herd, after having been correnced on one estancia, were sold and moved to another. For then the mare was likely to return to her former home, even if many leagues away—taking all her aficionados with her. It took about three weeks of careful guarding and training to so accustom a mare to her new surroundings that she would not flee.

If sheep had to be constantly watched by a shepherd, herds of cattle could be controlled either by men on horseback (gauchos if available), or kept reasonably close to the house by the *rascadero,* a highly visible scratching post planted in the earth near a source of water. The cattle gathered around it to scratch, to drink and to lick the salt blocks set out for them.

Henry Edwards and JG were provided with horses and some cattle by one Ciríaco Gomez. This man, an *estanciero* or rancher, was also an army commandant and the Intendente (mayor) of Tandil. As he had befriended them, the cousins were able to repay his favours on easy terms. His generosity was to continue.

According to Briton, they had, apart from their 900 sheep, a field of wheat that they harvested with a neighbour's threshing machine. Briton also tells us that the cousins even managed to get a *puestero,* a farmhand, to tame the cows that his wife then milked.[10] Milk cows were expensive and not easy to find. Reid, unable to afford one, dropped eggs, instead of milk, into his tea. Briton tells us that they also had some 200 head of cattle and were considering starting a dairy farm. Edwards was hoping that they

---

[10] He lived in his *puesto,* often with a family, in a house on his employer's land where he could also grow his own crops.

would soon have a flourmill so that they could 'consume some of their own wheat' as bread. For Edwards, bread was 'one of the great luxuries'.

Meat 'on four legs' was their main staple, while at home or while riding the range. The flesh of sheep, cattle or game, caught and slaughtered on the spot, was immediately roasted over an open fire. The *asado* usually came unadorned and un-garnished, supplemented only by whatever vegetables they could grow themselves. Reid gets thoroughly sick of this diet and throughout much of his stay in Argentina absolutely 'longs for fruit'.

Briton later outlines the difficulties of finding food and drink when travelling across the Pampas on horseback. He describes JG and Edwards driving cattle on a trip of about 150-kilometres to Bella Vista, northwest of the Sauce Grande in 1870/71.[11] They rely on river water for drink, but the streams are often dry and they go thirsty for days. Their only food is the usual meat 'on four legs'. Their guide kills a heifer but cooking at the height of summer, with no thistles or other vegetation, no dried horse or cow dung, is not easily done. They learn how to fashion a 'grotto' out of the animal's bones and to set it alight with a rag or shirttail saturated in grease. With the 'grotto' serving as a rack, they cook the meat for the evening meal and have enough over for the following day. Any uncooked meat is abandoned to the vultures.

There is also plenty of game: ostrich, deer, duck and, at a pinch, even armadillo. Years later, in the 1930's, Oliver Linley Adams was to opine that the *peludo*, the hairy armadillo, is the largest of the species 'but not so good to eat'. JG and his cousin regularly eat ostrich eggs, equivalent to a dozen hen's eggs, found for them by a small boy who strays on to their farm. With nowhere else to go the child is allowed to stay on although there is no real work for him.

In January 1870 the two cousins are hard at work. Henry Edwards had cut the barley that he, JG and a German peon are loading on to carts. One of the other settlers, Grieve, is reaping wheat with a new machine that they had, with great difficulty, managed to put together themselves. The machine proves effective. Their neighbour, Sinclair, is harvesting his crop by hand, but, even with the help of seven other men with scythes, he cannot match the new appliance. Mildred, another of the settlers, has a threshing machine that Edwards hopes to borrow. This lawyer's son remarks to his sister, in a letter of January 1870, that 'It is no joke to sow wheat from 5 in the morning to 11 at night.'

---

[11]   *Yarns from the Camp*, transcribed or recollected by JG's son Briton.

JG and Edwards, like the other settlers, plough, sow, scythe, and reap their own harvests. They shear sheep, sort wool, load carts, milk, sow and tend vegetables; they make bricks, build, plaster and roof their own houses, and even construct their own furniture. Edwards goes over to Sinclair's, where they have brought in the whole harvest by hand, but now are thinking of turning to machinery before the next harvest. Edwards thoroughly approves: 'I hope never to try it again . . . In a new country machinery is necessary or nothing can be done on a large scale.'

Edwards also describes the relentlessness and heaviness of the labour. Work in January, the hottest time of the year, begins at four or five in the morning and continues until eleven at night with a siesta break in the high heat of the day. According to Reid, 'it is impossible to move at that time'. The temperatures are so high that at night he sleeps under a tree because the 'house is unbearable'.

Working from sunrise to sunset, the cousins are exhausted. The two-hour siesta break in the heat of the day doesn't help much, according to Edwards. He has so much to do that he cannot sleep, neither then nor through the short nights. JG does all he can to help him. 'John', Edwards writes, 'is of very great use, he is working here as I never saw a man work, unpaid and not for himself.' By April 1870 the number of houses in the Colony have increased to nine. The settlers have also collected 60 oxen, 130 horses, and about 12.000 sheep, as well as a herd of milk cows.

The Return of the Indios

But it wasn't long before JG's experiences with the Indians began. He arrived in Argentina, when the country, in 'Triple Alliance' with Brazil and Uruguay was embroiled in the territorial war against Paraguay. The six-year turmoil left fewer soldiers to man the frontier lines and to protect the farmers; it would be followed by yet another outburst of serious civil rebellion, this time led by the Federalist caudillo López Jordán.

Nevertheless, by the end of 1869 the government had drawn up a plan to push the frontier some fifty kilometres forward and to build a couple more forts. The once abandoned *Fortín Pavón* on the banks of the Sauce Grande river was to be restored. About 20 kilometres eastwards, it would be the colony's closest centre of military defence. This steady pushing forward of the frontier into their hunting territory enraged the Indians as an injustice and a breach of promise.

In April of the following year, 1870, the much-criticized, incompetent and corrupt commander of Bahía Blanca, one Llanos, made the mistake of betraying the fragile peace that had been established with the Indians—after much killing on both sides—under the dictator Rosas. With his system of tributes and subsidies that supplied the Indians with basic necessities, Rosas had been able to buy a measure of peace. The Indians were desperately poor, so in need that they often stripped their victims of their clothing, leaving them stark naked.

The tribute system continued, but was rife with corruption and graft. Materials and animals due for delivery to the Indians were still substituted with inferior goods by middlemen or not delivered at all. Comandante Llanos himself first refused to hand over the monthly supplies and tributes promised to the representative of the Cacique Canumil, one of the friendlier Indian leaders. Then the officer attacked Canumil's tribe on a series of pretexts—robbing horses, harbouring deserters—that were, according to the settlers themselves, exaggerated if not trumped up. About 70 Indians were killed, their women raped, their horses taken, and Canumil, surprised in his bed, was captured. According to Ras, the military authorities in Bahía Blanca almost succeeded in concealing the facts of this piece of criminal stupidity, had it not been for the outrage of the English colonists. *The Standard* newspaper in Buenos Aires was able to get at the truth and published the story of what had happened and why.

On June 28, 1870, the Indians, who until the April attack by the military had been relatively quiet, struck back at Tres Arroyos, a recently founded town 200 kilometres north-east of Bahía Blanca and the Sauce Grande. Under the leadership of the charismatic and now septuagenarian cacique Calfucurá—both friend and father-in-law of Canumil—groups of Indians galloped in across a stretch of territory 100 kilometres wide. Some forty settlers were killed or captured; nearly 50.000 cattle, 4000 mares, 1500 horses and 7500 sheep were driven off.[12]

---

[12]   Rojas Lagarde, 1870, p.37-39

Calfucurá of the Puelches in military uniform

The news reached the settlers by *chasque* or post-chaise, but this first attack, horrifying though it was, did not much affect the Englishmen on the Sauce Grande. On the 20th of October *The Standard* reported one of JG's friends as saying that the settlers were all safe although a nearby estancia had lost 500 head of cattle. Crops were flourishing and sheep getting nicely fat. A flourmill was still a necessity, but some of the settlers had travelled to England and brought back farm machinery. However, more and more English, never there in large numbers, were leaving in disgust because land could not be bought at any price, and others, even after three years of back-breaking work, were unable to obtain, from the government, the long-promised titles to their property.

Reid clearly had more capital than either JG or Edwards. And, at the beginning of the 'terrible year' of 1870, he is still enjoying galloping across the Pampas at sunrise. Nevertheless, he writes to his father that he and several of his friends are 'ruined'. He had lost 4.500 sheep in two months. A couple of his gentlemen friends were so disheartened they had decided to move to Canada and look for work as labourers. His friend 'O'Dwyer and his wife have had their place seized and are left with three pounds in the world and everyone else is in the same sort of state.' George Reid was to give up on Argentina entirely and return home at the end of the year 1870.

On October 23, 1870, 2000 Indians of various tribes, newly united thanks to the treachery of Llanos, fell on Bahía Blanca itself. The sun rose to the tintinnabulation of church bells, the cacophony of cannon shot. These were coupled with the clamour of two thousand horsemen 'shrieking like demons' as they galloped into the town. Led by Namuncurá, one of Calfucurá's sons, they were accompanied by a horde of about 300 boys and women—*chinas*—whose job it was to drive off any stolen animals, leaving the men free to fight. The men torched houses, speared anyone in their way and rounded up animals. Llanos' cannons appeared to do more harm to the houses than to the Indians, but his 300 rifles were effective.

About 700 Indians then moved on to the Sauce Grande region where they attacked an estancia belonging to a German settler, grabbed his horses, smashed his machinery and destroyed his sacks of carefully tended, accumulated grain. They then raced on to Barber's in the northernmost area of the settlement. There they murdered an Irishman and drove off the animals. A few days later, an Indian was seen in Bahía Blanca sporting the Irishman's clothes.[13] Sheep, we are told by Briton, were killed and stuffed down the wells to contaminate the water.

The other settlers barricaded their doors and reinforced the parapets of their houses with sacks of grain as protection from the deadly hail of flying rocks. They stretched wires to trip up the approach of galloping horses. Again they were left alone, perhaps because they were not yet worth the trouble of attack. Norberto Ras reports a rumour circulating among the Indians that reflects both the precarious state of many English settlers and their danger to the Indians. 'The gringos have more lead than animals.' With their stones and spears, and in spite of the deadly accuracy with which they hurled them, the Indians were no match for the rapidity and accuracy of the newly efficient breech-loading rifles. Eventually they fled but not without having done considerable damage. The settler Mildred's later summary for the year 1870 was brief but precise;

October 23rd invasion of 2.000 Indians to Bahia Blanca. Deveridge and Nilson killed by them. Mildred's mares stolen, about 100.

---

[13] Rojas Lagarde, *Malón, 1870.*

Twigs of a Tree

In December, *The Standard* published a report describing the attack. Highly critical of their impotence and ineffectiveness, the article accused the authorities of having abandoned Bahia Blanca, the best 'seaport in the Republic'. The paper had discovered that the Indians, as long as Llanos remained in Bahia Blanca, would do 'everything in their power to destroy the district'. If the government continued deaf to the supplications of the inhabitants, all the foreigners would be driven out and they would be obliged to turn to their own ministries for help.[14]

On December 18th *The Standard* in Buenos Aires listed the overall holdings of the colony and their value. Among them are 8 *azotea* houses, 18 *ranchos*, 6 sheds, 15.000 bricks, sheep and cattle corrals, a selection of machinery, 16 wagons, 18.450 sheep, 6 Cotswold and 6 Lincoln rams, 215 milk cows, 16 tame oxen and 173 horses. Listed too are clothes, saddles, furniture, a canon, 2 Spencer rifles, and 62 Snider rifles. They have planted an astonishing 19.500 trees and are growing wheat, maize, alfalfa and vegetables.[15]

In October 1871 Edwards tells his sister Louise that eight of his horses have been stolen. Anastasio Sotelo describes a chase following the Indians, with Edwards and thirty men, that took them as far as the Sierra de la Ventana. Their mounts exhausted, they could go no further.[16] But Edwards had friends in relatively high places: the Comandantes Spika and Gomez, who had already given him 200 cows, now offered him 200 more. Edwards doesn't want them thinking he is 'sponging on them', but he is inclined to accept one or two horses.

The following month another attack left the colonists of Sauce Grande with no horses at all; Thomas, one of the Jordan brothers, was killed. He had made the mistake of going out unarmed to check some horses. Coming out of a river valley, he found twenty Indians lying in wait. When he took flight, the Indians, with better horses, managed to surround and lasso him. Jordan cut himself free and fled again. They then brought down his galloping horse with their *boleadoras*, tied him up and slashed his throat. The Indians made off with seven horses and ten oxen. The attacks continue, and in February Edwards loses more horses. After this the settlers were ready to plea with their embassies or consulates.[17]

---

[14] Lagarde, 1870, p. 77
[15] Rojas Lagarde, *1870* p. 78.
[16] Rojas Lagarde, *1870* p. 96
[17] Briton also tells the story in *On the Frontier*. Rojas Lagarde, *1870*, 98

Elinor Barber later adds the detail that Jordan was killed on her father's land on the 'spot they passed to the picnic place by the river'. Her father, she says, during the really bad Indian raids often abandoned his cabin of clay and wattle to live in a cave on the river bank, opposite Jordan's cottage.

The Indians were not the only danger. The soldiers of the army and its stragglers could be equally perilous to isolated settlers. Argentine soldiers, not unlike the Indians in their camps, often lived in conditions of misery, even starvation. Rojas Lagarde publishes a declaration from one army commander to his troops that shows the wretchedness of many of the military at the time: 'They are without tobacco, bread, clothing or cash. These conditions render even the soldiers dangerous.'[18]

Reid tells us that Colonel Gonzalez' men, marching through the country in huge bands, would sometimes camp next to an estancia and help themselves to as many as 100 bullocks. Slaughtered on the spot they would be roasted for dinner. Soldiers riding exhausted horses were always on the lookout for fresh steeds, and army men were not above robbing farms, or even killing their owners for a good horse. Reid reports that a group of army ruffians sacked the house of some friends leaving

> *poor little Mrs Burr with one petticoat and her husband a pair of trousers . . . the only articles they left them, they also took all the linen, sheets, tablecloths, in fact everything and 50 horses . . . worth £250, all picked horses, a hobby of Burr's.*

Hudson relates how his father hid his horses when groups of Rosas' soldiers approached. Twenty years later Reid was deliberately starving his own animals so that they would be too thin and frail to attract the eye of the roving military. The outcome of the war with Paraguay (1864-70)[19], in which infantry or foot soldiering was useless, was, according to Reid, 'entirely a matter of horseflesh'. Each soldier needed not one, but at least four horses, and most had to be stolen. Reid describes how during the civil uprising of 1870, led by Lopez Jordán, things were even worse. Horses not taken were often left permanently crippled. So they would not fall into the hands of the enemy the tendons of their hock joints were slashed:

---

[18] Rojas Lagarde, *1870*, p. 193
[19] One estimate puts Paraguay's losses at 1.2 million, almost ninety percent of its male population, in its war against the Triple Alliance of Brazil, Argentina and Uruguay.

Twigs of a Tree

> *At Spankenbenberg's they took 70 horses, hamstrung 30, I suppose to prevent them falling into enemy hands. It is a vile cruelty . . . and (they also) burnt the house to the ground.*

Weathering the Weather

The notorious unreliability and the wild swings of weather were also leaving their mark on men, animals and countryside. Attempting to keep cool in a darkened room that nevertheless registered a temperature of 102F (38.8 Celsius), George Reid describes the effects of a drought in February 1868:

> *The sheep are dying and dying and dying. The horses are nearly mad for want of water, and want incessant watching, and even so we keep losing them. The camp has taken fire and burns day and night, for leagues and leagues there is nothing but a black smoking wilderness.*

Mulhall reports that the drought of 1869 killed off four-million sheep. The grass they fed on burnt away by the relentless sun, cattle also starved to death. In 1870, the year of the huge Indian invasion, drought turned to downpour. In that year Edwards and JG lost most of their wheat crop to a *pampero*—one of those crashing Pampas storms that pour from the heavens with such suddenness and ferocious force that within minutes fields turn into lakes, and unmade roads into rushing rivers. The waters run so deep and fast that even modern SUV's and trucks come to a halt.

These are downpours that also shoot fire. Their force is such that a man, or even a horse, can only with the greatest difficulty remain on his feet: bolts of lightning crash from the skies with such speed and fury that the darkest night flashes into day. Men, horses and cattle can be felled forever. Reid tells us that if sheep shorn of their wool are hit by a storm, they die 'in scores'. Sometimes the rain hardens into hail with stones that fall so large and fast that grown men howl with pain as the ice beats them black and blue.

Perhaps this is the place to insert a few paragraphs of personal experience with Pampas weather. In 1994 or so, my husband Carlos and I went, with our son Sebastian, to visit Molly at the *Susana*. It was Christmas—which means summertime—and we had been invited to dinner at a neighbouring estancia. We set off in the car with Molly at the wheel. We carried Christmas puddings for the party and had also brought along a bottle of Scotch. There are no electric (or any other) lights on those earth roads even today, and, now, at nightfall, the horizon was turning inky black.

Suddenly, from one moment to the next, the skies opened. Molly, then in her mid-eighties, drove on as best she could through the sheets of rain, her nose to the windscreen. But soon the road vanished, a swimming duck appeared in the headlights; the car stopped, unable to move through water that was already halfway up its sides. We sat in the car and listened to the rain pounding down, the landscape appeared and disappeared as lightning struck and receded, the skies flashed for split seconds in an immense web of light. Then Carlos and Sebastian decided to go for help. With difficulty they pushed open the door and vanished into the night, running half-bent with the vague hope of avoiding a strike by lightening. I stupidly let them go, they could have been killed.

A saint of a man, a *puestero*, or tenant farmer, eventually rescued us. He was just about to sit down to his Christmas dinner with his family when Carlos and Sebastian appeared out of the darkness. Soaked, almost drowned by the downpour, they knocked on the door of his tiny farmhouse and asked for help. Realizing that they had had a long and dangerous run, the *puestero* abandoned wife, small children and Christmas dinner, got out his truck and, after much effort in the still pelting rain, pulled the car—with Molly and me still in it—out of the water. He then dragged us all to a garage in Venado Tuerto. We never got to our own dinner, but spent Christmas Eve at Molly's flat in Venado, consuming a somewhat unbalanced feast of plum pudding and whisky—all we had. Carlos and Sebastian, totally soaked, were decked out in whatever of Molly's garments they could squeeze into. Unfortunately, I had no camera to record that elevating sight for posterity.

Of Locusts and Other Plagues

Sometimes the *pamperos* are dry. Lightning and thunder are accompanied not by rains or hail but by furious winds that leave the air, for days, clogged and heavy with dust. For Elinor Barber, the dry storms were even more terrifying than the wet. She recalls one that left 'seven white horses lying dead by the lagoon'.

There were other natural blights. Maggots, foot-rot and disease; the scab could eliminate a flock of sheep in a few weeks. Rats (as well as frogs and toads) invaded the settlers' houses in such numbers that not only meat, but even saddles and other leather goods had to be hung high from the rafters to save them from the rodents. Reid says it was not uncommon to kill 100 rats a day. Giant ants ate at their clothes. Opossums, so fierce that the dogs ran from them, invaded the runs and devoured the chickens and their eggs. Snakes and spiders, some of them deadly, were common. In the summer there were so many insects and flies that, says Reid, 'You eat flies, drink flies and breathe flies, everything is alive with horrid insects.'

Then there was that plague of biblical times. Locusts that suddenly united into swarms so great that they blotted out the sun, stripping entire fields bare: wheat, maize and the contents of vegetable gardens all disappeared within a few minutes. I remember a day darkened by locusts beating on the windows of the *Susana* like demented drummers. Briton describes locusts 'bubbling out of the ground' as they hatched, and attempts to control them by setting up metal sheets, or digging trenches along the fields. Caught in the ground, the 'struggling millions' were squirted with burning *nafta*. The sight of the writhing insects was pure inspiration to the clergyman who at the time was visiting JG,

Mr Walker, what an illustration of Hell! Damned souls writhing in everlasting fire! What an illustration for my Easter sermon on the Fate of the Ungodly! [20]

Social life was meagre, nothing to write home about, but there were some highlights. One day, the Comandantes Gomez and Spika, including wives and attendant servants and soldiers, came to call at the Sauce Grande. On their arrival, their lunch was still contentedly grazing. As mealtimes loomed in those days of no refrigeration, dogs, guns and knives had to be brought out to chase down, slaughter and butcher the main—and probably the only—course. But there was no lack of freshly killed meat cooked over an open fire, often with the hide still on—*carne con cuero*, as it is still called. 'In two days,' reported Henry Edwards, the visitors and their hosts 'ate two cows and three sheep.'

Over this *asado*, the main topic of discussion with the military men was no doubt what to do about the expected Indian attacks. The authorities had received some reinforcements. 'I fancy that very soon the great expedition against the Indians will come off, as the weather is better and they have just received a thousand horses at Pillahuinco—enough to mount 500

---

[20] J.B. Walker, *Yarns from the Camp*.

Life And Death By The Willows

men,' remarks Edwards, adding *en passant* that his French bride, Hélène de Bernardy, was in Berlin and 'will learn German in a year'.

Edwards is now looking forward to a trip to England the following August, that is 1872. They have 100 acres of green, healthy-looking wheat supplied with an irrigation system made by themselves, so as to avoid another loss through drought like that of the crop of the year before. The cows are beginning to increase; the dairy farm seems imminent.

In January 1873, a few months before Alice Catty's expected arrival, Arthur Mildred, one of the settlers, reports in a letter to Goodhall, their agent in Bahía Blanca, a decent harvest of barley and a bad one of wheat—'the frost had got it'. Things are not too bad, but a gang of fifteen Indians suddenly attacks. In this world killing is a casual thing:

They came for Edwards' trot horse and Walker shot one in the back, and the natives (the farmhands) finished him. On the way back Herald (a farmer) met them on the other side of the Sierra, and killed six, and yesterday I heard that some of them came back with some more and that they killed four.

In spite of this, Mildred goes on to say that they spent a 'very pleasant Xmas day'. 'The Cobbolds were here and one or two others and we got up some races. I was very successful and I have lately made 700 pesos in racing.' The following January, the horse racing in Sauce Grande is honoured by an article in *The Standard*.

These races, an occasion for all the men to get together, had, because of the Indian attacks, become a rare event. They gather to race their best horses: Douner, Mildred, Cobbold and Catty, though not JG, are all mentioned. They have a cold lunch with all the important 'little etceteras' and then, after the racing, they 'call on Bacchus to rinse their throats so that they can toast the health of absent friends and wish them a swift return'. Then, after most had left, the rest sit down to play cards and sing songs.[21]

George Reid describes some of the strange, often lost, young Englishmen wandering in the Pampas. One had been meandering about the country for so long that he had forgotten how to speak English. Another was a

---

[21] Rojas Lagarde, *El Malón de 1870*.

very rough looking young man, skinning sheep, living in a filthy, mud-floored hut, sheep carcass hanging from the rafters, but with 'ivory backed brushes with gilt monograms' signalling his identity as the 'nephew of Lord Gough.'

Then there was Swinburne, the son of an army officer. He had given up a perfectly good job 'to seek his fortune in Argentina and was now grateful to be washing Reid's dishes and living with his servants.' The young men yearned for the company of women, but to Reid camp life—difficult enough for young fellows in good health—was 'completely unsuitable for females, except for those who were young and strong . . . unaccustomed to a refined style of society.' He adds, 'As to comforts or conveniences for a lady, there are none.'

On his way to Brazil in 1867, Henry Edwards mentions being 'introduced into society' in Buenos Aires. He exclaims on the 'treat it was to look at the English ladies—I had not seen one for ten months,' then, with a touch snobbery: 'Of course I had seen Mrs. Heeton, but she does not count, she is not very strong in aitches and does not go for a lady.'

In October 1871, lovesick Edwards is so anxious about how and when to get married that he can barely 'settle down to write letters'. His cousin John was to beat him to the altar. In April 1873, JG, by now engaged for over five years, set off on the long journey to Buenos Aires to meet his betrothed, Alice Catty.

CHAPTER VIII

ALICE IN MACHOLAND

We have a photograph of Alice Catty taken at just about the time she was going to travel across the globe to get married, the anonymous book in her hand testimony either to a love of reading or (who knows?) of her intellectual preparations for Argentina—with, for instance, Woodbine Parish's widely read *Buenos Ayres and the Provinces of the Rio de la Plata*.

Alice Catty Walker
(1848-1939)

Twigs of a Tree

Like most girls at the time, and unlike her brothers, Alice was probably given a rather cursory education. On the other hand, she certainly profited from her father's love of music. Frederick Adam or perhaps his wife Ann must have played that 'Grand Horizontal Piano-Forte' sold before he left England in 1837 to practice medicine on the continent.

Alice, his seventh child and fourth daughter, was born in Bad Ems in 1848 shortly before his return to England and his change of career. When Frederick Adam eventually became the 'Principal Clerk' in the Lord Mayor's office—he also presided over the music committee of the London Guildhall. Recognizing his daughter's abilities, Frederick Adam put Alice, according to Melrose, in the hands of an 'exceptionally good music master'. There was doubtless a touch of envy in my grandmother Melrose who grew up on the Pampas without any such musical tutoring. She too played the piano, probably taught by her mother, Alice.

Even if Alice had not read Woodbine Parish, it is very likely she already knew something about Argentina. Her mother Ann Edwards was, as we have seen, a cousin of George Alfred Henty. Henty, writer and journalist, was already famous for his dispatches from numerous European wars, including Garibaldi's battles for the unification of Italy in 1861.

In 1870, three years before Alice sailed for Argentina, Henty's first children's book—*Out on the Pampas*—appeared.[1] It was a tale that, curiously enough, dealt with emigration and with pioneering. Henty's protagonist, architect Frank Hardy, before setting off for Argentina makes sure that his family learn some Spanish. Although allowed to drop Latin 'which will be of no use', his boys go on with their ordinary curriculum. However, they must also learn to garden—plant vegetables, prune fruit trees—to ride, to carpenter, even to plough. The idea of battling Indians is an exciting, indeed, 'glorious' attraction to the two teenage boys in Henty's story, so they also learn to shoot, to handle Colt revolvers and Remington rifles. This military training, and the arms they are given by their father, is strictly secret. Neither their mother nor their sisters must know. Their young sisters, of course, have less to learn but they must abandon French for Spanish and drop their music—the piano—for cooking. They learn to

---

[1] Apart from the Crimea, Henty covered the Austro-Italian, Abyssinian, Franco-Prussian. Turco-Serbian, Ashanti wars and the Carlist war in Spain. He travelled to India and Palestine and witnessed the opening of the Suez Canal. He does not appear to have gone to Argentina.

'make puddings and boil vegetables properly', to 'attend poultry' and the other skills that later came to be rather grandly called 'domestic science'.

We know that Alice Catty, too, prepared herself for her new life in Argentina. Melrose frequently told me that her mother had gone to Wales to 'learn about farming and the milking of cows'. She too went into her father's well-staffed kitchen to learn how to cook, and by the time she left for Argentina she was obviously capable of riding a horse. What she did not do, like the Hardy girls, was give up her music. Before Alice's departure, not only clothing and furniture, but, above all, a piano was loaded onto the *RMS Boyne*. In early April 1873, she said goodbye to her father's seventeen-member household in Wandsworth—parents, brothers, sisters, nephews, assorted servants—and set off, seemingly alone, for distant Buenos Aires.[2]

One wonders why she did it. Why did she abandon her comfortable life to link herself to a man whom she had not seen for almost five years; a man who although clearly enterprising and adventurous, lived a highly precarious life? Through affection, no doubt—she had been engaged and presumably corresponding with JG for five years—but perhaps too because, at the end of her 24th year, Alice was already approaching the nineteenth century deadline of thirty, getting beyond marriageable age. At thirty women commonly gave up on marriage and reached for the lace cap. This particular sign of respectable female maturity, when worn by his spinster-aunt Marianne Walker, resembled, Briton tells us, an 'upside down boat'. Marriage was still, and would long remain, one of the very few options open to women.

It was a rather uncertain option in those days. In 1856, a census revealed that there were two million more women than men in Britain. Elizabeth Gaskell's novel *Cranford* is almost entirely populated by females, with so few 'gentlemen' that its ladies had almost persuaded themselves that 'to be a man was to be vulgar'. In the 1850's, during the Crimean War, Florence Nightingale had introduced the option of nursing. And the advent of the typewriter in the 1870's would eventually open up a few other professional fields to women. But, generally speaking, at the time that Alice sailed to Argentina, women from the middle classes could earn a living only by teaching as governesses or by sewing.

---

[2]   See 1871 Census

Twigs of a Tree

Without any social or economic alternative to marriage, many women were destined to remain spinsters, old maids, or, as they were then called, 'odd women', living out their lives, if they could, in the households of fathers or brothers. This was also the age of the so called 'fishing fleets' to India, where young women whose parents could afford the journey travelled during the English winter months in search of a mate, preferably a dashing young officer. Those who didn't find the man of their dreams, or any other for that matter, sailed home again as the 'returned empties'.

Like JG's sister Marianne, two of Alice's sisters—Jessey and Emmy—never married. They lived with their father into 'old maidenhood', until Frederick Adam died in 1891. They were eventually known as the 'Twickenham aunts'. Frederick Adam seems to have been able to keep them. According to Temple, he retired from the Guildhall on his full salary, a then comfortable pension of £750 per annum. This was just as well, for his other daughter Mary Shearman, soon widowed, and her three children, including the two little practical jokers Jack and Tont (Montague), also seem to have become part of his household.

The unmarried Catty sisters were fortunate. George Gissing's novel *The Odd Women*, published in 1893, shows the plight of the thousands of impoverished 'genteel' women, with neither husband, father, uncle nor brother able to provide them with 'accommodation and board into perpetuity'. With no possibility of making a living themselves, Gissing's ladies starve in garrets all over London. Frederick Adam's household was probably not too different from that of Gissing's charming Dr Madden, whose wife had left him with six daughters. The girls were a source of incessant worry. Dr Madden's daughters are cultivated, but none is a beauty. Two are downright plain, the others have no 'physical charm but that of youthfulness'. Poor Mrs Madden had 'known but little repose, and secret anxieties told upon her countenance long before the final collapse of health'. However,

> *The parents had omitted no care in shepherding their fold. Partly at home, and partly in local schools, the young ladies had received instruction suitable to their breeding, and the elder ones were disposed to better this education by private study. The atmosphere of the house was intellectual; books, especially the poets, lay in every room. But it never occurred to Dr Madden that his daughters would do well to study with a professional object. In hours of melancholy he had of course dreaded the risks of life, and resolved, always with postponement, to*

make some practical provision for his family; in educating them as well as circumstances allowed, he conceived that he was doing the next best thing to saving money, for, if a fatality befell, teaching would always be their resource.

Nevertheless, for Madden, the thought of his girls having to work for money was 'so utterly repulsive' that he could 'never seriously dwell upon it'. Gaskell's Miss Matty, ruined by her bank, is forced to open a shop, but this is seen as so unfitting for a 'lady' that the 'small-as-possible' sign reading 'Matilda Jenkyns Licensed to Sell Tea' is only reluctantly, even shamefully, displayed, 'hidden under the lintel of the new door'. One of Gissing's heroines is a Miss Barfoot who sets up, in the 1880s, a then revolutionary system for female independence by training young women for office work or 'clerkships', including the teaching of 'typewriting'. By the 1920's, as a result of efforts like Barfoot's, typing and secretarial work had been added to the meagre list of more or less acceptable women's professions.

Perhaps Alice Catty was as adventurous as J G Walker himself, or believed that, like Henty's pioneering family, she would be back in England in a relatively short time. Henty's tale ended well on all fronts: The beleaguered daughter Ethel—captured by the Indians, tied to a stake to be burned alive, but rescued at the last minute, virginity intact—eventually found her prince, 'a rising barrister in London'. Her sister Maud, later united to a 'wealthy country gentleman', was able to flourish in English rural life in conditions considerably more genteel and less perilous than those of the Pampas.[3] The fictional Dr Madden's attitude remained common for several generations afterwards, particularly among the English in Latin America. Melrose Goodbody, widowed when she was around forty, left with very little income and with no profession, moved in with her brother Briton. She lamented to the end of her life never having had, at the hands of 'ignorant governesses', a 'proper' education. Molly Dyson also complained about having been sent—unlike her sister Noreen—to a 'tin pot school'.

But my mother's short stint in her not-so-tin-pot Berkhamsted School also led her in the 1930's only to the typewriter. At 21, after the death of

---

[3] Henty's named his characters after his own daughters. His personal tragedy was that Maud and Ethel Henty both died before they reached twenty, felled, like their mother, by tuberculosis.

her first husband, a doctor, she wanted to chuck typing for medicine. Not having the means, nor perhaps the preparation, for a doctor's training, she settled for physiotherapy—and later did much useful and stimulating work with children in the days when polio still raged. However, in the still tight and conventional bridge-playing circles of São Paolo club society, she was if not disdained, certainly pitied for her work by the ladies gathered around the tea and bridge tables. As a result, she put up no resistance when I was removed from school at 16 by my decent, upright, but hardly nonconformist papa.

Long after having sat my A levels at the British consulate in Amsterdam when I was in my twenties, this particular bee coursing through my own bonnet was finally brought down on the 'twenty second day of December of 2002' when I finally crossed back to the United States from France and received my doctorate from the University of Maryland, by which time I had a foot pushed well into the threshold of retirement. A little late, but never mind.

It is perhaps, but only perhaps, a measure of progress that at a recent dinner party in Paris a group of young men were discussing their own and their sisters' education. One, a charming Vietnamese brought up in England, ticked off the professions of three of his sisters—doctor, academic, lawyer—adding that only the fourth and youngest had so far 'made nothing' of her education. She had become 'only a mother'. Today a new name has been coined for a very ancient position, the 'stay-at-home-mother'.

Arrival, Marriage—and Typhoid

We know nothing of Alice's voyage—only that JG Walker met his bride (and boarded her ship) in Montevideo. Because the steamer had passed through Rio de Janeiro, all the passengers were put into quarantine on the island of Martín Garcia. It was apparently 'an awful station with most primitive accommodation': quarantine was, however, often unavoidable. Epidemics—typhoid, cholera, measles, yellow-fever—were common and devastating. In 1867 alone, cholera had left 8.000 dead in Buenos Aires. It then spread into the rural areas as far as Santa Fé and the town where George Reid had gone, Gualeguaychú, northeast of Buenos Aires. It seemed to Reid that 'Death himself was stalking.'[4] Whole families died

---

[4] Reid, 91

in a single night, estancias were left without a soul alive, bodies unburied, animals abandoned to die of thirst in the terrible drought of the same year. Those who survived such an outbreak, like Reid, had to push aside their grief and labour like ten men just to keep the farms going and the animals alive.

I remember those bitter tombs in the graveyards in India, around the abandoned 19th century churches, their floors strewn with the pages from the Bible, with forsaken hymn and prayer books.[5] Headstones in these churchyards were commonly inscribed with the names of entire families: young mother, father, and two, three, four children, felled by a single epidemic, and often all buried on the same day. Cholera had struck Buenos Aires again in 1870.

After those long five years of engagement, April 28, 1873 must have been a joyous if somewhat bewildering day for Alice. On being released from the quarantine island, she and JG were married by the Reverend Francis Smith in Buenos Aires' St. John's Church. Among the witnesses were her brother, George E. Christie Catty, and E.P. Goodhall, one of the Sauce Grande colonists. Goodhall later became the British vice-consul in Bahía Blanca, and we have an assortment of letters to him by JG and other Sauce Grande settlers.

Unfortunately, there are no photographs or personal accounts of this wedding, but the immediate aftermath of the marriage ceremony was hardly a honeymoon, neither happy nor carefree. No Italian opera for this young couple. No sooner was he married than JG was hit by the latest epidemic. He was so ill with typhoid fever that, although he survived, he and his bride were unable to leave Buenos Aires for a full three months.

They lived in lodgings, and their son Briton relates how some friends of JG's came to the rescue and 'helped Alice get a doctor'. For this sheltered young woman, alone with a new and desperately ill husband in a strange and in those days somewhat savage city, it must have been a frightening time. They were soon almost penniless. Not only was JG's own money gone, so was the £100 he had taken to Buenos Aires to repay Gomez's office for the stock supplied from his estancia in Tandil. Gomez continued sympathetic and accommodating but nevertheless the young couple's

---

[5] In one church the leather cover of the large Bible still stood on its stand but its pages were gone. Later, while shopping in the market, I discovered them. My apples were handed to me in a bag roughly stapled together from pages taken from Leviticus.

funds all vanished in the expensive city; eaten up by doctors, food and accommodation.

Alice did not even have the consolation of her brother's company. After the marriage ceremony, George Catty had soon left Buenos Aires and sailed back to Bahía Blanca with most of his sister's heavy luggage. His ship grounded in the bay; its cargo was later transferred to bullock carts. Other belongings, including the piano, had gone on a second boat, but, having been mistakenly shipped to Patagones, they disappeared.

In July, three months after their marriage, bride and groom were finally able to travel to Alice's new home on the Sauce Grande. The steamboat service to Bahía Blanca had been suspended, but transport by *galera* or diligence had just re-started. Their *galera* was almost the first one running after many years of interruption. Briton tells us that this diligence set off from Las Flores, a small town 80 miles from Buenos Aires, and then followed the line of frontier forts. They took a full day to get to Las Flores and found 'little accommodation' there.

The diligence was a rough un-sprung carriage drawn by about a dozen horses, arranged in fan formation, some with a rider. At full gallop, whipped on by driver and riders, the horses were pushed hard, even 'unmercifully'. The diligence, careering across the rough ground, provided a hideously uncomfortable ride, but with a change of horses every few miles they were able to cover 50 to 60-miles a day.

The newlyweds spent their nights in the rough quarters of the forts but, according to Briton, were made as comfortable as possible by the officers. The 250-mile journey across the Pampas took five days and was relatively uneventful, but a few months later another diligence on the same route was held up: passengers, drivers and guards all left dead on the road.

If Alice was dismayed about the conditions in which she found herself, she courageously concealed it. In September 1873, after she had been in the Sauce Grande region for a month, Edwards writes to his sister saying that Alice found both the house and the life and behaviour of the men 'much better' than expected. His cousin's 'very good, jolly little wife' seemed, according to Edwards, very 'happy and contented'.

Although neither her piano nor the rest of the luggage had yet appeared, Alice was adding touches of civilization to the house: 'blue curtains' at the windows, guanaco rugs and matting on the floors, new chairs, and meals of 'nice little dishes', so good that the men were getting nicely plump under her care. 'I was seedy and unwell before they came and so thin, but now am all right again and weigh nearly as much as I did when I was in England,' writes Edwards to his sister. 'We are all so well attended to, having a lady in the house.'[6]

Like Edwards, George Reid is also delighted with the changes that come with Ada, his friend Clode's new wife. Sheets appear on the beds, cloths, clean glasses, knives and forks on the tables, pictures on the walls; dirty washing vanishes from the floors.

For quite a time, Alice was one of very few women in a rough macho world. JG's 'Yarns from the camp', transcribed or recorded by his son Briton, are crammed with accounts of the fights, knifings and shootings—once even a poisoning—that he observed around him. One of their neighbours, 'no friend of mine', knocks down Edwards's friend Lieutenant Brown. 'Very disgraceful', says Edwards,

'it would not have happened if I had been there, as no visitor should have the trouble of knocking down a man for insulting him in my presence. I should have done it myself and saved him the trouble.'

The men, notwithstanding their pride in their Britishness and belief in their own refinement, could be dangerously wild, fists, or worse, always at the ready. In 1875 Arthur Mildred records in a letter to Goodhall an eruption between two of the settlers that was almost fatal:

Colinson shot Barber . . . the ball (la bala, the bullet) *entered underneath the right nipple, lodged underneath the shoulder blade. It was a row about a dog of Collinson's that Barber wanted to kill because it had bitten him. It seems he began knocking Collinson about, who in self-defence drew his revolver. I am awfully sorry that such a thing should have happened amongst Englishmen. Barber is now convalescent.*

Briton Walker tells us that the locals were unable to get over the amount of 'washing and bathing' they did. They were also astonished by the men's idea of entertainment. Their games were mostly games of battle: single-sticks, or cudgel play, a type of fencing with wooden rods. Then there were under-water wrestling, boxing and target practice.

---

[6] Extracts of Edward's letters to his sister Louise.

Alice's blue curtains were set off by testimony to warfare. A large collection of 'rifles and cutlasses'—and a nine-foot Indian lance captured by JG—graced the walls of the dining room, at hand in case of a visit from the Indians. There were none of the conveniences we take so much for granted today: no running water, no bathroom and, no doubt, very meagre lighting from foul-smelling tallow candles (cheaper and more easily available in Argentina than wax) or lamps fuelled by mare's fat. The settlers were learning to make their own soap, still inexistent in Bahia Blanca.[7] Briton describes the scant offerings in the nearest store, attached to the soldiers' fortress: salt, sugar, yerba mate, and *galletas*, biscuits 'of cricket-ball size and hardness'.

There was no refrigeration, animals had to be killed and immediately consumed. There were no shops stacked with fresh goods; all vegetables and fruit had to be planted, grown and tended by themselves. But finally, many months after Alice's arrival, one of those huge-wheeled bullock carts swayed heavily into the settlement: the piano, given up for lost, had at last arrived. Alice's accompaniment to the sea shanties her husband enjoyed singing, and her own playing, must have invested the rough male household with some slightly gentler, more refined, even joyous entertainment.

Henry Edwards remarks that Alice sometimes went riding with her husband. Riding, as women did in those days, in long skirts, sitting side-saddle with one leg around a pommel, could be dangerous. Even jumping, if they were good enough, was done side-saddle. Briton describes how a woman in her long skirts had to be lifted on to her horse by stepping onto a man's clasped hands. Emmy, Alice's sister, who came to visit her in the 1880's, was accidentally lifted with such force that she flew across her horse's back, landing hard on the ground on the other side. After she had put her habit back together on the 'sewing machine', she was provided with a 'box with some steps' to help her mount.

Horseback apart, the only transport was an old un-sprung cart, a box fitted with wheels and hitched to the cinch of a horse with a rider on it. Primitive though it was, the 'cinch-cart' was a luxury compared to the 'sledges' made of cow-hides with which the gauchos, riding on horseback, dragged their own families across the rough ground into town.

According to Briton, there were no other English women nearby. Her daughter Melrose's later report that Alice 'didn't speak to another

---

[7] In November one of the colonists writes to Buenos Aires for the ingredients: soda, cal viva, and resin.

Englishwoman for five years' may, perhaps, be only slightly exaggerated. Nevertheless, for a long time Alice's only reasonably close female neighbour was Comandante Spika's wife. Whether the women could communicate with any fluency we do not know. However, the house was always full of men: her brother George, Edwards or other settlers of the group.

Alice's Pampas

Alice was soon introduced to the rich and strange animal life around her. Croaking toads, oven-birds or *horneros,* hopping in and out of their ingenious mud nests, usually stuck on a pole; ostriches with their beautiful feathers—then highly prized for ladies' hats—chasing in huge flocks across the Pampas, their nests brimming with as many as ninety eggs; deer, snakes and lizards—some of them highly venomous—and various species of armadillo. Vultures hovered over the dead animal carcasses strewn over the camp, stripping them to the bone in a cloud of flies.

As game for the table there was duck, swan, goose and even armadillo. There was the *puma,* or 'lion of the Pampas'. According to JG, if the puma got into a corral, he would, with blows of his fore paw, break the necks of as many sheep as he could.[8] Snakes, some of them deadly, settled under the furniture. Skunks—pretty little black and white creatures—according to Reid, continually wandered indoors, leaving a smell so terrible and invasive that foodstuffs like tea, coffee and even clothes and blankets had to be destroyed. He adds that

> *it is a dreadful country for creeping and crawling things of all kinds, it is not safe to put your foot outside the door without long riding boots; even the women wear them. The only two English ladies I have seen in the camp were wearing long boots and short dresses . . . I do not know what would become of a lady wearing ordinary boots.*[9]

Unfortunately, we have no record of Alice's own reaction to the exotic animal life that was so different from that of England. She must have been astonished by the vast skies and beauties of the Pampas, astounded by the violence of the weather. But she was drawn to some of the animals. Briton tells us that much later she nurtured, with a bottle, a pet guanaco through its babyhood.

---

[8] From *Yarns from the Camp* tales by JGW, transcribed or recollected by his son Briton.
[9] Reid, p.64

Twigs of a Tree

In certain stretches of the Pampas, if a man loses his horse, because of the difficulty of moving through the grasses that grow so thick and tall, he can die; he disappears as if into deep water, never to be seen again. Cunninghame Graham refers to the dangers of being marooned and horseless on the Pampas:

Afoot upon the plains . . . that was indeed a phrase of fear upon the Pampas of the south. No mariner afloat upon the waves, his mainstay but a little boat, was in a worse condition than the man who, from some cause or other, found himself horseless in the vast sea of grass. From having been as free as is a bird, he instantly became as helpless as the same bird with a wing broken by a shot.[10]

Diana (Eggar) McClure tells a 1930's story of two young Englishmen who set off on a hunting trip with local *baqueanos,* or trackers. 'They quarrelled with their guides, who left them in a particularly large field. They became totally lost, and died.' Around 1994 a peon at the Dyson's *Susana* told me that some weeks before, he and his friends had found the body of a man—by now reduced to bones. They had been searching for him since his saddled but rider-less horse had appeared at one of the estancia houses, many months before. His body was eventually found in the long grasses at almost no distance from the road.

The Pampas is a countryside of no trees. The *montes,* or woods, clumped around any small settlement or estancia house are not natural to the area. All the trees have been brought in, planted and lovingly nurtured into growth. The most magnificent aspect of the *Susana* today is not so much the house as the space around it, glorious with its now ancient trees. Apart from different fruit trees, the wide skirts of a variety of pines and firs sweep the lawns; vast magnolias show off their great white flowers against a backdrop of night-dark leaves. These keep company with lanky eucalyptus. Many are now marching majestically into the full glory of a second century of life.

The cousins' friend, Lieutenant Coronel Enrique Spika, the local military commander, had arranged for the *galera* to stop at their house in Sauce Grande for the night four times a month, and JG and Henry Edwards were beginning to build a post-house, a thatched *rancho,* to put up about five or six passengers. Not luxurious, this little inn was to

---

[10] La Pampa, in *Charity*, London, Duckworth & Co. 1912, p. 235

consist of a single room that served as dormitory, dining and drawing room. Briton tells us that the furniture consisted of a 'high table, some forms, and a few *catres*, or trestle beds. But it was better than having the passengers sleep in their own quarters'.

They make everything themselves. JG is able enough, and by now well enough, to knock together all the chairs, tables and bedsteads from pinewood brought in from Bahia Blanca. These city folk even make their own mattresses and pillows with wool shorn from their own sheep, washed and dried by Edwards.

Meals for the *galera* passengers are to be prepared by their own cook, whose services they surrender once a week. The small charge made to the passengers is expected to cover no more than their costs. This inn-like arrangement suited them in another way, for the *galera* brought and delivered their letters and small parcels at no charge.

In spite of the isolation of their home, Alice had no lack of visitors. Apart from Comandante Spika there was the ever obliging Ciríaco Gomez. He was in no hurry for his money from JG and told Edwards—now looking forward to a trip to Buenos Aires to meet his own bride, Hélène de Bernardy—to pass through the town of Tandil if he needed any extra funds. Edward's hopes, alas, were premature: Hélène was only to arrive much later.

Shortly before Alice landed in Buenos Aires, the Indians attacked again. The historian Norberto Ras mentions this small *malón* of January 1873. He describes how forty Indians carried off all the horses belonging to Edwards and Walker, then already known as Facón Grande and Facón Chico, and how they, with one Jordan (presumably the murdered Thomas's brother) and three peons followed the Indians and recovered all the stolen animals. Ras remarks,

The decisive action of these colonists in various serious incidents around Bahia Blanca was acknowledged by Commandante Spika and was to make them legendary.[11]

Indeed, this *Teniente-Coronel* Enrique Spika, 'Commander-in-chief of the Southern Frontier' and the cousins' great admirer, had sent on to them a note of thanks from the National Government in Buenos Aires for their

---

[11] *La Guerra por Las Vacas*, Norberto Ras, p.355

Twigs of a Tree

assistance in the recovery of the stolen herd. In a note dated February 2, 1873 Spika was instructed to

> *Give notice to Messrs. Edwards, Walker and Jordan, as well as to Captains Iralde and Mundo, that the Government congratulates them on the 'digna conducta' (*honourable conduct*) of their action in battle. Their activity on the frontier had been of such great use and effectiveness that both the National and the Provincial Governments wished to make known their deep indebtedness to them.*[12]

This official 'mention in dispatches' does not seem to have resulted in any tangible rewards, a Pampas knighthood or even the settling of their title deeds. The Indians soon attacked again and Alice got her first personal insight into her husband's fighting capacities. This attack—a 'high old *golpe*'—is described by JG himself in a letter to Goodhall, dated December 20, 1873.[13]

JG tells how he went up the hill to look around with his field glasses and, seeing nothing, returned, keeping the animals near the corral because a passing *chasque,* or post-chaise had reported the night before that 'the brutes were invading'. He suddenly hears 'A high old yell' from 'our friends (who) appeared all over the shop mixed up with the cows and driving them for the hills.' A couple of his friends are 'blazing away with rifles'. He hustles Alice from bedroom to roof. JG then gets his hands on a 'coon and hit him hard, but he got away'. The Indians flee, taking a point of cattle with them. He goes on:

> *Holmes and self got on horseback and followed them. Mac doing the infantry business—they camped in the alfalfa, on the highest point between here and Sinclair's, and stopped there about four hours, ate a couple of our cows 'carne con cuero'. We went out into the hills now and then and got stray pots at them at long distance, but I don't think did any harm except when they tried to take the flock. Then Mac gave one of them a quieter at about 100 yards. He did not come off then but Mac and Chevenzo found where they had buried him the next day with his horse 'parado' (*standing*) over him . . . . his throat cut right*

---

[12] Photocopy in my possession
[13] Goodhall by this time seems to have been in Bahía Blanca and might already have taken on the position of British vice-consul. In the same letter JG asks Goodhall to clear a debt by sending £8.00 to 'Mrs. Ann Catty', presumably his mother-in-law in England.

across as their custom is. Chevenzo knew the horse—I don't know how many there were to start with but when they left I counted 70 to 80.

JG sends Holmes to the army's Major Brio asking for help. The army, in spite of its genuine regard for the cousins, turns him down. There are too many Indians for the available military forces, also coping with attacks from other directions. JG, a courageous man, does not hesitate, Winchester under his saddle flap, to take on large groups of Indians single-handed. Once, while loading skins into a cart, he sees a number of Indians surround the house. He unhitches his gun, disengages his horse from the cinch-cart and rides alone towards the troop 'expecting bloody battle' but this time the Indians 'opened up their ranks' and let him through.

Briton describes another attack that shows JG's decency, an essential reluctance to kill. On this occasion, a few cattle were still outside the corral when a group of Indians got close. One Indian began to drive off the animals. JG, standing on the roof of the house, took a shot and hit him.

The man did not fall off but was evidently in difficulties. His companions did not desert him, but closed up on either side and took him away quite slowly. Dad thought it decent of them not to leave him alone, and let them go in peace.[14]

When the Indians attacked, the men were usually killed, left with their throats cut. The terror for women and children was to be taken captive into what Woodbine Parish calls 'slavery of the most horrible description'—and Briton, for the women, 'a fate worse than death'. Captives were also exchanged for ransom. This particular drama was much exploited by artists and writers, including G.A. Henty, who makes a story of his daughter's capture and rescue. In 1892, long after the attacks had come to an end, Ángel della Valle portrayed a band of triumphant Indians returning home after an attack. One Indian carries off a captured woman.

---

[14] On the Frontier p. 8

Twigs of a Tree

Angel della Valle Return from the Malón 1892
Museum of Fine Arts, Buenos Aires

She swoons, this damsel, half-naked, overcome and unconscious, against her captor, a cross around her neck. White, Christian virtue and purity are portrayed in deliberate contrast to the dark-skinned heathen carrying her off. Other Indian warriors clutch the booty seized from a desecrated church, including a second cross.

The reality of this kind of tragedy, so dramatically portrayed in this work, is brought home by a list, found by Rojas Lagarde, of the damages in Juárez after a raid in April 1876. Apart from 40.000 cattle and 3200 sheep lost and dozens of farms torched, 62 farmers were listed as dead. This time, however, the inventory of captives is brief: 'Doña Sabina César and her four children.' [15]

The battles continue. Around the Sauce Grande colony, two Indians are killed while robbing Barber's, George Catty's neighbour. Their fellow tribesmen, nevertheless, manage to carry away not only the corpses but all the cattle, too. Arthur Mildred, one of the other settlers, loses all his animals, but another, Villalba, retrieves his cattle, mares and horses. The upshot of this raid that spread across all the way to Bahia Blanca, was that,

---

[15] Rojas Lagarde, *El Malón Grande* 1875, p.205

although the Indians took all the livestock from some settlements, enough remained to make another attack likely.

A letter from George Catty to Goodhall, dated January 23, 1874, just over a month later, shows that the settlers still fear another incursion: 'We have been expecting the darkies here every day for the last fortnight . . .' But now the farmers have a contingent from the army camped nearby: 'Even if they do come we may be able to show our claws a bit and I rather think the darkies already know that our bite is worse than our bark.'

The following week, *The Standard* in Buenos Aires published a collective letter from the settlers, apparently drawn up, says Catty, by JG. *The Standard's* accompanying introduction was an admonition to the Government.

The settlement of English farmers at Sauce Grande, in the far south, has long been the admiration of natives and foreigners. It is an advanced post of civilization in Indian Territory and is worth a dozen frontier forts to the National or Provincial authorities. The farmers are men of good family (a phrase over which Briton snorted, 'For God's sake!') *and education, some having been officers in the British Army and have invested all their little fortunes in pastoral and agricultural industry among those remote region. Any reasonable request from these gallant and persevering pioneers of progress ought to find ready compliance from the authorities, and we trust the subjoined letter will be favourably considered at the War Office.*

The letter that followed, signed by JG, Edwards, George Catty, Arthur Mildred, one Dobson and twenty-five other settlers from the colony shows how many men were still hoping for a future in the region. It also shows that they no longer have the official protection of their old friend, Lieutenant Colonel Spika. Spika had been relieved of his duties. Their letter asks for his reinstatement.

Twigs of a Tree

Sauce Grande, Costa Sud,

January 24th 1874

To the Editors of the STANDARD
Gentlemen,

    We the undersigned English colonists residing in the Sauce Grande, feeling ourselves profoundly affected by the result of the last expedition against the Indians of Salinas, in December, which caused great loss in this colony and neighbourhood, beg that you will interest yourself on our behalf, to the end that the National Government lend its attention and protection to the valuable interests of this part of the province and send the reinforcements and elements necessary to keep the Indians in proper subjection.

    At the same time we believe it our duty to state that during the six years that have elapsed since the foundation of the colony, the only epoch in which we have felt effectual protection by the frontier forces has been during the administration of Lieutenant Colonel Enrique Spika; shortly before the invasion just mentioned, this officer was suspended from his command by reason of accusations preferred against him by one of his subalterns, which charges as far as the general public outside of official circles are in a position to judge, have not been substantiated.

    Believing that it would go far towards establishing a feeling of security if Lieutenant Colonel Spika were reinstated in his former position, we hope you will use your powerful Influence to the end that the cause may be brought to a termination as soon as possible.

    Begging that you will give this communication a place in the columns of your valuable paper.[16]

Briton tells us that Spika was suspended for 'backing the wrong horse' in the 1874 revolution and that Henry Edwards, after this, left for the Indio Rico area. In the meantime there were other, more immediate, problems to think about. But first a little Indian interlude.

---

[16] Lagaarde, 1870, 143.

CHAPTER IX

UNCIVILIZED CLASHES

Some 10.000 years ago, at the end of the last ice age, the ancestors of the natives of North, Middle and South America had crossed into the continent by way of Alaska, Siberia and the Bering Straits, gradually wandering into the whole of the New World as far as the southernmost tip of Patagonia. A few of these peoples—the Aztecs and Mayas and, further south, the Incas—turned, in time, into sedentary, complex, urbanized civilizations.

Most however remained—through an unfavourable combination of climatic, ecological, animal, botanical and other resources—nomadic or semi-nomadic hunter-gatherers. The inhabitants of Tierra del Fuego, whose primitive way of life was to astound Charles Darwin, evolved into 'boat people'.[17] The majority, however, including the peoples of the Inca and Aztec civilizations, remained literally 'foot-people': their own two feet their only means of locomotion. Of necessity, since—with the exception of the lamas and guanacos in Inca territory, not suitable for riding—there were no beasts of burden or draught animals in the Americas: no camels, no oxen, no horses, no donkeys.

The first great shock to this vast territory and its peoples, isolated from the Old World for millennia, came with the accidental arrival of Columbus in the West Indies on the 12th of October, 1492.

---

[17] See Jared Diamond's *Guns, Germs and Steel*

Twigs of a Tree

The five-hundredth anniversary of Columbus' stumbling onto the island of Guanahaní in the Bahamas—and of the vast conquering enterprise that followed—was commemorated in 1992 from Alaska to Patagonia. However, for the descendants of the thousands of indigenous empires, chiefdoms, tribes, and clans that once spread across the vast expanses of the Americas, there was little to celebrate. For their leaders and spokespersons October 12th is a date to remember as a day of misfortune and mourning, the anniversary of a shattering catastrophe.

Just as the Etruscans on the Italian peninsula vanished—with their language, religion and customs—before the Roman legions, the arrival of Columbus eventually led to the extinction—or near extinction—of almost all of the indigenous societies of the region. Whether treated well or badly, with sympathy, ferocity or indifference; whether enslaved, conquered by war or forced assimilation; whether lured by pacts, alliances or promises of a Christian heaven, the Indians all over the Americas eventually lost both their way of life and the lands over which they had roamed so freely and for so long. This was true not only for the Natives of the Americas, but also for the Aborigines of Australia and the Maoris of New Zealand.

After about five months of farming on the 850 acres they had been granted along the Canning River in Western Australia, John Adams and his wife Susanna Edgecumbe boarded the *Eagle* in January 1831 and sailed on, with, seeds, animals and 'indentured servants' to what they imagined would be an easier life on the island of Tasmania, then known as Van Diemen's land. There, too, the arrival of European settlers at the end of the 18th century had brought disaster. By the end of the 1870's, all 6.000 members of Tasmania's aboriginal population were dead. According to Jared Diamond[1], the last native Tasmanian man died in 1869, the last woman in 1876.

In 1494, the infamous Borgia Pope Alexander VI, while broad-mindedly acknowledging the Indians as human beings, made a 'donation' of the entire territory of the Americas to the Kings of Spain and Portugal with the order that all its peoples should be converted to Christianity. It took the Spaniards themselves another fifty years to acknowledge the American 'savages' as human beings. If they were not already jailbirds—the Spanish Queen, as the British were to do in Australia, at one point emptied her prisons to populate her new lands—the *Conquistadores* certainly became

---

[1] Jared Diamond, *The Third Chimpanzee*

rough and violent. Their much-vaunted Christian piety often went hand in hand with an insatiable thirst for silver and gold. This, and the necessity for control over slave labour to prise the metal from deep in the ground, and later to work the fields, turned many—objectively speaking—into bandits, monsters.

The Dominican friar Bartolomé de las Casas (1484-1566)[2] has left us appalled descriptions of the storming of indigenous villages by the Spaniards; the massacres, the disembowelling and 'the infinite number of souls killed and destroyed by the Christians' because of their passion for silver and their 'lust for gold'.[3] Columbus described the innocence and vulnerability of the peoples he had 'discovered.' They were

the best folk in the world, and certainly the most gentle They know no evil—neither killing nor stealing —, they love their neighbours as themselves and have the sweetest manner of speech . . . Fifty men would be enough to overpower them and force them to our will.[4]

Nevertheless, the lure of gold was too potent to resist. Columbus himself, according to his biographer Eliot Morison, enslaved the natives and hit on the idea of severing the hands of those who were unable to produce at least one nugget of the metal for his coffers. Driven to despair, many of the natives hanged or poisoned themselves.[5]

Yet in the Americas it was not the sword, but disease that caused the 'greatest genocide of all time'. An estimated 80% of the indigenous population succumbed, in the century after 1492, to new European-borne epidemics: among them smallpox, chicken-pox, measles, typhoid fever, syphilis, diphtheria, tuberculosis, influenza and yellow-fever. It has been estimated that one hundred and fifty years after Columbus first stepped onto the island of Guanahaní, the population of some 70 million natives

---

[2] Also known as Protector or Apostle of the Indians and the author of 'A short account of the destruction of the Indies'.

[3] *The Myths of Argentine History*, Felipe Pigna, p.52 quoting Fray Bartolomé de las Casas, *Historia General de las Indias*, México, FCE, 1951

[4] quoted by Pigna, p.35

[5] Pigna 37, quoting Eliot Morison, *A People's History of the United States: 1492—Present*, New York, Harper-Collins, 1995

Twigs of a Tree

who then inhabited the continents of the Americas had been reduced to a mere 3.5 million.[6]

The early Spanish Conquistadores, largely resistant to their own diseases, saw this devastation among the indigenous peoples as Divine retribution, punishment inflicted by a justifiably angry God whom only conversion to Christianity could appease. Depopulation by disease—since it deprived the conquerors of easily accessible labour for working the new lands, the gold and silver mines—was in turn a decisive factor in the development of that other sorrowful European-borne catastrophe, the African slave trade. It was not long before the silver mines of Potosi in Peru, the sugar plantations of the Caribbean, and the cotton fields of North America became the end destination for tens of thousands of Africans transported in chains across the Atlantic.

Columbus was right. In spite of their vastly superior numbers, the native populations, even the most sophisticated and urbanized, were no match for the deadly novelty of European cavalry, steel weaponry and musketry. The civilizations of the Incas and Aztecs fell within days to a mere handful of gold-hungry adventurers and the fanatically pious—sometimes even murderous—priests who accompanied them.

The Aztecs fell first, between 1516 and 1519, to stout Hernán Cortez of the eagle eye, romantically depicted, three centuries later by John Keats.[7] The fortunes of the last Inca Emperors turned, a decade on, at

---

[6] Eduardo Galeano, *Las Venas Abiertas de America Latina*, Catalogos, Argentina, 2001

[7] Much have I travell'd in the realms of gold,
And many goodly states and kingdoms seen;
Round many western islands have I been
Which bards in fealty to Apollo hold.
Oft of one wide expanse had I been told
That deep-brow'd Homer ruled as his demesne;
Yet never did I breathe its pure serene
Till I heard Chapman speak out loud and bold.
Then felt I like some watcher of the skies
When a new planet swims into his ken;
Or like stout Cortez, when with eagle eyes
He star'd at the Pacific—and all his men
Look'd at each other with a wild surmise—
Silent, upon a peak in Darien.

the hands of the *Conquistador*, Francisco Pizarro, and a ragtag bunch of thuggish companions.

It was before this illiterate representative of Charles V, King of Spain and Holy Roman Emperor, that—on November 16, 1532, in the main square of Cajamarca, in present-day Peru—the formidable imperial *cortège* of Atahualpa first came into sight. The Inca ruler, held aloft by eighty liveried councillors, appeared in a litter ornamented in gold and silver, lined with parrot feathers. Present, too, was the Emperor's army—but, for this ceremonial occasion before the 'snow faced' strangers from across the sea, it had left its weaponry, fashioned from bone and stone, at home.

After some cursory greetings, Atahualpa was presented with a Bible. Perplexed by its apparent uselessness—for Atahualpa ruled over a civilization unfamiliar not only with horses and steel, but also with paper and writing—the Emperor put the mysterious object to his ear. Hearing nothing, legend has it that he angrily dashed the Holy Book to the ground. At this, the Dominican monk, Vicente Valverde, signalled the band of about 150 Christians hiding around the square—some, according to an eyewitness, 'wetting themselves in fear'—to surge out with their horses, muskets and steel weapons. Before this whirlwind onslaught, accompanied by the din of trumpets and rattles—hung on the horses to make them more terrifying—the unarmed Inca army of allegedly 80.000 men fled in panic.

Dragged from his litter, the Emperor-God of the Children of the Sun was stripped of his gold and his emeralds. Promising the ruler his life for 'history's largest ransom', the Conquistador Pizarro demanded enough gold to pack, from floor to ceiling, the Emperor God's prison cell.[8]

Several months later, egged on by Valverde, the future bishop of the Inca capital of Cuzco, Pizarro broke his word. Atahualpa was offered another chance for life, this time through conversion to Christianity. But his reward was merely a different death. Atahualpa was spared the stake and the fires reserved for witches and heretics. Instead, Pizarro and Valverde extended to him the dubious dignity of that peculiarly Spanish form of dispatch—slow strangulation with the tightened screws of the iron collar, the garrotte.

---

[8] In the half century after 1492, this type of ransom—lives for lucre—transferred into the coffers of Spain some 30.000 kilograms of gold from the Caribbean alone, much of it made up of melted-down artefacts and artistic objects.

Twigs of a Tree

To be sure, it was everywhere an age of ferocity. At about the same time, the Protestant William Tyndale was hunted down by British agents and, like the Inca king, garrotted for the crime of having translated the New Testament from Latin into English; the great scholar Thomas More lost his head for refusing to acknowledge Henry VIII as leader of the Church in England. But More himself had not been above sending those he considered heretics to the stake or the execution block. Today, contemporary historians—not only of the former colonies—frequently label as genocide what the colonists merely called war.

The 'miraculous' defeat of so many by so few that left 6000 Indians dead in the square of Cajamarca was ascribed by the Spaniards to the direct intercession of their own—the Christian—God. Less than a decade on, in spite of intermittent rebellions, the empire of the Incas that had stretched some 9000 kilometres, from present-day Ecuador through Peru and Bolivia into Chile and Argentina, was declared the property of Spain in the name of Christ. Its people, like those of the Caribbean, were to be converted to Catholicism and ruled by the Royal House of Castille.

Such were the beginnings of the proud Vice-Royalty of Peru, directed from Pizarro's city of Lima, where the Cathedral still holds his embalmed remains. The older Vice-Royalty of New Spain, centred in Mexico City (formerly Tenochtitlán), was followed by the three Viceroyalties in South America. First Peru and New Granada (Colombia) and, finally in 1776, the vast territory that includes present-day Argentina, Bolivia, Paraguay and Uruguay, became the *Virreinato del Río de la Plata*, the Viceroyalty of the River Plate with its centre in Buenos Aires.

Fighting Back

Of the many semi-nomadic societies of the region, some—like the friendly Guaraní of Paraguay—submitted reasonably quietly to the invaders. With others, initial astonishment and amicability soon turned to fear, hostility and hatred. In 1516 a band of adventurers led by Juan de Solís arrived at mouth of the River Plate with the idea of founding a town; when their demands became too onerous, the local population slaughtered and then made a meal of the band and its leader. Pedro de Mendoza's Buenos Aires, founded in the same area twenty years later as the city of Our Lady of the Good Airs, had to be abandoned because of the hostility of the local Querandí Indians. The town's European inhabitants were driven hundreds of miles upriver, into Guaraní country, to the newly established township of Asunción. Juan de Garay, governor of Asunción, eventually founded the city of Buenos Aires for a second time in 1580.

Two centuries after this, in Lima, the half-Spanish, Jesuit-educated Incan Cacique José Gabriel Condorcanqui Noguera, who called himself *Túpac Amaru*, stepped in on behalf of his people. He first petitioned the Viceroy against forced Indian labour in the fields, mines and mills; against the inhumanity of their treatment, and against crippling taxation. Getting no results, he finally began gathering arms. A further increase in taxation spurred him—and his large Indian following—to a revolt that, with its first successes, led the Spanish to seriously fear the loss of their Latin American Viceroyalties. Eventually, however, Túpac Amaru was overcome and subjected to a barbaric execution: on May 18, 1781, after being forced to witness, in the main square of Cuzco, the torture and deaths—by hanging and garrotte—of his wife and children, Tupac Amaru's tongue was cut out. Then, this courtly descendent of Inca kings and Spanish noblemen, roped to four horses, was torn asunder as the animals galloped off in four different directions.

Evo Morales, the first Indian president of Bolivia and an icon of the *indigenista* movement in the Andean countries, might be forgiven for thinking that the barbarity was all on the side of the Spaniards and other outsiders: those who professed to represent civilization but who killed so casually for gold in the name of their god and king. However, the Aztec and the Inca civilizations—thoroughly 'totalitarian' societies, as expert in sacrificing humans to the gods and in exterminating their rivals as any other empire in world history—were not without their own enemies before the arrival of the Spaniards.

Mapuches and the Cattle War

The Mapuches, one of the Auracano tribes, natives of what is today's Chile, fought back hardest.[9] Their ancient hostility to incorporation

---

[9] By their own definition, Mapuche are the 'people of the land'—*Mapu* meaning land and *che* meaning people. They are also known as Araucanos, a name given to them by the Spanish colonialists. Before the "huincas" (Spanish) arrived in 1541, the Mapuches—who numbered one and a half to two million—were the original inhabitants of the Southern Cone of the continent, in a region that today stretches across both Chile and Argentina. The Mapuche nation comprised both sedentary and nomadic communities: hunters and gatherers, shepherds, farmers and fishermen. They lived in small family groups known as *lof*, which were under the authority of a *Lonko* (chief).

into the Incan empire was followed by a three-hundred-year resistance—interspersed by periods of fragile peace—to the Spanish invaders. The Mapuche resistance lasted through the wars of independence and through the military persecutions by the Chilean and Argentine governments of the 1880s. It continues in some way even today.[10] The Mapuches, although generally miserably poor, have organized themselves to claim rights to parts of the vast territory of Patagonia—lands that are now owned by wealthy outsiders like George Soros, Douglas Tompkins, Ted Turner or the Benetton company.

By the time JG Walker and his cousin Henry Edwards arrived, the great plains of Argentina had long been the habitat of herds of wandering sheep, horses and cattle, descendants of animals brought and then abandoned by Spanish adventurers. These had multiplied in the wild and, by the beginning of the 17th century, many of the Indian tribes that had formerly moved about on foot had become adept at catching and mastering the horses. They also developed a taste for beef and mare's flesh.

The Mapuches became highly skilled mounted warriors, their bows and arrows supplemented by twelve-foot lances that could be handled more efficiently on horseback. When JG landed in Argentina, they were ranging huge distances, moving from their native lands straddling the new states of Chile and Argentina into the vast territory of the Pampas. By the beginning of the 19th century, the Mapuches had conquered, subdued or assimilated many of the different peoples, collectively known as the Pampas Indians, that were native to Argentina.

In spite of Túpac Amaru's attempts and example, no land formerly in Indian hands has, to this day, evolved into an independent Indian state. At the end of the wars of independence from Spain that started after 1810, both the new states of Chile and Argentina claimed Mapuche territory for themselves. In the 19th century the Mapuches in the Argentine Pampas, under the forty-year leadership of the Cacique Calfucurá (died 1873), managed to form a relatively powerful Confederation of some 14.000 souls, including a warrior group of three thousand lances.

---

[10] The 1992 collection of essays about Columbus' arrival compiled by Indian intellectuals, entitled *The Shock of Two Worlds 500-Years On*. In this one reads: "We fought and lost a battle, but the war to recuperate what is ours is not over. We are in this war and we will not cease until we obtain justice and the rights that our people lost the day in which the first Spaniard stepped onto our land."

Uncivilized Clashes

Among the few interested in—and sympathetic to—the Indians were Thomas Falkner (1707-1784), a Jesuit missionary who lived among them for years,[11] and Woodbine Parish, the British diplomat (1796-1882); there was also a French lawyer, Aurèlie Antoine de Tounans (1825-78). The Frenchman, who had been living among the Mapuches in Chile and learnt their language, was hugely impressed by 'this noble race of heroes' and their three hundred years of resistance to the Spanish. In 1860 he declared a Mapuche state: the 'Kingdom of Araucania and Patagonia'. It had a constitution, universal suffrage and equality of rights for all individuals. The French lawyer was declared Araucania's elected king. It was a short-lived reign for Orellie-Antoine I. Two years later, with both Argentina and Chile determined to keep the Mapuche lands, Aurèlie was captured and tried. Although he conducted his own defence with elegant eloquence, he found little appreciation. With the argument that it was clearly "not normal for a 'white' person to claim rights for savages", Aurélie was declared insane and cast into the lunatic asylum in Santiago de Chile.[12]

Since the 1830's, the Mapuches had been running a profitable business capturing—for sale or for food—Argentina's free-ranging animals, especially the cattle. The historian Norberto Ras contends that the last decades of the 19th century, when JG and his fellow Englishmen were in the Sauce Grande area, represented the final years of a war for cattle that had evolved over three centuries.[13]

When wild animals became scarce, the Mapuches turned from hunting to depredation, pillaging the herds bred on the newly founded farms or estancias. By the beginning of the 19th century, they were regularly driving cattle stolen in Buenos Aires province across some 1500 kilometres to the Chilean border. In Chile the animals were sold, with no questions asked by either the buyers or by the Chilean government. Sheep that, unlike cattle, move at little more than walking pace, were usually left alone because they could not be herded at speed over long distances.

---

[11] Thomas Falkner, *A description of Patagonia and the adjacent Parts of South America* (London 1774) lived among them for forty years. Sir Wooodbine Parish, *Buenos Airesa and the Provinces of the Rio de la Plata* (London 1852).

[12] R. Marhiquewun, Alberto Sarramone *Orellie-Antoine I—Un rey francés de Araucania y Patagonia,* Editoria Biblios.

[13] Norberto Ras, *La Guerra por las Vacas*, Buenos Aires 2006. The area was home to groups of Mapuches, Pehuelches, Ranqueles and Pinzen. Further south there were mostly Ranqueles.

Twigs of a Tree

By the 1870's Argentina's three large indigenous groups, of which the Mapuches were the most important, had managed to press as far north as the Pampas territory of the Province of Buenos Aires and beyond. The neophyte republic of Argentina, beginning to emerge from political chaos (the long and ferocious rivalry between the Federalists and the Unitarians) and only just settling down, was desperately fighting to win nationwide recognition for its central government.

In their attempts to push the frontier forward, the various Argentine governments were decidedly lax in keeping faith with the Indians. Agreements for tribute and boundary lines were made and repeatedly broken. The Indians became enraged, unable to understand why, after a frontier had been fixed by treaty, the government did not keep the *Cristianos* from migrating beyond those lines to settle and plant inside their hunting territory. Hasbrouck quotes the opinion that the whites were frequently more to blame for the many breaches of contract than the Indians themselves.[14]

Throughout the 19th century, the 'frontier' kept creeping southwards and westwards from Buenos Aires. In 1875, the war minister, Adolfo Alsina, began digging his famous trench, punctuated with fortresses linked by telegraph to Buenos Aires. This trench, designed to foil the cattle rustling by the Indians, pushed the frontier even further forward.

In their eagerness to exploit the agricultural potential of the Pampas, successive Argentine governments found themselves in escalating conflict with Indian tribes and rural societies that neither recognized nor acknowledged the sense, legitimacy or justice of those two components of the modern state: territorial borders and the private ownership of land and property. The matter came to a head in 1878, five years after Alice's arrival, with General Julio Argentino Roca's *Conquest of the Desert*.

---

[14] Alfred Hasbrouck, *The Conquest of the Desert*, Duke University Historical Press, 1935. p. 205

CHAPTER X

BABIES, BULLETS AND BOLEADORAS

Alice Catty's first child, John Briton Walker, came into the world on July 2, 1874. It is difficult to imagine the sanitary conditions and the kind of assistance available to her on the Sauce Grande, particularly in that period of constant attack and upheaval. In that world medical support was meagre or non-existent. Elinor Barber, the daughter of one of the settlers, remarks that although her mother—an art student—loved the life on the camp, there were 'some big drawbacks'.

One of these was, according to Elinor, that the only means of communication, in those days before telegraph and telephone, was the once-a-week *chasque* or mail-coach. But the principal difficulty was that there were 'no doctors or dentists nearer than Buenos Aires, hundreds of miles away'. Elinor was describing conditions in the nineties, long after peace had been established.[15] In the eighteen-seventies, things must have been considerably worse. Molly Dyson recalled that Briton was born with the help of two Indian women. Pipes hanging from their mouths, they sat in a haze of smoke with only a sheepskin in which to wrap the baby as protection from the winter frosts.

George Reid recounts that his friend Clode's wife, Ada, far in the north, in Gualeguaychú, could not get to the nearby English doctor and for the birth of her first child was attended by two 'native' medics. One was 'hopelessly drunk' and the other, according to Reid, 'knew about as

---

[15] Elinor Barber's *Journal*

Twigs of a Tree

much of the business as I did'. Ada was 'in frightful agony, shrieking most dreadfully'. Nevertheless, she and her 'little wretch of a baby, very red', survived. Of Alice's delivery of baby John Briton we only know for sure that they, too, survived.

If doctors were rare, so were clergymen. Baptism, official admission into the church, was a luxury not easily available. Many years later, Briton reports that one day, when he and his little brother, Norman, were playing 'stark naked in the mud', his father approached them with the tidings: 'Get your clothes on, you are going to be christened.'

This rather scared us, but we were washed and dressed and next morning the ceremonial was performed in our big dining room with the swords and guns hanging on the wall. [1]

The Reverend Gybbon-Spilsbury, a former missionary turned itinerant chaplain, who roamed the Pampas baptismal font in tow, stood ready to perform the double christening. By that day in February 1880, when the holy water finally touched the two young heathens, Norman was three and Briton already nearly six years old.[2]

What with Indian invasions, floods, droughts, fires (Indians frequently torched crops that were ready for harvest) and perpetual uncertainty, life must have been tense for adults and bewildering for children. Shortly after young Briton's birth, one of the settlers, Arthur Mildred, drew up a summary of the past seven years starting with 1868, the year of JG's arrival. It is a litany of disasters, at least one for every year. The entry for 1874 shows that the year of Briton's birth was a perilous one: the settlers' mares were all lost to the Indians. This kind of theft is a reminder that survival for the Indians was also a continuous struggle: mares were stolen not for riding, but for food.

---

[1] *On the Frontier*, p.12
[2] In the records of the San Pedro Flores church the two little boys are registered as having been baptised together on the February 18, 1880—two of among 45 christenings performed between 1879 and 1886 by the Rev. Joseph H. Gybbon-Spilsbury. This document also includes their birth dates.

Arthur Mildred's Little History
1868:
>   Began to poblar on Sauce Grande. Sowed wheat and maize. Wheat nearly all lost by temporal.

1869:
>   All horses stolen by Indians, January 20th. A seca (drought) from March to September. Could not sow wheat till middle of September.

1870:
>   October 23rd Invasion of 2.000 Indians to Bahía Blanca. Deveridge and Nilson killed by them. Mildred's mares stolen, about 100, by Indians.

1871:
>   July. All the horses from up the River stolen by Indians. Nov. 18th Mr. T. Jordan killed by Indians about 10 squares from the house.

1872:
>   Nearly all wheat taken away by a creciente (flood).

1873:
>   January 1st Invasion of Indians to Sauce Grande. One Indian killed.

1874:
>   December 12th. Invasion of 1500 Indians to Sauce Grande. All horses and cattle cleared from Sauce G. Recovered some horses and cattle. Mares lost entirely.

1874:
>   Revolution. Invasion inside. Partidos (bands) of both parties coming for cattle etc.

1875:
>   January 29th. Lost all wheat, 500 fanegas by a quemazon (fire) after having nearly finished harvest.

What Mildred, writing at the beginning of 1875, could not include, were the devastating attacks that followed at the end of that year.[3] Adolfo Alsina, recently appointed Minister of War under President Nicolás Avellaneda (1874-1880), had decided to push the frontier even deeper into what was commonly known as 'the desert', the highly fertile territory inhabited by numerous sedentary and nomadic tribes, among them the Mapuches. Alsina's first step was to connect the city of Buenos Aires and

---
[3]   These attacks have merited an entire book by Rojas Lagarde., *El Malón Grande de 1875*, Editorial El Aljibe, City Bell, 1993.

the *fortines* (small fortresses) with telegraph lines. A peace treaty with the cacique Juan José Catriel, and with the Mapuche leader Namuncurá followed. The truce was broken shortly afterwards, when the Indian tribes launched a vast coordinated attack on Tres Arroyos, Tandil, Azul and other towns, as well as on large estancias, in Buenos Aires province. It was an even bloodier incursion than that of 1870.

Shortly afterwards, Alsina began his famous *zanja* (trench), designed to prevent the Indians from driving away stolen cattle. 374 of the 600 kilometres projected for the trench were actually dug. It was fortified with 109 small fortresses, each manned by about ten military men. The trench, 4.50-metres broad, sloped down 2-metres to a 60-centimetre wide floor; its eastern side was piled high with earth. Alsina later remarked that his trench was an attempt to populate the 'desert', not to destroy the Indians. The latter, however, did not see it this way.

By October of the same year—1875—things had become so difficult at the Sauce Grande that JG started discouraging the arrival of new settlers and expressing doubts about the area in general.

It is clear agriculture wont act. There is only a little bit of land along the bank of this river that is available for sowing I fancy the people in Bs. Ays. do not know what sort of camp this is . . . . . all the hill land here is no use and never will be any use for agriculture. Wells might be sunk to obtain water for the support of sheep, but for irrigation purposes impossible. The size of our camps may sound large, but considering the grasses they are not so, I have had about 2000 sheep running on a league of land and they can only just keep in pretty good order—so that there really is not room for a great many more pobladores.

To find or to bring more colonists is wrong in as much as nobody with any conscience under existing circumstances would advise a friend to come here—but if we get the lands in propriedad and others see us doing well, they will come spontaneously and moreover we shall be in a position to bring more, that is to give work to more.

He adds,
20 or 30 Indians took about 3.000 horses and mares from the Indio Rico a few days ago, leaving Edwards with one horse—150 men out from the Sauce Corto after them. Lets hope they'll catch them.

JG continues, however, still reasonably optimistic about obtaining the title deeds to the land.

From what the skipper tells me, things look well for the propriedad business, and every one with whom I have talked on the subject 'inside' seems to think our chance is very good.[4]

A few weeks later the colony is dealt another blow. Arthur Mildred reports to Goodhall:

Nothing but bad news: on Monday, November lst, poor Douner was barbarously murdered in his own house by a brute by the name of Alcorta. He used to be a soldier here and was afterwards in the Police . . . . There was caña (a kind of rum) *knocking about, and the swine gave poor Douner about 6 stabs all about the heart and two fearful 'hachazos'* (blows with an ax) *on the head, causing the brains to protrude. He then cleared out after robbing all Douner's money and his revolver . . . Prigged* (sic) *a tropilla* (herd of cattle) *and cleared out. Walker and Smith followed him to within a day's journey of Tandil and there lost trace of him . . .*

Full of courage and initiative, JG set out on a long and dangerous but ultimately fruitless attempt to track down the killers. He and his single companion returned about ten days later. On December 17th, he too wrote to Goodhall:

I am a few days back from my unsuccessful run after the brute that murdered Douner. It was very hard lines to lose him when we had him so close, only two hours ahead and yet I lost the track. For a week we tracked him, old Smith and I, and then to lose him at last was bad. I should like to have given the bad lot about here a lesson.

He remarks on the loss incurred by the 'burning of the stocks and now our harvest'. But he is pleased with the developments on the frontier, where the *fortíns* have been garrisoned and extra troops brought in. 'Maldonado (the current commander) swears they shall not take a cow and so far has kept his word . . . . '[5]

Desperate and infuriated by Alsina's trench and his new border policy, regarded as a monstrous breech of trust and treaty, the Indians continue

---

[4] Letter to Goodhall, October, 1875.
[5] Letter to Goodhall by JG, 17/12/1875

Twigs of a Tree

to resist the forward push of the frontier line. They even engage scribes to write letters to the government. One exquisitely polite but firm missive from the cacique Namuncurá himself, recently discovered by Rojas Lagarde, was written at the beginning of 1875. The chief was trying to broker a peace, but he also declares that,

> *if the Superior Gobierno is going to go into battle against me, I will defend myself as God wills.*

Namuncurá then answers a request to return a female captive. After asking for her name, he produces a list of items he wants in exchange for the woman's release. The list, though long, is almost touchingly modest, if in the circumstances a little frivolous. Although it contains one or two luxuries like '4 silk handkerchiefs', it indicates, on the whole, the overall neediness of the Indians. The requests include 6 pairs of socks, a pound of onion seeds, sugar, flour, 6 tin plates, 2 pairs of (ordinary) boots—sizes 4 and 5—as well as a pair of 'fine' boots size 5, and finally—the Indians, too, have musical yearnings—a guitar.[6]

But by January 1876 the settlers have suffered yet another invasion, and yet another death. Goodhall is told that the

> *savages had it all their own way. . . . Poor Calderón was brutally murdered by the Indians, four leagues from Azul. The Indians were driving away the galera horses and Calderon went with his two peones to stop them. But the peones, staying a respectful distance behind, Calderón went by himself. There were twelve Indians. They lanced him, then tied his hands and feet and cut his throat. The letters that he had on his person were, we expect, some of them lost. Mr Edwards, who passed yesterday, showed us a letter that he had received. It was covered with blood and either torn or cut.*[7]

Henry Edwards is still described in Mulhall's 1875 edition as a sheep farmer in the Naposta valley, while JG Walker is a 'settler'. But it seems that both JG and Edwards were already giving up on the colony. Edwards moved to Indio Rico, northwest of the Sauce Grande, and JG had by 1876 moved to San Carlos, a property belonging to a Dr Romero, about twelve leagues from Azul. On the journey to San Carlos, JG and his family appear to have stayed with Edwards at Indio Rico. If the two men had

---

[6] *El Malón Grande,* Rojas Lagarde, p.p 29-30
[7] Letter to Goodhall, 19/01/1876 by Mildred

not yet thought of actually selling out, they do seem to have turned to the management of other people's property. In general things do not look rosy, the colony is not doing well.

1876 was the year of a massive attack less than 250-kilometres from the city of Buenos Aires. The Indians made off with 300.000 head of cattle and no less than 500 captives. In March 1876, they struck nearer home, in Indio Rico, where Edwards had moved. H.S. Black, another settler, writes ironically to Goodhall.

*We have had a grand invasion of Indians down here. They have not done much harm, only robbed about 200.000 mares and horses, 50.000 cows, killed and skinned God knows how many thousand sheep and an odd hundred of people, and captured others. However, it will probably be called a 'pequena invasion' (*a small invasion*) in the papers'.*

In April 1876 the colonists pen a lament to the *Standard's* new editor, outlining their desperately reduced state. Their numbers have sunk from over a hundred to less than thirty. Some are dead, some murdered, and many have left or are leaving. Without help from the government those remaining see no option but to abandon the area and re-emigrate. After eight years of privation, their herds are reduced to almost nothing; they are now selling off cattle simply to survive. They will be obliged to leave the country, ruined: another proof that the Republic of Argentina with 'all its splendid advantages' is not a place for 'the honest, hardworking settler', for here there is no 'guarantee of life or ownership' and 'Justice is a term not understood.'

The letter to the *Standard* goes on with a description of Douner's murder in the kitchen of his own house—stabs around the heart, head open with brains laid bare; the fruitless chase by JG and his friends, and the failure of the authorities to bring the killer to justice. Moreover, the harvest has been a disaster and they have lost 300 *fanegas* of wheat to a fire.[8] They add that the only reason the Indians have not recently troubled them is that the colony no longer has anything worth the effort of an attack.[9]

On June 27th, 1876, Arthur Mildred writes to Goodhall describing yet another attack that had taken place ten days earlier.

A body of Indians, variously estimated at one to two hundred, passed about a league above Jordan's and after "carneando"(slaughtering)

---

[8] A fanega is variously described on the web as 'one half hectare of land' or 55.5. litres.

[9] Copy of article in my possession.

Abellino Aragues passed inside . . . All horses and mares with very few exceptions were cleared off these arroyos, and at the Indio Rico they took all Faraminnans cattle (2.000) and 700 of Edwards' . . . We have now received official news both from the Juez de Paz (Justice of the Peace) and the Comandante that they have news of a very large invasion for Bahia Blanca . . . It is to be under the charge of Namuncurá himself, and they will number from 2000 to 3500 lances. Please make this known in the papers.[10]

Mildred echoes the protests sent to *The Standard* two months earlier:
Truly, I do not know what this country is coming to. The Indians go about just as they like. Cerri (the Comandante) has from 100 to 120 men under his command to protect a town like Bahia Blanca. It is certain, too, that among the Indians there are many men armed with Remingtons, probably deserters. Our life here is a misery, now one can not go ten squares from the house without expecting to meet Indians. If this enormous force comes here, I do not know how we will get on, but I trust they will pass where there is more 'robo' (booty) to be obtained. The Indians are masters of the country now, and it is no use disguising the fact. This is the plain truth about the Indians, better than all the falsified reports you see in the papers.
With this wretched uncertainty you can be sure that we do not feel especially sanguine about anything . . . No one would be mad enough to come here now . . . We have no peon now. I am looking after the sheep and I am glad to say the lambing has been very satisfactory so far.[11]

In the same month, in spite of the constant threat of invasion by the Indians, the settlers draft yet another petition for ownership, this one directed to the Senators of the Province of Buenos Aires. It was presented in September and signed by Goodhall, who also included revealing statistics about the Colony, showing the precarious state and nature of their investments and property.[12]

For example, the partnership of Mildred and Goodhall himself had invested £6300 and $120.000 in machinery and tools. They had introduced 44 colonists—of whom one was dead and 30 had returned home. Only

---

[10] Copy of article in my possession.
[11] Letter to Goodhall, from Arthur Mildred June 27th 1876
[12] Rojas Lagarde, *El Malon de 1870*, p.181

13 remained. They had 1600 sheep, 20 horses and 13 *animales vacunos*, cattle. There are also 3000 sheep that belong to 'peons' brought out from England 'with their passages paid by the Company'.

The partnership made up of JG, Edwards, George Catty and Samuel Giles, on the other hand, had invested considerably less: only £2000. They had brought out nine colonists, of which two had left, two had been murdered and one had died. Only four remained. This group had 3500 sheep and a handful of cattle. They had five *azotea* houses, a barn and several rancho (adobe and thatch) houses. Their land was surrounded by a large ditch, dug by themselves, and by a wire fence.

Goodhall also reports that, on Barber's estancia, Barber himself was the only one left of an original group of six men; Jordan, who had lost his brother, Thomas, was now alone except for a labourer from England. The long petition in Spanish, presented in June 1876 and clearly not the first, consists of eight interminable, scantily punctuated sentences, one per paragraph. After an introduction and the presentation of all the accompanying documents, Goodhall writes:

In presenting the documents in support of our petition, in addition to the basic points that I described in our first request asking that we be accorded the ownership of the lands that we, with our lives, our work and our capital have snatched from the barbarians; converting desert territory into productive and fertile land, I cannot but add a few short observations that will not escape the attention of the Honourable Senate.

Our Government, like all those of South America, concerns itself with the settling of its vast territories, spending ever larger sums to contract settlers, transport them to their lands, provide for their survival during the first period of colonization, and extend to them the ownership of lands necessary to the settlement and prosperity of the colonists.

Our English Colony on the Sauce Grande has not demanded any of these facilities; the government conceded us lands to establish ourselves through our labour and capital; we founded the Colony in the hope that one day our sacrifices would be rewarded by granting us the ownership of the land that we have conquered in the middle of the desert.

In the Colony's saddest and most dangerous times, when the invasions of the savages were so frequent that the colonists could not have repaired the damages caused by the earlier invasions, before being attacked once again, the colonists of the Sauce Grande not only did not abandon the Colony, but they maintained it, at their own expense, without demanding anything from the Government and always animated by the hope of better times, did not give up the idea of going forward with their work to turn the Colony into a settlement both happy and prosperous. The Colony of the Sauce Grande now comes before you requesting the ownership to the territory, conquered and cultivated by its own labours and capital, as a fair recompense for its sacrifices and hopes that the concession of this request will be carried out as an act of justice. Signed E.P. Goodhall[13]

They received a sign from the Government in October 1876. It agrees to the sale—to each of nine members of the English Colony at Bahia Blanca—of 1.75 square leagues of land. The nine included JG Walker, Barber, Edwards and Jordan. Six others, among them George Catty and Giles, were to be sold 1/3 of a league of land. The buyers had to agree to sub-divide and measure the land, during the course of 1877, into nine sections of l.75 square leagues each and six of 1/3 of a league. The price, set at '40.000 pesos of current money per square league',[14] was to be paid in eight annual instalments, the first due in the year 1878.[15] On November 28th the *Standard* confirmed the good news:

The provincial government has been authorised to sell the lands known as the English Colony in Bahia Blanca to the following parties: Dr J. Mildred; B. Smith; A. Mildred, E.P. Goodhall, J.G. Walker; H.J. Edwards; J. Grier; B. Black; B. Barber and J.M. Jordan 1.75 leagues each; and 1/3 league each to Messrs C. Shuttle, C.J. Hutchinson, E.R. Hutchinson; G.E. Catty and N. Giles. The price is $25.000 per square league, payable in 8 yearly instalments, the first to be paid during the year 1876. The purchasers to sign hypothecary title deeds on receiving the first instalment.

Even in these hardship conditions, the Argentine government was not especially generous to its immigrants, possibly because—as Andrew Graham-Yooll suggests—the rich, highly influential *estancieros* discouraged

---

[13] Rojas Lagarde, *El Malon de 1870*, p.181
[14] The price in the *Standard* does not tally with that of the Government's announcement.
[15] Rojas Lagarde, idem, p.190

any influx of smallholders, and opposed any move that limited the expansion of their own vast properties.

A correspondent for *The Standard*, who signed himself ND, visited the colony in 1879. Unimpressed with its progress in agriculture, he compared the Argentine government's immigration policy unfavourably with that of the United States.

I have always thought that the only way that agriculture could be successful here is in the way it is done in the United States, where the land is above all cultivated by families who obtain donations of land from the Government, either near a fort or a cheap railway line.[16]

Graham-Yooll points out that Canada, also eager for immigrants, offered free passages and 200 acres of free land on the condition that a house be built, the land progressively cleared and sown and the immigrant family live there at least six months a year. The land itself, in return for this labour, was free.

In comparison, the Argentine offerings were meagre and uncertain. Partly as a result of this, writes Graham-Yooll, fully half of all immigrants gave up and either returned home, like Reid and Seymour, or re-emigrated to friendlier countries.

The cousins were probably gratified that the title deeds were finally within reach, but they may also have been disappointed that the land they had been working and defending for so long had not, after so many years of heroic effort, simply been ceded to them.

They had already begun looking at other options. Henry Edwards was by 1876 in charge of one of Keen's estancias at Indio Rico, considerably to the north and east of the Sauce Grande. Indeed, Briton Walker describes having been to Indio Rico (he can only have been about two years old then) to visit 'Uncle Harry' with his parents. He mentions that, a short time after that visit, Edwards finally went to Buenos Aires to meet his fiancée, Hélène de Bernardy.

Indio Rico being considerably behind both the old and the newly projected frontier lines, Edwards clearly felt safer. Eager for marriage, he went to the trouble of building an 'adobe house' in preparation for the arrival of his bride. Even the Indio Rico area was not completely safe, however. Indians occasionally arrived on horse-stealing expeditions,

---

[16] Graham-Yooll, p.168

and once they found Edwards alone, as Jordan had been. But Edwards never left the house unarmed, without 'his revolver in its holster and his Remington rifle in the saddle', and he was able to reach home safely.

It was not long, however, before Edwards stumbled on yet another reminder that the Indians were still at large. *The Standard* of November 11, 1876 reports an attack on the diligence coach from Bahia Blanca to Azul.

We regret to announce bad news from the Indian frontier, as reported by the brother of the murdered mayoral, Mr. Baker. Last Sunday 5th inst. a band of 47 indians attacked the diligence between Bahia Blanca and Azul. They dismounted in five groups to make the attack and proceeded to murder Mr Edward Baker, Jose Giminez and Regio Pouce. The first named was mayoral (overseer or mayordomo) and died fighting. The corpses were interred by Mr Henry Edwards, manager of the estancia of Mr Henry Keen, of Indio Rico: he recovered also the mail bags but the letters were torn to fragments. The Indians, after robbing the coach, went on in the direction of Quenquén, burning houses on the way. Such alarm prevailed that all the neighbours were fleeing in terror. The scene of the tragedy was close to Quenquén, 52 leagues beyond Azul.

At the beginning of December 1876, less than three weeks after this particularly gruesome burial, Edwards finally set off for Buenos Aires to meet his longed-for bride, Hélène de Bernardy.

Marriage and Murder

Alice's arrival in Argentina had not been easy. Hélène's was highly dramatic. On December 4, 1876 she and Edwards were finally married. The ceremony took place in the same church—St. John's—and with the same clergyman—Francis Smith—who had tied the knot for JG and Alice. Goodhall was again witness, together with Edwards' old friend, George E. Keen. Keen is described by Mulhall as the owner, on the banks of the Salado River, of 'one of the finest estancias in this part of the country'. Some years before, Edwards had already been planning his honeymoon in 'the Hotel in Belgrano, the prettiest place near B.A'. We do not know whether he ever got to this place of relaxation and repose, because Hélène fell ill and, while at her bedside, Edwards received a telegram telling him of an attack on his own estancia. On receiving the news, he abandoned his bride to rush back to the house that was to have been Hélène's first home in Argentina.

Edwards had prepared his absence from Indio Rico with care. Before he left to meet his fiancée in Buenos Aires, he carefully trained his *capataz* to handle the rifles, and while building the house had even constructed special windows from which to shoot at any attackers. Hélène many years later wrote an account of what happened.[17]

Edwards had left a capataz, a married man, looking after his house and guarding the camp. Having shown him how to load the various rifles, he advised him, in case of attack, to close himself up in the house with his wife, firing at (the Indians) from the windows made especially for that purpose.

Naturally, with the time to send a message to the many neighbours, they would all have been perfectly safe in the house, where there were plenty of arms and ammunition. But by a stroke of ill fortune, the Indians captured the man out alone in the camp; his wife also found herself alone in the house, because their only child had gone out into the camp in search of the flock. The Indians took the capataz to the house and after having frightened the poor wife almost out of her wits, made a small hole in the floor of the patio, placed the head of the unfortunate capataz over it, and slashed his throat. His wife was obliged to serve mate while this went on, and some of the Indians went out and brought back a young heifer that they devoured as an asado with its hide on.

Meanwhile, the unfortunate couple's extremely sensible and courageous small son was on his way home.

The boy . . . spotted the Indians, dismounted and led his horse up to the scrublands where he stopped on a small knoll that gave him a view of the whole house, the patio, and whatever the Indians were doing . . . The boy was unable to move from there until nightfall, when he followed the river route to pass the news to the neighbours. These were so alarmed that instead of going to Mr Edwards house, they fled

---

[17] There are several versions of the story. One by Briton Walker in *On the Frontier*, one by Henry Hogg written much later in his *Yerba Vieja*, and one by Hélène de Bernardy, translated from English into Spanish by her daughter. Here is Hélène's version, that presumably came from Edwards himself, translated back into English by me.

Twigs of a Tree

into the interior. The boy, on returning to his knoll, saw the Indians removing clothes, books, pictures and arms etc. from the house. They stayed two days, eating, drinking and sacking the house.

This was not all:
Some of them (the Indians) then set off into the camp in search of the flocks. They cut the throats of all the sheep, lay them in rows in the corral, and then went on to set fire to the house. What they couldn't burn they threw into the well. They also took all the horses, as well as some cows, to eat on the way in case they were pursued.

The little boy, still watching, then saw that one of them
wrote something on a piece of paper and then placed it in an easily seen spot on what remained of the walls of the house, and when the Indians left, the boy took the paper before leaving himself to tell the neighbours what had happened. He then took the road to Azul and reaching the shed of Mr Henry Fallenstein, told him what had happened and gave him the paper. This, it appeared, had been written by a man whom the Indians had taken prisoner,

The note was a dire and discouraging warning:
Facón Grande, we have given back something but not all. Where ever you may settle we will find you and we will return and give you another dose of the same medicine.[18]

Henry Hogg, who over half a century later was in contact with Briton Walker for the details of his book, *Yerba Vieja*, tells a prettier—perhaps even deliberately prettified—story that casts a different light on the Indian's view of Henry Edwards. Yes, people on the estancia, including women and children, were 'barbarously murdered' and the wells were filled with dead sheep, but the note left for Facón Grande alleged that
the damage was not the result of anger against the courageous Englishman, but rather because of hatred of the government.

---

[18] From the Spanish of Edwards' daughter, the only version available to me.

Babies, Bullets And Boleadoras

At that time, JG—Facón Chico—was organizing the estancia at San Carlos; it fell to him to tell his cousin the bad news.[19] The authorities had established a strict censorship system so as not to discourage immigrants and investment. JG telegraphed Edwards in Buenos Aires with a few terse words in English, designed to pass the censors unseen: 'House burned, all murdered by Indians, cattle stolen.' Such was, comments Henry Hogg, 'the wedding present from the natives to their persecutor'.

The attack at such a moment was a devastating blow. The loss of the capataz and of the animals was bad enough, let alone the house and all its contents. JG's son Briton remarks that 'after clearing up the mess', Edwards brought his bride from Buenos Aires to another estancia he was managing near Azul, also a long way from Bahía Blanca. This was a property that belonged to Tomás Chas, owner of a ranch called *Segovia*, six leagues from Juárez.[20]

Three years later, in May 1879—after General Julio A. Roca's first devastating successes against the Indians had brought some peace—the correspondent for the Buenos Aires *Standard*, whom we have already met as 'ND', rode to the destroyed estancia in Indio Rico. 'This very good house is still not rebuilt', he reports. 'It continues a shell with most of the doors and the wood of the roof gone, as they were after having been sacked and burnt by the *boleadores*', the Indians.

The *Standard* correspondent rather confirms the original version of the Indian motive for the destruction of the house: he remarks that Henry Edwards had been in charge of the place, and since the Indians

hated him with all their heart and he was absent in Buenos Aires, they attacked, killed the sheep and an old man and his wife and set the house on fire . . .

By the following year, 1877, the Colony was a shadow of what it had been. Frightened off, many men had returned to England. And after four deaths, two murders and three killings by Indians, the colony of some 45.000 hectares (around 111.000 acres) was by now reduced to only 21 men—some, like JG, with wife and small children. After a collective

---

[19] If, and this is not certain, this is San Carlos de Bolívar, JG Walker was far behind the frontier and almost halfway to Buenos Aires. It shows how far JG was prepared to go in search of work. Azul, where Edwards went after the attack on the estancia in Indio Rico, was almost as far removed from Bahia Blanca.

[20] Helene de Bernardy's account.

investment of £14.000 it owned 12.000 sheep with 'a few oxen, milk cows, and horses.'[21] Cultivation had almost stopped, only Mildred and Goodhall were still planting wheat, but in the two years before 1877 they had lost their entire crop.[22]

Unfortunately, we have no testimony of what effect all this was having on Alice. In such circumstances—the danger, the insecurity, the constant moving about—Mozart and Chopin could have provided only the most scant relief. In the midst of the uncertainty, on November 4, 1877, Alice's second child, William Norman, was born. He was to endow his brother with lively company and much, if somewhat exasperating pleasure. In Briton Walker's memories of his youth, the mischievous young Norman was to play an important role. Briton was to name his own son, Angela's father, after him. JG and Edwards, however, had no option but to go on with their battles. On July 13, 1878, the newspaper *La Nación* reports on yet another attack in which the cousins and various other colonists—twenty men altogether—take part under the leadership of Comandante Spika himself. They recover some two thousand mares and horses, and the Indians leave behind two hostages and their dead.

The paper describes JG as 'one of the most famous colonists' of the Bahía Blanca frontier praising him for his courage and assistance to the campaign with both horses and arms:

The disaster caused by the Indians in one part of the country of the South was not complete, since the savages suffered a defeat as they left. The attention of our readers will have been caught by the term Facón Chico. We shall explain. Walker is one of the most famous of the settlers of the Sauce Chico on the frontier of Bahia Blanca, settlers who lived in daily battle with the Indians. Walker was so intrepid in combat with the Indians that he once entered a fight with only a small knife and emerged as a victor. He is known in all of the southern Buenos Aires by this nickname of Facón Chico... He with various other Englishmen and Argentines fought as volunteers against the Indians, led by Comandante

---

[21] One Hectare = 2.47 acres
One Hectare = 10,000 sq. meters or 107,600 sq. feet
One Acre = 4,050 square meters or 43,560 sq. feet

[22] Rojas Lagarde, *El Malón de 1870,* p.188. The dispatch remarks that Walker is a capitalist landowner in Juarez, but that is a mistake. It was Edwards who went to Juárez, and he was no 'capitalist landowner' but a manager. Half a century later, Henry Hogg was to repeat this journalistic mistake.

Babies, Bullets And Boleadoras

Spika. The following Englishmen took part in the battle: J.G. Walker, Harry Edwards, William Cobbold, landowners of those parts.

The dispatch continues:
A thousand congratulations. Comandante Spika, Facón Chico, Farías and other neighbours recovered all the mares. The Indians only took some forty mares. The herd is complete and only one or two horses have been lost.

The jubilation, however, ends on a sombre note:
Burgos, who was lost, is dead. We found his body lanced through. He leaves ten orphans.[23]

Briton, by now nearly six years old, retained a vague recollection of this attack. He remembers
a lot of men coming with my father into our dining-room at San Carlos one afternoon. They took all the rifles and arms from their hooks on the wall . . . Dad had heard that his old friend Comandante Spika was in the neighbourhood on private business. He was not in uniform, but Dad had got in touch with him and he agreed to take charge of operations . . . Dad left Sam Giles to look after the house and he joined Spika with a supply of arms and horses for volunteers who wanted them. They had a hard chase and got back nearly all the raided cattle . . . It was too dark to continue the chase. He had told Giles to put a lantern on the Mirador of the house, but Sam knew better and made a bonfire which went out. But mother got a lantern onto the roof which guided the party back.[24]

The Man on the Hundred Peso Note

By the time of this expedition, the youthful General Julio Argentino Roca, who became President Nicolás Avellaneda's Minister of War (1878-1880) after Alsina's death in 1877, was already in charge of the 'Indian problem'. Alsina's trench may well have been, as Rojas Lagarde believes, a terrible 'mistake that brought much bloodshed and desolation to the region.'[25] The frontier had been continually pushed forward over many

---

[23] Lagarde, *1875*, p.201
[24] JBW. *Yarns from the Camp*, "Yeguada Recovered."
[25] Rojas Lagarde, *El Malón de 1870*, p.65

years. Roca, nevertheless, decided to push his immediate predecessor's frontier plans even further, to finish off what Rosas in his own *Campaign of the Desert* of some forty years before—and Alsina after him—had begun.

In view of this, Andrew Graham-Yooll seems a trifle overwrought when he pays the cousins the (dubious) compliment of laying the destruction of the Indians almost entirely on their shoulders. He invests these courageous men, struggling to make a living in extremely difficult circumstances, with powers they certainly did not have. Graham-Yooll writes:

Walker and Edwards' letters to Goodhall about the attacks by the 'darkies' and the 'brutes' as well as comment on the incompetence of the local army garrisons in protecting colonists eventually were to bring about, not just stronger censorship, but the decimation of the southern Buenos Aires and the Patagonian native Indians by the Argentine army.[26]

A more powerful and immediate influence may have been that of the tycoon Ernesto Tornquist, JG's future employer. He seems to have exerted pressure on his close friend, General Roca, for a solution to the 'Indian problem'. He invoked a simple arithmetical axiom: 'With the *malones* Buenos Aires is worth ten. Without them, it is worth one hundred.' [27]

General Roca's three-part campaign of 'liberating, punishing and colonizing' was a long-term, carefully thought out strategy that involved the whole government. Highly efficient and ultimately brutal, the operation involved five military divisions armed with the latest Remingtons. These were provided by the United States, a nation still dealing with its own 'Indian problem'. Besides Remingtons, Roca also took with him surveyors, naturalists and explorers to study and map the topographical features of the 'desert', the hitherto unknown territory over which the Mapuches and their fellow Indians had roamed for centuries.[28] After much preparation, the first part of Roca's plan, the *Campaign of the Desert*, was launched on April 5, 1879.

Historians have described Roca's five divisions as a vast and deadly net that took the lives of thousands of Mapuches and other Indians—men, women and children. As the military swept across the land, the Indians

---

[26] *The Forgotten Colony*, p.170
[27] Ernesto Tornquist (1842-1908). *Escenario y circunstancias*, Lucía Gálvez
[28] Alfred Hasbrouck, *The Conquest of the Desert*, in The Hispanic American Historical Review, Vol 15, No. 2 (May 1935), p. 214

in their path were killed, captured or set on fruitless flight into Chile. At the Andean frontier, the passes had been blocked to prevent the Mapuches from either leaving or entering Chile. This was achieved in part by the Chilean government, itself eager to appropriate Mapuche lands west of the Andes. Indians fleeing from Argentina were forced by Chilean troops back into general Roca's trap.

Roca's divisions set out, Alfred Hasbrouck tells us, from various points on the frontiers of the provinces of Buenos Aires, San Luis, Córdoba and Mendoza, marching generally south towards the Rio Negro and converging on its island of Choele-Choele in Patagonia. The idea was that the Indians who managed to escape one division would inevitably encounter the scouting parties of another. Those who tried to flee across the Rio Negro or through the mountain passes into Chile would be driven into the trap of the 4th division under Colonel Uriburu. The 4th division blocked the passes and advanced to the junction of the Neuquén and Limay rivers with the Rio Negro.

Those Indians who fled south would inevitably run into the 1st division under Roca as it advanced to the Rio Negro from Puan. Roca himself quickly cleared the area around Bahia Blanca.[29] The national holiday on May 25th was celebrated on the island of Choele-Choel in the Rio Negro, far south of Bahía Blanca. 14.000 Indians had already been conquered, 480 hostages released and 15.000 square leagues of land had been opened up.[30] Colonel Lavalle, commander of the 2nd division that had advanced from Carhué and onto the Colorado River, reported on August 15, 1879:

Not a single Indian is left in over a thousand leagues of desert which have been scoured by my patrols, except those wandering in abject misery. The savages have been completely demoralized by previous expeditions. They have fled to the farthest lands of the Pampa. Some have been captured, the rest driven across the Rio Negro. [31]

Two subsequent campaigns—in 1882 and 1885—rooted out all the remaining Indians, whether friendly or hostile, who had escaped into the Chilean passes of the Andes or to the beautiful Lake Nahuel Huapí in

---

[29] Hasbrouck, p. 195-228
[30] Hasbrouck, p. 221
[31] quoted by Hasbrouck, p. 217

Twigs of a Tree

Patagonia, where the tourist centre of Bariloche now stands. By 1882, the 'problem' was solved. In 1885, the last caciques surrendered.[32]

Roca's results came at terrible cost to the natives. Historians are still debating whether the conquest was a justifiable and inevitable move in the name of 'civilization' or a particularly perfidious example of mass murder.

The Argentines of the period had no doubts in this matter. As soon as the campaign was over, Julio A. Roca was elected to the presidency. He served from 1880 to 1886 and again from 1898 to 1904. As the hero of the 'pacification of the desert' he was credited with the liberation of hundreds of white hostages, with the end of cattle rustling and payment of tribute to caciques; with the end of the war itself. On coming into the presidency, general Roca—the 'last of the conquistadores' was a mere 35 years old—suppressed a political uprising and declared Buenos Aires the centre of government and capital of the republic. This finally resolved the old Federalist/Unitarian controversy over which so much blood had flowed. The following year, Roca signed a peace treaty with Chile, securing for Argentina some conquered and hitherto disputed territory in the Andes and in Patagonia. The newly formed provinces of La Pampa, Neuquén and Rio Negro alone added some 460.000 square kilometres of territory to the Argentine map.[33]

Roca could not have known this beforehand, but his campaigns, by opening a vast expanse of the some of the richest agricultural land in the world, heralded over three decades of unprecedented development and progress for Argentina and its agro-business. For this, Julio Argentino Roca was honoured in 1941 with a monument of colossal proportions.

Others place the emphasis elsewhere. Andrew Graham-Yooll records the horror of the Welsh colonists in Patagonia at the merciless persecution of the Tehuelche Indians with whom these settlers had established reasonably amicable connections. Historians like Sabine Kradolfer point to the storming of the Indian encampments and the slaughter of their inhabitants, women and children included. Whole families were torn

---

[32] The word *desierto*, a misnomer for the dry but exceedingly fertile Pampas that would soon burst into life with the irrigation supplied by its many rivers, is better translated as 'wilderness'. The implication of the word was that the territory was un-peopled. Roca used it deliberately. The land was, of course, merely devoid of a 'civilized' white population.

[33] 1 square league = 17.9211 square kilometres = 1792.11 hectares.

asunder and destroyed, men and women separated so they could not 'procreate'; Indian men were imprisoned by the thousands on the island of Martín García. Others were pressed into the army and navy, into forced labour on the estancias and the sugar plantations of Tucumán, or into the extension of the railway network being built by the British. Indian women and children were distributed among Buenos Aires' well-to-do as domestic servants. Those who escaped death or exile were incorporated into the lowest strata of society, losing their language, culture and identity.[34] The numbers of Mapuche killed have been estimated as high as 20.000.

It is a sorry tale, not improved by the fact that a vast amount of land—some 15.000 leagues secured for agriculture—was appropriated, under Roca's corrupt tenure, by some 400 families. The generous general donated 30.000 hectares to himself.

The "Civilization/Genocide" debate continues. Both sides of the argument proffer irrefutable truths. The Indians were, indeed, almost wiped out. And, yes, Argentina did suddenly take off. As with so many in human history, the moral dimensions of this particular period are fraught with ambivalence and ambiguity.

In the long struggle for territory, who can blame the settlers for defending themselves and their families? But who today cannot feel regret, even outrage, that the Indians in their own struggle for a living, for their own way of life, were virtually destroyed? General Roca is still celebrated, although historians like Kurt Jonassohn class his campaign as mass murder.[35] There are also large numbers of Porteños—Buenos Aires citizens—still angry enough at the injustice perpetrated on the Indians to want the general's imposing monument in the capital removed. In the meantime, Roca's image continues to grace Argentina's hundred-peso note.

---

[34] Sabine Kradolfer, « Les autochtones invisibles, ou comment l'Argentine c'est « blanchie » », Amérique Latine Histoire et Mémoire. Les Cahiers ALHIM, 16 | 2008.

[35] *Genocide & Gross Human Rights Violations in Comparative Perspective* Kurt Jonassohn, Karin Solveig Bjornson. Transaction Publications, New Jersey, 1998.

CHAPTER XI

REALITY AND LITERARY LICENCE

It was when the fighting was at its height that Robert Cunninghame Graham (1852-1936) appeared in JG Walker's life. He had arrived in Argentina in 1870, barely out of Harrow, at the tender age of seventeen. Graham's mother, whose Scottish husband had become 'dreadfully rash with his money', seems to have arranged for young Robert to 'be a partner in a ranch'. The spendthrift Major had by now given up his ambitions of an army career for his son—and hoped, in sending him out to Argentina, for 'quick returns'.[36] Robert himself, much like JG and Henry Edwards before him, was in search of adventure.

The thrills of Argentina enticed him back to the country again and again. Graham's third Pampas exploit took place between 1876 and 1878, at the height of the Indian attacks around Bahía Blanca. Bloomfield tells us that this 'descendant of Scottish kings', after selling horses in Brazil, 'went south, bought a Ranch, *El Sauce Chico*, and raised cattle'. From its name his property cannot have been too far from JG's territory, Sauce Grande. The newcomer, like everyone else, had to put up with the Indian *malones*.

Robert Cunninghame Graham would only begin writing his long series of successful books many years later, after he reached forty. In one tale, he describes an evening with the Naposta valley settlers, the constellation of the Southern Cross hanging in the night-skies above

---

[36] *The Essential R.B. Cunninghame Graham,* selected with an Introduction and Preface by Paul Bloomfield, Jonathan Cape, London.

their heads. The men, after a fruitless attempt to retrieve a herd of horses taken by the Indians, sit around the light of the fire exchanging tales of camp life. One speaks of the woman he had loved and lost. She, whose *estanciero* father, mother and brothers had all been murdered in an Indian invasion, had been captured—like the half-naked virgin in the famous della Valle painting—by a wanton cacique. This wild man had fathered three sons on his unwilling captive. Rescued by the narrator, she falls in love with him, re-acquires her civilized ways, her dress and her Spanish name, Nieves Lincomilla. However, in spite of her hatred for the Indian father of her children, she cannot remain with her new suitor. The call of motherly love and duty overcomes her newfound freedom and happiness, and she returns to her children and the tribe that had captured her. The ocean metaphor for the Pampas rebounds as Graham describes Nieves' departure, her horse fading from sight as if into the seas,

> *just as a ship slips down the round edge of the world. Her feet went first... Lastly, the glory of her floating hair hung for a moment upon the sky, then vanished, just as a piece of seaweed is sucked into the tide by a receding wave.*

Among those listening to this tale in the light of the fire, were
> *two cattle-farmers, English by nationality, known as El Facón Grande and El Facón Chico from the respective size of the knives they carried, (who) talked quietly, just as they would have talked in the bow-window of a club...* [1]

By the time Graham got around to completing his story *Facón Grande*—published in 1936, the year of his death—Graham was a well-known figure, the first socialist to be voted into the House of Commons, a writer acquainted with George Bernard Shaw. But Briton could not forgive him for having virtually morphed him into one of Nieves' 'half-Indian, half-Christian children'. Alice Walker was to dismiss Cunninghame Graham as a *farsante*, a fantasizing buffoon. She brushed off his friendly description of her as a 'douce Scottish-Argentine' as the hallucinations of dotage.

Nevertheless, Graham's late recollections of the two cousins living the 'wild, dangerous and lonely life' of the frontier are not without interest. He

---

[1] In the short story, *The Captive*, in *Hope*, Duckworth, London,

Twigs of a Tree

describes the area, since the government gave the colonists no protection, as one where

> *only men of resolution . . . or outcasts from society would settle, a region where a man could be ruined in a night by raiding Indians.*

Graham then goes on with an extensive description of the cousins that is perhaps worth reproducing. The names are not right (Hawker, a perhaps misremembered Walker, for Edwards), but the descriptions refer unmistakeably to the cousins. Edwards would not have approved of being called a *desperado*, in Graham's description of the desperate or outcast nature of many colonists. He remarks of Edwards:

> *Still, there were some who, neither desperate nor outcasts, resolutely took up land and settled down. Of such the most remarkable was a tall Englishman whose name, I think, was Hawker, but better known as "Facón Grande" from the sword bayonet that he wore stuck through his belt and sticking out upon both sides, after the fashion of the lateen yard of fishing boats in the Levant. Tall, dark and wiry, his hair that he wore long and ragged beard gave him the look of a stage desperado, but in reality he was a brave and prudent man who knew quite well the danger that he lived in, but was determined to hang on, for he had faith in the country's future where he had made his home. As he had lived for many years upon the frontier, he dressed in Gaucho fashion, with loose black merino trousers tucked into high boots . . . .*

JG Walker, on the other hand, might have smiled at being sketched as an avenging archangel:

> *A short half-league away, his cousin lived, one Ferguson, known to the Gauchos as "Facón Chico", was about middle height with sandy hair and a short well-cropped beard. His face was freckled and his hands, mottled like a trout, had once been white, of that unhealthy-looking hue that exposure to the sun often impart to red-headed or to sandy-coloured men. For all his quiet appearance and meek ways till roused, he was perhaps the bolder and more daring of the two. The Gauchos said, although he looked like an archangel who had lost his wings, that in an Indian skirmish his porcelain coloured eyes shot fire and he became a perfect devil, the highest compliment in their vocabulary . . .*

From Facón Chico to Cortaplumas, Small Knife to Penknife

Graham follows with the lines describing the irregular union ascribed to JG, and his son, Briton, as the 'perfect type of the half-bred urchin' that, understandably, so irritated Alice Walker and her eldest son.

Curiously enough, he spoke Pehuelche fairly fluently, for he had lived some years with an Indian woman, who, when she went back to the Toldería, had left him as a pledge of their love . . . a boy the Gaucho humorists had christened Cortaplumas (Penknife)—to the delight not only of his father, but of the whole neighbourhood. The boy grew up amongst the peons neither exactly tame nor wild. Like other boys born in that outside 'camp' upon the frontiers, he ran about bare footed, lassoed the dogs and carts, and brought down birds with little 'bolas' that he manufactured by himself out of old strips of hide and knuckle-bones. By the age of six or seven he, like all the other boys, was a good rider, climbing up on the saddle, using the horse's knees as a step-ladder for his bare little toes.

Cunninghame Graham, no mean horseman himself, is hugely impressed by young Cortaplumas/Briton's riding abilities:

Once mounted, he had come into his kingdom, whirling his whip round his head and drumming ceaselessly with his bare heels upon the horse's side, he would set off at the slow machine-like gallop of the plains, either to help round up the horses for the day's work, or to snare partridges with a noose at the end of a long cane.

Briton, according to the writer, is dressed in rather wild a fashion:

He naturally, perhaps to prove his lineage, carried a knife large enough for a grown man to use, stuck in the Pampa Indian waist-band that kept up his ragged 'chiripá'. His wiry jet-black hair stuck out below his hat, and fell upon his shoulders like a mane . . . Had his Pehuelche mother not gone back to her own people or his father not married a douce Scottish-Argentine, most likely Cortaplumas would have grown up a Gaucho without education, and perhaps have disappeared one day to join his mother in the "Toldos", taking some of his father's best horses with him.[2]

---

[2] R.B. Cunninghame Graham, in *Facon Grande* from *Mirages*, Heinemann, Toronto. Pp.169-182

Twigs of a Tree

John Briton (Cortaplumas) Melrose, Harold Saxon and William Norman circa 1887

Briton's own comment on this literary embroidery was dismissive. *Graham writes that I was the son of an Indian princess, and that mother had found me nearly naked, being dragged up in the Peon's kitchen, quite neglected by all, and grudgingly given an odd bone. She had changed all that, and very kindly had had me dressed, fed and sent to school.*[3]

In 1943 Briton was still irritated enough with Graham's descriptions of the cousins in his *Mirages* that he went to the trouble of composing a full refutation. According to Briton, everything Graham wrote, not only names, was incorrect or trumped up. Edwards was not dark and wiry with ragged mane, but rather tall, robust and blond, with short beard and hair.

---

[3] *On the Frontier*

Reality And Literary Licence

He spoke Spanish well, and dressed not like a gaucho, but like an English country squire. He carried the knife only when he had work to do in the camp, and it was no more than 35 to 40 centimetres long. The knives were never used for fighting. They had more faith in their rifles.

Briton then moves on to Graham's descriptions of his own father—blond, medium height, with yellowish skin; he doesn't give the writer an inch. Facón Chico was not blond, but dark, and had neither a natural child nor an Indian mistress. Dismissing Graham for good, he adds that his own sobriquet *Cortaplumas*—Penknife, to match those of Facón Grande and Facón Chico—had nothing to do with Gaucho humour but came, instead, from Facón Grande, Large Knife, himself—'Uncle Harry' Edwards.[4]

---

[4] JBW note on *Mirages* by Cunninghame Graham, 1936, in Spanish, translated by me.

CHAPTER XII

BETWEEN BOOM AND BUST

By the time general Roca arrived on the scene in 1878 the cousins seem to have become exhausted by the chronic danger, insecurity and uncertainty. The difficulties of severely under-capitalized ownership were multiplied by the periodic loss of their crops—by fire, rain or drought—or by the theft or cruel destruction of their animals.

The complications around property titles seem to have come to something of a conclusion—though not to an advantageous one. *The Standard* of November 11, 1877 announced the success of Senator Gache's mission to move the government to finally relinquish the title deeds. But although the province had released the land and set a price that was reduced, according to Rojas Lagarde, to that of eight years before, the expense of actually buying the land might have entailed sacrifices the cousins, both now family men, could no longer take on. Even at reduced prices—after the losses caused by the Indian raids they may simply not have had the necessary financial resources.[5]

---

[5] The cost of the land is something of a puzzle. Seymour in 1867, admittedly nine years earlier, says he bought land for the equivalent of a few shillings per square mile. Mulhall, in 1878, cites land in Argentina as worth £1000 sterling a square mile. At this rate, a league being about 5.25 square miles, the price of the 1.75 leagues allotted to the colonists by the government could have been as high as £9.000. ND, the *Standard's* correspondent who went to look at the Keen's burned out estancia in 1879, remarks that the majority of the colonists had 1.75 leagues each, bought for 25.000 pesos a square league, to be paid off in 10 years. This does not tally with the 40.000 pesos first asked for by the government.

Nor could they, at the time, have had any certainty that the Indian danger would eventually be permanently crushed.

Commenting on the 'statistics' submitted by Goodhall, Rojas Lagarde observes how very precarious the colony seemed to be as early as 1876, and how very few animals it then owned:

12.000 sheep, a few oxen and a few milk cows is really extremely little for so large a piece of land . . . It shows the critical state of the Colony. The hope that the Indians would not attack because there was nothing to steal was no exaggeration.[1]

Three years on, in 1879, we get another insight into the plight of the Colony from the travelling *Standard* correspondent, ND. After visiting Edward's destroyed estancia, the reporter sets off for the Sauce Grande, arriving at John Cobbold's house at about midday. Noting that sheep breeding is the settlers' main occupation, he adds that, 'Agriculture seems to have been a failure.'

For ND this failure is the result of the colonists not being 'men of the plough' and unused to heavy labour. He remarks that in spite of much investment in a 'good metal plough . . . saws and other machines', all the labour had to be contracted, so that every *fanega* of wheat cost the settlers more than they could ever get for it in Bahía Blanca.[2]

ND then moves on from Cobbold's to see Alice's brother, George Catty, who had just ridden all the way to Pillahuinca and back by himself, a journey that, according to the correspondent, showed great courage. It might also have indicated that the Indian danger had somewhat abated. George Catty, still a bachelor, is very busy building. He shows his visitor around, puts him up for the night, then gives him two fresh horses to continue his journey to Barber's.

Barber subsequently surprises the *Standard* reporter by serving cocktails with the unexpected ingredient of Angostura bitters, especially imported from England. ND remarks on the beauty of Barber's land adding that Jordan, brother of the murdered Thomas, was on the point of selling out whatever rights he had and returning to England.[3]

With a wife and a small child, JG appears to have begun looking for an alternative to the Sauce Grande as early as 1875, two years after

---

[1] Rojas Lagarde, *El Malón de 1870* p. 193-4
[2] *idem* p. 209
[3] *idem* p. 213

Alice's arrival. In his letter of December 17th of that year, written after Douner's death, he remarks that he had sent someone to 'pay the stamps' for the deeds to a 'league of land transferred by Keen to my name.' We also know that he was at the San Carlos estancia at the time of the 1876 attack on Indio Rico, where his cousin Edwards had moved. By the time of ND's visit to the Indio Rico in 1879, JG and Edwards appear to have abandoned the Sauce Grande area if not actually sold out.

Briton writes that in about 1876 his father—tired of wasting his energies on a place where there was no security from constant raids, no help from the authorities, and no probability of getting titles to the land he had settled—sold out for whatever he could get, taking on a job as 'manager on a camp near Olavarria, about twelve leagues from Azul'.

This seems to have been the San Carlos estancia. According to Briton, it belonged to a Dr Ernesto Romero. Like Edwards' Indio Rico estancia, it lay at a considerable distance from the Sauce Grande colony.

In this country where ownership of land had long been and remained a ticket to prestige, my grandmother Melrose—with a touch of ruefulness—believed to the end of her life that the government had not honoured its promises, that her father had somehow 'lost' his land at the hands of corrupt officialdom. Her daughter Molly Dyson believed the same thing into her great old age, as we can see from the filmed interview she gave her granddaughters Tania and Susie in 1995.[4]

Rojas Lagarde has cleared up the question through his investigations into the archives in Bahia Blanca. Edwards, Walker and Jordan, none of whom had much capital—or any way of knowing how successful Roca's brutal campaign would be—all sold whatever stake they still had in the Sauce Grande properties to one Juan Henesterosa in 1879. It is not clear whether they had initiated their buying rights or not.

'A pity they didn't hold on for one more year!,' Rojas Lagarde remarked when I visited him in his home around the corner from Molly's flat in Buenos Aires. That the sell-out of their 4.5 leagues was in the long run a mistake seems now fairly obvious. When JG, Edwards and Jordan gave up on the Colony in 1879, land in Olavarria was going for $350 a square league. Thirty years later, the same area of land sold at $400,000.[5]

General Ignacio Fotheringham, the commander of one of Roca's divisions, was, 'like most army officers, a poor business man', writes

---

[4] Tania Dyson made a DVD of this long and interesting interview.
[5] Hasbrouck, p. 227

Hasbrouck. Fotheringham was to 'bewail' until the end of his life the blunder of selling off—for the 'infinitesimal price' of $600 a square league—the eight leagues with which he was rewarded by the Government after the end of the Indian campaign.[6] But this is hindsight; there was at the time no way of knowing that the Indian raids were finally over.[7]

On the other hand, with little capital, Edwards, Walker and Jordan may all have found themselves in a situation where they simply had no choice. Be it as it may, all three—JG, Edwards and Jordan, though not Alice's brother George Catty—had certainly abandoned the area of the Sauce Grande colony by the end of 1879.[8]

JG and his family could not have been immediately aware that the eighties, with the Indians defeated, hailed the beginnings of great changes in Argentina. The fifty years between 1880 and 1930 were the years of Argentina's first great boom, of vast agricultural and economic expansion. These were the years of *las vacas gordas,* the fat cows; the period when agriculture and cattle raising turned the country—for a while—into the fifth richest nation on earth. The 'desert', newly freed from the Indians, turned out to be some of the most fertile farmland in the world. Commercial, even industrialized agriculture and cattle- and sheep-farming, in the hands of men who bought up vast tracts of land in the newly opened provinces, became very big business.

Julio A. Roca's electoral winning formula called 'force and fraud' was to be operated to the advantage of the great landowners—often men who had only recently acquired vast stretches of camp—and the military itself. The area around Bahia Blanca is richly scattered with townships founded by and named after military commanders who, after the defeat of the Indians, had been awarded the land on which the towns now stand. Among them are the well-known towns of General La Madrid, Colonel Pringles, Colonel Dorrego and Colonel Suarez.

By 1900, Argentina's exports of agricultural goods—beginning with wheat in the 1880's—had become as important to the economy as its earlier animal products of salted meat, hides and extracts. In turn, with the invention and development of refrigerated shipping, meat exports flourished as never before. Landaburu tells us that in the Argentina of the

---

[6] idem
[7] It is interesting that the daughter of JG's fellow colonist, Elinor Barber, tells us much later that her father was 'given' his land in return for helping the military defend it.
[8] Rojas Lagardc, *El Malón de 1870*, p.211,

1880's, the professional on his salary, the simple tradesman, the politician without land and the incipient industrialist all counted for very little. What counted was land, and the people who owned it, those with great investments in territory.[9]

Nevertheless, some of the very rich future landowners—among them Adam Altgeld and his brother-in-law Ernesto Tornquist—were also involved in commerce and enterprise, much of it dominated by the British. The boom years ushered in an unprecedented extension of the new electricity and water supply systems, drainage and railway networks, as well as a rush of over-wild financial speculation. It was, naturally, also a period of massive immigration.

Large-scale agriculture and animal ranching, supported by the new railways, by refrigeration and the new meat-packing companies turned Argentina into a 'magnet of labour' for young men from all over Europe but also from neighbouring countries like Chile, Bolivia and Peru.[10]

Koebel explains how the eighties heralded a whole new range and intensity of employment, including the business of running other men's estancias. He describes the profession of *mayordomo* or farm manager as that of 'revising camp' and keeping a watchful eye on fence-lines, pumps and the progress of crops.' It was into farm management that several men of the family—various Goodbodys and Diana McClure's father, Martin Eggar—would later enter. By the time Koebel was writing in 1910, it was no longer the lure of free land that counted, but that of a rural life based on farm management. The manager, he writes in distinctly over-rosy terms,

> *was in all probability a public school man, since it is a curious fact that, the more costly the education, the greater is the probability that its recipient, in straits for a livelihood, will seek the land. This blending of the public school-boy and the agriculturalist is frequently responsible for astonishingly successful results. The height of his ambition is to become manager of one of the great pastoral and agricultural concerns where cattle and sheep are counted by the tens of thousands, and where all else is upon a similar scale. Once in this position his material reward is substantial. His own master to a degree unusual in other professions, both as regards his private life and estancia operations, in receipt of a liberal salary, a dweller in a luxurious home, with a host of tried men careering to and fro at his orders—the broad leagues, for*

---

[9] Roberto E. Landaburu, *Gringos,* Fondo Editor Mutual Venado Tuerto, 1991
[10] Landaburu, *Gringos,* p. 16

all practical purposes might well be his own . . . Many such managers of the greater estancias are themselves owners of properties that, in turn, are manipulated by equally independent managers . . . and the overlooking of one estate with another of his own goes no small way toward lessening the precariousness of livelyhood (sic).[11]

The newly freed Indian territory north of Bahía Blanca soon caught the eye of the rich businessman Adam Altgeld, who then passed land on to his brother-in-law, Ernesto Tornquist.[12] Tornquist was to become one of Argentina's great landowners, acquiring, after Roca's campaign, some 52 leagues (240 square kilometers) of land on the Sauce Chico—in the area of Roca's fortress, the *Fuerte Argentino*, and near a section of the old Alsina ditch. Ten leagues of this land were later donated for the founding of a colony that eventually developed into the town and railhead of Tornquist. Briton tells us that, in 1881, JG Walker began to *poblar*—to organize and man—Ernesto Tornquist's land on the Sauce Chico.

Henry Edwards, on the other hand, after the 1876 disaster at Indio Rico, spent first a year on Tomás Chas's estancia *Segovia*, some six leagues from the Juárez station. Two years later, however, in 1879, still times of turmoil, he accepted an offer by Ernesto Romero, the stepbrother of the current Minister of Finance. Edwards was to set up and manage Romero's estancia *La Larga* on a system of halves—profits to be shared equally between the owner and his manager. Edwards then went into the purchase of stock. He seems to have had no regrets about having gone into management. His ties to his cousin, JG, remained strong. In October 1882, still settled at *La Larga* after Hélène gave birth to their third child, Edwards offers us an insight into his and JG's lives (and the management business) in a long letter to his sister Louise. He seems content with his lot:

Our home is very comfortable and we are very happy and doing well. They are trying to entice me to take the management of another large estancia like the one John manages, and the new one is also on the Sauce Chico, touching John's. It also will be nearly 40 leagues of camp. They will put on 20.000 head of cattle and only 10,000 sheep. I was in

---

[11] W.H. Koebel *Argentina Past and Present*, Trubner & Co. London, 1910. p.102-106

[12] Altgeld came from a Hamburg family with many international business connections (and the capital that the cousins lacked). He had interests that eventually ranged from sugar refineries, meat salting plants and beer breweries to shipbuilding, railways, steel, ceramics, refrigeration and whaling.

B.A. last month and Tornquist introduced me to Altgeld, the head of a new company here, brother-in-law to Tornquist.—Capital 150.000, London. I have neither accepted nor refused the management as yet, as Altgeld has not told me the terms, but they have got John to use his influence with me and get me to take it. He says I shall be offered (illegible) or $500 a year and a share of the profits.

Altgelt has had some misunderstanding with the London directors and consequently is not able to settle anything, but said he would want to see me in about a month. I have many objections to the new concern, it is not like John's who has only Tornquist to consult in B.A. And a London Board of Directors who know nothing about cattle will want to have their say in everything. I should much like to be near John but I also like a good camp, and here at La Larga I have 'the flower of the camp', and there it is very hilly and sandy, no black earth—here I get such an increase in my flocks as none of my neighbours ever do. I get on well with Romero, and I might with the new people. I wont go there on the <u>chance</u> of getting £1000 a year if things go well. What I want and why I did not tell them once and for all that I would not go, is because I don't wish to break off all business. For if I can only get the buying of the stock for them I shall make a good thing of it. They have to pay about £900 for some commission agent to buy stock for them, and I can do it and still keep on La Larga. I have bought, since John started, about £9000 worth of sheep and cattle for him, and now I am getting orders for other people as well and, be sides, the place now pays well. We have 10,000 sheep now and 1700 cows, half the produce being for me. I prefer a small place on halves to large place with 10% or 5% of the profits.

Edwards goes on with a description of the new railway line and station planned for Tornquist's territory

The railway from Azul to B. Blanca is being made very fast now. The earth works are done past here. The station will be 5 leagues from La Larga and will be on the land John manages. In December it will be opened to Olavarria, a small town 10 leagues from Azul and ten leagues from here. Shearing is coming very soon, in about 3 weeks time I hope to begin. I fear the railway will run us very short of peons as the supply is rather limited and the demand for the railway is unlimited. One contractor near here has 500 peons and wants more.

I am glad to see that mother is doing well and hope to be home in a year and a half, as things are going well here and from what Alice tells me the cost of a trip for a family is not very dreadful—she only spent £240 and was nearly a year away.[13]

Eventually, when Ernesto Romero died, the Finance Minister offered Edwards the management of his own estancia, *Santa Clara de Romero*. It must have kept Edwards busy, as it covered nine leagues and had 20.000 sheep, 10.000 cattle and 1000 horses. He was to remain there for ten years. Tornquist was, in time, to subdivide his enormous property, selling off small parcels of land on easy terms. We do not know whether JG Walker himself took advantage of the offer.

---

[13] *Datos sobre la vida del Sr. Henry John Edwards*, translated into Spanish from originals by Edwards' widow.

CHAPTER XIII

OLD ENGLAND, NEW ARGENTINA

Alice Catty Walker in the 1880's

Some time in 1880—and once again expecting a child—Alice Walker gathered up her two young sons and set off to visit her family in England. According to Briton, they travelled first to Azul and caught the new train from there to Buenos Aires. JG then saw them off on the *Iberia* on its way from

Chile to Liverpool. Alice's stay in London, as we have seen from Edwards' letter, was a long one of almost a year, and she was still there in 1881.

Almost eight years had passed since Alice had seen her parents, brothers and sisters. She and her two small boys stayed in the house she knew so well: Antwerp House in Wandsworth. The household was still an enormous one of sixteen people, but the family had changed. According to the 1881 census, Frederic Adam and his wife Ann now lived in the company of four daughters—two unmarried, one widowed—with six grandchildren and four servants. The grandchildren are fifteen-year old Mary Shearman and the two practical jokers, her brothers, now in their twenties. Young Montague ("Tont", 1858-1930) had already completed his MA at Oxford and was now reading for the Bar.

With Alice came her children, Briton, then 6, Norman, 3, and eventually Alice's new baby, Harold Saxon, born on February 14, 1881, during her stay in England. Alice was to have five children in all. Alice Melrose, born in 1884 in Argentina, followed Harold. Finally came Alfred English, known as Eric, born in 1891. By the time of Eric's birth Alice had reached the relatively ripe old age of forty-three. By today's standards, five is a large brood, by those of the 19th century it was not. Susanna Goodwin and Benjamin Bovill, a wine merchant—grandparents to Ann Edwards (1812-1896), Frederick Adam's wife—had sixteen children. Of these, a full seven did not reach adulthood: six died before they reached three and one died at eighteen. Frederick Adam himself had nine surviving children, four sons and five daughters. My Adams great-grandfather, Charles, produced thirteen children, and my husband Carlos' Bavarian grandparents had ten. Briton Walker tells us that their neighbours in Argentina, the Pettigrews, where he often went to play, had brought no less than twenty children into the world.

Many years later, shortly before her death on November 12, 1977, Melrose (Walker) Goodbody gave an interview to Rosalie Benguria. In it she made a point of her father's patriotism, his devotion to his country of birth. The names chosen by Alice and JG for their children appear to indicate a longing for the home and the peoples they had left behind. The stress on their Britishness seems to include the implication that, in spite of their own position in Argentina, they made scant distinction between the conquered and conquerors of their own native land.

John *Briton* was named after the original Celts, first overcome by the Romans and then by the Germanic Angles and Saxons. These, in turn, were subsequently conquered by the—originally Viking and later French—Normans. After John Briton came William *Norman*, named after the conquerors first of Britain in 1066 and then of Ireland. Briton and Norman were followed—while Alice was in England—by Harold *Saxon*, and then, last of all, by Alfred *English* or Angle. Only their daughter did not fit into this pattern of all-encompassing historical conquest, defeat and re-conquest that constituted the British nation. She might have completed the pattern as *Icena*, after the ancient rulers of present-day Norfolk, or—as Molly also observed—as *Boudicca*, their Queen, who with her two daughters led a revolt against the Roman occupiers of Britain.

As it was, Alice and JG's only daughter became Alice *Melrose*. Even here there may be a touch of nostalgia or a special meaning. Melrose was, curiously enough, the name of the London street on which Frederick Adam's *Antwerp House* stood. Or perhaps the name Melrose was a nod from the Pampas to the border town in Scotland, an ancient city in originally Pict territory that has endured, through the ages, its own cycle of invasions: by Angles, Jutes, Saxons and Romans.

At the time of the 1881 census, Frederick Adam Catty—although now 77—was still employed as 'Guildhall City Of London Principal Clerk'. It is possible that he kept his job so long because of his linguistic abilities. As Briton remarks,

lots of big swells from France, and many German Princes and Dukes who were related to old Queen Victoria, used to be entertained at the Guildhall, so the Secretary who could talk in their languages was very useful.

Frederick Adam's 'white side-whiskers' and the 'gold watch and chain across his waist-coat' impressed young Briton; his wife Ann, less so. Briton remembered her as an old Granny, 'round like a ball' and so strictly religious that little Briton was dismissed from the room for the shocking sin of choosing to play a game of dominoes rather than 'sing a hymn or go to Sunday school'.

Young Briton, the first of a long and steady line of 'South American' children to be housed and boarded by generous and long-suffering English relations, is impressed with the numbers of aunts in the house.[1] Other

---

[1] Briton's tale *A trip to England in 1880* is one of many, all in a style addressed to children, that he writes for his own children and grandchildren. Briton's writings are the only evidence we have of that period of JG and Alice's life.

aunts came to visit 'the strange people from South America' and they were all, he says, 'very kind to him'.

He remembers lying in bed, listening to the emanations from one of his grandfather's 'swell dinners'. Later he recorded how Alice shocked a respectable gathering of dinner guests into open-mouthed silence. Her account of a fatal Indian attack came, after eight years on the Pampas, to what seemed to her—if not to her guests—a perfectly logical conclusion: 'Since there was no churchyard, we had him buried in our back garden.'

Briton, at six although stoutly defended by young Norman did not easily assimilate into English life. Other 'boys who lived in the street', constantly teased him for being different, for being a 'foreigner'. Once, while carrying some of the Aunts' books back to the library, he was taunted first for not being able to read, then for not being able to run. He laid down the books to demonstrate his sprinting abilities—when he returned the books were gone. This painful experience, for which no doubt he was soundly punished, was, he tells us, his first experience of the 'confidence trick'.

Briton had a wonderful time playing with his many cousins, but once he was hit accidentally in the eye by a bat as he was being taught to play cricket. Surprised that he did not 'yell the house down', his kind-hearted grandfather, Frederick Adam, rewarded him for his bravery with a 'very nice silver watch and chain'. Briton's modesty, one of this gentle and delightful man's characteristics to the end of his life, already showed through: 'I wasn't very brave, just stunned.' His quietness and gentleness was to be passed on to his son Norman, Angela's father.

We have no record of the visit from Alice or from JG, and Briton says nothing of his father's family or of his other grandmother. Perhaps they were among the 'Aunts' who came to visit. But he goes away with fond memories of Frederick Adam, by then known as 'the Guvnor'. He, at Christmas, hid silver shillings under the children's helpings of plum pudding. The children, thrilled with these easy takings, pushed their plates forward again and again until the 'interfering Aunts' stopped the game, saying they would be sick. The truncated diversion of silver shillings may have driven Briton to the remark that, in Frederick Adam's household, 'the women ruled'.

They spent a few days in Devon with Aunt Robin Wilson (née Mary Barbara Cross), a widowed friend of Alice's and sister of one of JG's rowing friends. Aunt Robin's husband, James Wilson, a ship's captain, had been lost at sea. She had two children of her own, Leslie and Sidney, and two Wilson stepchildren, Jean and Lillie.[2] Aunt Robin would a few years later marry Alice's brother, George Catty, and join him in Argentina with her children and stepchildren.

After almost a year in England, Alice and her three small boys—Briton, Norman and baby Harold Saxon—left for Buenos Aires in the *Valparaíso*. They were met in Montevideo by JG and then, according to Briton, took a two-day journey on the steamboat to Bahía Blanca. As they neared the shore the ship struck a mud bank and caused such alarm that, fearing the boat would be overturned, 'Everyone started screaming and fainting.' The two little boys ran around gleefully, singing pointedly of a clock that stopped short never to go again. They were told to 'shut up': the noise they were making, their father scolded, was worse than the shrieks of the passengers.

The family, having finally arrived safely, drove out in carts to their new home on the Sauce Chico, apparently a 'much bigger estancia' than San Carlos. For JG and his family it was a new life, no doubt hard, but at least almost free of the anxieties provoked by the Indians.

Their new home on the Sauce Chico stood near general Roca's *Fuerte Argentino* and was at a considerable distance from the San Carlos estancia. About fifty miles away were the hills that Briton remembered rising from the ocean of the plains like an island, peaks standing 'out sharp like teeth of a saw'. The highest of these, with a large window—*ventana*—cut into it, gave the mountain range its name of Sierra de la Ventana.[3]

We have a picture of the relatively modest house that JG had prepared for his family while they were in England, presumably on the newly acquired land belonging to Ernesto Tornquist. What is striking in the picture is the rawness and the isolation, the lack of trees. Those trees so popular in Argentina: the fast-growing eucalyptus, the magnolias, *jacarandás*, various conifers and the beautiful native *ombú*, also known as the 'lighthouse of the Pampas'.[4]

---

[2] According to Patrick Brady Mary Barbara had married Captain James Wilson, after the death of his first wife, in Gibraltar on December 20, 1870.
[3] Ride to the Chilenos, 86
[4] The ombu, phylolacca dioca, is strictly speaking not a tree, but a bush, belonging to the same family as the pokeweed. It needs almost no moisture but can grow to massive heights, storing water in its huge spongy trunk.

When Alice arrived, the trees that signal human habitation on the bare plains of the Pampas—house, estancia, or small settlement—were still to be planted. Behind the house the very slight undulation indicates the proximity of the Ventana hills. No longer necessary—the Indians having been quelled—there is no *mirador* or lookout-tower, as there had been at San Carlos, from which to keep watch for raids or *malones*.

There is an account in Spanish by Briton of the enormous difficulties that JG confronted, now for a second time, in setting up an estancia: fencing off the vast territory, building corrals and barns, and putting up the house. All materials had to be carried in across long distances: wiring, fence-posts, bricks, corrugated iron for the roof, as well as everything else necessary for putting up and furnishing a house and lodgings for the many people who worked on the camp. Including the *capataz,* or overseer, there were some fifty peons and even a schoolmaster on the ranch. Workshops—for iron mongering, horse shoeing, carpentry and shearing—all had to be built with imported materials.

The Fuerte Argentino c. 1882. The barely visible figures are listed on the original as: AW (Alice), MAW (Marianne Walker) NW (William Norman Walker) JGW, and Harold

JG seems to have found a set of navigation maps in a bookshop—maps drawn up by none other than the talented Robert Fitzroy, commander of Darwin's *Beagle*. With these, he managed to persuade a ship's captain—unsure and fearful of the waters—to load his boat with all the necessary building materials and sail them in to Bahía Blanca. JG had to plant trees for shade, for fruit, for fire and building wood as well as a vegetable and, for Alice, a flower garden. He had to fence off the fields with the relatively new barbed wire that was now imported into Argentina by the mile, and, once the building was done, stock the place with animals: sheep, cattle, horses and poultry. He even had to construct roads that the bullock carts could handle. Briton describes the Walker's own eight-room house as being well-built, with bricks made on site and a corrugated iron roof. The floors and ceilings were made of a mysterious material, that Briton calls *chumbre*.[5] He makes a point of the fact that they now also acquired the rare luxury of a bathroom.

JG seems to have had a quantity of people helping him, including several *mayordomos*, managers of his own. Some, like 'Mr. Murie', lived on the vast property in estancia houses that, presumably, they erected with their own hands. On the grounds of the *Fuerte Argentino* was a construction, dubbed *Adobe Hall*, with its own kitchen. It was here that the farm assistants and *mayordomos*—one of whom was Richard Pettigrew, that prolific father of over twenty children—and other *transitorios* or people passing through, took their meals.

Water, whether in surfeit or shortage, was often a serious problem. A project for an irrigation system was drawn up, but Briton—sent off to school in England in 1886 when he was twelve—never knew whether or not it had been carried out. In the meantime, they used what he describes as a *noria*, advertised in the *Standard* of January 14, 1874 as the 'Salvation of the Camp.' This system of two connected wheels, one slung with buckets was a 'perfect machine for drawing water from wells'. A horse or donkey walking in circles, hour after hour, day in day out drove the machine. Briton describes the *noria* placed near the roses that Alice had planted.

If scarce above ground, water could be drawn from deep in the earth by windmills, those great Eiffel-like constructions topped with a huge bladed wheel. At the time relatively rare, they soon became a common part of the landscape around every estancia house in the Pampas.

---

[5] Neither Carlos, nor the dictionaries, nor our various Argentine friends have been able to tell me what 'chumbre' is.

A Pampas Windmill

The main house of the *Fuerte Argentino* was about 300 meters from the banks of the Sauce Chico River. Generally relatively gentle, this temperamental stream sometimes swelled into a flood so ferocious that it invaded the house itself, driving its inhabitants not out but up onto the roof. Briton remembers the rescue of a family whose rancho, near the banks of the equally unpredictable Sauce Grande, had been hit by the water. The flood rose so fast, so furious that it tore off the roof, casting it and its cargo of passengers—mother, father and children had all fled to the rooftop—onto the roaring waters. They survived, dragged to safety with ropes thrown to them by George Catty. Pasturing animals, too, could suddenly find themselves in water so deep that heaving on lassoes thrown around the animals' heads or horns was the only way of saving them.

With life on the camp less dangerous, it was now possible for the Walkers to have guests. In 1881, JG received a visit from his sister Marianne, and in 1883 Alice's sister, Emmy, arrived. Several of the colonists decided to settle down and marry. Among them was Henry Alfred Barber who returned from England to his estancia *La Lena* on the Sauce Grande with his bride, an art student.

Twigs of a Tree

His neighbour, George Christie Catty (1850-1936), Alice's brother, in 1882 travelled to Bath in England and married, in October, 'Aunt Robin', Mary Barbara Cross (1849-1888). She arrived at his estancia on the Sauce Grande with her two children, Leslie and Sidney Wilson, sons of her former husband, the lost sea captain. She also brought with her two stepdaughters, Lillie and Jean Wilson. The boys would be Briton's play- and classmates at the lessons conducted by Mr. Dauber.

A year later, on August 8, 1883, George Catty's daughter Annie Alice Catty—to be known as Elsie—was born. She was only to be christened about five months later. Her brother George Frederick Gordon, born on June 5, 1886, was to wait over a year, until September 1887, for his official entry into the church.[6] On January 10, 1884, my grandmother Alice Melrose Walker—JG and Alice's only daughter—was born in Bahía Blanca and registered at the British Consulate nine months later.

Briton, Melrose, Harold and Norman, photographed in England some years later.

George Catty's two new stepdaughters, Jean and Lillie Wilson, were soon off his hands. On September 7, 1887, Jean Wilson, now 19, married

---

[6] Baptism 7/9/1887 Catty, George Frederic Gordon, (birth 5/6/1886) father, George Ernest, mother, Mary Barbara, Estancia El Divisorio, Partido Pringles Estanciero

Charles Upton Cazalet[7], and the following June young Jean Wilson Cazalet was back in Buenos Aires with JG and George Catty at St. John's church. There they witnessed the marriage of Jean Cazalet's 21-year old sister Lillie Wilson, to an Englishman, G.A. Baldock.[8]

For George Catty much of the joy over these unions and the recent births of his own two children, now around five and two, was soon to be shattered. By the end of 1888 his wife, Mary Barbara, aka Aunt Robin, was, after seven years of marriage, dead at the age of 38. Like her first husband, she seems to have died at sea.[9] The next we hear of Alice's brother George—now suddenly left, no doubt more than bewildered, with four young children on his hands—is his somewhat precipitous marriage to his housekeeper, Enid Lawrence, in about 1890. Many years after George's own death in 1935, Enid Lawrence was still living at one end of the Moldes house in Belgrano, with the widowed Briton and Melrose.

---

[7] 07/09/1887 Cazalet, Charles Upton, 25, Bahía Blanca, Estanciero Peter Grenville Cazalet Wilson, Jean, 22, Estancia Divisorio, Coronel Pringles James Wilson Ed. Chance, M. B. Catty, George E. Catty Estancia Divisorio, Coronel Pringles RobtA

[8] 7/6/1888 Baldock, George Arthur 22, England, Buenos Aires Wilson, Lillie Sharpe 21 Cape of Good Hope, Buenos Aires, M. B. Catty, F. C. Pembroke-Jones, Maud Pembroke-Jones, J. G. Walker, Jean Cazalet, George E. Catty Pelham Ogle after banns St John's Church

[9] Death notice NOV 18th 1888 aboard the S.S.HEVELIUS Mary Barbara wife of George E. CATTY Sauce Grande, Bahia Blanca Buenos Ayres only daughter of the late James L CROSS, Liverpool

CHAPTER XIV

CHILDREN'S PARADISE
Estancia life between *Fuerte Argentino* and *La Susana*

In the eighteen-eighties the entrepreneur Ernesto Tornquist was settling, with the help of JG, the land previously roamed by Mapuche tribes near the Sierra de la Ventana. In 1883, Tornquist founded the town that still carries his name. At the same time an enterprising Irishman, Edward Casey (1842-1906), was occupied in a similar manner some six hundred kilometres directly north of Bahia Blanca. In this part of the 'wet' Pampas—on the southern tip of Santa Fé province, now also safe from Indian incursions—Edward Casey that same year founded his own township. It carried the curious name of Venado Tuerto, the town of the One-eyed Deer. According to Landaburu, this good-looking and morally upright Irishman bought up, with backing from English banks, some 170-leagues of land that he later vigorously advertised and auctioned off at enormous profit to himself. Like Tornquist, he subdivided the land into small plots of about a league each and sold them off on easy conditions. Casey also bought up some 100 leagues around Loreto, east of present-day Venado Tuerto, and even ventured for territory as far south as Bahia Blanca.[10] Baring Brothers & Co. was one of the banks that helped finance Casey's acquisitions.

Among the men who attended Casey's land-auctions was William Davison (1836-1898), great grandfather to Derek and Brian Dyson. Described as a 'contractor', Davison had arrived in Argentina—Rosanna

---

[10] Landaburu, *Gringos*, 1991, p.30

Davison tells us—from Sheffield in 1884, at the relatively advanced age of forty-eight.[1] In 1885, on land that he had bought from Casey, William Davison founded the estancia *La Susana,* near San Eduardo in Santa Fé province. Molly Dyson believed that Davison also acquired interests in the Buenos Aires dockyards and considerable property in the capital city.

A number of still familiar names appear in Landaburu's book, *Gringos.* He tells us that Frederick Bridger did a survey of the territory for Casey and was rewarded with the two leagues that today make up the estancia *Bentworth,* one of the *Susana's* immediate neighbours. The daughters of the last male descendant, Frederick or 'Bicho' Bridger, have recently taken over the property. Landaburu mentions the *Beatriz* of the MacNie family, also acquired in the 1880's—and ultimately inherited (and sold decades later) by my childhood playmate Robert MacNie.

The bungalow-style houses of the *Susana* and *Bentworth* appear to have been designed by the same architect. Each is a charming variation of the design then used for the many train-stations that were, during the 1880's, springing up all over the country with the expansion of the British-built railway network. Today, the houses are set off by lovely park-like gardens, their verandas overlooking bright lawns streaked with shade from the—now gigantic—trees.

Another view of La Susana

---

[1] Rosanna Davison's DVD entitled *Where we Come From,* sent to me by Susie Cogan, Brian Dyson's daughter.

For a while, the only insight we have into JG's family estancia life comes from the childhood recollections of his son Briton[2] and of Elinor Barber, the first child of the recently married Henry Barber. George Catty, their neighbour, was still in the Sauce Grande area on his estancia *El Divisorio*. The estancia managed by JG, *Fuerte Argentino*, was at a considerable distance to the west, on the Sauce Chico river; Briton cannot have seen his maternal uncle, or his young cousins—Annie Alice/Elsie born 1883 and Frederick Gordon born 1886—very frequently.

Briton describes the 'very nice house' of the 1880's near the Sauce Chico as a 'lovely place to live in'. The children apparently all have their own horses, although it is not really surprising that—as Briton writes—'Melrose did not do much riding before she was two . . .' The children go on picnics with guests, while the men go shooting. It is now safe for the children to ride very long distances by themselves. One horse called Chico Blanco sometimes carried as many as five young ones at once, 'including Norman's two brothers and his sister'. The children ride through Alsina's ditch, which was dug—as Briton says with his perennial sense of the ironic—'to keep the bad Indians from killing the good—or not so bad—white people.'

The children ride to the river to bathe, passing through a gate labelled: 'Cerrá la puerta, sonso' or 'Shut the gate, you fool'—a piece of JG wit directed at his illiterate peons, but that could only be read by his (presumably literate) guests. Elinor Barber has a canoe to play with and they all swim in the streams and lagoons. Briton and his brothers watch—as I was not allowed to do—the branding of horses and cattle with a T—presumably for 'Tornquist'. They cringe in horror at the agonised bellowing reverberating across the countryside as the red-hot branding irons come down on the animals' flesh.

The young people make excursions for sweets and biscuits to the shop near the soldiers' camp—perhaps in those days correctly, rather than ironically, named the 'Sin Nada'—Nothing to be Had—or to the new telegraph office. Briton basks in the salutations of 'Hola, patroncito!' or 'Como te va, Cortaplumas?'—'Hi, little master' or 'How are you doing, Penknife?'

They revel in the antics of Nancy, their pet guanaco. Nancy 'could jump higher than any horse', but once, while foraging for food in the

---

[2]   J.B. Walker, *Children in the Camp, A Long Time Ago*.

kitchen, gets her head stuck in a biscuit tin. She survives the mishap with nothing worse than sore ears, but was much later shipped off 'on a passenger ship' to the Antwerp Zoo by JG's successors at the *Fuerte Argentino*. When this was, who the successors were, and why JG left the *Fuerte*—Briton does not say.

Forbidden to Nancy, 'who got in the way' and 'burned her tail on the oven', the kitchen always welcomed any number of baby ostriches. The *ñandus* with expert flicks of their long and elastic necks, performed the useful task of ridding the kitchen of clouds of flies. The children rewarded the birds by caressing their feathers. When they grew too big for the kitchen, the *ñandus* were set free to roam the estancia with their wild brethren. There were dogs, armadilloes and skunks, and Briton recorded the children's delight in the birds: redbreasts, woodpeckers and swallows. They rode about visiting JG's various *mayordomos*—most apparently British—who managed different parts of the vast property: there was Mr Murie, Mr Barnes with his dogs, a Mr MacFarlane and the prolific Mr Pettigrew with his twenty children. But the English were not everywhere. Elinor tells us that the Barbers had a nursemaid, Amelia, 'who speaks no English, while the children speak no Spanish'.

JG seems to have left an impression and inspired considerable affection among the military. One day in 1881 Briton was arguing with his 'very tall, thin and severe' Aunt Marianne, JG's unmarried sister, visiting from England. He was contesting her spelling of the word 'house'. While young Briton, still unfamiliar with the inconsistencies of the English language, insisted that the third letter of the word house could only be a W, as in 'how', his sound but refutable logic was suddenly lost in the music of a loud band. Trumpets, flutes, clarinets, trombones, drums and bugles assembled by the local soldiery had been marched several miles across the Pampas to surprise Facón Chico with a celebration of his fortieth birthday on the 5th of April.

Wine and an *asado* by the river with musical accompaniment followed. Aunt Marianne, who now wore the confirmed spinster's lace cap like an 'upside down boat' and kept 'everyone in his place', threw in the towel over the spelling argument and left. 'She, disliking the music, retired to her room . . . The little boys were not very sorry, as they preferred the band.'

The boys enjoyed watching the circling horse working the waterwheel—the strange *noria*—in the garden, where Alice had planted her flowers. They also helped with the dipping of the sheep, Briton's 'silly animals', in tobacco juice to save them from the scab.

Like the other children, Elinor Barber cowered in terror when the *pamperos* hit. The dry storms of tearing wind with not a drop of rain were particularly frightening. But generally, for the child Elinor, life on the estancia was—as for Briton and Norman, for me and my cousin Diana over half a century later—often an enchantment or, as Elinor described it, 'free and wonderful'. Elinor tells us that the only 'nearby' friends of her own age were Elsie and Gordon Catty.[3] They lived on the next camp, George Catty's estancia *El Divisorio*, a 'very long ride away'.

Elinor Barber has a keen eye for the beauties of the 'hot and dry straw-colorations of summer', the 'sparkling icicles and frost ferns' of winter, and for the

brilliant flower-studded greens of spring that also brought with it whole acres of lavender-coloured verbena and myriad other wild flowers, including the morning glories.

These were so beautiful and abundant that she and the other children tried, but gave up, the effort of trying to count them. The 'sharp-peaked clear blue of the Sierras (that) danced and twisted like a mirage' were as enchanting to her as they were for Briton.

Elinor describes the admiration, the sheer thrill of watching the young horses being broken in, the extraordinary, often dangerous riding. 'The Gauchos could ride . . . they rode until the horse had bucked to a finish . . .' But this courageous horsemanship seems to have had a price. 'It was said', she goes on, 'that few of these horse-breakers lived to any age owing to their internal injuries.'

Once a year, JG's now huge flock of 50.000 Tornquist sheep had to be shorn. Elinor describes the bands of Italians who crossed the Atlantic for the season's work. They so shattered the quiet of the camp with their 'shouting, singing, accordion-playing, fighting and near-murdering' that all were delighted when they finally left. Among the *quintas* (small market gardens) around the city of Buenos Aires she notes other 'grinning Italians making wine, dancing barefoot in barrels of grapes to squash out the juice'.

Briton tells us that Eusebio was one of the Tornquist 'shearing gang'. After an excess of celebratory drink at the 'pay-day party', he actually

---

[3] Annie Alice Catty (1884-1918), known as Elsie, Briton's cousin and future wife, and George Frederick Gordon Catty (1886-1949), known as Gordon.

fell into the cooking pot, a 'cauldron the size used . . . to boil asphalt'. Eusebio was so badly scalded that JG, after sprinkling the burns with flour, wrapped up the injured man and sent him to the British Hospital in Bahia Blanca and then on to Buenos Aires. There the volatile Italian went for the doctor with a knife, so he was returned to the estancia, but his back remained 'so shrivelled that he never walked well again'.

Briton delights in the 'dark, chocolaty-coloured eggs' of partridges, the swallows' nests in the riverbanks and the call of the *tero-teros*. Then there are the round and mysterious mud-nests built by the ovenbirds, the *horneros* that I, too, used to admire and get off my horse to inspect. The eggs inside the little mud globes, sitting on fence posts like brimless bowler hats, could never be seen beyond the curve so cleverly engineered by the birds. Later young Harold Walker collected a nest and sent it to London, where it and its post were displayed in the city's Natural History Museum.

One of the estancia delights for me were the long solitary rides to the lagoon, home to the eccentric flamingos. Flocks stood, as they still do, in the waters, ruminating philosophically on one leg, barely moving, for hours at a time. If anyone approaches to take a closer look, they rise into the skies with a noisome flapping of wings—glorious clouds of pink streaked with scarlet.[4]

The flamingo

---

[4] The old mystery of the single leg has recently been solved. Nature's arrangement of a single leg in the water, the other folded under the body, keeps the birds warm.

There were the exhilarating gallops through the fields. Once, near the house, I was thrown into a cowpat with a messy splat and had to submit to an ignominious wipe-down by my tut-tutting grandmother. There were the butterflies hovering in great clouds of colour—yellow, white, purple, pink, depending on the species—over Molly's flowers; the blue-black skies studded with all the stars of the universe; the squirt of milk into a steaming bucket as dark hands pumped at long pink teats in the milking shed; the treasure of a smooth brown egg found under a hen—or the tiny ones, nested like jewels—blue, yellow, white or speckled—swaying in their nests high on a tree. I, at first resisting temptation to take more than one for a little collection, then left them all. Sometimes the high nests offered not eggs, but just a mass of open mouths and beaks, clamouring for food, for life.

There was the music of the croaking frogs from the side of the veranda and the fireflies that I once collected into a glass jar to see if they could produce a glow strong enough to read under the sheets after my lights had been firmly turned off. They did not, so I crept out and released them into the night. Crumbs stolen from the bread-bag hanging in the kitchen sometimes enticed the mysterious goldfish upwards from the dark and silent depths of the round 'Australian' tank near the windmill.

There were the sleepy journeys in the back of the car after a day of cricket and tennis for the grown-ups at the club in Venado; rides on the horse-pulled lawn-mower. Once the feeding of my linen hat (those irritating garments we had to wear) into the whirring blades of the mower—a strictly scientific experiment on my part—got me into trouble. The green trail behind the mower indeed suddenly burst magically into textile flower; Jackie Dyson, the kind warden of linen hats, was not entirely convinced by the hopeful but consciously guilty suggestion that it had all been the fault of the wind.

There were the huge gates—*tranqueras*—that, with practice, could be opened from a horse's back even by a child; the tap of croquet mallets, the thump of tennis ball and racquet. There were the books in the back room—two whole cases of children's books. The more difficult ones I read with the help of my grandmother, Melrose. The garden of the *Susana* was then, in the 1940's, fully grown into the full beauty of its maturity. A child could read hanging in the fruit-trees, or pretend the branches were ships sailing the seas. There was the wood where we dug a 'house' into the ground and then thatched with branches.

There was a swimming pool. Built, according to Molly, by the Goodbody brothers in 1919, it was placed not in, but rather on the ground, standing like a shoebox between orchard and tennis court. One end had a wooden platform reached by a steep staircase, the other end looked into the woods. There were then possibly few or no chemicals, not even a filtering system for keeping the water clean. The pool was regularly emptied and refilled with a thrilling rush and fall of fresh water, pumped from the ground.

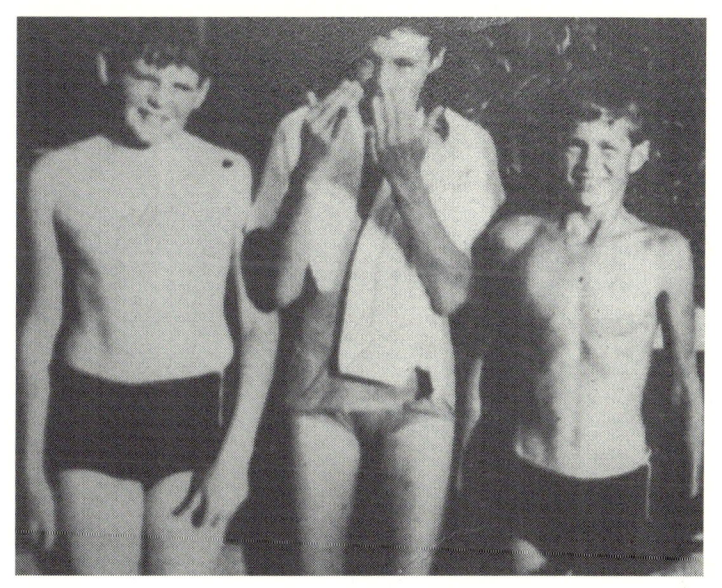

Robert McNie, Lin and David Adams at the Susana Pool c.1952

Diana McClure recalls the still relatively primitive conditions of the estancia near Tandil that her father Martin Eggar managed in the 1940's. Even then, there was often no electricity and no refrigerator or 'ice chest'. As in the laundry shed of the Susana, clothes were still washed and scrubbed by hand on wooden boards and smoothed with huge black irons heated by placing them near a stove or with smaller hinged irons filled with hot coals.

Diana looks back on visits from JG's son Briton—by then her grandfather—the 'kind old man who told us stories':

My grandfather was our most frequent visitor, and we loved his visits. He wrote stories for his grandchildren, made us a wigwam and a canvas hammock, and made each of us a wooden farmhouse. Christie and I spent happy hours playing with those farms. He was the *ideal grandfather. Sometimes friends from Tandil or a neighbouring estancia would come and stay, and in January 1949 our cousin Lin stayed with us . . . She introduced us to a new game, cowboys and Indians. We were* the *Indians and* the *other children* on the *estancia were* the *cowboys. We captured Carlitos, a small boy, and tied him to a tree.*

Choosing to be Indians was the ticket to wildness; I hope that Carlitos did not sustain any lasting psychological injury. Like Elinor fifty years before, Diana also describes the scarcity and distance of doctors; how her mother Betty kept a book listing the symptoms of the most common childhood illnesses, so that she could self-diagnose and do any necessary doctoring herself.

There was an outbreak of aftosa (foot-and-mouth disease) in the *Friesian herd. My mother never boiled* the *milk and we all came down with aftosa—a most unpleasant illness, with a high fever and swollen gums. I was back in Buenos Aires when I got aftosa, and kind Dr Cooper came round and injected me with a new medicine that had just arrived from Europe, called penicillin. He told me that* the *illness only affected my mouth—and not my feet—because I didn't have hooves.*

My own earliest introduction to the fearsome mystery of death and disease was on my solitary rides. Every now and again the beauty of the sounds and sights of the swaying Pampas was overwhelmed by a terrible stench. Then, inevitably, in the long grasses appeared the body of a cow, a horse or other animal. Pullulating with microscopic, crawling life, the carcasses were guarded by ferocious vultures crouched in such numbers that the sight of the birds sitting on their foul-smelling meal could set a horse rearing onto its hind legs.

Once my tall handsome cousins, Derek and Brian, took me with them on a shoot, and I learnt how easily the glorious arc and sweep of flight could be wiped from the sky. Consigned to the role of bearer, I noted how different a flying bird looked from the limp iridescent object hanging dead from my hands. For several days after that I avoided speaking to my cousins.

Latin and the Three 'R's

One of the huge problems of life on the camp was the schooling of children. For Elinor Barber—born in 1884, the same year as Melrose[5]—the only boredom was lesson-time. Children didn't attend school but were taught at home by parents or relations. The Barbers had a young unmarried aunt who for five years gave lessons from 'little reading books she had written herself'. Briton, his two young brothers and their newly arrived cousins-by-marriage, Sidney and Leslie Wilson, were first taught by Alice, then for a while by JG's sister, Marianne. Very strict and religious, she was not too popular with the children, but she spent three or four years on the Pampas staying with JG's family or with her missionary friends, the Spillsburys. Finally, as they grew bigger, the children—or at least the boys—were schooled by a tutor, Mr Dauber.

A surgeon by profession, Mr Dauber had been to college with a nephew of Alice's. In Argentina, he had become a 'bear-leader', a schoolteacher, supplementing his teaching with the treatment of the victims of 'accidents, illnesses, or fights' on JG's camp. One of his patients was a cart-man run over by his own brick-loaded wagon, another was the unfortunate wife of a gaucho whose husband stabbed her 'in twenty places, all calculated to finish her off'. However, under the ministrations of Dr Dauber, the resilient gaucho lady—as Briton dryly remarks—'got over it'.

Since Briton, on the Sauce Chico, and his cousins Leslie and Sidney, on the Sauce Grande, did not live close to one another, the young Wilson boys were 'packed off to the *Fuerte Argentino*, moving in with JG and Alice'. Here they attended Mr Dauber's classes of 'Arithmetic, Latin, and *The curfew tolls the knell of parting day . . .* '. Once Dauber, whose interests and skills clearly ranged well beyond the inflections of Latin nouns and the poetry of Thomas Gray, discovered the corpse of an Indian. After having dug up the body and 'boiled him in a big cauldron', he carefully linked the bones into a skeleton. With this Dr. Dauber clearly envisaged some serious instruction in anatomy.

Diana (Eggar) McClure—living near Tandil on an estancia in the 1940's—began school at the relatively late age of nearly seven. She shows us that, over half a century later, schooling on the Pampas had not progressed enormously:

---

[5] (Born) 7/10/1884 (Christened) 16/11/1884 Barber, Elinor (sic) (father) Henry James Alfred, (mother) Agnes Ashby, La Leña, Sauce Grande, (profession) Estanciero.

There were two other children of school-age on the estancia when I started school in March 1947: Titina and Negro, the foreman's children and a boy from a nearby puesto (outpost)

We usually rode together to school through a potrero, along the track down to the main road, which was a narrow dirt road with wide grass verges. The school was about an hour's ride down the road. It was very unusual to see any motor traffic, but we occasionally met cattle being herded along the grass verges . . . . Many of the children helped their families with the milking. Because of this, school began in the early afternoon. With the exception of one family of five children, who came to school in a light cart pulled by one horse, we all rode to school. The horses would have a sheepskin tied on with a girth, and no saddle or stirrups (considered unnecessary for a child), and they'd wait patiently, tied up to the fence outside the schoolhouse until lessons finished, three or four hours later. There was no school on very rainy days. About 30 children, aged between six and fourteen, sat in one large classroom and were taught by one teacher. The teacher, Srta. Echevarria (of Basque descent), would arrive early and write out work on the blackboard for each year (there were seven years of primary education). She would ring a bell when lessons were due to start, and we'd line up outside, boys on one side, girls on the other, smallest children at the front, tallest at the back. We had to place a hand on the shoulder of the child in front, to make sure we were the correct distance apart. The Argentine flag would be raised, we'd sing the national anthem, and then we'd go in to school in an orderly file. Before we entered the school-house, we had to show our hands to the teacher, who'd check that they were clean.

We wore the standard Argentine school uniform: a long-sleeved white overall. The boys' apron buttoned down the front, the girls' apron had a fitted bodice and a pleated skirt, and did up at the back. When we reached school on Monday, the aprons were white, starched, beautifully ironed. By Saturday (we went to school six days a week) they were a very dirty grey . . . . I think Argentine education at that time was based on the French system. It involved a lot of learning by rote and was something of which the country could rightly be proud: illiteracy was almost unknown. All the children left that small country school with a good grounding in written Spanish and in arithmetic; we were also taught Argentine history and geography, the catechism, and in the last period on Saturday afternoons the girls did some sewing . . . Our teacher was strict on discipline. Any girl or small boy who misbehaved had to stand in the corner; older boys (who rather gloried in standing in the corner) had to kneel on maize . . . The horses looked forward to the end of lessons almost as much as the children did, and would gallop home much faster than they'd jogged along to the school. When we got home, we'd remove the sheepskin, take our horse to the Australian tank and pour a bucket of water over her back (we rode a mare), remove her bridle, and she'd race off and roll in the dust before settling down to graze. Horses on an estancia didn't get much TLC. [6]

In 1886, when Briton was barely twelve, he was taken to England to the 'Catty ancestral home' in Bournemouth and placed in Wimborne School.[7] We do not know whether or not he was a boarder. The Wilson children attended a school in Buenos Aires run by the Spillsburys, Marianne Walker's friends. It is possible that Marianne also taught there for a while. Norman, according to Briton, was eventually sent to King's College School, Wimbledon. Melrose, still only two, stayed behind with her five-year old brother Harold and presumably went on as a student of the women she called, until the end of her life, 'those ignorant governesses'.

Elinor Barber, however, tells us that, for her family, school in England was a luxury far beyond its means. The Barbers had been on their estancia *La Leña* on the Sauce Grande since the very beginnings of the colony in 1868. But as his children grew, Elinor's father began studying copies of the *Auckland Weekly*, sent to him by his sister. Unable to incur the expense of sending his children to school in England, he was attracted by New Zealand's 'good free primary education and the beautiful scenery'. Barber and his whole family—after thirty years of effort in Argentina—pulled up roots in 1898 and re-emigrated to New Zealand. Their descendants are still there today.

Ruin in the Belle Époque

In 1890, under the presidency of Miguel Juárez Celman (1886-1890), a financial crisis caused by the 'most scandalous political corruption in the nation's history', bankrupted the Argentine government, destroyed

---

[6] *Growing up on the Pampas*, by Diana McClure, February 2010
[7] Where this 'ancestral' home was or why it was in Bournemouth I have no idea.

Twigs of a Tree

many private fortunes, and—had it not been rescued—almost brought down the London Bank of Baring Bros.[8] This big bust in the middle of the boom years brought many to their knees, but Ernesto Tornquist himself remained relatively unscathed. He went on to build, in 1902, a palatial neo-gothic estancia house that he called *La Ventana*, after the range of hills that broke the flatness of the Pampas north-east of the Sauce Chico.[9]

Edward Casey of Venado Tuerto, however, was ruined. Returning to England he managed, through his share in the Midlands railways, to recoup part of his fortune. This he then, on his return to Argentina, proceeded to distribute among the victims of his speculations. In 1906, forgotten and impoverished, he laid himself down on the tracks of a railway line. He is buried in the cemetery of Venado Tuerto, the town he founded.[10] William Davison too, like so many others, lost almost everything. All he retained, Molly tells us, was the *Susana*.

It is not quite clear what course JG's own life was taking at this time. In the year of the financial bust, 1890, he was in Adrogué near Buenos Aires, but whether he was living there or merely visiting is not clear. It is also not clear whether he was still working with Ernesto Tornquist, or whether he had already moved to the estancia *La Mancha*, near Las Colinas in the province of Buenos Aires. However, on November 5, 1891, Alice's youngest child, Alfred English, always to be known, somewhat illogically, as Eric, came into the world.[11] If he was born in England, this would indicate another visit by Alice to her family and to her two oldest sons after their departure from Argentina around 1886.

Briton and Norman were still in England and at school. In the census of 1891 Briton (16) and Norman (13) are registered in their grandfather's household as 'scholars'. Frederick Adam Catty by then had moved from Antwerp House to Meadow Lodge, Cambridge Park, Twickenham. He was now, according to the census, living with

---

[8] Argentina *Gesta Britannica*, Tomo II, parte B, Emilio Manuel Fernández-Gomes.
[9] This was somewhat in the manner of the great landowners, the 'silver chamber pot' crowd who had long been importing, at vast cost, the materials to build grand estancia houses, some of them modelled on French chateaux.
[10] Landaburu, p. 36.
[11] I cannot find his birth registered on the Arg. Brit. Site. It may be that he was born in England as stated on Claire Dulanty's Ancestry site which gives his birth as '. . . . England, 1891', with no further details.

a somewhat smaller family: his wife Ann, his daughter Emmy, two grandsons, and two servants.

In February 1892 JG lost his beloved cousin, long-time friend and fellow-adventurer. Henry Edwards had fallen ill in November of 1891 and in spite of all medical efforts died on January 24, 1892, of a 'cerebral congestion' at the relatively early age of fifty. The publication *River Plate Sport and Pastime* of the following Wednesday, gave him an admiring obituary with a somewhat clumsy conclusion:

It is with great regret that we have to announce the death of Mr Henry John Edwards, which occurred on the 24th *inst after a long and painful illness. Mr Edwards, perhaps better known by his sobriquet Facón Grande, was one of the earliest pioneers in the Southern camps and, in company with his friends and companions in arms, did more to protect life and property against the frequent raids of the Indians than whole regiments of soldiers could have done. Always living outside the lines of defence, many are the stories told of his pluck and daring, combined with the promptness of action in saving the lives of settlers further in, and he was held in such awe by the Indians, they feared his revolver to such an extent, that it is related on one occasion he scattered a whole crowd of them by simply pointing a pipe case at them. Genial, hearty, courteous and brave, we can ill spare men like Harry Edwards, and of few can it more truly be said: "He has done his level best".*

John George Walker and his cousin Henry Edwards[12]

---

[12] Wrongly identified, since JG on the left was Facon Chico, and Edwards, Facon Grande, is on the right. The photo comes from a historical article about the two men published in the Bahia Blanca paper, *La Nueva Provincia,* on January 15, 1984

Edwards was, it seems, buried in Azul, but some years later his wife, Hélène, moved his remains to the Chacarita cemetery in Buenos Aires. We lose sight of Edwards' family after his death, but, according to Briton, Hélène and her six children were left 'stony-broke'. Two of the girls, Elena and Louise, were sent to live with JG and Alice, probably at the *La Mancha* estancia. Their daughter Ninette moved in with George Catty, and Lucie was sent off to a 'de Bernardy' aunt who lived in the Argentine. Hélène began a boarding house with the help, at first, of her unwilling children, who, as Briton put it, were made to 'slave in the kitchen, make the beds and put up with the attentions of the indifferently mannered paying guests'.

Death hit again two months later, on April 3, 1892. Alice's father Frederick Adam Catty, according to his friend A.G. Temple, was, in spite of his 89 years, still working on his Italian and reading novels to his wife, Ann. When he died, they were enjoying a work by Ouida, the novelist known as the 'passionate Victorian'.[13]

Briton was then old enough—and the right gender—to attend Frederick Adam's 'stately funeral' at Twickenham cemetery. At that time in England, women who were not corpses themselves, were not generally admitted to funerals. As Briton remarks drily: 'no women'. He sat in the fourth coach with George Henty, the journalist and novelist. Frederick Adam's death was acknowledged with a long obituary. It may have given his daughter, Alice, far away in Argentina, a small measure of comfort.[14] The *City Press* of April 6, 1892, p.5 reads:

> Many of our readers, especially those who are old Corporators, will learn with sincere regret of the decease, on Sunday last, of Mr Frederick A. Catty, F.R.C.S., the late chief clerk in the Town Clerk's office at Guildhall. After long and faithful service, the deceased, it will be remembered, retired a few years since on full pension, which was unanimously granted to him by the Court. Mr Catty, who was 89 years of age, had been ailing for some few weeks, but until a very short time before the end the family had no idea at all that he would so soon be taken from amongst them. The interment takes place tomorrow at Twickenham Cemetery, at one o'clock.

---

[13] Maria Louisa Ramé (1839-1908), otherwise known as Ouida, was a hugely successful novelist.

[14] The obituary has been generously passed to me by Meryl Catty.

Three days later, on April 9, 1892, the paper continued:
Many of our readers, we doubt not, will be glad to learn further particulars concerning the life and interesting career of Mr Frederick Adam Catty, whose decease on Sunday last it was our melancholy duty to record in Wednesday's issue of the City Press. Mr Catty, on the paternal side, was of French nationality, being the son of Monsieur Louis Catty, who in the year 1793 came to England in order to accept the position of Professor of French at the Royal Military College, Woolwich. The mother of Mr Catty was Miss Mary A. Christie, the sister of the late Professor Christie, of Cambridge. Born at Woolwich in the year 1803, Mr Catty, after receiving his education at a local school, studied at Guy's hospital with the object of entering the medical profession. Subsequently he visited Paris, with a view to studying the treatment of gunshot wounds. As a boy, it is of interest to note, he was a constant visitor to Paris, staying while there as a guest of Talma, the great tragedian, and M. Belard, the eminent advocate. On returning from France, fully qualified to enter upon the practice of his profession, Mr Catty took up his residence at Cambridge, where he practised for some years, subsequently migrating with his wife—the daughter of the late Dr Edwards, of Putney—to Ems, in which City he resided until his return to England in the year 1851. He then became private secretary to Sir John Musgrove, afterwards entering civic life and acting as secretary at the Mansion House to several Lord Mayors. Eventually, in the year 1859, he bid adieu to the Mansion House and accepted an official position under the Corporation, being appointed managing clerk in the Town Clerks' office, a post he filled with distinction until the year 1881, when he finally retired, being granted a full pension by the Court in recognition of his long and honourable services. Though then advanced in years, Mr Catty, unlike not a few who relinquish office, did not wholly abandon his active pursuits, for he entered with spirit into the study of the Italian language, in which he eventually became as fluent as he was in French and German. Up to within a few days of his decease, Mr Catty enjoyed all his faculties, and was able to enjoy life to the very full. To mourn their loss he leaves behind a widow and nine children, besides a large circle of friends, amongst whom are numbered many who still have fond memories of the old days when he was one of the most respected and zealous servants the

Corporation possessed. By them, indeed, he will be fondly remembered so long as life lasts.

Not long after Frederick Adam's death, JG and Alice received what was the first of a series of particularly terrible blows. [15]

A bare two years after his grandfather's death young Norman fell horribly ill. On May 27, 1894 he died at Frederick Adam's residence, in the arms, not of his mother, but of his widowed aunt, Mary Shearman. His death certificate cites him as having been diagnosed with an accumulation of medical calamities, 'Scarlatinal Rheumatism, Pericarditis, Endocarditis, Dilation and valvular disease of Heart'.

Only sixteen years old, there were no published obituaries for young Norman, but he was laid to rest next to his grandfather in Twickenham Cemetery. Meryl Catty tells us that the grave is damaged, the cross, broken, the inscription largely effaced. This can, however, still be read in part: 'In Loving Memory of (on broken off part of cross) . . . Frederick Adam . . . born July . . . Died at Twickenham . . . Ann widow of the . . . .' A second inscription reads:

In memory of William Norman Walker, Grandson of the above, born November 1877, died May 27th 1894.[16]

We know little about Norman, apart from Briton's descriptions of his mischievous antics on the camp, his courage with animals—including the story of his fearless capture of a snake while swimming in a river. According to Angela Walker Huber, there are a couple of cups in the family that carry the King's College School crest, tokens of boat races won by Norman at school. The effect on Briton, nearing twenty, was dire. He never forgot him. When Briton had a son of his own—Angela's father—he named him 'Norman' after the little brother he had so much enjoyed as a child.

By the time Norman died in 1894, John George and Alice Walker seem to have left Ernesto Tornquist's estancia *Fuerte Argentino*. At least for some time after 1890, JG seems to have continued managing other men's

---

[15] The parents who had sent their 9 year-old son, William Norman, to school in England some six years before seem never to have seen him again. There is no record that Alice, unless Eric was indeed born in England in 1891, ever went to England in the years after Norman and Briton left Argentina around 1886. There is also no record of how, or with whom, the children reached England.

[16] This information comes from Meryl Catty's, *Descendants of Pierre Mignolet*,

farms. According to Briton's South Africa tale, JG 'ran for some years' an estancia for a Walter Congreve. Norman's death-certificate describes the place of his death as Heidelberg Lodge, Twickenham, and his father as 'John George Walker, a landed proprietor'. This last point is still something of a mystery, since *La Mancha* is not mentioned.[17]

In 1906, however, when, Eric, their fourth and youngest son, joined Bedford school, JG and Alice were still in Argentina and, by then were definitely on the *La Mancha* estancia.[18] The original building no longer exists. However, the present owner of *La Mancha*, Don Mariano Correa, has very kindly provided me with an old photograph of the British-style main building, or *casco*, before it burnt down many decades ago. We do not know the date of the fire or the photograph. It therefore does not necessarily show the estancia exactly as it was when JG and Alice lived there.

La Mancha, JG's property in Argentina

---

[17] The 'oficina del catastro', the archives office, in the municipality of La Madrid in Buenos Aires province cannot confirm when JG actually bought the estancia La Mancha, near the Las Colinas railway station; it claims no longer to have any records that go further back than 1944.

[18] The Bedford School records claim that Eric, born 5 November, 1891, entered the school in June 1906 and left at the end of the summer term 1910. His parents are given as J.G. Walker Esq and Mrs A. Walker of La Mancha, La Colina TCS, Buenos Aires. It was eventually sold, according to Alice's obituary, in 1910.

CHAPTER XV

BRITON, BOERS AND BULLETS

It was with his nickname or honorific of Facón Chico that JG Walker became a figure of popular legend and entered the Argentine history books. From Briton Walker's annotations we have no evidence that the son was in any way aware of his father's potential for a small slice of immortality. After all, Facón Chico had only defended his family and his property, assisting the Argentine army in punitive expeditions after attacks. JG's courage and determination can be explained by his need for his own and his family's survival.

But what impelled young John Briton Walker, to sail from Argentina across the South Atlantic to join a war in the southern tip of Africa? And what motivated his father, who had already lost one child—now that the terror and hardship of the Indian *malones* were over—to encourage his son in this enterprise by handing him three valuable horses to carry into battle?

By 1899, Briton Walker was about 26 years old. He had long left school and finished his engineer's training in England. By October of that year, when war broke out in the south of Africa, Briton had settled down in Argentina, the country of his birth and much of his early upbringing. Nevertheless, when the news of the war reached him, he almost immediately volunteered, ready to fight not just for England, which was not exactly under attack, but for the Queen and the expanding Empire.

Briton must have known that his uncle, Alfred Walker, JG's long deceased brother, had gone to Africa as a ship's doctor in 1866. By then the Cape had already fallen into the hands of the British, who were living in uneasy proximity to the two recently founded Afrikaner States of Transvaal and the Orange Free State.

In 1620, two British ship captains, in the manner of the *Conquistadores*, had, at a stroke of the pen and a wave of the sword, laid claim to 'all Africa' for their King, James I. It was not the British, however, but the servants of the Dutch East India Company who eventually founded a 'refreshment' station on the Cape for ships plying the spice-route to the Far East. This in time, with the erection of a fort and the cultivation and stocking of the land, developed into a god-fearing little Calvinistic community—mainly Dutch and German. The revocation, in 1685, of the Edict of Nantes that had guaranteed Protestants freedom of worship in France, added exiled French Huguenots to the European population mix. The whites traded with the nomadic Khoikhai or Hottentots and with the San or Bushmen. Many of these were also, together with other African tribes, forcibly incorporated into the pioneering community as slave labour.

By the end of the eighteenth century, the Dutch East India Company was bankrupt, but the population in southern Africa—descendants of the original Company servants around the Cape—now numbered about 20.000. Some 30.000 slaves attended them as field hands and domestic servants. Their language was Afrikaans, a derivative of Dutch. There was also a considerable mixed race population, known as 'Coloureds'.

Some of the Afrikaaners, the burghers, resided in the city of Cape Town under a governor, but about half of this Afrikaans-speaking population still lived a semi-nomadic life as pastoralists and subsistence farmers. Groups of these *trekboers* moved in their ox-carts through the countryside, constantly expanding the area of white settlement. As a result, 'a few thousand persons were scattered across an area as large as England'. As in Argentina, the natives—the San, Khoikhai and other indigenous tribes—often plundered the Boer laagers, or ox-cart settlements. Other tribes, including the Zulus in the east, would, like the Indians on the Argentine Pampas, later go to war to stem the incursion of the whites into their lands.

The Dutch and the British had fought four wars by the end of the eighteenth century. Having changed hands several times during the Napoleonic Wars, in 1816 the Afrikaner Cape Colony was declared British territory. This was followed, in 1820, by the settlement in the area of some 5.000 British. They were not easily assimilated. The Boers remained unhappy with English, the new official language, and with the new foreign government.

By then, British 'liberalism', with its Quaker and Wilberforcean anti-slavery ideas, was suspected of placing 'slaves on an equal footing with Christians, contrary to the laws of God'. When slavery was finally outlawed by London in 1833, the promised compensation to the slave-owners did not always materialize. As a result, many Boers and burghers loaded their ox-carts and set off on what is known as the 'Great Trek' in search of territory and independence in the western area of Natal and in the northeast, on either side of the Vaal river.

Massacres and attacks on the *trekboers* by the Zulu and the Matabele tribes followed, as well as further tussles with the British. Eventually, after the annexation of the new Afrikaner Republic of Natal in 1843, the British, in the 1850's, recognized the independence of two other recently founded Boer republics: the Orange Free State and the Transvaal, or South African Republic. Southern Africa was now divided into British Colonies, independent Afrikaner states and two Griqua—mixed race—states.

This was the situation when young Alfred, Briton's deceased uncle, made his trip to South Africa in 1866. In the 1870's, things changed. The still somewhat tepid British interest in the states around the Cape Colony was suddenly stirred into life and then fired into conflagration: first by the discovery of diamonds around what became the town of Kimberley in West Griqualand, and then by the discovery of gold. The British quickly claimed the Griqua state, but an attempt in 1877 to capture the Afrikaner Transvaal was soundly repulsed by the Boer General, Piet Cronje.

In the scramble of the 1880's, Germans, French, Belgians, Portuguese, British and Italians all laid claims to parts of Africa. Cecil Rhodes, who had become a mining magnate almost overnight, dreamed of a British Imperial Africa stretching 'from Cairo to the Cape'. More immediately, he aimed at a federated Southern Africa under British rule. The discovery of gold in 1886 in the Afrikaner states not only made the bankrupt Transvaal suddenly rich, but it also attracted thousands of mostly British prospectors. Alarmed at being outnumbered in their own territory, the Afrikaaners attempted to restrict the voting rights of the swarms of gold-hungry *uitlander*s, or outsiders. The franchise restriction became the pretext, first for the failed British Jameson-raid on the Transvaal in 1895 that cost Rhodes his job as head of the Cape Colony, and then for the clash that turned into the South African War, or Second Anglo-Boer War. It lasted from 1899 to 1902.[1]

At the outbreak of hostilities on October 11, 1899, the British immediately began casting about for volunteers in the furthest reaches of the globe: Australia, New Zealand, Canada and even in Argentina. Eventually some 90.000 Afrikaner forces faced a British army of 500.000 regulars and volunteers. Bystanders—African, Coloured and East Indian—were also drawn into the war: about 100.000 into the British Army and some 10.000 into the Boer forces.

After several months in the army, Briton was to find himself on a patrol with a force of Q.I.B's—Queensland Imperial Bushmen—from Australia. Among them was an Adams granduncle, Edward Buse Adams (1874-1946) who, although wounded, lived on and later joined the Australian troops in the First World War. These Q.I.B's, fighting in a war in which they had almost no stake, would hardly have appreciated their nickname: they were known, Briton reports, as the Queer Ignorant Beggars.[2]

The Boers began the war by laying siege to the towns of Ladysmith, Mafeking and Kimberley, where diamonds had been found. They inflicted a series of serious setbacks on their enemy, including the cutting of the railway and telegraph lines. However, during the year that Briton was in South Africa, the new commander Lord Roberts, with his vastly more numerous forces, managed to cut through much of the fierce Afrikaner resistance. Roberts launched a successful attack on the Orange Free State, putting Paul (or 'Ohm'—Uncle) Kruger, the Transvaal president, to flight. He then dispatched General Piet Cronje to commune with the ghost of Napoleon on the island of St. Helena and captured the Afrikaner capital cities of Bloemfontein and Pretoria.

---

[1] Sir Arthur Conan Doyle gives a blow-by-blow account of the war and its battles in his *Great Boer War* of 1902. The entire book can be seen on the net. Winston Churchill wrote an account of the campaign in which Briton Walker took part in *Ian Hamilton's March* (The Boer War).

[2] Briton has left a set of letters to his mother, father and his sister Melrose, as well as an account of the South African adventure that he wrote much later. All quotations come from these.

Twigs of a Tree

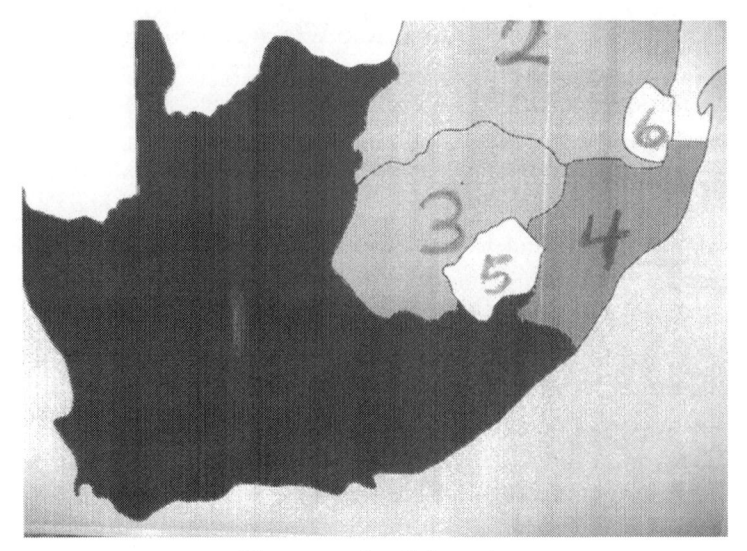

The geography of the region

1. British Cape Colony
2. South African Republic/Traansvaal
3. The Orange Free State.
4. Natal Boer State annexed by British in 1843
5. Basutoland
6. Swaziland[3]

Briton does not say why he decided to go from the Pampas to South Africa. Seeing an appeal in the Buenos Aires papers, and pricked, perhaps, by what seems an inherited sense of adventure, he took a job as a 'cattle man' on the *S.S. Mab*. Once at the Cape, he would volunteer for a stint in the British army. Briton felt fortunate to be one of the twenty-four chosen (out of some fifty applicants)—an honour extended to him, in part, he thought, because he had those three horses of his father's.

This band of young men from Argentina was—with a couple of New Zealanders and Australians thrown in—a motley, multi-national crew. Among them were the Jacobs brothers, Norman and Edgar, friends of Briton's; a ship's steward; a veteran of the Indian wars; several office clerks;

---

[3] Map published by Wikipedia.

and a Divinity student who had been 'rusticated', expelled, from Trinity, Dublin. A very amusing fellow,' says Briton,

> who had gone onto the stage and finally disgusted his people by marrying an actress who supports herself in England while he makes his living out here.

Some were horsemen, good enough to be polo players. One, Clarke, is dubbed 'The millionaire' because he is always broke. Briton appreciates him, nevertheless: 'He's a little slack—though, if you consider that he has never done any work in his life, he is very good.'

Their leader was a Henry Somervell, 'a queer cuss' who had got together a load of cattle, sheep and horses that he intended to sell to the army in Cape Town. Enthusiastic supporters provided them with horses, vaguely military dress and 'Mexican' saddles that turned out to be useless.

JG Walker, one of the 'patriotic estancieros', had donated horses to the cause, but one of these—a ten year old 'goose-rumped roarer'—suffered a rejection that saved its life. Unlike the other horses sent to Africa, almost none of which survived the year, the rejected horse lived, says Briton, another 20 years. After the effort of loading their ship with sheep, cattle, horses, bales of alfalfa and other fodder, the 'Somervell Scouts' were paraded, partied, and even photographed by the press. A concert 'where popular songs were shouted until late' preceded an emotional send-off from Buenos Aires harbour.

The journey to the Cape was, for Briton—consigned to feeding and watering the sheep and mucking out their pens—hard work, though, he claims this was easier than looking after the cattle. Once they are put to shifting bales out of the coal bunker: 'No room to stand up, plenty of coal dust . . . we've been washing ever since.' Food is meagre and rough: 'a mash of potatoes and yesterday's scraps'; except when he takes 'tea like a Christian with the engineers'. They try to exchange some of their daily ration with the cook for slightly better food. 'But all is vanity and vexation . . . the cook takes your beer and gives you nothing in return.' The crew, spending much of its time peeling potatoes for its somewhat unwelcome guests, is unfriendly. The captain is so disagreeable, that this 'picturesque crew of pirates with hardly a clean shirt among them' fantasize jokingly of starting a mutiny and putting Somervell in irons. 'The crew could go on peeling potatoes, and Morris and I could work the engines, with the Parson and Clarke as stokers,' remarks Briton. The

Parson, more ambitious, refuses, threatening to 'split unless he can be Hangman'. However, when a 'Maltese' actually did attempt to throw the Captain overboard, some of Briton's friends come to the rescue and put the aggressor in irons. Briton spends his nights either on deck or with the cattle, 'sleeping just by my bunk'.

Rules regulating the very dangerous overloading of ships had been recently introduced.[4] The *Mab*, however, had clearly not yet been marked with her load—or Plimsoll line. The ship listed dangerously and the cargo had to be constantly shifted from side to side to balance the vessel. Nevertheless, after a little over two weeks at sea, they sail safely into the harbour. Table Mountain rises before them. In the sunset it looks, remarks Briton poetically, 'like Doré's illustrations of Dante's Inferno, the Gates of Hell, the Land of Lost Souls'.

The young men join up for 'Three months or the duration . . .' and are incorporated as a company into Kitchener's Horse. It is not clear why Briton did not attempt to get a commission as an officer. Possibly, for a volunteer, this was not—as it would be in the Great War—then possible.

Briton's pay is 7/6 (seven shillings and sixpence) a day, reduced to 3/-(three shillings) after deduction of the cost of rations. These cavalry types were reasonably fortunate: ordinary soldiers were paid a third of the amount. Their horses—Briton's two supplied by JG—are bought for £28 each by the government. The money is given not to the men but deposited with Somervell. Briton manages on a mere ten shillings a week. Visiting a woman called Sybil, to whom he had an introduction, he leaves most of his small hoard of cash with her.

Ten days later, decked out in their 'rotten—worse than Somervell's'—army issue of 'helmets, forage caps, khaki tunic, rough riding breeches, enormous . . . boots and puttees', they load themselves, their *Enfield* rifles and their horses into a train for 'Orange River'.

Briton spends much of the journey sitting in the train corridor writing letters—to his mother, his father and to his sister Melrose. A few weeks later he writes to 'Alice' (possibly Annie Alice or Elsie, his cousin and future wife), and once to a friend in Hopetown, 'Ina'. The other men in the train amuse themselves with poker. But after a three-day trip this newly minted Argentine 'Squadron F' of Kitchener's Horse finds itself at Enslin on the Modder river near the town of Kimberley. They are in 'a

---

[4] Pointed out to me by Patrick Brady.

large, dusty, unattractive camp', where the country is like the 'worst parts of the Pampa Central'. Briton is singularly unimpressed with the scenery of the African Veldt, although sometimes it reminds him of the Argentina of his youth.

> *The country here is awful, no grass, a few shrubs, and hilly, almost mountainous; the hills close by are rather like the hills at the sides of the Sauce Chico after a long drought, and in the distance blue and misty like the Ventana.*

The besieged towns of Mafeking, Kimberley and Ladysmith have not yet been relieved; all are still holding out against the Boer forces. Briton soon notices that the Dutch are very 'anti-English'. His nights are disturbed by the sound of distant gunfire reverberating across the veldt from Lord Robert's invasion of the Orange Free State, launched just two days before his arrival in Enslin. They get news that the Boers had got another squadron of Kitchener's Horse 'in a bad position' and had 'killed three and wounded twenty-one men'.

The defence of the area where Briton found himself was in the able hands of the Afrikaans General, Piet Cronjé, who had in 1896 distinguished himself by rounding up Rhodes' friend Jameson after his abortive (and illegal) raid on the Transvaal. More recently, Cronje had directed the sieges of Kimberley and Mafeking, the last ably defended by Colonel Robert Baden-Powell. It was during the siege of Mafeking that Baden-Powell, in 1900, developed his idea of turning adolescents into helpful, self-sacrificing 'boy scouts'.

Mounting Kitchener's Horse

Briton soon gets his first taste of shelling. Alice Walker cannot have been delighted to read her eldest son's report from Jacobsdael of February 16, 1900. He writes that a group of colleagues had ridden back from a patrol 'in a hailstorm of bullets, we also being under fire'. He adds that he immediately volunteered to take ammunition to the firing line, that he 'was in front and had a most exciting time, as we were the marks for the Boers'. Then he goes on to say that arriving at the telegraph office, 'we were properly bombarded by Boers in kopjes overlooking the camp.' Further on in the letter, Alice reads that 'Staunton and my horses were lost.' The horses turned up, but Briton's colleagues 'thought I was dead'.

Moving on from Jacobsdael, they arrive at a camp on the Modder river. By February 20th he remarks that, 'After a battle . . . . Cronje is trying to break through the lines, and we lost a lot of men.'

If Briton had ever imagined himself as a horseman charging through battle in the chivalrous glory of the storybook medieval knight, he was to be sadly disillusioned. As a member of the ranks, his year in South Africa is one of hard, often disagreeable, even humiliating work. There is the 'wood fatigue', the 'water fatigue', the 'latrine fatigue'; there is wagon loading, the constant pulling down and setting up of tents—when they have them—as they move from camp to camp. There is cooking, acting as look-out from the hilltops or 'kopjes', picketing and patrolling in search of the enemy; there is sentry, grazing and guard duty; scrounging for food—any sort of food—and the delivery of cartridges and telegrams often with shells falling about their ears. 'I'll never get used to these shells,' he says.

In the lowest reaches of the military hierarchy, Briton is the butt of command, of constant ordering about. By March he remarks that 'It will be nice to be independent again some day.' A month later he feels, 'it will be nice to be free, and not to have to stand being cursed and nagged at in silence'. He goes on with an insight into his own prudently tractable character: 'I am more fortunate than other fellows, principally because I do stand it in silence.'

Kitchener's Horse, though warmly commended a few months later by Lord Roberts, seems somewhat chaotic. The men are given no drill or even musketry instruction. Briton's friend, Traill, finds himself in battle without a clue as to how to re-load his *Enfield* rifle when it runs out of ammunition. Nor do they, the various squadrons of Kitchener's Horse, have any riding instruction. For Briton, long an experienced rider because of his Pampas background, this did not matter. For the majority who 'do not know one end of a horse from the other', this is a not insignificant omission. The inability to get on a horse without the aid of boxes or fence rails is followed by an inability to stay in the saddle. Very few of the volunteers of Kitchener's Horse, Briton tells us, knew how to ride at all. The horsemanship of Squadron C 'is disgraceful', he says.

Once a whole squadron of horsemen bolts off in all directions. The riders are unable to control their steeds, driven wild, not by battle, but by a group of patriotic children and a brass band that bursts into 'Onward Christian Soldiers' as the soldiers leaving the Cape march past. However, the Argentine contingent or Rough Riders, as they came to be known, seem better. 'Great things are expected of us,' he writes to JG in February 1900.

Men with difficulty in controlling or even staying on their horses' backs soon find the problem of their bad horsemanship solved: starvation drained their steeds of all spirit. But as a fighting force they were badly crippled by the deterioration of their mounts. 'It's a beastly shame, they take us scouting all day and give our unhappy mokes (sic) nothing to eat.' A famished animal could charge into battle at a pace no faster and more furious than a reluctant trot. Briton describes chasing after the formidable Boer leader Christian de Wet on 'our broken nags'. A good horse became so rare that it was either requisitioned by soldiers of higher rank, or simply stolen. Without a horse, the troops, particularly those at the bottom of the military hierarchy, had no option but to 'foot-slog'. Briton once has to get rid of the mare he had been riding because it had foaled. It was not deemed apposite for a cavalry man to be followed about by a colt in the manner of 'Mary and her Little Lamb'.

Somervell suddenly falls from his horse while crossing a river. Briton, ever ready to help, strips naked, leaps into the water and brings the horse, 'very far gone', ashore. He seemed to know the horse: 'It was Hilda's horse, she may like to hear that it is still going strong,' he writes. Animals too famished to continue were not fed but shot dead. Briton is appalled at the shooting of a number of horses that could easily have recovered their spirit with a proper feed.

If the horses are starving, the men, too, are almost always on short—half or even quarter—rations. Mostly, even when in a town, they lack the means for any supplement. As early as February Briton complains, 'We get even less food than the horses . . . 2 biscuits, coffee, and a little soup, and no chance of buying more.' He worries, however, more for the animals than for himself and he tries to feed his horse biscuits. In June he remarks, 'I have very little to write about except marching and feeding . . . We walk miles in search of jam and seldom get any.' Part of his 'fatigue' work is to roam through the countryside scavenging for food: sometimes only rusks or 'dog biscuits' can be found; when lucky there are chickens, geese or even cattle. These are cooked over fires fuelled by stolen fence posts or dried cow-dung. Once 'We got some vegetables and the pen, ink and paper I am writing on—(riding) about 9 leagues—on half starved horses.'

Deserted Boer camps are raided and searched for 'grub for the troops'—flour, sugar, salt, coffee, anything. In one camp a 'decoy' of 35

Twigs of a Tree

hens is 'massacred'. After Pretoria they travel 'light, hungry and cold'. Water, too, both for men and horses, is often scarce. An outbreak of enteritis sends many men into field hospitals from which they only emerge feet first.

Scavenging for clothes is rife. The army, as time passes, can barely keep its men in clothing. Limited in what they are allowed to carry, the soldiers usually have no change of dress. In an April letter to Alice's sister, his Aunt Jessey, Briton asks for some of

Harold's old underclothing, anything . . . as we can get no kit and my spare things, when I do get a change, can only be kept until we shift camp.

Later the threadbare young man is delighted to be given a pair of socks. Briton's friend, Staunton, is in 'rags, his worn-out uniform full of holes badly stitched up'. So tattered is Staunton that he is dubbed 'The Long-lean-wibbly-wobbly beggar'. In Rhenoster, Staunton runs into his younger brother recently arrived from England as an officer of the Royal Horse Artillery. This officer, 'very smart in his new uniform', is much dismayed at his veteran brother's condition and hands over whatever spare clothes he can lay hands on. Briton is thrilled when he manages to scavenge a 'waterproof sheet, a khaki coat, a pipe, writing paper and envelopes'.

In spite of the surrender, at the end of February, of the Afrikaans commander Piet Cronje, and the capture of the capital of the Orange Free State, Bloemfontein, in March, the news in April is still 'very despondent'. 'We are to be here till Xmas and everyone is sick of waiting.' Briton is short of money but 'Harold sent me a postal order of £1 and it is very handy, tho' the sixpence cakes make it vanish pretty quickly.' He adds, 'I am afraid we shall never distinguish ourselves much.'

The men are constantly shifting from camp to camp. From the Cape and the Kimberley area they move on to Jacobsdael, Bloemfontein, Tabanchu and Pretoria with many stops on the way in places with 'unpronounceable names'—Schuurpoort and Nooitgedacht among them. They soon find themselves covered with lice, so thickly infested that they are forced to boil their clothes. Briton leaves us a picture of his friend Staunton, sitting in his shirt, trying to spear, with a thorn, the swarms of lice in his trousers.

The men amuse themselves by designing a piece of humorous heraldry with nothing particularly glorious about it. Under the motto 'Hurry Up' a shield bears a ragged coat in the top left corner; underneath this a stubborn horse is dragged up a hill with much swearing. Top right a man digs a grave before an audience, and below this is a line of chevrons decorated with chickens, symbols of the non-commissioned officers, the NCO's. Beside these stands a tree hung with mealies (corn cobs) for the men.

Kitchener's Horse Crest with its motto Hurry Up

The side supports show, on the left, a mess orderly bent under the weight of his buckets, 'heavily grousant' (loaded, grousing?) over a pennant that reads 'Half Rations or Sweet F.A.' On the right a scruffy Boer stands smiling over another pennant reading 'Trust in the Lord'. The lines are ornamented not with the traditional heraldic ant, symbol of 'great labour and wisdom', but with the louse—so much a part of the uncomfortable life of Kitchener's Horse.[5]

Much of the time the men have little idea of what is going on or even of where they are. Rumours are, however, rampant. 'One gets to believe nothing on this job, as almost everything is false' writes Briton.

---

[5] The original of this crest has come down to Barbara Brady from her father, Briton Walker. Her daughter, Gillian Finlay, has managed to decipher the wording on the pennants.

Twigs of a Tree

The Captain is anxious to keep the Argentines with him for a future police force, but as early as March the men are already 'fairly fed up'.

Briton is taken by Somervell—as his orderly—into the town of Bloemfontein, wrested from the Boers in March. It is a 'pretty little place, like a small English county town', and the shops are all English. Somervell treats Briton to lunch—'awfully decent of him'. But his boss has quarrelled with the rest of the officers and usually eats on his own, ignored by his colleagues.

Not an easy man and disinclined to take orders even in a military situation, by April Somervell has clashed seriously with the squadron's leader, Captain Cheyne. In spite of the meal he had shared with Somervell, Briton's sympathies lean towards the Captain, who 'has stood more than he would from anyone else'. Somervell resigns and tries to get his men to leave with him. Some of his men—'anything to get out of this'—depart with him. But Briton, although clearly tempted by home, feels that he cannot abandon the cause, cannot 'leave in the middle of things'. Although 'sick of the job', he determines to seek out, should the dismembered squadron be disbanded, another position as a volunteer.

Briton's descriptions of the exploding shells, the danger, the raids, shootings and inevitable killings are dry, undramatic: 'Macarthy shot in the heart.' Or, 'I was with the ambulance and so missed quite a successful little fight.' Once they have 'no end of a fight' trying to take a 'kopje'. They lose fourteen men. Captain Cheyne gets 'a scalp wound and a bullet through his cheeks'.

In May the squadron is paraded before the commanders themselves. Lord Roberts with Kitchener—alumnus of the Woolwich Military Academy where Francis Lewis Catty had taught a century before—inspects the somewhat 'unwashed and lousy lot' that was Briton's group of Kitchener's Horse. Lord Roberts heaps them with praise. Kitchener, however, says nothing, but looks 'very fed up . . . his red face made him look like a hard drinker', which, adds Briton kindly, 'he certainly is not'. This attention from the military bosses does not earn them a 'half-holiday' or 'anything else worth having'. But the rest of the squadron, which had not been seen for days, suddenly reappears with Briton's friends, Norman and Edgar Jacobs. Captain Cheyne, now somewhat miraculously recovered from his head injuries and the bullet that had coursed through his cheeks, accompanies them.

Nothing is comfortable. Often, even in heavy rain, 'we have no shelter'. At other times, soaked blankets having been discarded, the only refuge is a 'waterproof sheet'. There are nights without even that. In April, Briton writes to Aunt Jessey that 'it rains every night now, and we have no tents, so we get wet.' His stoical conclusion to this piece of news is: 'But as the sun generally shines next day we get dry again.' However, many men fall sick through the double shortage of food and shelter.

Once, after a battle, they stumble into tents abandoned by the enemy and find quantities of bibles. Unimpressed by this evidence of Afrikaner piety, they do not hesitate to turn the separate pages of Holy writ to more immediate and better use. The 'fellows,' says Briton, 'found them useful for making cigarettes'. On another occasion they are promised tents. But the tents fail to appear and they continue as 'open-air gypsies'. He accepts the vastly more easy conditions of the officers with grace, 'we do not grudge them their luxury as most of them are very good fellows.'

By June the Transvaal Free State had been overcome and by August they are marching to Pretoria, its captured capital. At first, they think the war is over, but they are soon marching to another tune.

. . . . we thought the work was done
All the Free State conquered and the Transvaal nearly won
But we soon discovered that the job was just begun
While we were marching to Pretoria.

So goes the ditty of the day that underlines the defiance of the formidable Boer general Christian de Wet:

De Wet! De Wet! He's got away with Steyn
Cut the blooming railway and wrecked our Armoured train
Tho' he's quite surrounded he eludes us once again
While we were marching to Pretoria.

De Wet's defiance would go on to the end of the war; but shortly afterwards they arrive in the Boer capital of Pretoria. Briton is sent for. He cleans himself up and calls in on the quarters of officer Major Congreve. The major's uncle, a Walter Congreve, whose estancia JG had apparently been 'looking after for some years', had asked him to give Briton some special attention. [6]

---

[6] I have found no trace or evidence of this estancia or JG's part in it.

Briton leaves the Major, happily clutching a shirt and a badly needed pair of socks. The additional gift of a £10 note is 'like manna from heaven' since the men's pay was 'very seldom forthcoming and we depended on spare cash to supplement our rations'. Shut out from the eating houses in the town—all reserved, respecting the inimitable British class divisions, for 'Officers and Civilians'—Corporal Walker and his low-ranking friends content themselves with 'some tinned stuff' eaten as a picnic in 'someone's backyard'.

A little later their hungry colleagues in the camp welcome them with enthusiasm. Briton has no illusions: the fervour was cupboard love, 'not for ourselves' but for the sudden and unexpected abundance of supplies, the 'jam etc.' he had purchased with the £10 note. On the way back to the camp he gets a glimpse of Baden-Powell, 'just arrived from Mafeking'. The town had finally, after 217 days of siege, bombardment and starvation, been relieved from the Boers, on May 17th. The elation in London is so exuberant that a new verb—'to maffick', or celebrate boisterously—enters the English language.

On one occasion they reach a Boer camp, but the mechanism of their 'Pom pom' jams and does not fire; 'a few shots do some damage, bringing down a man and some horses.' The subsequent search for booty in the abandoned camp is disappointing. It yields no more than a few leaflets declaring the Afrikaner intention to 'Fight to the End'.

This squadron of Kitchener's Horse had been attached to the division of the commander Ian Hamilton. Briton is not far from the crucial confrontation of Diamond Hill on June 11th and 12th. The young war correspondent, Winston Churchill, in his book about Hamilton's progress through South Africa, would declare that the battle of Diamond Hill was the turning point of the war. Briton's group loses a few horses but otherwise sees little of the battle. He does record however the battle's 'hard fighting and a good many losses'.

When on patrol, Briton suddenly encounters a troop of Boers who open fire. His horse rears up in terror and Briton lands flat on his face on the stony ground. His split tongue and injured face keep him on the sick lines for a couple of days, eating nothing but suet since everything else was as 'hard as bricks'. Shortly afterwards his friend Staunton is hit, 'but not badly wounded'. By this time the squadron, with much work to do, is feeling the loss of over half its men—those who had gone off with Somervell.

By August, Briton is near the Crocodile River, South of Pretoria, in an area they name the Happy Valley. He admires the fertile farmland, the richness of the crops, the rural beauty. They carry out raids, capture wagons and once are about to open fire. At the last minute a 'doubtful' officer, unsure about whom they have in their sights, stops them. The officer's hesitation is well founded; the 'enemy' they are about to mow down turns out to be a brigade of their own men. The modern euphemism for the cause of that narrowly avoided massacre would have been 'friendly fire'.

They search abandoned farms for arms, supplies and ammunition. They burn the wheels of wagons and, when leaving, set the farms alight. But they have an 'easy time' in the valley and eventually are even supplied with new tents. All in all, however, they do 'not do much good'. Briton finds the three months from September a 'waste of time'. He comes across an acquaintance in charge of an escort for a Sergeant Major. This man, in a quarrel, had turned his gun on his officer and shot him.

The killer is awaiting Court Martial. Briton finds him a 'nice fellow'. So nice indeed that he takes pity on the man and gives him a book to read. It will pass the time, he says; it is a 'dreary outlook waiting for the trial'.

At the end of November, the men are offered a choice between an immediate discharge: a month's leave plus another three months service or a bonus for an extra month. Most, including Briton, grab the immediate discharge. A fifteen-day journey finally brings them back to the Cape. Briton is paid for one of his two horses but, mysteriously, not for the other. He finally sets off for home—not Britain, but Argentina.

The decision to leave immediately may well have saved Briton's life. On December 12, 1900, only a few days later, his squadron, caught in a serious battle, suffers heavy casualties. One of his friends, Sergeant Berdoe, writes to him ten days after the battle, on December 22nd, describing the attack:

There were 4 companies of infantry holding the top of the range and every man of them was either killed or taken prisoner. They kept up firing until all their ammunition was expended, charged 3 times with the bayonet, and then clubbed their rifles. All no good, the Boers just swarmed everywhere. Talk about a hail of bullets! Diamond Hill was a fool to it. I never expected to get back alive. The bullets were zip-zipping all around and the ground strewn with dead and wounded men and horses. The guns were shelling the top of the range and you could see our men and the Boers falling over the edge of the rocks as they were killed. 300 killed and wounded and 3000 prisoners. The Boers admit to having 200 killed and 300 wounded and missing. It is some consolation to know that they suffered as heavily as we did.

After this, Berdoe is delighted to tear open the '3 or 4 parcels' addressed to Briton and other departed friends. They contain some welcome *grub, plum pudding, tobacco and clothes. They came in very handy, seeing that I had nothing except what I was wearing, and not even a horse.*

By the time Briton left Africa, at the end of 1900, the war seemed over. Lord Roberts, thinking his job well done, returned to England, replaced by Lord Kitchener, the recent 'conqueror of the Sudan'. However, the Boers, in spite of their defeats and the huge numerical odds against them, do not surrender—they instead intensify their guerrilla campaign. Kitchener, the bold and ruthless new Commander-in-Chief, retaliates with war tactics of draconian dimensions.

The 90.000 Afrikaaner forces—set against 500.000 British troops—were eventually crushed, not by superior numbers but by Kitchener's fortress-line of block houses and barbed wire that isolated them from one another. The fortress-line was accompanied by a scorched-earth policy that resulted in the torching of some 30.000 farms and the driving of women, children, older men and African forces into that new invention of war: disease-ridden concentration camps.

This war, where the Afrikaners—unhappy about federation under the British—were defending their autonomy against the British assertion of hegemony, was afterwards highly criticized. And although feted and raised to the peerage for his victory in the Sudan, Kitchener had already been faulted for an unnecessarily brutal slaughter of Arabs at and after the battles of Omdurman. The Irish, Catholic though they were, had loudly supported the Calvinist Boers because of their own hatred of British domination. Liberals in England had been against the war and in favour of continued negotiation. After her visit to South Africa in 1901, Emily Hobhouse raised a resounding and widely reverberating protest over the appalling conditions in the concentration camps.

As a war veteran, Briton became aware of all this—and of course disliked it.

It has been the custom of late years to condemn the Boer War as a War of Aggression by the Brutal English against the poor down-trodden Boers.

He somewhat curiously compares the war against the Boers to George Washington's uprising against George III.
We were fighting for the same principle that actuated Washington and his Republican Heroes in their rebellion against the English.

He wonders why the Americans are 'now amongst our most severe critics'. In his fierce defence of the war, Briton has no doubts about the justness of British policy in South Africa. Making no mention of the camps, he ends with:
The British very rightly objected to the Boers oppressing British subjects, and endeavoured to persuade them . . . to make concessions. The Boers were even more pig-headed than the British . . . it was they in the end who declared war.

Rudyard Kipling apparently remarked that this war taught the British 'no end of a lesson'. John Briton Walker was fortunate: over 20.000 British troops were laid to rest in the heat and dust of the South African veldt by warfare and disease. Almost 23.000 were wounded. The total casualties seem to have been over 90.000, of which some 27.000 were Boer men, women and children who perished in the concentration camps.

CHAPTER XVI

THE ENGLISH TOWER

Gold had been on John George Walker's mind some forty years before, in 1862, when the *Queen of the Mersey* carried him from Gravesend as far as New Zealand and Australia. In the early years of the 20th century, fantasies about gold were still alive and kicking. Gold's glint would now lure JG's eldest son into the hostile environment of the Brazilian jungles. His parents, Alice and JG—who had given him their blessing for his venture into the war in Africa—also seemed to have had no objection to this new and risky enterprise.

Briton, trained in England as a civil engineer, was susceptible to the recently revived idea of mining gold from difficult and inaccessible sites in Argentina. This now seemed plausible through the invention of more efficient machinery, combined with cheaper means of discovery, dredging and transport. A slump in tin mining in other parts of the world not only put many prospectors and miners out of work and freed their machinery, but also fomented a keen new interest in gold.

Groups of prospectors formed companies, attracted investors and imported unwieldy machinery. This sparked a prospecting boom in Argentina that eventually spread to the Mato Grosso in Brazil and beyond. Gold was the main objective, but diamonds and other precious stones were also in their sights. As an engineer, Briton was engaged by the Este Mato Grosso company to organize the transport of cumbersome dredging machinery to the concession site of Jaurú and to supervise the plant. He has left a long description of this fifteen-month misadventure. As in other

The English Tower

projects of its kind, most of the promoters and shareholders were 'left lamenting'.[7]

Briton records the steamer trip from Rosario, the nights spent in hammocks, the mosquitoes, the difficulties of moving the heavy machinery. He meets an assortment of colourful characters—ranging from Indians 'with filed pointed teeth' to Paraguayan and Italian mechanics, a German officer, a number of Australians, a Scotsman and a 'patriarchal old Jew'. He 'shattered' an English companion—an aristocrat vaunting his connections to the Duke of Fife—by owning that 'my grandfather had kept a livery stable in the City of London'.

The boats were inadequate, and one sank under the load of machinery. The captain was enraged—less about loss of the ship than about the cash he had left in his cabin. Briton, ever courageous and willing to help, appeased him by tearing off his clothes and diving into the flooded cabin to rescue the captain's wallet and its contents.

After passing many obstacles in the Taquary and Paraguay rivers, the journey continued by land: on roads the men had to hack through the forest themselves, moving most of their equipment on bullock carts. At one point, the horses all died and they had to continue on mules. Sometimes they went hungry for days. There were 'mosquitoes that left us no peace', beri-beri fever and malaria; there were 'jiggers that laid eggs' in their toes, and no let-up in the chronic problem of scarce food supplies. Mysterious uprisings in the surrounding territory did not help. Briton shot at—but missed—a giant anaconda; he developed boils, suffered from ticks and became acquainted with some 'dangerous little fish', the piranhas.

The only doctoring for these hopeful gold-diggers came from packets of capsules, numbered from 1 to 120. There was no indication as to what exactly the capsules contained. They had to be swallowed on faith: N° 9 for influenza, n° 19 for measles, and for stomach aches they swallowed a n° 3 pill, followed by a n° 25.

Briton enjoyed the adventure, the men he met, and even the work, although it turned out to be fruitless. Never having seriously believed in the project, he was disappointed but not surprised that the company was eventually closed down and that the shareholders were cleaned out. He writes to his mother just before leaving 'this sad little place', ending his tale with a piece of doggerel by one of the participants:

---

[7] *A Year in Mato Grosso* 1905-1906 (On the Road to the Jaurú)

Twigs of a Tree

I don't know the moral of all this Lament
For the time is all gone and the money's all spent
But one thing we all hope—that, whatever we do
We may never go back to the Bonny Jaurú.

Briton returned from Brazil to Buenos Aires at the end 1906, at a time when JG and Alice were still in Argentina, just back from yet another trip to England.

Alice Walker seems to have made several trips to England, sometimes, as in 1880, on her own. She seems to have been there shortly after young Norman's death at the age of sixteen in 1894.[1] Apart from visiting her son's grave, Alice perhaps needed to see to the education of her third son, Harold Saxon. Harold, born in February 1881, had by then—at 13—arrived at middle-school age.

Brian Dyson has found at the estancia *La Susana* a copy of a book by Charles Lever, dedicated to Harold Saxon Walker by his mother. Inscribed May 14th 1895, Heidelberg Lodge, St. Margaret's-on-Thames, it must have amused, perhaps encouraged young Harold. Charles Lever was an adventurous Irish doctor and storyteller who had enjoyed student-life in Germany, apparently met Goethe in Weimar and created a number of highly popular characters in *The Confessions of Harry Lorrequer*.[2]

We have found no records of Harold's schooling in England. It seems possible, however, that Alice took her son across the channel, as far as the University town of Heidelberg—to the English-language 'Heidelberg College', still run by her brother, Arthur Bovill Catty, in Germany.[3]

Alice seems to have been in England yet again, this time with JG, in 1906. Briton writing to his parents in England during the Mato Grosso adventure mentions a telegram of April 1906 telling him that the family was 'all going home'—that is, back to Argentina—in the *Aragon* on April 21st. Eric, about to enter Bedford, 'won't like being left behind', Briton says.

---

[1] See footnote below.
[2] "The Confessions of Harry Lorrequer", by Charles Lever. inscribed "H.S. Walker, from Mother, 14.5.95, Heidelberg Lodge, St. Margarets on Thames." Heidelberg Lodge may, after the death of Frederick Adam, have passed to the widowed Mary Beardmore Catty Shearman, and her two unmarried sisters, Jessey and Emy, the 'Twickenham aunts'.
[3] Heidelberg College was taken over by the Americans after World War II and all its records have been destroyed.

Harold himself, now 25, was by 1906 living at *La Mancha*, dipping sheep and handling the peons.[4] But he found time to travel to Buenos Aires to take part in rowing competitions on the Tigre River near the city.

La Mancha, Las Colinas, was the address registered for Alice and JG when their youngest son, Alfred English Walker—always called Eric—entered Bedford School in 1906, the year of Briton's Mato Grosso adventure. By 1908 Alice and JG are registered as living in Oxfordshire. A recently found document shows that on September 18, 1909 Alice and JG boarded the ship *Tuonese* in Liverpool for a journey to Buenos Aires. It was presumably in the following months that they sold their *La Mancha* estancia. But, according to the Bedford archives, by the end of the 1910 summer term, they had become residents of Teddington, near Richmond-upon-Thames, in southwest London.[5] Eric left school that year, having passed the entrance examination to read engineering at the City and Guilds Institute of London.[6]

Like his father JG, he too became an enthusiastic oarsman. The school records tell us that young Eric as a neophyte

. . . is erratic in his sliding, lets his back give way at the beginning, gets a slovenly grip of the water and is often lamentably lacking in length . . .

By the standards of the rowing community, his anatomy did not seem to predestine him for glory on the water:

Walker with a few inches more of body and rather less legs would be a good oar. He is not yet quite with stroke, but is rowing well. He is long in the water and should make a good seven,

Even years later, in 1909,

E.A Walker's . . . body form is not great but he rows a fairly long and hard blade as he has long legs and long arms.

---

4 Incomplete letter to 'Madam' signed H.S. Walker, dated May 4th 1906.
5 As mentioned Alice Catty's obituary of 1939 also tells us that the estancia was sold in 1910.
6 The school, founded in 1878, for 'vocational and engineering training', records his parents as JG Walker Esq. and Mrs. A Walker of La Mancha, La Colina TCS, Buenos Aires. JG's later address in the Register is given first as Crowmarsh, Wallingford and then as BroomWater, Teddington.

Nevertheless, Eric was in the team that won the Grand Challenge Cup at the Bedford Amateur Regatta in 1910. His vast improvement can still, over a century later, be read in the school records. Eric is now

a good seven, rows long and hard. Although his body form suggested that he was not in time with his stroke, a glance at his blade showed that they were absolutely together at both ends of the stroke.[7]

For all the school's reservations, Eric, a very handsome young man, looks more than all right to me in this photo taken about four years later.

Eric Alfred English Walker around 1914

The young people were now all growing up and marriages began taking place that eventually would connect the Walkers to three other British families that had recently settled in the Pampas.

In April 1897, in the church of San Salvador in Belgrano, the 'contractor' William Davison's daughter, Katherine Rose, married, Charles Harding

---

[7] These records were passed to me by the secretary of the Old Bedfordians.

Dyson, a 29-year old 'broker'.[8] The couple's first child, daughter Jackie (1898-1975) christened Maria Luisa, was born on February 24, 1898. Jackie's brother, Charles William Dyson (1902-1977) came into the world on October 9, 1902.[9] Their grandfather William Davison owned the land on which the present-day estancias of *La Beatriz, La Susana* and *Las Magnolias* are situated, near the village of San Eduardo, not far from Venado Tuerto, in the province of Santa Fé. This town had, over the past ten years, developed into one of the most active centres of British country, social and sporting life in Argentina.

Three years after his return to his country of birth from the Boer war, Briton Walker was probably a witness at the marriage of his twenty-year old sister, Alice Melrose to William Robinson Goodbody Jr (1876-1928).

Alice Melrose Walker at about the time of her marriage to William Robinson/Patrick Goodbody in 1904

---

[8] Marriages 1896-1900 in the church of San Salvador, Belgrano:
6/4/1897 Dyson, Charles Harding, 29, Broker, Belgrano, father of groom, John Dyson, Contractor, to Davison, Katherine Rose, 28, Belgrano William Davison, Contractor, W. Davison, A. Davison, S. Ficlsy? AOT

[9] 158 24/2/1898 6/4/1898 Dyson, Mary Louisa, Charles Harding, Catherine Rose Rosario British Stockbroker JTS

Twigs of a Tree

Melrose's husband, great-grandson of Margaret and Robert Goodbody, writer of the journal, came from a Quaker family in Tullamore, Ireland. His own father, William Robinson Goodbody Sr (1849-1929) grandson of Robert, and son of Thomas Pim Goodbody, (1814-1890) had, after several not hugely successful business ventures in Tullamore and Liverpool, emigrated to California where, among other things, where he had opened the 'Puritan Dining Room', a Godfearing eatery ornamented with Biblical texts. His son, William Robinson Jr. already knew something about Argentina through the Goodbody business ventures. At the beginning of the century, carrying a well-thumbed copy of Tennyson's Complete Works, presented to him by his grandmother Elizabeth Goodbody in June 1896, William Robinson seems to have decided to go into farm management. In order to learn, he perhaps apprenticed himself to JG, or one of his friends, and thus met JG's daughter, Melrose.[10]

William Robinson Goodbody Jr.—always known as 'Patrick'—and Alice Melrose Walker were married November 12, 1904.[11] They eventually moved to an estancia, *Las Conchillas*, dept. Colonia, in Uruguay, managed by Patrick, where their first child, Molly, christened Kathleen Mary, was born in February 1907. She was followed by Patrick, born in England in 1909, and later by Noreen Melrose, born in Uruguay in 1912.

William Robinson/Patrick was neither the first nor the last Goodbody to arrive in Argentina. His cousin Edward Gaynor Goodbody (1852-1927) is recorded in the archives of St. John's parish in Buenos Aires as a witness to a marriage in 1878. In 1880, by then 28, Edward Gaynor was married in the same church. He eventually returned to Ireland, where his Quaker ancestors had fled in Cromwell's time and where many of the Goodbodys still live or are buried.

When William Davison died in 1898 only five of his huge brood of twelve children were still alive. After a married daughter sold off her share of the inheritance to her siblings, Davison's lands near San Eduardo were divided among the four remaining heirs. *Las Magnolias* went to William's son Henry and is still in the hands of the Davison family. The *Beatriz* estancia passed to Davison's daughter, Beatrice Amy, and her husband John MacNie. Davison's son and daughter, Willie and Katherine Rose, took over the *Susana*.

---

[10] Michael Goodbody has written an extensive account of the Tullamore Goodbodys and their businesses.

[11] Date from Michael Goodbody's *The Goodbody Family of Ireland*

The *Susana* was for some years run jointly by Charles Harding Dyson, Rosie Davison's husband, and by her brother Willie. According to Molly Dyson, these two somewhat unhappy young men were unsuited to the rigours of estancia life. After tippling their health away, they died within three months of one another in 1906. Charles Harding Dyson was thirty-eight years old. His widow Rosie was left with Jackie, eight and Charles, only three-years old.

After this heavy blow, Rosie Dyson left, according to Molly, with very limited means, prepared to move back to England to see to the education of her two small children.[12] She may have met the brothers Jonathan and Ebenezer (Eben) Pike Goodbody through their cousin, Patrick Goodbody—Melrose Walker's husband. For when Rosie Dyson left Argentina for England, she placed the management of the *Susana* in the hands of the brothers. Jonathan and Eben Goodbody would run the estancia for twenty years.[13]

In England, just one year after JG's son Eric Walker left Bedford School in 1910 to study engineering, Rosie's son, young Charles Dyson, from *La Susana* in the province of Santa Fé, joined the very same boarding school.[14]

Two years before, in 1908, Briton Walker had turned his back on the adventures of foreign warfare in South Africa and gold dredging in Mato Grosso and decided, at age thirty-five, to settle down to marriage. He did not look far for a wife. *The Times* announces his marriage on October 25, 1908 to his twenty-five year old first cousin, Annie Alice (Elsie) Catty, in St. John's Church, Putney. The groom's father, John George Walker, 'late of Buenos Aires', is by now registered as living at The Limes, Crowmarsh,

---

[12] Katherine Rose, 28, daughter of William Davison, contractor, is cited as having married Charles Harding Dyson, 29, broker, son of John Dyson, contractor, in Belgrano on April 16th, 1897.

[13] Ebenezer Pike Goodbody (1880-1957) emigrated to Argentina in 1906. Jonathan (1883-1957) after reading law at Clare College, Cambridge joined him in 1907. They later established the Dairy Farm, Derrynane, near the *Susana*. (M.E. Goodbody *The Goodbody Family of Ireland*, p. 61)

[15] Charles William Dyson (b. 9 October 1902) entered the School on Jan 17, 1911 and left nine years later at the end of the summer term 1920.

Twigs of a Tree

Wallingford, in Oxfordshire. But the bride's father, George Ernest Christie Catty, is still 'of Buenos Aires'.[15]

In Argentina, during their twenty years as estancia managers, the Goodbody brothers tried several times to buy the *Susana*—without success. Rosie Dyson—who was, presumably, receiving some income from the land—wisely resisted. Evidence of their serious interest in the property are the swimming-pool and tennis court they left behind. Rosie's son, Charles, would eventually take over the *Susana* in the 1930's. He became the estancia's very effective boss and later married Melrose and Patrick Goodbody's daughter, Molly, sister to my mother Noreen and my uncle John Patrick (Pat) Goodbody. It was this connection that was to render me, Molly's niece, the brief estancia experiences that so enchanted my childhood and early youth.

After his own wedding, Briton Walker had also returned to Argentina—with his new wife, Elsie Catty. Their oldest child, Alice Elizabeth (Betty) Walker, was born in Córdoba in 1909. A son, John Norman, also born in Córdoba, followed in 1912. Briton was now an employee of the construction firm of *Hopkins & Gardom*. As an engineer with this company, he would soon be working on the *Torre de los Ingleses* that was to be erected directly in front of Buenos Aires' main railway station, Retiro.

This 'English Tower', a gift by the British community to the Argentine government, was intended to commemorate Argentina's liberation from Spain a hundred years before, in May 1810. The first stone was laid on November 26, 1910. The inauguration of the building took place nearly six years later, in 1916, while the war in Europe still raged. On July 9, 1816, Argentina had formally established itself as an independent country, and the construction of the tower a hundred years later coincided with the period between Argentina's liberation and its declaration of independence. By the time Briton's son Norman was born in 1912, the Tower was already well underway, and when Mary Barbara was born, on September 14, 1916, it had just been inaugurated.

---

[15] The wedding certificate tells us that Elsie's brother Frederick Gordon and Fanny Cross (sister-in-law to Elsie's deceased mother) were among the witnesses. George Henry Cross, Fanny's husband, had rowed with JG at Henley in 1868. JG is cited as 'Farmer' whereas George Catty is now, curiously, a 'merchant'.

The English Tower

*Buenos Aires' English Tower now
The Torre Monumental*

Designed by Sir Ambrose Macdonald Poynter, the Tower was constructed by the firm of *Hopkins & Gardom* with materials, including Portland stone, imported from England. As an engineer and employee of this company, Briton seems to have been in charge of the building operations. Molly never forgot the terror of being taken, as a child, to the top of 'Uncle Briton's tower' on a 'platform-lift with no sides'.

The four-fold entrance of the 70.5 metre clock-tower is embellished with emblems of the British Empire: the Thistle of Scotland, the Rose of England, the Red Dragon of Wales, the Shamrock of Ireland. A statue of George Canning ornamented its interior, the bells replicated those of Westminter Cathedral, and the tower was inscribed

Al gran pueblo argentino, los residentes británicos, salud! 25 de mayo 1810-1910 ('A salute to the the great Argentine people, from the British residents, May 25, 1810-1910').

This very English clock tower stood on a square named, for the occasion, the Plaza Britannia. These manifestations of mutual respect

Twigs of a Tree

were already something of an irony at the time the tower was built. Irony was later to turn to bitterness.

If the Spaniards did not accept Argentina's secession for over three decades, until 1842, the British government also took its time. It was only in 1823, with the signature of Sir Woodbine Parish, in the name of British Foreign Secretary George Canning, that London acknowledged Argentina's independence from Spain, although Britain had quietly—the Spaniards would have said underhandedly—promoted independence from the very beginning. Ten years after recognizing Argentina as an independent republic the English appropriated the Falkland Islands, known to the Argentines as the Islas Malvinas.

These islands had at various times been claimed by the Italians, the British, the Dutch, the French, the Spanish and finally, after independence, the Argentines themselves. Nevertheless, in 1833 the British flag was raised over the islands, and the Argentines, for all their respect for the British (as the most powerful investors in their economy throughout the thirty years before the Great War) never forgot the humiliation of the loss of the Falklands. Diana McClure tells us that as a small child in the 1940's she was at school on the Pampas. There, under Juan Perón's nationalist dictatorship, all the children were obliged to inscribe *Las Islas Malvinas son Argentinas* (The Falkland Islands belong to Argentina) at the top of every page of their exercise books.

Almost forty years later, on April 2, 1982, the military junta in Buenos Aires under General Leopoldo Fortunato Galtieri (an officer blessed, in spite of his middle-name, with little *fortuna*), launched its ill-starred attempt to re-conquer the islands. A blood-soaked two-month war in the South Atlantic brought Galtieri's brutal military regime to an end.

My husband Carlos—then a correspondent in Rome—was in Buenos Aires with Pope John Paul II just before the end of the war. There he had a conversation with Molly Dyson. Not out of sympathy with the military, but rather to prevent possible retaliation against British *estancieros*, she had donated a steer from *La Susana* to the Argentine war effort. Carlos' reflections on the Falklands' war were published in Munich's *Süddeutsche Zeitung* under the headline: *Ein Stier von Tante Molly*—A Steer from Aunt Molly.

The *Torre de los Ingleses* of course survived the war, but its name was later changed to *Torre Monumental*, and the square on which it stands is no longer *Plaza Britannia* but *Plaza Fuerzas Armadas Argentinas*—square

The English Tower

of the Argentine Armed Forces. George Canning's statue, toppled during a hooligan attack after the war, was rescued. Today, the tower faces a memorial to the Argentine dead of the Malvinas/Falklands war.

Tower and Memorial scowl at one another across a wide avenue and the space of the renamed Plaza. Of the Argentine navy and air-force officers who died for the Malvinas, many have English, Scottish or Irish names. To keep George Canning from further harm and indignity, he now resides in the safety of the British Embassy.

CHAPTER XVII

DEATH IN THE TRENCHES

'Uncle Briton's Tower' was still under construction when, on June 28, 1914, a nineteen-year old Bosnian nationalist, Gavrilo Princip, shot dead the heir to the Austro-Hungarian throne, Archduke Ferdinand, and his pregnant wife, Sophie. This act, during a royal visit to Sarajevo, was secretly planned by Serbia's military intelligence. It was intended to break Bosnia away from Austria's multi-national Hapsburg Empire. The assassination sparked what has been called a 'mindlessly mechanical' and deadly series of responses. There were threats—Austria-Hungary against Serbia; previous alliances honoured—Germany's with Austria, Russia's with Serbia; and alliances betrayed—Italy entered the war in 1917 against her former allies Austria and Germany. Old resentments surfaced—Turkey's entry into the war on the German side was a shake of the fist at Russia; while France dreamed of reversing the 1870 loss of Alsace and Lorraine to Bismarck's Germany.[16] Colonial and imperial envy also played their part: Germany's desire for a 'place in the sun' equal to Britain's.

Austria mobilized against Serbia for what was at first seen as a limited skirmish. Germany invaded the neutral territory of Belgium provoking the entry of Britain to uphold an almost forgotten treaty made seventy-five years before. The concatenation of these and other events and circumstances

---

[16] The poet Rupert Brooke fell ill on the way to Gallipoli for the disastrous invasion of Turkey and died on April 23, 1915 at the age of 27.
But see Niall Ferguson's reassessment of the causes of the war. *The Pity of War*, 1998.

Death In The Trenches

turned increasingly ferocious. Two months after the assassination, on August 4, 1914, the first global, the first industrial war was unleashed on the world. Britain came in with her colonies—among them Canada, Australia, New Zealand, India and South Africa. Germany's submarine attacks on American commercial shipping eventually, in 1917, brought in the war's decisive factor—the armed forces of the United States.

This 'Great War for Civilization', also known as a 'grotesque absurdity', a 'piece of evil folly', a 'monstrous massacre', was the most deadly in history—until outdone by Hitler and Stalin in World War II. The monuments to the slain are scattered across the world; ranging from the meadows of Flanders and Verdun's ossuary of Douaumont, looming over its field of 130.000 crosses, to the India Gate in New Delhi, to South Africa and beyond in far away Canada, America, Australia and New Zealand. Tiny villages all over Europe—like our Acqualoreto in the hills of Umbria—rise around memorials inscribed with names still current among the present inhabitants; the shopkeeper, the surveyor, the postman, the young woman who sometimes comes in to cook—all carry names inscribed on the village monument; memorial to their ancestors, the countless young men slaughtered in this most terrible of wars. A cenotaph in a small town in Puglia displays the name of the current mayor, 'Salviano' no less than twenty-nine times.

In 1914, Alice and JG—he by now in his mid-seventies—were living out his retirement in Teddington, by the Thames. JG read his novels—Dickens, Scott, Kipling, Hardy—and sang his songs. He occupied himself with his beloved boats—one was later, according to Barbara, called *Kathleen* after his young niece Molly. He rowed his family to the shops down the river and, in 1911, even became a 'non-rowing', i.e. non-competing member of the Twickenham boat club where his son Eric also rowed.

Alice, according to Molly, at first may have been less happy. In Argentina she had lost touch with many of the friends she had left behind in England so many years before. 'She was very quiet', says Molly. For Alice, however, household duties and any sadness were relieved, according to Barbara, by the pleasure of her music. Later, when JG's eyesight started to fail, it was Alice who read him the books he so enjoyed. They both loved the theatre and the concerts from which they had been sundered by so many years on the Pampas, and later introduced their grandchildren to Gilbert and Sullivan.

Twigs of a Tree

Alice and JG were, like so many people of their age and times, well acquainted with grief, having lost their second son, Norman. But by now, although two of their sons were still unmarried, they had collected a bevy of grandchildren.[1] Briton, their eldest son, now forty, had survived the Boer war and his misadventures in the Mato Grosso—and, as we have seen, had settled down to marriage with his first cousin Elsie (1879-1919), daughter of Alice's brother and JG's fellow pioneer in the Bahia Blanca area, George Christie Catty. Briton, at that time although still working on the famous Tower in Argentina seems to have been in England at the outbreak of the war. Melrose's husband, Patrick Goodbody, was probably still managing the estancia in Uruguay, since it was there that Noreen was born in 1912. Alice's and JG's son Eric (1892-1916) may still have been completing his 'civil and mechanical' engineering training at *City and Guilds,* or beginning work in the construction and maintenance business for the Great Western Railway. He continued to row for Twickenham in its Thames Cup crews. In 1911, 1912 and 1913 he took part in the Henley Regatta, where JG had distinguished himself so many years before.

Harold Saxon Walker as a schoolboy

---

[1] Their son Briton had two children: Betty (1909-1966) and Norman (1912-1992). Their daughter, Melrose Goodbody, had three: Molly (1907-2009), John Patrick (1909-1975), and Noreen Melrose (1912-2005).

After his schooling at his uncle's Heidelberg College in Germany, Harold Saxon Walker (1881-1917) does not seem to have attended university. He appears at the age of twenty in the 1901 census as a 'clerk', living in Twickenham with his two unmarried aunts, Jessey and Emmy Catty. Briton was also there at the time. Not mentioned in the 1911 census, Harold may very well—like Briton—by then have returned to South America. He was certainly in Argentina in August 1914, when the Great War broke out. Unfortunately, that didn't prevent him from being drawn into its deadly vortex.

Already thirty-three years old, Harold had fallen in love. He asked his sister Melrose to choose an engagement ring for him. Molly tells us that young Hilda Bulman—the lady in question—was not much appreciated by the family: 'A flighty piece,' according to Molly, 'no better than she should be and not nearly good enough for Harold.' Relieved when the engagement was suddenly broken off, the family—somewhat unfairly—later blamed poor Hilda for 'Harold going off to the war'. The reason: 'If they had been married and had had a family, he might not have been able to go.' It seems that the young woman's irresistible flightiness was short-lived. Many years later, Molly met Hilda and was unimpressed: 'She had become a dull, fat, elderly widow, hardly the *femme fatale* I had heard so many exciting stories about.' [2]

Molly adds that Harold was Melrose's most beloved brother. It was to her that he passed on the emerald and diamond ring, presumably returned to him by Hilda after the break-up of their engagement. The last time I saw my grandmother, in 1974 at the *Susana*, three years before her death, she shyly and touchingly made a little ceremony of passing the ring on to me. I wore it for many years as a precious reminder, of her warmth, the reading lessons she had given me, the stories she had told and all her manifold kindnesses. But one evening, at a concert, the emerald fell out and was lost among the rows of seats at the Salle Pleyel in Paris. I replaced the stone; then passed on the ring, with its little history, to my daughter, Christie, on her fortieth birthday.

We know that about five months after war broke out, Harold Saxon Walker again crossed the Atlantic from Argentina. There is a record of an H.S. Walker, aged 34, arriving in England 'first class' on the *Highland Brae* on December 21, 1914. Here his profession is given as 'farmer'. [3] We have already seen him on the *La Mancha* estancia. It is very likely that Harold

---

[2]   Molly Dyson, letter to Barbara Brady, July 1985.
[3]   A record cleverly discovered by Patrick Brady.

by then was indeed farming or managing somewhere on the Pampas. However, on hearing Lord Kitchener's call for volunteers, he, like so many others, sailed home to enlist in a war he could easily have avoided.

Molly tells us that, when the war began, she found herself actually on the high seas, with her mother, Melrose, and her brother and sister, Pat and Noreen. Their father Patrick Goodbody had stayed behind in Uruguay. The family, with the three children, arrived in England to find Briton, his wife Elsie, and their two children, Betty and Norman, living in JG's Teddington house. They stayed in England for about six months. The children all came down with measles. Her handsome young uncles, Eric and Harold, in their military uniforms made a great impression on young Molly, then about six years old.

Several months later—in February 1915—the war and its dangers did not prevent the two families—Briton's and Melrose's—from boarding yet another *Highland* ship together, all five children in tow, to return to Argentina. The perilous wartime journey back to the South Atlantic remained in Molly's memory as rather a gay affair of shipboard parties and dinners. She remembered Melrose, blushing with mortification, racing into her cabin to tear off her evening dress. Even as the war gathered momentum, a sartorial solecism could still disturb an evening: Melrose had appeared at the dinner table in a new frock, 'deep purple', that turned out to be identical to the one her cousin Elsie was wearing.

In 1914, Alice Walker's brother Arthur Bovill Catty (1854-1920) was still, with his friend Dr Albert Holzberg, in Heidelberg running the school they had founded together in 1887. Arthur Catty was briefly detained at the outbreak of war but then allowed to return to England with his wife and their youngest son, Frederick Robert (1903-1980). His two older sons, Francis Bovill (1891-1972) and Norman Arthur (1894-1978) were also students at the school. However, since both were of military age, they were interned for the duration of the war. With other civilians caught working or holidaying in Germany, the boys were moved to the internment camp of Ruhleben, just outside Berlin.[4] For Francis and Norman Catty, those

---

[4] The National Archives in London holds documents from 1916 at FO383/207 "regarding permission granted to Mr Arthur Catty to send money to his sons at Ruhleben via Holland, the provision of information on the poor rate of exchange being given, and suggestion of reprisals. Permission to send coupons instead of money is also discussed, as well as a subsequent enquiry when the coupons were found to be not valid in neutral countries".

four years of relatively benign incarceration may have turned out to be a piece of luck that probably saved their lives. Their father was to lose his share in the school, but it continues today in the hands of the Holzberg family, descendants of Arthur's founding partner.[5]

Niall Ferguson discusses the mood in the European capitals in 1914—why and how men joined up. Although he qualifies the old myth of general Germano-phobia and joyous enthusiasm for the war, he concedes that Lord Kitchener—known to us from Briton's South African adventure and by 1914 Secretary of State for War—eventually managed to enlist almost 2.5 million men into his territorial or volunteer forces. Ferguson adds that 'there is ample evidence' that women did send white feathers, the symbol of cowardice, to young men wary of enlisting. The Pankhurst sisters, leaders of the feminist suffragettes, believed that the victory of a 'male nation' like Germany would be a 'disaster for the women's movement'.[6] Jingoistic verses from feminists like the journalist Jessey Pope implied that war was a game that only cowards did not play.

---

[5] The ousting of Arthur Bovill led to a court case in 1924. The Michigan Law Review, vol 43, No. 6. (June 1945) carries an article *Legal Liability for War Damage* by John Hanna that discusses Catty's legal case after the war, A.B. Catty v. German Government (Trib. Arb. Mixte anglo-alemand, 1924)

"The late Mr A. B. Catty, English national, and Dr Holzberg, a German, were the owners of the "Heidelberg College." The partnership property consisted of buildings, land, a sports ground, furniture and fittings, boats and a number of trophies. On July 31, 1916, the liquidation of the claimant's property was ordered. Dr Holzberg bought Mr Catty's personal belongings for 1,000 marks, Mr Catty's half of the furniture for 2,000 marks, and Mr Catty's half of the property, including good will, for 88,000 marks. Moreover, he took upon himself the liability for Mr Catty's half share of mortgages which totalled 120,000 marks. An architect of Heidelberg valued the property at 483,232 marks as of July 31, 1916. Mr Catty's share was, therefore, 181,616 marks of which he had received 88,000 marks, leaving a balance of 93,616 marks. The claimant was held entitled to receive the balance at the rate of exchange prevailing through a neutral currency on July 31, 1916. The rate through Zurich was 26 Mk. 75 pfg. to the pound on that date. Hence, £ 3,499.13.3 were awarded. The award in respect of the college furniture, boats and trophies was £ 305.12.2. The value of the personal belongings was assessed at 10,000 marks, representing £336.9.0. Claimant's demand of £3,000 in respect of the goodwill of the college was granted to 1.66 per cent, i.e., £ 50 . . . . A. B. Catty v. German Government, (Trib. Arb. Mixte anglo-allemand, 1924)

[6] Ferguson, p.205

Twigs of a Tree

Who's for the game, the biggest that's played,
The red crashing game of a fight?
Who'll grip and tackle the job unafraid?
And who thinks he'd rather sit tight?

Kitchener's conscription poster

A letter home from Geoffrey Pether touches on the same subject. Pether, also a student from Heidelberg College, was interned in Ruhleben with Alice's two young nephews, Francis and Norman Catty. As early as July 31, 1914 highly literate young Pether, admirer of Goethe, Schiller, Mozart and Bach and not yet eighteen years old, gives us an insight into the thinking in Arthur Catty's school:

To my mind the Liberal government is responsible for the blackest stain in our history . . . Russians, Germans, Frenchmen, Austrians whom I have met, all blame England (i.e. Sir E Grey) . . . . I hear that the Govt are trying to raise a "Volunteer" army by means which practically amount to compulsion . . . A lot of news comes over Holland referring to the 'white feather campaign' etc. to induce men to join. It's all rather disgusting I think. The Govt keeps people in the dark to save its face.

Young Pether would have been even more appalled by the methods later applied by the Italian General, Luigi Cadorna. To get his troops to fight, Cadorna revived the ancient Roman method of random decimation. On occasion, when his own units did not perform to his standards of fervour and ferocity in battle, he pressed them by randomly executing every tenth man.

The volunteer reserves of the regular British army—since 1908 known as the Territorials—and originally destined only for the home front, were soon pressed into service abroad. The initial torrent of volunteers quickly evaporated to a trickle, and in 1916 conscription—obligatory service—was introduced. This, in time, pulled men as old as fifty into the fighting forces. Like so many other young men, Alice and JG's younger sons, Harold and Eric Walker, immediately lined up in the initially enthusiastic, even jubilant queues to join the volunteer forces. Harold, now 33, after a stint in the Artists' Rifles, eventually joined the volunteer brigade of Queen Victoria's Rifles. His young brother Eric, still only 22, joined the Royal Fusiliers.[78]

Eric was recorded, on March 25, 1915 as one of fifty-five members of the Twickenham Rowing Club serving in the King's forces. Both brothers got commissions as officers. In 1917, when Briton—now in his forties—arrived from Argentina, Harold, by now at the front, was to advise him to apply for a commission to save him from being conscripted into the 'other ranks'.

We have a couple of pictures of the brothers: Eric with young Betty, Harold in his uniform. Whatever their mood when they joined up, they would—like so many others—not survive long.

---

[7]   He enlisted in the 20th (Service) Battalion of the Royal Fusiliers (3rd Public Schools Battalion) at Westminster on September 15, 1914. "He was 22 years and 9 months old, 6'2" tall and weighed 172 lbs., medium complexion, eyes blue and dark hair." He was soon promoted from corporal to lance corporal and then in May 1915 to lieutenant.

Twigs of a Tree

Eric on leave playing with his niece Betty Walker

Harold Saxon Walker ready for the front

A Visit to the Graves

In 2006, on the way to a Christmas visit to Amsterdam, Carlos and I drove from Paris through the beautiful countryside of Picardy bordering the northern bank of the River Somme. The Western Front, one of the four great battle-lines of the war, stretched from the Swiss border through France into Belgium, passing through this part of Picardy. The 'front' where 'six months could wipe out a generation' consisted of two parallel lines of trenches separated by a 'no-man's land' across which the stalled armies fired at each other from their respective ditches. In 2006, after almost ninety years, the battlefields of this line—where an advance of a few metres through the desolation and tangles of barbed wire was paid with the death of thousands—were now meadows for peacefully grazing cows.

The only sign of the ferocious trench warfare that left the vegetation stripped and splintered, the ground burned and broken, barren as the surface of the moon, are the innumerable monuments and little cemeteries that everywhere spring into view, by the side of woods or like islands afloat in the fields.

The smashed and shattered trees are now healed. The blasted countryside again sways scarlet with poppies, those sad symbols of a lost generation of young men. Small groups of identical white gravestones stand at lonely attention in the sun, in cold contrast to the exuberance of the meadows in which they are set and to the lush beauty of the woodlands around them.

Thistledump Cemetery near Longueval

Twigs of a Tree

With some valuable previous assistance from Angela and Matt Huber, and after some wandering in the Longueval area, east of Amiens in Northern France, we found first Eric's, and afterwards, near Ypres in Belgium, the grave of his older brother Harold.

It was in this area of Picardy, mainly within the triangle formed by the towns of Peronne, Albert and Bapaume, that the advance into the German lines—now called the First Battle of the Somme, or the Somme Offensive—took place in the five months between July and November 1916. Six divisions of the regular army, the British Expeditionary Force, had been almost wiped out by the advance of the Germans in 1914 and 1915. As a result, the professional units were largely replaced by the Territorial or volunteer forces made up of eager young men like Eric and Harold, entirely new to soldiering. The Somme Offensive was designed to push the German line of the Western Front, just north of the River Somme, back and eastward as a means of countering the German pressure on the French forces further south around the area of Verdun, east of Paris.

The five month struggle was to become a 'byword for futile and indiscriminate slaughter'. The many battles of the Somme offensive would cost the British 420.000 and the French 200.000 casualties. The Germans lost nearly 500.000 men. Altogether, over a million young men were slaughtered for a negligible advance—a ten-kilometre bulge in the German line that failed even to reach the town of Bapaume. Both Edward Buse Adams, (1874-1946) a great-uncle who had survived the Boer war, and his younger brother Raymond Axford Adams (1882-1916) had volunteered from Australia and were in France at the time. Edward Buse Adams, although wounded, returned home. His brother did not.

The offensive was launched on July 1, 1916 with a massive artillery attack against a thirty-kilometre stretch of the German line north of the river Somme. George Coppard, a machine gunner, describes the scene between the trenches and the less than glorious deaths, on the day after the first—and unsuccessful—artillery attack:

The next morning (July 2nd) we gunners surveyed the dreadful scene in front of us . . . (The British) attack had been brutally repulsed. Hundreds of dead were strung out like wreckage washed up to a high water-mark. Quite as many died on the enemy wire as on the ground, like fish caught in the net. They hung there in grotesque postures. Some looked as if they were praying: they had died on their knees and the wire had prevented their fall. Machine gun fire had done its terrible work.[8]

The first day's killing was a sorry record: 60.000 Englishmen dead or wounded including 60% of the officers. Two Australian divisions managed to capture—between July 23rd and August 5th—the village of Poizières, just east of Longueval. The battle included, for the Australians, a first: merciless German bombardment from the air. It claimed some 11.000 casualties, dead and wounded. Great uncle, Raymond Axford Adams, was killed on August 5, 1916 not long before Eric met his end. Raymond was twenty-four. He lies in a cemetery dedicated to the Australians, one of the 243 graveyards that are the legacy of the Somme offensive.[9]

The battles raged on, and in the Longueval area the Germans eventually had to retreat onto the elevation of High Wood, the Bois de Fourcaux, a wood of 'sweet chestnuts used locally,' David Payne tells us, 'for making pitchforks.'[10] One of the many battles for position, for villages, woods, copses and elevations, was the long battle of High Wood—now known as the Hell of High Wood—that raged for two months, until the middle of September.

---

[8] Taken, like the picture of High Wood, from an article on the web. The site by Alan Jennings has a detailed account of the fighting in the area.
[9] The battle for the village of Pozieres high on its ridge left it—in the words of historian Charles Bean—'more densely sown with Australian sacrifice than any other place on earth'.
[10] Dr David Payne, *Woods and Copses Natures—Fortresses on the Somme on the Western Front*. Internet Site of the Western Front Association.

Twigs of a Tree

*Aerial view of High Wood looking north-east.
Photo Mike Insall, Alan Jennings*

Astride the battle-line, High Wood lay 500 ft high on the Bazentine Ridge. On July 15th, two weeks after the first assault and in spite of the hideous losses, the battle-line had moved eastwards. High Wood then became the object of numerous murderous forays that lasted two months, into the middle of September.

One of the insanities of the 'first modern war'—a war of tanks, planes, air balloons, stokes mortars, cannon, machine guns, barbed wire, not to mention poison gas and flame throwers—was that the commander, General Douglas Haig, ordered a cavalry attack. This disastrous action on High Wood by soldiers on horseback would be the last of the war. This was not the only mistake to be laid at the feet of commanders with antiquated (and possibly romantic) ideas of warfare, commanders with scant concern for the lives of their men.

It has been pointed out that modern weaponry 'artillery, machine guns, barbed wire and the spade' made World War I essentially a war of defence, but that commanders, on all sides, persisted in viewing the war as an exercise in offence, launching attacks that resulted in huge and unnecessary loss of life. The troops rarely saw an officer above the rank of captain and it was rare that a high-ranking officer ever entered the trenches. Another assault provoked Sergeant Bill Hay of the 1/9th Battalion, Royal Scots, to remark on both its horror and its foolishness

... a stupid action because we had to make a frontal attack on bristling German guns and there was no shelter at all ... There were dead bodies all over the place where previous battalions and regiments had taken part in previous attacks. What a bashing we got. There were heaps of men everywhere—not one or two men, but heaps of men, all dead. Even before we went over, we knew this was death. We just could not take High Wood against machine-guns. It was ridiculous. There was no need for it. It was just absolute slaughter.[11]

By the end of July, the German defenders of High Wood had lost almost 10.000 men, of whom nearly 2.000 were dead. It was now, Payne tells us, that

the British decided to forgo set piece battles and their tactics turned to sapping, mining, and, as always, trench excavation, using new hydraulic technology. (The Bartlett Forcing Jack) to deploy explosive charges, plus the new secret weapons, tanks and flame-throwers ... On the 7th August, 33rd Division relieved a totally exhausted 51st Division who had lost over 2,000 men in just two weeks of fighting in and around High Wood, including a devastating number of officers—120. However, 33rd Division had received drafts totalling over 400 reinforcements and was rested, retrained and back up to wartime strength.

The first use of the new technology took place on the 17th August. From the outset it was a fiasco, the huge, two-ton flame-throwers being buried by a misdirected British preparatory barrage. Nevertheless, despite also having suffered from this heavy 'friendly fire,' some elements of 33rd Division made their infantry charge in the wood whilst 1st Division attacked the north-western corner. Outnumbered and out-gunned, 33rd Division were soon back in their own trenches with many casualties. 1st Division made some progress but was halted on the fringes of the Wood by the inaccurate British shelling and determined German resistance. With one exception, the new hydraulically pushed sapping charging had failed to explode on time. Once again gloom descended on 33rd Division HQ. And well it might: on the night of the 19th/20th August, 33rd Division had one more aborted attack; many of the new draft of men failed to leave their trenches.[12]

---

[11] Quoted by Steve John, below.
[12] David Payne, see above.

Twigs of a Tree

JG, Eric on leave, and Briton

In the next abortive attempt on High Wood, on the 22nd of August, Eric Walker was hit and killed, just seventeen days after the death of Raymond Axford Adams. Then, two days later, followed an assault with a barrage that in 'twelve hours fired over one million shells from ten machine guns'. By September 14th, the eve of the final and successful attempt to capture High Wood, the British had lost 6.000 soldiers. Further 'blunder and sacrifice' cost the British division another 4.500 lives and the demotion of the commander for 'wanton waste of men'. The slaughter in the battles for High Wood alone eventually added up to 10.500 British lives. Among them was handsome young Eric, who died ten months after his arrival in France.

High Wood and the adjacent German Switch Line were finally taken by the British after two months and three days of almost incessant shelling and fighting. In the four days it took to actually capture High Wood, the British suffered another 4.500 casualties. Payne tells us that the bodies of an estimated 10.000 British and Germans soldiers still lie unrecovered and unidentified within the bounds of the wood. In effect, High Wood became, and remains, a vast, anonymous mass grave.

Eric Alfred English Walker.
Lieut. Royal Fusiliers

We know too little about Eric but I found this photograph and these lines with a picture of his tombstone.

Eric was the Son of John George and Alice Walker, of 11, Broom Water, Teddington, Middx. Eric was commissioned into the Royal Fusiliers and served with the 20th Battalion, which was attached to the 98th Brigade, 33rd Division. In November, 1915 the Battalion landed in France and was subsequently transferred to the 19th Brigade of the 33rd Division. The Division moved into positions at the Somme, where they took part in the Battle of Albert, and the Battle of Bazentin, where they attacked High Wood. Eric was killed in action during the attack on High Wood on the 22nd August, 1916. He was 24 years old, and is buried at Thistle Dump Cemetery, High Wood, Longueval. [13]

---

[13] See web-site by Steve John, dedicated to the Pembrokeshire County War Memorial. Eric's name is inscribed on the Memorial of Fishguard Harbour, Wales. John remarks that many young men were in Pembrokeshire at the time working there on the railways.

Twigs of a Tree

We stumbled up the lane to the Thistledump cemetery on that windy December day, just before Christmas in 2006, and after some searching stood for a long while by Eric's grave. He shares his place in the fields of Flanders with 106 comrades and 43 members of the enemy, Germans and Austrians. Carlos has an eighteen-year old uncle buried somewhere in the area. In these graveyards it is difficult to find anyone over thirty. The horrors of their last days are beyond imagination. A considerable number, having probably lied about their age in their eagerness to join up, are under eighteen. In a box by the gate a notebook, nearly a century on, still contains details of Eric's parents and their address in Teddington.

Tombstone inscribed Lieutenant E.A.E. Walker
20th Battalion, Royal Fusiliers 22 August, 1916.

Eric is also commemorated on the Fishguard Memorial in Wales under the sign 'Lest We Forget'. In 1920, JG and Alice may have reaped some pride, if not comfort, seeing their son's name with those of other young sportsmen felled by war on the walls of the Twickenham Rowing Club.

The memorial at Twickenham Rowing Club carrying Eric's name

Bidding Eric goodbye, we drove sadly on from Longueval past Arras—Robespierre's birthplace—to Ypres, an ancient and beautiful market town in Belgium. From the windows of our hotel room we now admired the medieval cloth hall and the lovely 'ancient' buildings in the main square. Though the buildings look as if they have been there for centuries, they are reproductions. All were built after the war, as close to the design of the destroyed medieval originals as possible, paid for with German reparation money. In 1914, after the German and British armies clashed in Belgian territory over the rush to the North Sea coast, the Flemish town of Ypres had the misfortune of finding itself a few miles from the battlefields. The parallel lines of German and British trenches of the northern Western Front curved around the town a short distance from its centre.

Henry Edgar Goodbody (1884-1915), son of Thomas Henry Goodbody, a wholesale tea merchant, partner in the firm T.H.& E. Goodbody from Tullamore, was first cousin to Mel's husband, Patrick Goodbody. He was one of the early victims of the deadly battles around Ypres.

The Quakers, as pacifists, did not usually fight. They, including some members of the family, took part in the war—not fighting, but helping the wounded: nursing, doctoring, ambulance driving. Possibly influenced by his father-in-law, army General T. Beaumont, young Edgar, in spite of being a Quaker, joined the Irish Leinster Regiment in 1913 and was sent first to West Africa. When war broke out he returned and soon found himself in Belgium.

In Ypres he took part in a battle marked by a new low in the horror of warfare. When Henry found himself in the forces fighting for Ypres he was introduced to an entirely new means of mass slaughter: chlorine gas. Half of the 10.000 men enveloped by the gas died of asphyxiation within ten minutes. Two years later the weaponry had expanded to mustard gas and flame-throwers. Young Captain Goodbody was killed at Hill 60 in the last stages of the second of the five battles of Ypres. He died on May 12, 1915, aged 31. His name is inscribed on the Menin Gate.[14]

A new accoutrement of war, the 'helmet' or gas mask

The year after Harold's young brother, Eric, was killed, the third attack began on the trench system projecting towards the German lines, the Ypres Salient. By the time Harold arrived in the area in January 1917, the town of Ypres was already gone; bombed completely flat and evacuated.

---

[14] I was very kindly passed this information by Michael Goodbody.

Gas, Lice, Rats- and Yerba Mate

Like the poet Wilfred Owen, Harold Walker left a collection of letters written to his parents from the day of his arrival at the front on January 12, 1917. JG later copied these letters from his son into a notebook. They are nothing like as harrowing or as outraged as Owen's. Not only because Harold did not have Owen's literary gifts or ambitions, but also because he seems to have been trying to shield his parents from the true horrors of the war. They were still reeling from the loss of one son on the Western Front and, one imagines, desperate with fear for the other. Molly many years later recalled Harold's own outrage about the war.

> *There are odd things I remember that Mother used to tell me. One was that in one of the last letters to her from Harold, who was her favourite brother, he told her that for some reason they had had a truce, and as he had been to school in Heidelberg, he had enjoyed fraternising with the German soldiers and had got along fine with them and said in his letter how stupid it was and how he couldn't understand the stupidity of it all. Naturally he spoke German so he was one of the few who could communicate with the Germans.*[15]

Chirpy, even optimistic, Harold's letters are those of a man doing a job. The day he arrives is a 'ripping day' and he thinks he is going to 'enjoy' himself. Between time in the trenches, he looks forward to a promotion, to a 'captaincy' and the command of a company of his own. Later, as 'adjutant' to the Commander, he deals with transport, railway building and training sessions for the battalion. He handles a communication system between tanks, airplanes and men; billets for the soldiers, finding duck boards for the trenches and making roads and walkways through the deep mud. He's happy with the extra five shillings a day he earns with the work. In April he is 'fearfully busy learning new things'.

Lieutenant Harold Walker, now the professional soldier, has a low opinion of Kitchener's volunteers, also known as Kitchener's mob. 'We look upon Kitchener's army somewhat as we look upon the army of the Free Republic of Haiti,' he remarks. In June, Harold has some fun reading Punch's *Ballad of Incipient Lunacy* and recommends it to his parents with a quotation as 'The best description' he has read of an orderly room—'only

---

[15] Letter to Barbara Walker Brady 17th July 1985.

Twigs of a Tree

orderly to a military mind of limited vocabulary'. Thanks to the Web, here is the 'ballad' and the introduction that struck so familiar a note.

<u>The Ballad of Incipient Lunacy</u>.
A Battalion "Orderly" Room in France during a period of "Rest."

Runners arrive breathlessly from all directions bearing illegible chits, and tear off in the same directions with illegible answers or no answers at all. Motor-bicycles snort up to the door, and arrogant despatch-riders enter with enormous envelopes containing leagues of correspondence, orders, minutes, circulars, maps, signals, lists, schedules, summaries of all sorts. The tables are stacked with papers; the floor is littered with papers; papers fly through the air. Two typewriters click with maddening insistence in a corner. A signaller "buzzes" tenaciously at the telephone, talking in a strange language, apparently to himself, as he never seems to be connected with anyone else. A stream of miscellaneous persons, quartermasters, chaplains, generals, batmen, D.A.D.O.S.'s, sergeant-majors, staff officers, buglers, Maires, officers just arriving, officers just going away, gas experts, bombing experts, interpreters . . . Doctor drifts in, wastes time, and drifts out again. Clerks scribble ceaselessly, rolls and nominal rolls, nominal lists and lists. By the time they have finished one list it is long out of date. Then they start the next. Everything happens at the same time; nobody has time to finish a sentence. Only a military mind, with a limited descriptive vocabulary and a chronic habit of self-deception, would call the place orderly. The Adjutant speaks, hoarsely; while he speaks, he writes about something quite different. In the middle of each sentence his pipe goes out ; at the end of each sentence he lights a match. He may or may not light his pipe; anyhow he speaks:

"WHERE is that list of Wesleyans I made?
And what are all those people on the stair?
Is that my pencil? Well, they can't be paid.
Tell the Marines we have no forms to spare.
I cannot get these Ration States to square.
The Brigadier is coming round, they say.
The Colonel wants a man to cut his hair.
I think I must be going mad today.

Harold, always on the move, allows himself a small complaint: 'We have never stayed a day in one place, on the whole had a fairly strenuous time.' But then he brushes off the difficulties with: 'Everyone keeping fit.' Once he is in a freezing train with only a primus stove to keep him and his companions warm. There are endless marches through the mud, often ankle-, sometimes knee-deep. While reconnoitring the line, he gets 'severely shelled with gas shells' . . . 'No harm done,' he writes.

Not Harold, but others describe the hell of struggling—knee- or thigh-deep—through 'ubiquitous mud, thick, slimy and glutinous'. When the mud is thick an 'exhausted man in full kit carrying a rifle can take many hours to traverse a hundred yards'. He can even drown. Otherwise the men move through the trenches on tracks of 'duckboards over shell-holes' with the 'unburied dead much in evidence'.

Harold looks out for lice, gets bored in the office, and often works far into the night, grabbing whatever time he can to write letters. Sometimes he has to sleep through sub-zero nights: 'Two nights without blankets and heavy snow.' Chronic sleeplessness is a problem.

Because of censorship strictures, we never know, from his letters, where he is. If he puts down the name of a town or village by mistake, he scratches it out. But once he gets as far south as Arras. He is delighted with the pies, dates, socks, chocolates and other small comforts he gets from home and asks for some blankets and a 'groundsheet'. Once his family, old Argentina hands, send him *yerba mate*. Later he wants a watch and special box, marked 'H.S.Walker', for his 'secret' papers. He remarks that the countryside looks 'like Wiltshire' and is splendid for the horses he sometimes has to ride.

He spends long periods in the freezing, mud-filled, blood-soaked, rat-infested trenches. In these cramped quarters the men, many mere boys, stand, sleep and wait, hour after hour, day after day, dead comrades lying around and under their feet. Then the silence suddenly explodes into the deafening clatter of bombardment, artillery shelling, sirens and screams. It has been remarked that trench life was essentially tedious. So slow, so boring, that an attack, no matter how foolish and dangerous, was welcomed.

The trenches, those ditches of 'mud and blood' even when quiet, are dangerous and disease-ridden. An inadvertent glance over the top can mean death by sniper fire. There are lice, frogs, and nits, but also rats; black, and worse, brown. These can eat themselves into the size of cats.

Twigs of a Tree

There are millions of them. They run across the faces of sleeping men and feast on the bodies of the dead, with a preference for eyes and livers. To Harold, the rats are the worst horror of the trenches. He spends every night hunting them down. 'They killed our cat 2 nights ago. I think she died of fright.'

The lice bring trench fever that takes some twelve weeks to cure. The damp and the cold cause trench foot, a gangrenous condition that often leads to amputation. Visitors to the trenches are horrified by the stench: a nauseous mixture of gas, latrines, chlorine, cigarette smoke, food, putrid sandbags and rotting corpses.

Life in the Trenches

Although Harold hates the rats, he takes the boredom of the long days in these gutters of modern warfare—the cold, the wet, the discomfort and even the danger and death—in his stride. 'Had quite a good time . . . men were excellent . . . didn't mind the bullets at all and soon got used to shells.' In this modern, new form of warfare anything that had to be done was done after dark, since it was too dangerous to venture out during the day. Men in balloons, presumably out of the range of rifle shot, surveyed the scene from the air.

In February, 'I altogether thoroughly enjoyed myself in the trenches and shall not be sorry to return.' A perilous crossing of territory to get to his platoon through bursting shells and grenades is to Harold 'most amusing'. In the same month, 'my orderly room in the village had the stove blown through the wall into the garden . . . We had some casualties up here. So long. P.S am enjoying my job very much.'

Or again, after a stint away from the trenches: 'Hope we go into the line again soon, am getting fed up with this peaceful life. We are building a railway.' The billets where they sleep are 'not the best' and often can only be reached through ankle-deep mud, so bad that the soldiers sometimes lose their shoes and gum boots and have to march barefoot or with feet wrapped in the cloth of their 'puttees'. Harold displays his sense of irony in his description of a general, a 'most extraordinary fellow', who

was here to tea today, very fed up, thinks the war may soon be over. When he is feeling very well he thinks the war may last another 3 or 4 years, but if he is feeling bad . . . he thinks peace may be declared at any moment.

Not all the commanding officers are as gung-ho about warfare as this general, or as cool as Harold himself. 'Personally, I have had a fairly easy time, but some of them have had it pretty thick.' Five officers are so incompetent that they are sent home. Another is so traumatized by what he has seen that 'he went to pieces after 4 days and has been in hospital ever since'.

Once Harold encloses a special letter to be sent on to his sister Melrose. He pokes affectionate fun at his older brother by describing a stranger who is 'rather like Briton but more intelligent looking'.

At the Mercy of a U-Boat

Briton's own year in Argentina was not uneventful. 'His' tower was inaugurated in Buenos Aires on May 24, 1916, in the presence of Argentina's president Victorino de la Plaza and a slew of British dignitaries. Three months later, Briton received the news of Eric's death in the fields of France, and, less than a month after that, on September 14th, his youngest child Barbara was born. Seemingly appalled and worried by the effect of Eric's death on his parents, Briton, in spite of the war, is soon back on the Atlantic, sailing to England from Argentina. With him are his wife, Elsie, his two young children, Betty and Norman, and his new baby daughter, Barbara, not yet nine months old.

The family have an adventurous and no doubt dangerous voyage, during which their ship, Spanish and therefore neutral, is nevertheless

Twigs of a Tree

stopped by a German submarine. Barbara heard later that some of the British were hidden in a lifeboat; others were put into a ship's boat to be taken away. The story goes that, as the Germans searched through the passenger list for British names, young Norman, Briton's five-year old son, piped up with: 'If they are going to shoot us, why don't they do it now?' In her *Memories of Broomwater,* Bar adds: 'But they didn't, and the British were allowed back on board.'

On June 12, 1917 the young Walker family from Argentina arrive—after a month at sea—in the harbour of Santander in Spain and then make their way by land across the war-torn continent to England. Alice and JG have been frantically getting the Broomwater house ready for Briton's arrival. On June 17th, after a relatively short but no doubt dangerous trip of five days, the whole family finally arrives in Teddington—'in time for lunch'.

Eager to see his brother again, Harold manages to get leave, travels two days and gets home on July 6th, just over two weeks after the arrival of Briton and his family, for a nine-day break from the trenches.

Betty, by then eight, clearly enchanted both her young uncles. When Harold travels back to the lines on July 15, he writes to her from Folkestone, telling her that he has arrived safely, and has been to see a film. He hopes that she had a 'nice swim' and tells her he will be boarding ship at 6.30 pm. He is sent straight back to the lines, but has time to write: 'Tell old Betty I use her pencils constantly . . . everybody admires the colours.' Like many soldiers, he took photographs while on the front and he asks the family to fetch some film he has left to be developed at the Kodak shop in the Strand. Promotion is in sight, for he writes that he is pleased to be receiving command of his own company, a group of anything between 60 and 190 men divided into platoons.[16]

As adjutant to the commanding officer, Harold signs the preparatory plan for a raid on 'Mow Cop' on the 22nd and 23rd of July. On the 31st, Harold writes to young Betty again: 'Please tell Granny that the Brigadier has ordered me to put three stars on my shirt, and tell her she may now address me as Captain. I must now go and powder my nose as the sun makes it so red.'

---

[16] The numerical army hierarchy ranges from squad, (9 to 10 soldiers) platoon, company, battalion, brigade, division (10,000-15.000) and corps (45.000). The company consists of anything between 62-190 men, sub-divided into 3 to 5 platoons.

On July 31st, the same day that Harold writes to his niece, General Haig launched the operation now known as the 'Third Battle of Ypres'—or Passchendaal. It was yet another attempt to move the trench line forward along an eighteen-kilometre flank. The advance was to last two months, until November. Harold now has a company to command.

For Harold, the action is a welcome 'treat to do decent work again after 5 months office work'. He is delighted with his new command. 'I should never have got a Company without being adjutant first. As I am so junior in the regiment—there are about 40 Lieutenants and 2nd Lieutenants senior to me—I must clean myself for dinner.' He is now very busy organizing practice attacks with 'five tanks to help us'.

Harold moves briefly to Amiens, admires its cathedral and has breakfast at the Officers' Club. On August 22nd, he has a 'big day': 'The whole division operating . . . with tanks, aeroplanes was quite amusing'. He is happy that Briton, who obviously tried to join up in spite of being over forty, managed to get a commission,

It will keep him out of the ranks in case they increase the age limit, which they wont do anyway, as I think we may finish the war this year.

After his Boer War experience, Briton no doubt was delighted not to be a member of the ranks. Harold has some sympathy for the enemy. 'The Huns are getting a most putrid time. Their losses are from 5 to 10 to one of ours, and they can't keep that up much longer.' He appreciates with some irony that 'the weather has turned fine again, we are having quite a pleasant time in this peaceful spot.'

But by the beginning of September the weather is absolutely 'stinking', with constant rain pelting down day after day. He sends home a photograph of a Cathedral in a nameless town. He and his men try to bring down a circling plane with rifle fire but fail, so afterwards cheer themselves up by watching one of his officers 'do the Ghost in Hamlet'. He still hopes to be put into a 'real high-class attack and drive the Huns right out of Belgium'—a task he feels quite up to if the weather clears, 'But it rains all the time.'

The opportunity of a 'high class attack' arrives soon enough. The operation to capture German positions on either side of the St. Julien Winnipeg Road, near Poelcapelle just north of Ypres, began 9.45pm on September 7, 1917. The raid plan contains orders like:

Twigs of a Tree

Every man, except Lewis gunners, will carry either a pick or a shovel. Each man will carry twenty-four hours food rations and 2 bottles of water. Password and Distinguishing Marks: each man will wear a piece of white tape tied round above the elbow on each arm. The Password for the night will be 'Bully'. Gas. Provided the wind is favourable on the afternoon of September 8th, there will be a projection of gas from 'Livens' projectors on the area to be attacked.

The force is divided into three Companies, A, B, and C. Harold, now Captain Walker, is commander of B company. His orders are to capture Jury farm, occupied by the enemy. The farm is slightly north of Ypres, on a crossing of the Winnipeg and St. Julien Roads. C. Company is to take the cemetery that lies across the road to the east of the farm as well as the 'mebus'. This mebus or concrete pill-box is a small but heavily defended, well-manned fortification standing between the cemetery and the farm.

In his history of the Queen Victoria Rifles, Keeson includes several descriptions of the operation by survivors. Jury farm, first demolished by the fire of 'our heavies', was successfully captured; seven Germans were taken prisoner, others fell to the bayonet. He tells us that 'Captain Walker shot 2'.

C Company set off under Captain Griffith. The Company had lost twelve men before the operation began. The men had been 'gassed in the afternoon', not by the Germans but, accidentally, by 'our own gas shells' when they arrived at the cemetery. 'A considerable proportion of the men went into the attack suffering from the effects of gas.' As a result, Griffith's C Company failed to capture either the cemetery or the Mebus.

After B Company under Harold, had dealt with Jury farm, 'the attack proceeded to just beyond the crossroads, where we dug in.' Harold's company then sent a patrol to find C. Company. The patrol returned forty minutes later to say that the cemetery was still in the hands of the Germans with their machine guns, and that C. Company was nowhere to be seen. The narrator, Lieutenant McAdam of B. Company, then tells us:

It was then we decided that we should make good Jury Farm. We got back to the farm and tried to dig in. It was impossible, however, to enter the dug-out as it had been blown in by the barrage and it was equally impossible to dig in around it, owing to the state of the mud and shell-holes filled with water. On the way back Captain Walker was hit by a sniper's bullet from the Mebus, and owing to the enemy's accurate MG (machine-gun) fire it took two stretcher bearers over an hour to get him to a place of safety. We heard later that Capt. Walker had died in hospital near Poperinghe, which was not only a great blow to the company, but to the whole battalion.

McAdam goes on:
While the men were occupied in digging in at Jury Farm, they came under cross-fire from M.G'.s from the Mebus on either side, which made it impossible to hold the farm as there was absolutely no cover, and even if the men attempted to remain in the shell-holes, they would sink in the mud. The company was thereupon ordered to return to its former positions.[17]

Keeson records additional details by Rifleman A.E. Mills who, though severely wounded in the chest, seems to have survived:

Two platoons of B. Company and the whole of C. Company were taking part in the operations, and B Company succeeded in accomplishing their task. Capt. Walker called for a volunteer party of four (presumably he wished to know what had happened to C. Company on our left), and Riflemen Farmer, Ellis, Mills and Wainwright went with him. Captain Walker stopped to talk to a wounded German and it was then discovered that something had prevented 'C' Company from carrying out their programme. In rapid succession Mills, Ellis, Captain Walker and Rifleman Farmer were hit from a machine-gun which C. Company would have mopped up, had they been able to advance. Captain Walker then sent Rifleman Mills forward to the platoon for assistance, and when he returned Ellis was dead and Captain Walker was being got on to a stretcher. This gallant gentleman died shortly afterwards in hospital. I shall never forget his action after he was wounded; he lay on the stretcher directing us (his local knowledge seem to me wonderful) and we dragged him over the rough ground, just two stretcher bearers and myself, until we were back to our starting-point where my wound was dressed. One could not judge from his quiet and decided manner whether he suffered any pain, but the rough ground and the shaking he got must have been all against him.

---

[17] Keeson, C.A. Cuthbert, *History of Queen Victoria's Rifles 1792-1922*. Constable & Company Ltd., 1923 p. 329

Twigs of a Tree

The Brigadier General commanding the Brigade ends his account of the operation of Harold's B. Company with:

> *I consider that this Company was exceedingly well handled. C. company was not so successful. At dusk, when the Company Commander arrived at Springfield, he found that 8 of the garrison (Lieut. Spenser Pyrse's platoon) had been gassed by our gas shells, and had to be evacuated. Lieut. Wightwick's platoon had lost 9 men the previous night during a company relief, and had to be reinforced by a section from another platoon who did not know the ground at the last moment. They thus started seriously handicapped. In addition, our barrage was very short on this flank.*

The Brigadier concludes that the failure was the result of the platoon commander and his sergeant being hit at the same time:

> *I much regret that this attack should have so nearly succeeded, and yet failed, but I am confident that we will succeed next time.*

The battalion commander, Lt. Colonel Langworthy Parry, is recorded as describing

> *the loss of Capt. Walker and Lieut. Wightwick as a serious one for the battalion. No two officers . . . were more highly esteemed and loved by all ranks, and they were indeed very gallant gentlemen.*

Langworth Parry was later congratulated on the 'very near success' of the operation. B Company, finding it was being fired into from the back from the Mebus that C Company had failed to take, returned, bringing another six prisoners and leaving about two more badly wounded Germans behind. On September 14, their granddaughter Barbara's first birthday, Alice and JG Walker receive a casual note from Harold, dated September 10th:

> *Just a line to say I am going strong. I took 2 platoons of B company to raid the Huns and got my right thigh bone fractured with machine gun bullets. We got 12 prisoners and have one man killed and 4 wounded. So long.*

So long it was; this was Harold's last letter. By the time they received it, Alice and JG's third son had died of his wounds in Poperinge hospital. A telegram from the War Office dated the 13th followed:

We most deeply regret to inform you that Captain H.S. Walker died of wounds 12th September.

Perhaps no-one has left so powerful a picture of the sheer horror, the indignity of the war than the poet Wilfred Owen. In October 1915, he, like Harold before him, enlisted as a volunteer (with the Artists' Rifles) and, after training, arrived—again like Harold—in France at the beginning of 1917, the worst winter of the war. He was to spend a total of only five weeks on the lines. From what he saw in those five weeks he fashioned the poetry that epitomizes the war's waste, misery and desolation. Hospitalized in Edinburgh for four months with trench foot, he wrote a now famous lament for the slaughter he had witnessed:

<u>Anthem for Doomed Youth</u>

What passing-bells for these who die as cattle?
Only the monstrous anger of the guns.
Only the stuttering rifles' rapid rattle
Can patter out their hasty orisons.
No mockeries now for them; no prayers nor bells;
Nor any voice of mourning save the choirs, —
The shrill, demented choirs of wailing shells;
And bugles calling for them from sad shires.
What candles may be held to speed them all?
Not in the hands of boys but in their eyes
Shall shine the holy glimmers of goodbyes.
The pallor of girls' brows shall be their pall;
Their flowers the tenderness of patient minds,
And each slow dusk a drawing-down of blinds.

Back on the lines the year after Harold's death, Wilfred Owen was killed only seven days before the butchery came to an end. On November 11, 1918, when all England, the world itself, was rejoicing, celebrating the end of the war, his mother's relief was cut short. On that day she received the news of her son's death. He was a mere twenty-five years old. One of the very greatest of the war poets, Owen emphasizes not the glory but the horror, the ignominy, the loss, the grotesqueness of modern warfare, where soldiers, stripped of any glory, move 'knock-kneed, coughing like hags'. In

Twigs of a Tree

this poem he rejects the bitter fraud of Horace's line that there is beauty in the sacrifice, that 'It is Sweet and Right' to die for your country. [18]

<u>*Dulce et Decorum est*</u>

Bent double, like old beggars under sacks,
Knock-kneed, coughing like hags, we cursed through sludge,
Till on the haunting flares we turned our backs
And towards our distant rest began to trudge.
Men marched asleep. Many had lost their boots
But limped on, blood-shod. All went lame; all blind;
Drunk with fatigue; deaf even to the hoots
Of tired, outstripped Five-Nines that dropped behind.
Gas! Gas! Quick, boys!—An ecstasy of fumbling,
Fitting the clumsy helmets just in time;
But someone still was yelling out and stumbling,
And flound'ring like a man in fire or lime . . .
Dim, through the misty panes and thick green light,
As under a green sea, I saw him drowning.
In all my dreams, before my helpless sight,
He plunges at me, guttering, choking, drowning.
If in some smothering dreams you too could pace
Behind the wagon that we flung him in,
And watch the white eyes writhing in his face,
His hanging face, like a devil's sick of sin;
If you could hear, at every jolt, the blood
Come gargling from the froth-corrupted lungs,
Obscene as cancer, bitter as the cud
Of vile, incurable sores on innocent tongues,
My friend, you would not tell with such high zest
To children ardent for some desperate glory,
The old Lie; Dulce et Decorum est
Pro patria mori.

---

[18] Ferguson, p.205, writes that Owen 'reserved a special hatred' for Jessey Pope, author of the jingoistic calls to arms including *The Call. Who's for the trench/Are you my laddie/Who's going out to win?/ Who wants to save his skin?* He originally entitled this poem: *To Jessey Pope.*

Carlos and I found Harold's grave in Dozinghem cemetery near Poperinghe, just outside Ypres. Afterwards, while looking through a bookshop in the city, I discovered, by sheer chance, an account of how he died.[19]

Dozinghem Cemetery, where Harold lies

On the night of 8 September 1917, the Queen Victoria Rifles launched a raid against the German positions at Winnipeg Cross Roads. Initially all went well. B Company, under Captain Harold Walker, quickly occupied Jury Farm, where Walker himself shot two Germans with his revolver and took several others prisoner. Hereafter, however, things began to go wrong. As Walker and his men approached the crossroads, they came under fire from an old cemetery to their left, which should have been neutralized by their comrades in C Company. Calling for volunteers, Walker set off to find out what was going on.

The account goes on with Rifleman Mills' report, quoted above.

---

[19] *At the Going Down of the Sun 365 Soldiers from the Great War*, p.229. The book commemorates the death of one soldier for each day of the year. Harold represents September 12th. Much later I discovered that this account had probably been taken from C. Keeson's 'History of Queen Victoria's Rifles

Twigs of a Tree

Captain H.S. Walker Queen Victoria's Rifles
12th September 1917 Age 36

It is impossible to imagine how Alice and JG Walker received this terrible blow, the loss of yet another, the third of their four sons. That Harold was awarded an MID, Mention in Despatches, from General Haig must have been scant comfort.

Eric and Harold's deaths were not to be the last family tragedy in this second decade of the 20th century. Briton, still in England with Elsie and his three small children, was possibly, in those difficult days, still living with his parents in their suburban house in Teddington. As the war drew to an end, another disaster began unfolding.

The Spanish flu epidemic, once called 'the greatest medical holocaust in history', began to ravage the globe. In the two years from June 1918, it is now estimated, the flu killed anything between 50 to 100 million young adults, a toll infinitely larger than the approximately 16 million who lost their lives in the war. Among the victims of this avian flu were Austrian painter Egon Schiele and his young pregnant wife, as well as the French poet Guillaume Apollinaire.

Closer to home, in England, the flu carried off Elsie, the young mother of Briton's three small children Betty, Norman and two-year old

Barbara. Molly tells us that Elsie was again pregnant, and that she died on November 19, a week after the Armistice. She was thirty-four years old.

The devastation, the psychological and spiritual toll on Briton, after the loss of two more brothers and then his wife are beyond contemplation. But left with three small children, he could do nothing but go on. Molly remarks of Briton that he never spoke of his wife or of her death. 'Nobody ever mentioned her', said Molly. Years later, it was not to her father but to Molly that Elsie's youngest child, Barbara, turned for information about the mother she never knew: 'What was mother Elsie like?'

Like Wilfred Owen's mother, and thousands of other grief-stricken families, Alice and JG had little to celebrate at the end of the war. Three sons, and the young woman who was their niece and daughter-in-law, were gone. Bar reports that 'when Elsie died in 1918, we all moved in with them.' Alice, now nearing her seventies, was to begin a new and certainly not easy life. For it was she who was to take charge of the three small children—Betty, eight, Norman, six and Barbara, only two years old.

CHAPTER XVIII

YOUTH BETWEEN THE WARS

On his return from Argentina to England in September 1917, shortly after his brother Harold's death on the front, Briton Walker, now in his forties, had the good fortune of being taken on as an experienced civil engineer. Otherwise, on volunteering for an officer's commission—as Harold had recommended—he might very well, in spite of his age, have been sent into the mud and blood of the Flanders trenches.

Briton looking none too happy in his military uniform

Instead, the Air Ministry in London kept him at home—'building aerodromes'—which not only may have saved his life, but also made it possible for him to stay in England until his three small children had grown up. He must have done his job extremely well. Only two years later, in October 1919, Lieutenant John Briton Walker was awarded an O.B.E. By then a widower, he was only to return to Argentina in 1929.

Alice with Norman and Barbara, Teddington, circa 1920

Briton's sister Melrose, in the meantime, was still living with her own three offspring and her husband, Patrick Goodbody on the Conchillas estancia in Uruguay. In the first post-war years, the young cousins, Briton and Melrose's respective children, were oceans apart, but in 1922 Melrose landed in England on the *Holbein* accompanied by Molly, Pat and Noreen.[20]

---

[20] The ship's record of the landing is on Ancestry.com

Twigs of a Tree

Pat, then about twelve, was enrolled for four years in Leighton Park, the Quaker School near Reading. Founded in 1890, it became a favourite for the children of 'Quaker industrialists'. He seems to have had a difficult time at school, perhaps in part because he had no immediate family in England, apart from his grandparents, JG and Alice, and his Uncle Briton. His own family, far away in Argentina, according to the school records, seems to have been in these post-war years somewhat financially strapped. It is possible that by that time his father had lost his job.

Barbara remembers Pat setting off for school in a horse cab to Twickenham station for the train to Reading. She recalls his teasing threats to put the family cat in the 'ice chest'. David Lean, director of many successful British films (*Brief Encounter, Lawrence of Arabia, Doctor Zhivago*, etc.) was at Leighton Park at the same time as Pat. Lean remembers that 'my closest friendship was with a very glamorous fellow called Patrick Goodbody, an Irishman who came from the Argentine. Frightfully good looking and sort of dashing.'[1]

We learn from Lean that, if sexual education for girls at Berkhamsted was no more specific than 'lie back and think of England', the Quaker school's was equally laconic. Lean tells us that the headmaster's sporadic 'wine, women and gas' lectures were launched only when his wife left the dinner table. Having covered the subject of chickens and eggs, the headmaster went on to menstruation, followed by advice 'never to insist that girls should bathe if they put up any sort of objection'.

---

[1] *David Lean*, by Kivin Brownlow, discovered by Angela and Matt Huber. The school records tells us that "At Athletics he performed well at the Weight and High Jump. He played in goal for the Football XI in 1926. He was not promoted to responsibility as a School or a House Prefect. Initially he hoped to become an Electrical Engineer, but this seemed beyond his reach and he then decided to return to Argentina and become a Rancher."

Patrick Goodbody in his twenties

    This extracurricular tuition left young David Lean not much the wiser. After one such lecture he sauntered across the playing fields with his friend, Pat Goodbody. Pat, though not older than Lean, was nevertheless already 'very sophisticated', able to explain the mysteries of nature more intelligibly than the headmaster. 'What's he talking about? Blood?', Pat asked. 'Oh yes, I've got a sister . . . He then explained it all to me.'

    Pat's older sister, Molly, now fifteen, was sent to what she always called the 'tin-pot school', Summerleigh, where Barbara was later educated. Pat was necessarily a boarder, but Molly must have joined the fairly large number of children—including Briton's motherless brood—now living in the Teddington house under the tutelage of their grandparents, Alice and JG.

Twigs of a Tree

Alice in the late 1920's at Broomwater with Noreen's dog Roo

Barbara, in spite of the loss of her mother in the post-war flu' epidemic of 1918, the personal tragedies her father and grandparents had endured, has very happy memories of the Teddington household.[2] 'We had a lot of fun, always a full house, lots of friends visiting . . .' For Alice it was a delight to be sculled by JG along the river to the Saturday market in Kingston. There he would moor his boat in front of *The Sun* pub.

JG still enjoyed sea shanties, the theatre, and reading to himself and the children. Those being still very early 'radio days', he had a 'cats-whisker wireless' with two sets of earphones. Although her grandparents in their old age went out only occasionally, Barbara recalls an outing with Alice and JG to the Richmond Theatre to see *Lilac Time*, an operetta based on Franz Schubert's life and compositions.

Alice shunned the 'popular press' for the more respectable *Times* during the week and the *Observer* on Sundays. Barbara remembers her grandmother taking an inordinate amount of time cleaning books and shelves in the spring. Suddenly absorbed by the volume in her hand,

---

[2] Barbara Brady, *Memories of Broomwater*

Youth Between The Wars

temptation too fierce to resist, she would sink into a chair and read on, dusting entirely forgotten. She posted magazines—*Punch* and the *Illustrated London News*—to friends and relations abroad, among them a 'Mr Moroney', Briton's comrade from the Boer War—whom Molly later described as 'one of Briton's foul friends'. Alice generously put up with Mr Moroney, and others, coming to stay. She played the piano in the evenings, and later she tried to teach both Betty and Barbara the mysteries of the keyboard. She 'despaired' of Bar's sister Betty, who was very energetic, independent and 'good at everything' in Bar's eyes—sports particularly.

Barbara has fond memories of the boat rides up the Thames with JG, a 'fine old man' who taught the children to play cards, to swim, to scull, to sit up straight in his beloved boats. During the summer the children revelled in swimming and boating parties.

Briton, Pat and Noreen Goodbody with Betty, Norman, and Barbara Walker circa 1922 with friend Tom Heslop

I still have a little book containing a single poem—Coleridge's *The Ancient Mariner*, a gift to JG's 12 year old grand-daughter. It is inscribed, 'Noreen, with love from Grandad, July 1924'.

But by then JG had reached the age of eighty-three. His eyesight was failing, and books he enjoyed had to be read to him by Alice. The following year, on September 24, 1925, he died. His performance at Henley so many years before had not been forgotten: an obituary in the rowing magazine of the London Club extolled him as

> No. 3 in the winning Grand Crew of 1868—one of the finest fixed-seat eights ever seen on the river.

JG Walker in his seventies

Alice seems to have retained a deep respect for his rowing trophies. These she polished, according to Bar, every Friday. At night his collection of silver cups, in a wicker basket, accompanied her upstairs to bed. After her husband's death, Alice travelled to Kingston not by boat but on the tramway, followed by a walk to the local shops. John George Walker lies in the cemetery at Teddington.[3]

---

[3] We have not yet found an obituary in the local papers that might have mentioned his pioneering life in the Pampas, his role in defending the British colonists against Indian attacks—in short: his role as the legendary Facón Chico.

Bar at JG's tomb in Teddington c. 2008

Effects of a Roving Eye

My mother, Noreen, who had returned to Argentina with Melrose in 1922, never saw JG again. The *Ancient Mariner* must have been posted to her. Sent to school at Berkhamsted five years later, in January 1927, when she was already fourteen, she is recorded as having left school in July 1929, a mere two and half years later, just before her seventeenth birthday. Her father, Patrick Goodbody, whom she also never saw again, is described in the school records as a 'cattle rancher'.[4]

---

[4] The address is given as Estancia San Jorge, James Craik, Argentina. James Craik is a town near Cordoba. When she left Berkhamsted, Noreen's address is given as JP Long, Esq, 6 Bolton Gardens, Teddington.

William Robinson/Patrick Goodbody 1876-1928

In November 1928, only three years after JG's death, Molly, Patrick, and Noreen's father died at the early age of fifty-two. It is possible that because of this sudden demise Noreen was obliged to leave school earlier than originally planned. According to Bar, Noreen's last year at Berkhamsted was funded by the Freemasons.

When she enrolled in the usual secretarial course Noreen must have been living with her grandmother, Alice, or in rooms near the house in Teddington. Both Molly and Noreen had been sent to school rather late. It is very likely that all their primary education took place on the pampas, presided over by 'governesses' or by Melrose herself.

According to my mother, her father had a habit of rising very early. Before taking on his estancia work he would spend two or three hours reading while drinking strong *mate*. She believed that the *mate* gave him the throat cancer that killed him so prematurely. Melrose herself was then in her early forties, alone in Argentina since all her children were far away in England. Some of her husband's wide-ranging collection of books are still at the Susana.

We know very little about the elder Patrick Goodbody. He, like his son Pat (as described by David Lean) was a 'dashing' figure: perhaps too much so, for, although a Quaker, he also seems to have been something of a rake. After a Lady Chatterley-like extramarital affair with, so family gossip goes, the wife of the owner of the estancia he managed in Uruguay, he lost his job. When exactly this was, how long it lasted, or whether his sudden lack of employment was a result of an affair or of the difficult post-war economic times, we do not know.

My mother, his youngest and possibly most spoiled child, adored him: for his affection, wit and wide interests. Molly, however, did not. Possibly she, being older, had already noted—and felt the consequences within the family—of her father's roving eye.

*Young Molly, Melrose and Patrick Goodbody
in the early to mid 1920's*

Melrose was now, at forty-four, a widow. As was usual for women, she was without a profession, and was left, according to my mother, 'almost penniless'. At one point, she began dressmaking and became something of an expert at the decorative stitching called 'smocking', used to ornament the frocks of little girls. The letters she wrote to me throughout my childhood and youth were always cheerful, but I know that she had a difficult life, carried with courage, stoicism and grace.

Shortly after the death of her husband, Melrose returned to England, moving in with her widowed mother. Alice was now in her eighties; left after JG's death, with her one remaining son, Briton, and his three motherless children. Betty, Norman and Barbara, were now in or nearing their teens. Towards the end of the twenties, Melrose was diagnosed with breast cancer. Her second mastectomy took place around 1931. Although she survived well into her nineties, the operations affected her arms and she, an amateur pianist like her mother, was never able to play again. I never heard her at the piano and there was no instrument in the house in Calle Moldes, in Belgrano. I do remember her standing before the looking glass, padding out the emptiness of her brassière with folded handkerchiefs before arranging her hair.

Melrose was to remain in Teddington with her mother and young Barbara until Alice's death in 1939. Barbara appreciated Melrose's care and modernizing influence on her appearance and wardrobe. Through Melrose's intercession she was finally able to circumvent Alice's veto on the latest fashion: she was finally allowed to bob her hair.

In the years between the wars, Argentina and life in the pampas remained an attraction for many of the younger members of the family. Much land was now in the hands of large meat packing companies—among them Liebig's, Swift's, Bovril and Magnasco, a company that specialized in dairy products. Pat Goodbody, having left Leighton Park School, returned to Argentina and eventually found work with the meat extract company Bovril—first as an estancia manager and later in its Buenos Aires offices. Diana McClure's father, Martin Eggar, after Eton, had left England in about 1929, when he was twenty, and went to work as a trainee manager on a *Liebig* estancia in the Paraguayan Chaco. He was to meet his wife, Betty Walker, years later in Argentina.

In 1929 Briton gave up his 'aerodrome-building' work for the Air Ministry in London, accepting a position in Argentina with his old company, *Hopkins and Gardom*. He was now supervising the construction of bridges for the expanding railway network. Betty, now twenty, and Norman seventeen joined him, at least for a time. Melrose remained at hand in England to keep her mother, Alice, and young Barbara company. Barbara's sister Betty, having gone through a secretarial course was working in London and Molly was engaged in the same type of work.

Molly, however, seems to have been back in Argentina by the mid-twenties, and young Norman Walker—after finishing his own studies in engineering—joined his father, Briton, in Argentina in 1933, where the two of them worked together on the construction of a railway bridge. In the same year, Barbara visited them in Pinto, in the province of Santiago del Estero, far in the northwest, where a version of Quechua, the ancient language of the Incas, was still spoken.

Living conditions in Pinto were primitive, but Barbara thoroughly enjoyed her three-month visit, in spite of frights with the local insects and other fauna. She delighted in the swimming, or rather floating in the salt-laden river, the long walks and the books she read in English instead of, she says guiltily, settling down to learn Spanish. Barbara celebrated her sixteenth birthday in 1932 with an *asado* and was present at the ceremony that marked the completion of the bridge. She then journeyed all the way to Venado Tuerto—to visit the newly-weds, her cousin Molly and Charles Dyson, before returning to England on the *Highland Monarch*.

Betty Walker also returned to Argentina at about the same time as her brother Norman and began work at the British Embassy in Buenos Aires. She stayed, at least at first, with her uncle—Elsie's brother—George Frederick Gordon Catty (1886-1949) who had, at thirty-two, volunteered for the Great War and, unlike his cousins Harold and Eric, survived.

Gordon, as he was known, made various trips to the United States and eventually, in 1924, returned with an American bride, Corinne Cochrane Mendinhall (1896-1984). In the forties he ran the Argentine branch of Elizabeth Arden. He and his wife lived in considerable style in a beautiful house with a large garden in Buenos Aires. Derek Dyson remembers the good deed that disgraced him at table there. As a child at one of their elegant luncheons, Derek picked up his empty plate and—just to be helpful—handed it to the butler himself. He was thoroughly scolded. I recall wondering how the same butler's gloves remained so white, whether he kept them on when he cleaned his teeth or polished his shoes, indeed why he bothered to wear them at all. Gordon and Corinne Catty had no children.

George Catty, Gordon's father, seems to have long given up *Il Divisorio*, his estancia on the Sauce Grande, and was living in the Moldes house in Belgrano with his second wife, Enid. He died there in 1936 at the age of eighty-four. His nephew, Briton, then bought the Belgrano house and lived there for many years. When Melrose returned to Argentina after

Alice's death, she too moved into the house. Enid, George's widow, by then very old, was in the 1940's still in the rooms at the far end of the veranda, tending to her plants. When I was there as a child, she sometimes invited me to tea and plied me with lemonade and delicious ginger biscuits.

Takeover and Marriage

The first marriage of the younger generation—after Gordon Catty's to Corinne Cochrane—seems to have been Molly Goodbody's to Charles Dyson.[5] After over nine years at Bedford School and completing—like young Eric Walker—a civil engineering course at *City and Guilds,* Charles, in about 1926, had also returned to South America.

English women in Argentina had long travelled to England to give birth, as a means of avoiding the indenture of an eventual son into the Argentine military service. This had not been the case with Elsie and young Norman Walker. Angela tells us that Briton's son, Norman, J.G's second grandson, was born in the Rio Cuarto region of Córdoba Province. After his father's return from Argentina in 1917, he passed all his youth in England. In 1930 Norman left King's College School for London University where he read civil engineering. Like his grandfather, a keen oarsman, he rowed in the London University crew and at the Kingston Rowing Club, near the Walker home in Teddington.

When Norman, now in his early twenties, returned to Argentina in 1933, he was drafted into the military and served one year in the Argentine Horse Artillery. Norman then briefly returned to England and, at a Kingston regatta, met his future wife, Gladys (Joan) Hills. However, he was soon back in Argentina working with his father.

Although born in Argentina, Charles—like Norman—had spent most of his youth in England. But when he returned to Argentina in

---

[5] Bedford School still has these records of him. 'Charles William Dyson (dob 9 October 1902) entered the School on Jan 17th 1911 and left at the end of the Summer Term 1920. His father is cited as Charles W Harding Dyson (Deceased added at a later date) and Mrs Katherine Rose Dyson. Their address was 45 Ashburnham Road, Bedford and later 73 Ashburnham Road. His previous school is given as Miss Gillions', 8 Rutland Road.

He joined the OTC, or Officers' Training Corps, in January 1918 and there is a further annotation 'm. 3.3.30' which I take to mean married in March 1930. The school magazine, the Ousel, for October 1920, notes that C.W Dyson 'failed to obtain School Certificates but passed with a credit in the subjects named: History and Elem. Mathematics.'

around 1926 he somehow managed—according to Molly—to talk or pay his way out of military service. He also had little stomach for the work he had been offered on the 'construction of the Burma Railway'. However, after visiting the *Susana*, which he had left so many years before, Charles, according to his son Brian Dyson, 'had his own epiphany'. He would

> *apply his brand new degree in civil engineering to the practice of farming and really make the land flourish. He would also begin to pay down the debt and then send for his mother, Rosie, and sister Jackie: this would lift them out of their lives of genteel poverty and justify their sacrifices in putting him through Bedford College.*[6]

The lease of the estancia in Santa Fe province was to remain, for another four years, in the hands of the Goodbody brothers, Jonathan and Eben. In the meantime, young Charles, eager for some practical training in agronomy, seems to have apprenticed himself to several estancieros. One of these could have been Molly's father, Patrick Goodbody, second cousin to the brothers, who was at that time running an estancia in Córdoba province.[7] Charles was willing to work hard. Brian tells us that he joined one estancia as a 'second':

> *The term meant that you were at the very bottom of the management ladder and got all the dirty work on a large 15.000 hectare estate. There, between rising at dawn and drinking and playing cards into the night with the Manager and his staff, he learned the craft of farming in Argentina. And he bided his time for when he would be able to apply his skills to his own promised land—the 2.200 hectares at La Susana.*

Briefly returning to England, Charles announced, to his mother Rosie and his sister Jackie, that he wished to farm on the Pampas. If this was something of a shock to Charles' mother, it was also a disappointment to

---

[6] Brian Dyson, *Estancia La Susana in the 1930's*, 2011.
[7] Melrose's husband William Robinson and the two brothers, sharing a great-grandfather, Robert Goodbody of Clara, writer of the journal, were second cousins. Their respective grandfathers were two of Robert Goodbody's five sons: Thomas Pim (1814-1890) and Jonathan, (1812-1889). Eben and Jonathan of Venado Tuerto were sons of Richard Goodbody of Belair, grandsons of Jonathan. William Robinson was the son of William Robinson Goodbody of Elm Field (1849-1929), grandson of Thomas Pim (1814-1890)

Twigs of a Tree

Jonathan and Eben Goodbody, who had been running the *Susana* for some twenty years. Having built a swimming pool and expanded the house, they were still interested in buying the estancia. There was, however, an amicable handover, and the Goodbody brothers remained friends and neighbours on their dairy farm *Derrynane*, near Venado Tuerto.

Molly Goodbody in the late 1920's

By the time Molly and Charles's marriage took place on March 3, 1930, when Molly was 23, Rosie and Jackie were back in Argentina. The *Susana* was officially returned one month later, on April lst. The picture below shows the marriage party. A still youthful looking Melrose, who must have gone out to Argentina for the occasion, stands next to her son, Pat Goodbody; next to him is Rosie Dyson, who later taught me the subtleties of embroidering French knots. Molly, looking beautiful, stands next to Charles, in formal dress, and a little further along, the second woman from the right, is his very pretty sister, Marie Louise—Jackie Dyson.

Molly Goodbody's wedding to Charles Dyson March 3, 1930

Jackie and Rosie lived on the estancia with the young couple and their soon to be born children—Derek (1932), Brian (1935)—for over ten years. Jackie firmly believed that, where Molly could be 'wife' to Charles, she, Jackie, could be 'mother' to their sons. She would run to obey the boys' any order. I remember Derek and Brian inspecting the drinks she would bring them while they were lying reading on their beds. If they were not satisfactory (not enough ice) Jackie would charge off to correct the deficiency; still not right, she would race off again. But when life with three women in the household became too difficult, with—as Molly put it—'too many cooks in the kitchen', Jackie and Rosie moved to a flat in downtown Buenos Aires—not far from 'Uncle Briton's tower', the *Torre de los Ingleses*. Derek and Brian must have missed their aunt's loving ministrations.

Jackie, according to Molly, had once been engaged, but she never married, 'because she never found anyone as good as her brother, Charles'. She too had no profession and lived with her mother until the end of Rosie's life. Although she always insisted that I wear one of her large stock of despised linen hats, as protection from the 'dangerous' sun, I remember her with fondness and feel she must have had a somewhat constricted life. Carlos and I had an amusing meal with her in Buenos Aires at the

Twigs of a Tree

Claridges' Hotel, many, many years later on a visit to Argentina from India. She died July 22, 1975, about a year after we last saw her.

Jackie on the Susana veranda, watching Lin dangling from the magnolia. 1940's

Brian Dyson describes the 'enterprise and excitement' of his young parents, this new generation of pampas 'pioneers':

During the lease, La Susana *had languished: now, every thing had to be done. Charles, in "bombachas" and short, wide boots, used theodolite and compass to map out a model working farm for crops and Shorthorn cattle. Molly tended to the vegetable and flower gardens around the house, and armed with a dog-eared edition of Mrs. Beaton's Cook book, started down the path to becoming a first rate cook of hearty fare.* [8]

In her 1996 videotape interview with her granddaughters, Tania and Susie Dyson, Molly describes the early difficulties of life on the camp. Charles himself had very little capital and, in order to stock what was now a 'bare' farm, had to take on four *colonos*, tenant farmers, who in exchange

---

[8] Brian Dyson, *Estancia La Susana in the 1930's*, 2011

for building their own houses and sowing the land gave their landlord a percentage of their profits. He also let fields as pastureland for other men's cattle, including animals that belonged to the Goodbodys. Molly remembers that at first there was no car, no tractor, and no money.

But, as Brian explains, over the years things gradually took shape.
Like a painter stepping back to admire his canvas, Charles could see staunch new fencing marching into the distance; windmills turning briskly to feed the round Australian tanks, and then to nourish the cement drinking troughs with cool, sweet water; a handsome troop of steers trudging home after being vaccinated, weighed and dipped; and immaculate lines of young corn, affirming the vigour of life cycles; here and there, a clump of young saplings huddled together, knowing they must stand against the cold Pampero, whistling up from the long limb of Patagonia; or even the solitary, stubborn thistle, still clinging to life in a freshly ploughed field.
Life was good in the early years. Hard, hands-on work from early light and then back to drinks and dinner with scratchy, wavering news from the BBC and a Book of the Month selection from Harrods. Then gradually nodding off, knowing you have left your mark on the soil.

As with JG so many years before, nature periodically turned savage: *Yet there were times when life gave you pause and the grim face of nature bore down hard. Waves of locust would darken the sky, killing the crops and denuding trees, and even chickens and eggs became inedible. There were traditional foes: foot and mouth disease; plagues of single minded insects, worms and flying green bugs that simply ate, reproduced and died; and rodents and birds who paid no heed to human husbandry. But the worst was drought: to watch young crops wither and burn, and see cattle having to eat leaves and bark of trees, was more than a strong man could take. People became surly and short tempered, attendance in church rose, and all would be covered by a layer of fine dust. Eventually, balance would be restored. Dead fields would spring to life, and the fundamental optimism of farmers would be rewarded, albeit with a vague remembrance that what is given can also be taken away.*[9]

---

[9] Brian Dyson, *Estancia La Susana in the 1930's*

Twigs of a Tree

For many, life on the camp remained tough, relatively basic. Alice and JG Walker would have recognized much of the camp life of even the forties and fifties, as described by Martin Eggar's daughter Diana,

The estancias I lived on as a child in the 1940s and 1950s were almost self-sufficient. Meat, milk, butter, cream, fruit and vegetables, all were supplied from the land, or from the cattle which were raised on that land. Horses were the most usual form of transport. We had no need of public utilities: the wind pump pulled up the water, firewood came from the estancia trees, there was a cesspit for sewage, and a pit was dug for the disposal of any rubbish. There was very little waste—scraps were fed to the poultry—and it took a long time to fill the rubbish pit, which was then covered with earth, and a new one was dug.

Alice and JG would also have been at home with the lack of electricity, the wood-burning kitchen stove; reading by the light of kerosene lamps, clothes still washed by hand, still smoothed with irons filled with 'red hot cinders' from the kitchen stove. They would not, however, have recognized the startling modernity of the 'tiny wind pump on the roof, which supplied power for a radio.' Nevertheless it was only around 1985 that the *Susana* was equipped with a proper telephone line; before that, it merely had what Molly described as 'a radio-telephone, good for messages but not very good for direct talking.'[10]

When Charles took over the estancia in 1930, in those days of the Great Depression, money was scarce, and the value of beef and currency was steadily falling. But there was, as Brian points out, also much fun and social activity. Household help was plentiful; there were dinner, lunch and bridge parties, riding, cricketing, croquet, tennis, swimming, and, for those so inclined, even polo.

Although the needs of a working Estancia are an everyday affair, there was time for socializing and fun. Venado Tuerto, only 25 kms away, flourished as the young and restless could catch the overnight sleeper train from Retiro station, in Buenos Aires, and awaken to a week-end of racing, polo and inebriation. But most entertainment was centred on the Estancias and would range from the modest dinner and bridge

---

[10] Letter to Barbara July 17th, 1985

Youth Between The Wars

invite, to big blow-outs with dining tents and music, where even the dogs had more than their fill.
Some Estancias had a swimming pool of sorts, maybe a tennis court, and croquet was a natural. The crisp winter months were perfect for gymkhanas, shooting ducks or partridge, or a ragged football match on a pasture with no boundaries or referee. Occasionally a priest on his appointed rounds would bring the word to Venado Tuerto; or sometimes an old movie, reels in metal canisters that needed to be spliced together, would make it to a makeshift screen. Sometimes a couple who had gone "home" to England would return with a trunk of riches; bright yellow Colman's mustard; round tins of Players Navy Cut cigarettes and Ronson lighters; Tate and Lyle Golden Syrup, Kepler's malt and such; but, above all, the real stuff, bottles of Scotch whisky. And then, if the harvest was good, the whole family would pack into the car, with luggage on top, and either go East to the beaches and casino at Punta del Este, Uruguay, or West to the cool hills of Cordoba

Partying on the Pampas, Charles standing on left behind Jackie, Molly and Betty seated in the middle among friends.

The club in Venado Tuerto—allegedly still closed to non-British, to Argentines, as the British São Paolo club was then closed to

Brazilians—provided more than adequate entertainment to a rural society of English or Irish families.

To our generation it seems beyond belief that the Anglo community, as Molly said, 'never bothered with the Argentines', and that Jackie used to vaunt not knowing a single 'Argentino'. Her brother Charles has gone down in family legend as once having remarked of a friend: 'He's a bit of a twerp, he married an Argentine.'

Diana McClure, looking back on her forties' childhood, remarks on the same insularity of the British community around the estancias where she lived. 'Nearly all our close friends were British, or of British descent.' Children were sent to English schools in Buenos Aires or to boarding school in England, often at considerable financial sacrifice. It was then inconceivable to send one's child for secondary education to even the best of Argentine or Brazilian schools.

Jean Bazán, the English wife of Brian's friend Pardo Bazán, told me that, when she married her Argentine husband, she had to make a point of 'learning to speak Spanish properly'. The very good English school to which she went in Buenos Aires did not think Spanish worth the trouble of thorough teaching. Spanish was the language for the 'help'. Jean had been in Argentina all her life and spoke Spanish fluently, but with her marriage she decided to try and match the speech of her highly educated husband. The effort, she told me, took her several years.

Although this was not true of every Englishman, it was common enough. Gustavo Monacci in his book about the British in Bahia Blanca writes that

This small group of immigrants is characterized by an innate tendency to isolation. It does not behave like the other groups of Europeans who sooner or later do integrate into the Argentine community, making up a new and original cosmopolitan society. Of the tendency to introversion typical of so many similar groups; the English is the group of foreigners most protective of its customs, its language and its traditions.[11]

Even today, although many English estancia houses are crammed with books—poetry, fiction, history, philosophy—it is still rare to find anything in Spanish. No Spanish-language classics, either ancient or modern; no

---

[11] Gustavo Monacci, *La Colectividad Britanica en Bahia Blanca*, 1979

Borges, Sábato or Cortázar, not even García Márquez or Isabel Allende. Neither was it common in Brazil, for that matter, to find Camões or Eça de Queiroz, Jorge Amado or Clarice Lispector in households of English descent. Generations of British first sent their children to local English schools, and then pushed them on, at the tender age of eleven or twelve or even earlier, into boarding schools in England.

My father had the same ideas about what he considered the virtually unbridgeable distinctions between his own Britishness (actually Australian) and the Brazilians. These ideas were to be blasted in his extreme old age when he—revelling in the hugs and good-night embraces of the pretty nurses—was cared for with so much warmth and affection in the Brazilian nursing home in which he died.

My mother, who worked with the Brazilian poor—victims of cerebral palsy and polio—and their families for much of her life, was considerably more broadminded. When my youngest brother Jim, born in Brazil, reached his 'boarding school' age, my parents gave in to a little pressure from me (just back from school in England myself, and eleven years older than Jim) and, instead of sending him to Britain at eleven or so, placed him in an excellent Brazilian school. As a result, my brother became perfectly bi-lingual, as I did not. He can not only speak but also write like a cultivated Brazilian. Nevertheless, Jim was also sent to school in England—much later—to do his A-levels at Atlantic College in Wales, around the age of fifteen, before going on to University, not in England but in Canada.

Diana McClure describes how her father Martin Eggar arrived in Argentina. Although his own father had taught at Eton, Martin, according to his daughter, was 'not academic' and decided on a career in agriculture. Potential estancia managers did not, then, bother with the study of agronomy; like Charles Dyson, they 'apprenticed' themselves. It was a profession that still attracted many young men. Life as a manager on these vast 'industrial' farms, owned by companies rather than individuals, could be comfortable—with perks like 'home leave'—but the jobs were also precarious, subject to the fluctuations of supply and demand in the world commodities market. Diana tells us that her father left England in about 1929, when he was 20, and went to work as a trainee manager on an estancia in the Paraguyan Chaco, belonging to Liebig's Extract of Meat Co. It was beside the River Paraguay, about 200.000 hectares in size (half a million acres), very flat, with enormous fields of savannah and thorny scrub with palm trees. He worked there for a couple of years. His father told him that he must insist on being sent back to England on leave, in accordance with his contract. Liebig's duly sent him back to England, but said that, as it was the height of the recession, they no longer had a job for him.

Martin nonetheless returned to Argentina:

He invested the little bit of money that he had in an enterprise called "El Dorado", an orange-growing scheme in the province of Misiones, in north-eastern Argentina. It turned out to be a scam, he lost all his money and worked for a while as a children's tutor on an estancia, and then as a cadet for the Southern Land Company, in Patagonia, in the foothills of the Andes. It was there that he met my mother, Betty Walker . . . She was visiting her father, John Briton Walker, who was, I think, building a bridge . . .

Noreen Goodbody

Sudden Death

My mother, Noreen Goodbody, had remained in England after her schooling at Berkhamsted, living in Teddington and working at a secretarial job.[12] In 1931, when she was about nineteen, she attended a Christmas party given by the Roylance family, neighbours of Alice's. There she met a young doctor from Cork in Ireland, Eric St. John Emerson. Eric, about to finish his medical training, had no time for young women and said so. However, they made an appointment to meet six months later, after his final examinations.

They were soon engaged, tooling around antique shops collecting the bits of vintage furniture that Eric loved and that my mother kept until the day of her death, including a little sideboard with shelves above it, always known in the family as the 'Aunt Mary'. In July 1932 they went off alone together, rather surprisingly for those times, on a camping excursion. Noreen travelled from Waterloo to meet her fiancé in Basingstoke.

Noreen Goodbody & Eric St. John Emerson c. 1932

She was not on the expected train, but Eric's long and anxious wait was finally rewarded:

---

[12] According to Bar she lived in Teddington but worked for the United Potash Co. in Fenchurch Street in London. When she gave up her job to marry, Bar joined the company, staying with it until her own marriage just before the outbreak of war.

Thank goodness there was the tall erect figure walking gracefully towards me, and as she got nearer I saw the half-shy smile and my dreads were set at rest . . . I might have done God knows what mad thing if she had not been on that train.[13]

They then set off through 'enchanting Hampshire', driving from Basingstoke to Winchester, Romsey, Lulworth, Dorchester—the 'Casterbridge' of Hardy's *The Mayor of Casterbridge*—Bridgeport and Exeter. They slept either in 'Pheemus'—Eric's car—or in a tent. Eric poetically noted of Noreen how
the wind played strange tricks with her hair, blowing it straight back till she looked like the spirit of nature.

They stopped regularly to get something to drink, beer for Eric and lemonade or 'soda pop' for Noreen. Doctors then thought nothing of the dangers of smoking, and at the end of the year Eric gave my mother a silver cigarette case as a Christmas present, engraved: 'For Noreen 1932'

By then Eric was sufficiently interested in Noreen's exotic background to acquire W.H.Hudson's *Far Away and Long Ago*. I still have the volume, inscribed 'Eric Emerson January 21st, 1933'.

Several months later, on Saturday July 15, 1933, Noreen and Eric were married in St Alban's Church at the end of the High Street in Teddington. Francis Berry, an old friend of her father's, gave Noreen away.[14] Matt and Angela Huber have unearthed a report of the wedding in *The Surrey Comet* of July 19, 1933.

---

[13] I have an account of the trip written in diary form by Eric.
[14] I have a postcard showing Francis Berry and his wife (in demure ankle-length skirt) on a tennis court, sent to Patrick Goodbody in Uruguay for the New Year of 1911. Francis Berry ran the old family firm of Wine Merchants, Berry Brothers; founded in 1698; it still exists. An engraving we have shows Francis Berry standing in his office contemplating a couple of bottles of, presumably, more than acceptable wine.

BRIDE AND BRIDESMAID IN ORGANDIE
WEDDING OF MISS NOREEN M. GOODBODY
AT ST. ALBAN'S CHURCH

The wedding took place at St. Alban's Church Teddington, on Saturday, of Miss Noreen M. Goodbody, younger daughter of the late Mr. W.R. Goodbody and Mrs. Goodbody of 11, Broomwater, Teddington, to Mr. Eric C. Emerson, elder son of Mr. and Mrs. Edward Emerson of Cork, Ireland. The bride, who was given away by Mr. Francis Berry, wore a dress of flowered organdie with hat to match and her ornaments were a pearl necklace and brooch to match. She carried a bouquet of golden roses. Her only bridesmaid was Miss Marcia Emerson (sister of the bridegroom) who was attired in a dress of green organdie with hat to match, with an ornament of a pearl and sapphire brooch, a gift of the bridegroom. She carried a Victorian posy of yellow flowers. The bride's mother wore lace and white crepe de chine and a blue hat and the bridegroom's mother chose green with a beige hat trimmed with black. Captain T. T. Rody (?) was best man. The Vicar (the Rev. H. William) officiated. And Mr. Alex Rowley (Master of Music) was at the organ. A reception held at 11 Broomwater was attended by 35 guests and the bride and bridegroom afterwards left by car for an undisclosed destination for their honeymoon.

Barbara was present and wore a dress made for her by Melrose. Bride and groom then set off in 'Pheemus' and, as the report says, got as far as Salisbury, where Eric had recently been working in an infirmary during a rheumatic fever epidemic. In Salisbury the groom suddenly felt so ill that he checked himself into hospital. The following day a friend from the infirmary drove the young couple back to Teddington.

Eric did not have the rheumatic fever for which he was first treated, but septicaemia, or blood poisoning, his bloodstream invaded by bacteria. Septicaemia is still life threatening, but in those days, before antibiotics, it usually killed. The young doctor died the following Saturday, aged 28, on the anniversary of his wedding of the week before. He is buried in Teddington cemetery not far from where JG lies. Curiously, Noreen's own death at 93, in 2005 in Sao Paulo, was also on July 15, the seventy-second anniversary of her first short-lived marriage .

Twigs of a Tree

The announcement of Eric's death appeared in the *Surrey Comet* of the following Wednesday, July 16, 1933. It reads:

BRIDE FOR A WEEK ONLY
DOCTOR HUSBAND'S TRAGICALLY SUDDEN DEATH
ILL FIRST DAY OF HONEYMOON

Taken ill on his first day of honeymoon, a young Irish doctor died at Teddington exactly a week after his marriage. He was Dr Eric Emerson aged 28 years, and his home was at Mount Verdon Villa, Cork. On Saturday July 15th he was married to Miss Noreen M. Goodbody of 11 Broomwater Teddington. The ceremony took place at St. Alban's Church, and a report of it appeared in last Wednesday's Surrey Comet. Although the destination of their honeymoon was not disclosed, the bride and groom set off by car towards the West of England. It was on the next day while on the way to Salisbury, that Dr Emerson was taken ill. He was brought back to the bride's home at Teddington, and on Friday was taken in an unconscious condition to Teddington Memorial Hospital, where he died the following morning. The elder son of Mr and Mrs Edward Emerson of Cork, Dr Emerson took his degree at St. Mary's Hospital, London. He was in practice at Leighton Buzzard, Bedfordshire, and it was his intention to open a practice in Portsmouth. The funeral took place at Teddington Cemetery yesterday morning, when the service was conducted by the Rev. L.C.R. Smith (assistant priest at St. Alban's).

We have no visual records of the wedding. Photographs must have been taken but, after Eric's death, it might perhaps have been too painful to have them developed, pasted into albums, admired. We have a photo of a happy-looking Noreen in what may have been her wedding dress, taken before the occasion.

Noreen Goodbody c.1933

Shortly after Eric's death, Noreen, going through his papers found a stamped, addressed envelope. It contained forms filled out for his life insurance. Never posted, Noreen, still shattered, had to go straight back to work. According to Barbara Brady, Noreen—still not twenty-one years old—then briefly worked for 'Poppy,' as she was known in the family. The redoubtable Poppy, born Lucy Radmall, and now divorced, had become Lady Byron in 1901. She then turned suffragette and was later awarded the medal of Commander of the British Empire (C.B.E.) for her support of a home for nurses who had served in the First World War.

Once divorced and again widowed in 1917, when her husband Lord Byron died, she then remarried, in 1924 at the ripe old age of 67, a millionaire shipping-magnate described in the Oxford Dictionary of Biography as 'a hard, ruthless, unpleasant bachelor'. Sir Robert Paterson and Lady Houston lived on the island of Jersey as tax exiles. He died on his yacht, *Liberty*, in 1926 and left his wife some £ 5.5 million.

Barbara claims that Poppy made a small monthly contribution to Alice after JG's death. After Eric's death Noreen seems to have become Poppy's secretarial assistant, she then decided to move in the direction of medicine. However, perhaps for reasons of time and expense or possibly for lack of the necessary preparatory schooling, Noreen settled for physiotherapy. Poppy seems to have underwritten part of her studies at the University of London's, Kings College Hospital. She once gave my mother a triangular diamond brooch—now with Maria-Lucia Ferreiro, my brother David's wife. Lucy Radmall, Brinkman, Byron, Houston died in 1936. Time magazine published a not entirely flattering article calling her the 'country's reputedly wealthiest woman'.[15]

After three years of study at King's, Noreen worked for a while in England and then she too, eventually, returned to Argentina in 1938. According to Bar, she left her dog, Roo, in the hands of kind-hearted Alice, who was now approaching her nineties. The training Poppy helped finance was to enrich Noreen's life with a great sense of fulfilment. In Brazil she was able to alleviate the usual women's club life of tennis, bridge, and tea parties with many years of work with children suffering from the consequences of cerebral palsy or poliomyelitis, a disease then still rife all over the globe. Whenever in England, she returned to her college to update her training.

The Tasmanian Connection

I never met my paternal grandfather. Oliver Linley Adams (1870-1949), who was born and lived on the island of Tasmania, off the southern tip of Australia, had arrived in Argentina a few years before Martin Eggar, in the late 1920s. He was involved not in estancias, nor in the meat-packing business of companies like Bovril, but in that other staple of contemporary British employment abroad, the railways.

Oliver Linley Adams travelled from Tasmania to Spain after having been recommended to set up a railway line that included the cities of Burgos and Valladolid. After this, instead of returning to Tasmania, he went

---

[15] Lady Houston gave generous support to British Aviation, providing 'valuable impetus to the development of engine technology that would ultimately be vital in the Second World War, in particular during the Battle of Britain.' Apparently she had extreme political ideas; admired Mussolini and Hitler and in 1933 financed the Houston-Mount Everest Flight Expedition. This first ever flight over the summit of Everest was intended as a sign of opposition to the granting of independence to India. It seems she was so upset by the abdication crisis that she stopped eating and died on December 29th, 1936, aged 79.' This information comes from an article about Lady Houston I found on the internet. The *Time* magazine article can also be found there.

on to Argentina, where he spent about ten years on railway planning and construction. Later, in 1935, he directed a *galeno* or lead-sulphide mining venture at the Anca Mahuida mines in the southern Andean province of Neuquén. His wife, two of his sons—including my father—and his daughters Sheila and Berna eventually joined him in Argentina.

His oldest son Noel Darwin Adams (1906-1989), who held a BA in English and History and had already done newspaper reporting for the Hobart *Mercury,* arrived in South America in about 1930. Noel worked for two years for Mulhall's English-language paper, the Buenos Aires *Standard.* When Noel returned to Australia in 1933, he developed into a journalist of national stature.[16] During World War II he became a war correspondent on several fronts, where he also befriended his colleague, the writer Alan Moorehead, whose works—among them *The White Nile, The Blue Nile*—graced my parents' bookshelves. After the war, Noel Adams broadened his journalism into radio and television broadcasting. And, *piccolo mondo*: half a century later, in our neighbourhood in the Umbrian hills, we met—and became friends with—Alan Moorehead's daughter, Caroline, another writer and biographer.

Noel Darwin Adams' son, my first cousin, is also a friend. My husband Carlos met Dr Anthony Adams in 1973, many years before I did. I was not in Delhi at the time. Tony had come to India on a preventive medicine programme for the World Health Organization. He later became—and was for nine years—the Chief Medical Officer of Australia.

---

[16] The Australian Dictionary of Biography tells us that Noel worked as a 'leader writer' in the editorial section of the *Adelaide Advertiser.* He later became the Advertiser's war correspondent and eventually its foreign editor.

Twigs of a Tree

Oliver Linley Adams at his desk

Our grandfather Oliver Linley Adams, who died in Australia in 1949, left many papers and accounts of his life and interests. His wife Leonora Battanta, however—in the manner of the silly widow of Richard Burton, translator of *The Arabian Nights*—seems to have destroyed many of his writings. All that remain are a few affectionate letters (closing with long lines of x's) to his daughter Sheila—and a short account of some of his time in Argentina.

The Growth of the Tortoise

Oliver Linley says nothing of his work or his domestic arrangements in Argentina except for remarking to his daughter that he is building a house to receive his wife in the mining area of Neuquén, and that he hopes she will not feel too isolated. An avid naturalist, he spends much of his time collecting and sending specimens to the Natural History Museum in London. In October 1935 he writes to Sheila from Neuquén and, in passing, mentions that—after Charles Darwin and Thomas Huxley, whose surnames he passed on to his sons—his third hero was the 19th century scientist John Tyndall, the man 'who explained why the sky is blue'. To Sheila he adds: 'You can thank your stars that you were not a boy or you would be known as Tinny or Tin-can or something equally irreverent.'

Oliver Linley's account of his period in the Neuquén province gives us an idea of the man. His observations on the flora, fauna and geology of the area expand a little on the untouched world that JG Walker had known half a century earlier:

Spring clothes the desert with a carpet of annuals among which a small species of helianthus (sunflower) covers large areas with a sheet of gold . . . To conserve water the desert shrubs have resorted to many expedients. Some, like the 'sampa', have leaves covered with minute hairs that give them a silver-grey colour, others like the 'mataceibo' have discarded leaves altogether, but the branches are green and varnished.

He comments on the mason bee,
a big hairy fellow, like a bumble bee, found in great numbers in the sandstone cliffs and in the walls of the adobe houses made of sun baked brick. The bee, with his strong mandibles, tunnels into the sandstone and at the end of the tunnel makes a nest of grains of sand cemented together, about the size of a walnut . . . The bee fills it with honey, lays an egg on top and seals the cell. Almost all the bees in the colony die in the autumn, but a few females survive in sheltered crevices to found another colony in the spring.
A striking feature of the desert are the mounds made by the leaf cutting ants (Atta) with roads leading away from them in all directions. The ants excavate their nest more than a metre below the surface and the mound consists of the material extracted plus innumerable small sticks with which it is covered.

One species of ant, he explains, cultivates a fungus that is its only food:
When a queen leaves the nest, accompanied by a swarm of winged males, to found a new colony, she takes a small piece of the fungus with her in her crop.'

He makes some surprising finds:
The sandy plains are intersected by cliffs often of sandstone, belonging to the Upper Cretaceous, and the huge bones of Dinosaurs are quite common in them. All this country has been under the ocean at least twice since Jurassic times and the sea reached to the foot of the Cordillera. In many places the plain is covered with a cap of lava, and extinct volcanic craters are common. The most easterly one of these

Twigs of a Tree

was called by the Tehuelche Indians 'Anca Mahuida', which means the yegua madrina or bell mare that leads the tropa. These Indians were not entirely without imagination.

In the 20's moving about the country had not changed much since JG's day—nor had that collective equine infatuation that made possible the domination of a whole troop of Pampas stallions by a single mare.
The best and most exhilarating way to travel about the desert is with a 'tropa' or tropilla. If you are 3 or 4 in the party you take 6 or 8 spare horses and a 'yegua madrina', a bell mare with a small bell attached to a strap around her neck, often accompanied by a yearling foal. With shouts of 'Yegua' the men urge the mare forward at a gallop. If she swerves from the desired course the bolas whiz by her ear and turn her in the right direction. Your horse needs neither whip nor spur. He will not lose sight of the mare . . . You can change your horse as often as you please and when you camp you have to hobble only the mare. The horses will never leave her. One travels by night if there is a good moon or early in the morning and rests during the heat of the day at some water hole to be nearly eaten alive in the summer by the tábanos known in Australia as March flies.

He enjoys riding about with the gauchos:
The gauchos may not be the equals of the Australian aborigines as trackers, but they are very good and it is interesting to ride with one over these sandy plains and get him to interpret the innumerable tracks. Even the tracks of small beetles do not escape his sharp eye.

Oliver Linley Adams in his inexhaustible curiosity also takes a baby tortoise, reputed to have a life-span of a hundred years, into the house—to study its eating and laying habits and to record the speed of its growth. Result: 1.5 cms in breadth and 2 cms in length after 25 months. By this time, the sturdy little beast had become so affectionately attached to him that, when called, it came scuttling across the room like a handicapped puppy.

From Pianist to Lady Gaucho

Pat Goodbody married the elegant Inez Margaret Thompson in October 1939. She was a superbly talented and accomplished pianist, good enough to have been taken on as a student, in London, by the great

Solomon (Solomon Cuttner), master of master-pianists. Inez was, however, so shy a person before an audience that she almost died of stage-fright and few people ever, except presumably her teacher or her husband, heard her play. Many years later she inherited an estancia in the Venado Tuerto area, moved into the pampas, donned breeches and boots—later bombachas and alpargatas—and 'went native' all the way, smoking black-tobacco cigarettes, eschewing dental work and talking rough like a gaucho.

The mystery of her personality will never be solved. She and Pat Goodbody eventually divorced and he married Angel McClintock, an attractive and eloquent lady of conservative inclinations. Carlos and I had lunch with them, around 1971, at the British Club in Buenos Aires. After Pat, like his father, died of throat cancer in 1975, Angel moved to London and helped in Margaret Thatcher's electoral campaigns. Unfortunately Alzheimer's disease switched off her lively brain within a very few years. Derek Dyson has fond memories of Patrick appearing with 'very nice, expensive toys for me . . . It was not my birthday, and I thought he was God.' Pat Goodbody was not only my uncle but my godfather—yet, thanks to our gipsy life, I barely knew him. He left no children.

Barbara Walker, Joan Hills, Noreen Goodbody c. 1933

Twigs of a Tree

More Marriages and the Shadow of the Looming War

Angela Huber tells us that her mother, Joan Hills, waited two years before joining Norman Walker in Argentina. They were married in Buenos Aires from Corinne and Gordon Catty's house on December 19, 1935. Part of their honeymoon was spent with Molly and Charles Dyson at the *Susana*. They then moved further south to live in Rio Negro where Norman was working for a company of Argentine Fruit Distributors. Joan, no doubt conscious of the imperatives of Argentine military service, returned briefly to the UK for the birth of their son, also a John Briton, on December 4, 1936. Two years later, in 1938, Norman and Joan left Argentina with two-year old Briton and moved back to the UK.

Betty Walker had met Martin Eggar at the Argentine bridge works her father, Briton, was directing, but they did not marry immediately, as their daughter Diana McClure explains:

They had a fairly long engagement, as they had to wait until my father became a manager—a trainee wasn't entitled to married quarters in those days. They married early in 1939, after my father got a job as an estancia manager for the dairy firm Magnasco . . . Magnasco had a number of dairy estancias near Tandil, and all the managers were British.

A rather gloomy looking group photo of Betty Walker and Martin Eggar's wedding in St. John's, Buenos Aires, 1939.

Diana, their daughter, remarks of the photo,
My father looks like a condemned man. Reminds me of a wedding for which I rang wedding bells—instead of the traditional wedding march at the end of the service, the organist played: "another good man bites the dust". My mother also looks pretty grim.

My Australian-born father Oliver Huxley Adams—always known as 'Hux'—was already in Argentina by 1929. His father, Oliver Linley, mentions reading the papers' accounts of his son's successes on the rugby fields of Montevideo and Buenos Aires, but says nothing about his job or his whereabouts.

Oliver Huxley Adams on the rugger pitch, Argentina

My father, in spite of his remarkable memory for everything he read, had for some reason decided not to go on to university, as his brother had done. Instead he joined a bank. In Argentina Hux in all likelihood found early employment in the meat-packing business—he certainly worked for *Swift's* in Rosario in the forties—and joined the sporting life of the

Anglo community. How my father—a 'jock' of many sports with a talent for cartooning—met my young widowed mother, I do not know. They were married on November 11, 1939 in Argentina, but it is not quite clear where. The war had already broken out. Noreen's mother Mel might already have been back in Buenos Aires. Presumably Molly and Charles Dyson, Betty and Martin as well as Pat and Inez Goodbody were all there. Again there are no photographs or accounts.

Laying the Foundation Stone of the School in 1846 by O.H. Adams, published in the Launcestonian 1923

Marriage of George and Barbara

Barbara, Betty's sister, the youngest of JG's grandchildren, met George Brady at a St Patrick's Day dance in Kingston. They were married on August, 26 1939 at Canford Magna Church near Wimborne in Dorset, where George's mother and brother lived.

Barbara Walker and George Brady on their wedding day
August 26 1939

Barbara and George barely spent any time in the flat they had bought in Broom Road, Teddington, for six days after their marriage the war broke out. George, already in the Territorial Army, was called up the day after the declaration of war, on September 2nd. The planned honeymoon (cycling in Cornwall) never took place and the Teddington flat was sold the following May. Daughter Gillian was born on September 27, 1940. By the time Patrick came into the world, on September 24, 1941, his father had left for the Middle East with the Cheshire Regiment. He was to return only four years later.

Norman, back in England, continued his work on ordnance factories, Air Force maintenance depots, airfields and dockyards throughout the War.[17] Barbara, to this very day, is still grateful for all the help and support she had during the war years from Norman and Joan Walker while George was in the Middle East.

---

[17] Angela tells us that after the war he specialised in concrete engineering with innovative systems for bridge constructions.

Twigs of a Tree

Martin Eggar abandoned the 'very pleasant estancia' he was managing in Buenos Aires province and, he too, like many other young British men around the world, joined up. Pat Goodbody volunteered for the RAF from Argentina.

Pat Goodbody in military uniform c.1939

Sheila Adams joined a woman's unit of the army. Her brother, Hux, my father—who had had typhoid fever shortly before he was married—was rejected 'for weak lungs'. Those weak lungs carried him into his ninety-second year. The brush off by the army, for this man who was above all a sportsman, remained a source of ambivalent distress for the rest of his life.

Charles and Molly Dyson remained on their estancia *La Susana*, but Brian tells us that with the war and the subsequent election of General Juan Perón as President in 1946,[18] the good years of the thirties were over:

That life-style would never return. Many men and women of English descent would enrol and go to war; then Perón came to power and started a class war between employers and employees; and then a long

---

[18] Perón began a populist movement that included an attempt to break up the great estancias, by raising wages and generally setting the 'descamisados' or shirtless ones against the landowners.

siege was brought by the Government over farming values that lasted for years.

When Martin joined up in 1942, his young family—Betty, with Diana, born September 4, 1940, and pregnant with her second child—left the estancia he was managing and moved into the Moldes house with Briton and Melrose in Belgrano. They remained there for the duration of the war. I was born eleven days after Diana, on September 15, 1940, and was followed a year later by a second child, John Richard Adams.

My mother came home one day and found the baby in an alarmingly deep sleep. She lifted him out of his cot, leapt into a tram to race him to the doctor, crooning to the 'sleeping' child as she went. The doctor pronounced the little boy dead. Difficult to imagine the dreadful trip home, baby in arms, to arrange for his burial. On November 23, 1943 Noreen gave birth to a second son, my brother David Patrick Adams.

Shortly after Martin left for Britain his second daughter, Christie, was born. Martin spent four years with a Gurkha regiment on British India's North West Frontier territory (today in Pakistan) and returned from the war in 1946. He immediately went back to farming and estancia life in Tandil, in the province of Buenos Aires.

My only memories of the war are the patriotic fund-raising get-togethers in Buenos Aires, with all the women wearing red, blue and white aprons designed after the Union Jack.

Childhood and Tragedy

After the war, in 1946, my father was transferred to Brazil by *Swift's*, but later joined the Canadian Light and Power Company in Sao Paulo. The company offered him, an Australian, the perk of home leave to England. My mother and I—once together with my brother David—returned twice to Argentina. In 1949, we stayed in the Moldes house in Belgrano, at the *Susana* with Molly and Charles, and with the Eggars in Tandil. Below are Diana, Christie and me on the estancia *La Suiza*, the toy-farms that Uncle Briton had made for us in the background. I look rather wild and uncivilized compared to my cousins—the two demure and properly shod little girls next to me.

Christie and Diana Eggar, Lin Adams at Tandil 1949

Diana tells me that her grandfather Briton Walker had been very badly hit by the depression, the general downturn of the nineteen-thirties and the post war years. In 1952 he was forced to sell the Moldes house. It stood on a piece of extremely valuable property in Belgrano, and when I went to look for it in 2005 the house had been replaced by an expensive-looking high rise apartment building. However, since times were bad, Briton received very little for it. He and Melrose then did not buy, but rented the Calle Patricios house in the suburb of Hurlingham. Their neighbours' front garden—I remember—was ornamented by a pair of life-sized animal statues of singular gracelessness—deer perhaps, but only marginally better than dwarfs.

At the beginning of 1953, shortly before going to England, I was back in Argentina, staying mostly at the *Susana*. My mother had left me there with Molly and Charles, and I, as usual, was having a most wonderful time: keeping cheerfully out of the way of the alarming grown-ups, digging a 'house' into the floor of the woods, swimming, riding, helping with the milking, smoothing the nose of 'my own' *Petisa*; feeding her lumps of sugar, stolen from the kitchen. That was when I fell flat on my face into a patch of nettles while I was trying to retrieve a badly aimed croquet ball. I think my screeching tempted Charles to wring my neck, but he gallantly refrained. I took comfort with the maids who were sitting outside the kitchen door with bowls of hot water at their feet, gossiping and plucking the chickens that would later appear on the dinner table.

Those were the pre-Dr-Spock, spare-the-rod, sit-up-straight and seen-but-not-heard child-rearing days, elbows required to be glued so fast to their sides that wielding knife and fork from a too low chair was more than a challenge. Children were then, by definition, 'pests'. Later Molly would often declare 'I do not like children'. I would argue with her: 'At least you must appreciate the beauty of extreme youth, the loveliness of movement, of enthusiasm, curiosity and wonder at the world'. She was not convinced. 'I like them when they are grown up.'

This British attitude was markedly different from the Italy I came to know in 1978, where children are greeted, even by strangers, with *Ciao, bello* and *Come sei carino!* and *Amore mio!* I, enchanted with this entirely un-British approach to children, when I arrived in Rome from India with our four-year old Sebastian, immediately started applying what I was learning. Perhaps too avidly: years later, when Sebastian came up against some of the inevitable cussedness of real life, he suddenly turned to me with a look of withering reproach: 'The trouble with you, Mum,' he said, 'is that you made me feel I was God's gift to the world!' Ah, parents, you can't win.

But in late 1952, Diana tells me, Betty and Martin Eggar were themselves going through hard times. The *Magnasco* farm Martin had been managing in Tandil was expropriated in 1951 by the populist government of General Perón. Even I remember Molly and Charles' voluble disgust with this man. Brian remarks that

> *Charles, in particular, was deeply disillusioned by Perón's misguided poling and believed that it would undermine the grand vision for La Susana to which he had dedicated his life.* [19]

Martin at the time managed the 'show farm' of an influential Argentine family—until there was some disagreement about when to vaccinate against foot-and-mouth; the whole family—if not the stock—caught the disease. Martin, Diana tells us, lost his job.

---

[19] Brian Dyson, *Estancia La Susana in the 1930's*

Twigs of a Tree

The Patricios House, Hurlingham, Buenos Aires

Martin and Betty then stayed with their four daughters at Melrose and Briton's house in Hurlingham, while Martin went in search of employment.

Diana with her sisters, Elizabeth, Veronica and Christie

One afternoon, just after my mother's arrival from Venado Tuerto, the grownups—Betty, Melrose, Briton, Noreen—were sitting in the garden over tea. Diana describes how, that afternoon, the joy of her childhood came to a terrible end:

One hot afternoon in January 1953 my grandfather gave Christie and me money to buy bread, with a bit extra so we could buy ice creams. We walked back eating our ice cream cones. Christie always had a water ice, lemon, and I had dulce de leche. We each had a lick of the other's ice cream, and then took the footpath that crossed over the railway lines. A train was travelling southwards. We'd recently read an English story book in which one of the children was a train-spotter, and we wondered what numbers he collected—every carriage had a different number. Christie was standing on a railway line. I was just behind her. Neither of us heard the train that was coming from the opposite direction. It hit Christie and she flew into the air like a doll, and was thrown down onto the rails on a siding, a limp, lifeless body. She was ten years old. Our happy childhood was over.

My own mother never forgot the shock of little Diana's sudden appearance in the garden, her cry that Christie had been hit, the race with Betty to the heart-breaking scene on the tracks. Some time later, probably by telegram, the news reached the *Susana*. Molly was completely distraught.

I, who had been playing with Christie the week before, began to cry. Charles, although no doubt as upset as everyone else, told me fiercely to stop 'blubbing'. I fled, sobbing; wandered alone about the garden, not knowing what to do, what to think, where to go. Molly finally came to fetch me, and sitting down on one of the old wrought-iron veranda chairs that years ago had come all the way from England, took me on her knee, soothing my sobs with tales of immortality and the delights of heaven that I was then only too happy to believe. Molly's kindness and gentleness to me after the shock of Christie's tragedy was in a way the real beginning of our intermittent but very long friendship.

My own connections with my cousin Diana were only restored when we were in England. We did not, being at different schools, see much of each other. Once we spent a holiday together at Aunt Mary Eggar's in Bentley, where I discovered *Gone with the Wind*, a book that—according to Bar—Alice launched into in her late eighties, remarking with periodic disapproval on Scarlett O'Hara as 'that woman'. Even then the pain, the blight of Christie's death was still present. When Diana wrote me letters she signed them with two names, her own—and that of her sister. Little Christie was never forgotten. I was to name my own daughter after her.

This tragedy, the loss of her great-granddaughter, was one that Alice Walker did not have to endure. Nor, fortunately, did she have to live through the tribulations and horrors of yet another World War.

Lively and active almost until her final days, Alice Catty Walker died on January 23, 1939, in Teddington at the age of 90, eight months before the outbreak of the Second World War. After her death, according to Barbara, the house at 11 Broomwater was sold for £750. It was then that Melrose Goodbody returned to Argentina and moved into the Moldes house in Belgrano with her brother Briton.

Although her obituary is largely devoted to her husband's exploits in the pampas and on the Thames, things had changed somewhat: unlike her grandmother Mary Ann Christie so many years before, Alice is, at least, not recorded as a nameless 'relict'. Alice lies in Teddington cemetery, alongside her husband, John George Walker. Her obituary reads:

*Mrs. Alice Walker's Eventful
Life Closes at Ninety*

Widow of a pioneer settler in the Argentine, Mrs. Walker, died on Monday at her home, 11, Broomwater, Teddington, aged 90 years. In spite of her advanced age, she had been ill for only a week.

Mrs. Walker had had an eventful life, for in 1873 she joined her husband, Mr. J.G. Walker, who five years earlier had gone to the Argentine with the early settlers. For several years she never saw another white woman, living many miles from civilization and being exposed to considerable hardship and danger.

Gradually, however, things became more secure and Mr. Walker was appointed manager of a large cattle ranch. Later he acquired a ranch of his own, which he sold in 1910, when he returned to England.

Love of the river—he was a member of the eight which won the Grand Challenge Cup at Henley in 1868—brought him to Teddington, and before he died in 1925 he became a well known figure on the Thames, Two sons of Mr. and Mrs. Walker were killed in the war and one son, who is in the Argentine, and a daughter survive. The funeral will take place at Teddington Cemetery at 2.pm tomorrow.

> **Mrs. Alice Walker's Eventful Life Closes at Ninety**
>
> Widow of a pioneer settler in the Argentine, Miss Alice Walker, died on Monday at her home, 11, Broom-water, Teddington, aged 90 years. In spite of her advanced age, she had been ill for only a week.
>
> Mrs. Walker had had an eventful life, for in 1873 she joined her husband, Mr. J. G. Walker, who five years earlier had gone to the Argentine with the early settlers. For several years she never saw another white woman, living many miles from civilisation and being exposed to considerable hardship and danger.
>
> Gradually, however, things became more secure and Mr. Walker was appointed manager of a large cattle ranch. Later he acquired a ranch of his own, which he sold in 1910, when he returned to England.
>
> Love of the river—he was a member of the eight which won the Grand Challenge Cup at Henley in 1868—brought him to Teddington, and before he died in 1925 he became a well known figure on the Thames.
>
> Two sons of Mr. and Mrs. Walker were killed in the war and one son, who is in the Argentine, and a daughter, survive.
>
> The funeral will take place at Teddington Cemetery at 2 p.m. to-morrow.

Alice's Obituary

So much life, interest, kindness, courage, quirks of character vanished into the abyss, the enigma of that 'undiscovered country from whose bourn no traveller returns'. So little, so very little that we know about the mysteries of identity, of personality, so much that we would like to know, to have seen, to have asked.

SOURCES & BIBLIOGRAPHY

MANUSCRIPTS
Barber, Elinor, *La Lena, Recollections by Kitty and Nelly*, Memoirs of her childhood from a copy given to me by Rojas Lagarde in February 2006.

Bernardy, Hélène de, *Datos sobre la vida del Sr. Henry John Edwards*, translated into Spanish by her daughter.

Brady, Barbara *Memories of Broomwater*

Catty, Meryl, *Descendants of Pierre Mignolet*

Dyson, Molly letter to Barbara Brady, July 1985.

Dyson, Brian *Estancia La Susana in the 1930's*, 2011

Goodbody, Robert, (1781-1860) *Journal*, found in the attic of his house by Tony Lynch. Can be seen on the internet.

McClure, Diana *Growing up on the Pampas*, February 2010

Talma, Michel, *Letter to his wife Anne,* The complete text (in French) of this letter was very kindly sent to me by Madeleine Ambrière in 2009.

Walker, Alfred, *Journal of a trip to South Africa,* 1866.

Walker, Harold Saxon *Letters to his parents from the front—12th January 1917 to September 1917*, later hand copied into a notebook by his father J.G. Walker.

Walker, J.B.

Letters from South Africa, Children in the Camp, A Long Time Ago, Yarns from the Camp, transcribed or recollected Briton's tale *A trip to England* 1880, is one of many, all in a style addressed to children, that he writes for his own grandchildren.

An Account of his experiences in the Boer War

A Year in Matto Grosso 1905-1906

Note on *Mirages* by Robert Cunninghame Graham, 1936,
On The Frontier
Journey to Jauru,
Walker J.G. *Journey to New Zealand, 1863*
Various Letters to Goodhall, October 1875.
Walker, William
Letters from New Zealand transcribed by Gillian Finlay.

DVD's
Davison, Rosanna, *Where we Come From*, kindly sent to me by Susie Cogan, Brian Dyson's daughter.
Dyson, Tania, Interview with her grandmother, Molly Dyson.

INTERNET SITES
Jennings, Alan, on the *Battlefields of World War I*.
John, Steven on *lst World War memorials*
Payne, David Dr. *Woods and Copses Natures Fortresses on the Somme on the Western Front*. Site of the Western Front Association.

BIBLIOGRAPHY
Adams, Keith, *Crocodile Safari Man*, Strategic Book Publishing, 2008
Ambrière, Madeleine et Francis, *Talma ou l'Histoire au Théâtre*, Fallois, Paris, 2007
Bengoa, José, *Historia del pueblo Mapuche*. LOM-Ediciones. Santiago de Chile,
Brownlow, Kivin *David Lean*, 1997
Casas, Bartolomé de Las, *Historia General de las Indias*, México, FCE, 1951
Casas, Bartolome de Las, *A Short Account of the Destruction of the Indies*
Catty, Frederick Adam, *Handbook for Ems and its Environs*, Bad Ems, 1844.
Catty, Meryl, article in *Guardian* on Last Wills and Testaments April 14, 2007.
Churchill, Winston, *Ian Hamilton's March, 1900*, N.Y. Longmans, Green & Co. for an account of the Boer War campaign in which Briton Walker took part.
Clacy, Mrs. Charles, Thompson, Patricia (ed): *A Lady's Visit to the Gold diggings in 1852-1853,* Lansdowne Press Pty Ltd, 1963.

Conan Doyle, Sir Arthur, *The Great Boer War of 1902.*
Connerty, Ian, *At the Going Down of the Sun 365 Soldiers from the Great War*, Lanoo, Tielt, 2001
Cunninghame Graham, Robert Bontine, *Mirages*, Heinemann, Toronto, 1936 *The Essential R.B. Cunninghame Graham, selected with an Introduction and Preface* by Paul Bloomfield, Jonathan Cape, London, 1952 *Charity*, Duckworth & Co., London, 1912 *Hope*, Duckworth & Co., London, 1915
Conan Doyle, Sir Arthur, *Great Boer War of 1902*. London, Smith, Elder & Co., 1902.
Darwin, Charles, *Voyage of the Beagle*
Diamond, Jared, *Guns, Germs and Steel*, Penguin, 2005
The Third Chimpanzee, Penguin, 1991
Dodd, Christopher, *Water Boiling Aft,* London Rowing Club, *2006*
Falkner, Thomas *A descriptiom of Patagonia and the adjacent Parts of South America* (London 1774)
Ferguson, Niall, *The Pity of War*, Penguin Books, 1998.
Fernández-Gomes, Emilio Manuel *Argentina Gesta Britannica*, Tomo II, parte B,
Galeano, Eduardo *Las Venas Abiertas de America Latina*, Catalogos, Argentina, 2001
Gálvez, Lucía, *Ernesto Tornquist (1842-1908). Escenario y circunstancias*, 2008
Goodbody, Michael, *The Goodbody Family of Ireland.*
Gordon, Richard, *The Alarming History of Medicine: Amusing Anecdotes from Hippocrates to Heart Transplants,* St. Martin's, New York, 1994
Graham-Yooll, Andrew, *The Forgotten Colony*, Hutchinson, 1981
Hanna, John, *Legal Liability for War Damage, A.B. Catty v. German Government*, 1924. The Michigan Law Review, vol 43, No. 6. (June 1945)
Hasbrouck, Alfred, *The Conquest of the Desert,* Duke University Historical Press, 1935
Heilbroner, Robert, *The Wordly Philosophers: The Lives, Times, and Ideas of the Great Economic Thinkers*, 7th edition, Touchstone, 1981
Henty, George A., *Out on the Pampas, or The Young Settlers,* Wildside Press, Donahue, Chicago
Hicks, Peter, *Napoleon on the Théâtre,* e-book on Google Previously unpublished. German version in Was für ein Theatre!: Krönungen un

Specktakel in Napoleonischer Zeit, eds Dominik Gügel and Christina Egli, Verlag Huber, Frauenfeld, Stuttgart, Vienna, 2004

Hogg, Henry, *Yerba Vieja*, 1936

Hudson, W.H., *Far Away and Long Ago, A History of My Early Life,* J.M. Dent & Sons, Toronto, 1931

Jonassohn, Kurt, Karin Solveig Bjornson. *Genocide & Gross Human Rights Violations in Comparative Perspective* Transaction Publications, New Jersey, 1998.

Keeson, C.A., 'History of Queen Victoria's Rifles 1792-1922. Constable & Company Ltd., 1923

Koebel, W.H., *Argentina Past and Present*, Trubner & Co. London, 1910.

Korzelinski, Seweryn, *Memoirs of Gold-digging in Australia*, Stanley Robe (ed. and trans.), University of Queensland Press, St Lucia, 1979.

Kradolfer, Sabine, « *Les autochtones invisibles, ou comment l'Argentine c'est « blanchie* » », *Amérique Latine Histoire et Mémoire. Les Cahiers ALHIM*, 16 | 2008.

Landaburu, Robert E., *Gringos*, Fondo Editor Mutual Venado Tuerto, 1991

Lastra, Dionisio Schoo, *El Indio del Desierto 1535-1879*, Goncourt, Buenos Aires, 1928.

Marhiquewun, R. Alberto Sarramone, *Orellie-Antoine I—Un rey francés de Araucanía y Patagonia,* Editoria Biblios.

Meyer, Karl, *Dust of Empire*, Abacus, 2004

Monacci, Gustavo, *La Colectividad Britanica en Bahia Blanca*, 1979

Morison, Eliot, *A People's History of the United States: 1492-Present,* New York, Harper-Collins, 1995

Mulhall, Michael George and Edward Thomas, *Handbook of the River Plate,* Buenos Aires, 1863,1869, 1875

Parish, Woodbine, Buenos Aires and the Provinces of the Rio de la Plata, (London, 1852)

Pigna, Felipe, *The Myths of Argentine History,* Planeta, 2006

Ras, Norberto, *La Guerra por las vacas,* Buenos Aires, 2006

Reid, George, *A South American Adventure, Letters from George Reid 1967-1870,* edited by Valerie Boyle, London, 1999

Rojas Lagarde, *El Malón Grande de 1875*, Editorial El Aljibe, City Bell, 1993. *Grande, Malones Y Comercio de Ganado conChile Siglo XIX,* Buenos Aires, El Elefante Blanco, 2004

Rock, David, *Argentina 1516-1992,*

Seymour, R.A., *Pioneering in the Pampas, or the First Four Years of a Settler's Experience in the La Plata Camps,* Stockero, 2002, first published 1869

Stow, John, *Survey of London,* '1603

Talma, Joseph Francois, *Mémoires de J.F. Talma,* 1850, ed. by Alexander Dumas.

Temple, A.G., *Guildhall Memories,* London, John Murray, 1918

* * *

Printed in Great Britain
by Amazon.co.uk, Ltd.,
Marston Gate.